April 12th 1941.

" Love „

But love is a durable fire
In the mind ever burning
never sick, never old, never dead
From itself never turning!

Jeanne

115

THE BLUE HILLS

Cornelius Weygandt Dies

Cornelius Weygandt, visiting professor of contemporary English poetry at Ursinus in 1952 and 1953, died on July 31 in Wolfeboro, N. H. He was in his eighty-sixth year.

A distinguished scholar, beloved teacher, and noted author, Dr. Weygandt was graduated from the University of Pennsylvania in 1891. Following this he did graduate work for one year, then spent four years as a newspaper man. In 1897 he became a member of the Department of English at Pennsylvania where he taught for fifty-five years before he permanently retired in 1952. He took his Ph.D. degree in 1901.

He discovered the Irish Literary Renaissance and in 1913 presented it to the world in the first book about it—*Irish Plays and Playwrights*. During the first summers he spent at his summer home in New Hampshire he became acquainted with the poet Robert Frost, and it was in 1915 at a tea at the Weygandt home in Wonalancet, N. H., that Frost was first presented to the public.

Dr. Weygandt's full length published books number eighteen. Four of these are critical treatments of English literature. *The Time of Yeats* (1937) is the last of these, and is considered to be the finest consideration of contemporary English poetry. One book is autobiographical, and thirteen are books of essays having to do with the American scene.

Best known of all his works that do not deal with literature is *The Red Hills* (1929), the first of two books he wrote to deal entirely with the Pennsylvania Dutch Country and of three more that presented it in part. One presents South Jersey, and four more deal in whole or in part with New Hampshire. But he remained always the devoted Pennsylvania Dutchman he was by birth. His books brought him the distinction of being one of the foremost American essayists of the second quarter of the twentieth century.

A

Certainly!

It was there, in the ground, in the
always had been. There are no more
today than there were when Rome rule
The only thing new is knowledge

AUTUMN IN THE STARUCCA VALLEY

THE BLUE HILLS

ROUNDS AND DISCOVERIES IN THE
COUNTRY PLACES OF PENNSYLVANIA

BY

CORNELIUS WEYGANDT

"The skyline is a promise not a bound"

NEW YORK
HENRY HOLT AND COMPANY

To

S. M. W., C. N. W., AND A. M. W.

Will you seek afar off? You surely come back at last,
In things best known to you finding the best, or as good as the
    best,
In folks nearest to you finding the sweetest, strongest, lovingest,
Happiness, knowledge, not in another place, but this place, not
    for another hour but this hour.

WALT WHITMAN.

THE APPEAL OF PENNSYLVANIA

IT is instinctive with man to love what he knows best. It is by birthright the Pennsylvanian is more the fellow of the hills than of the sea. Summer vacations may have taken him, from infancy, to Cape May, or Beach Haven, or Barnegat, to East Hampton, or Nantucket, or Bar Harbor, but somehow or other, the sea islands of New Jersey, and their kindred coasts northeastward, despite their familiarity and charm, remain for him places to visit rather than to live in, outing grounds for a season rather than home.

There are few Pennsylvanians born out of sight of the hills, for there are few places in Pennsylvania in which their level ridges, high or low, fail to hang blue in the offing. Conjure up before your mind's eye your lifetime's goings and comings hither and yon through the state, and there is no landscape of all you traveled through in which there are not hills, hills and valleys, running water, postwoods and forested slopes, stone houses with dooryards of flowers and fruit trees. Look at a contour map of the state and it tells the same story of highland and lowland. There are mountains over half the state and hills over nearly every bit of the other half. The ridges run from northeast to southwest, innumerable ridges, with seven dominant over all.

Two of these seven, the Stone Hills and the South Mountain, rose blue to the northwest from many places of my boyhood's rambling afoot, and in the drives of that remote time by horse and phaeton that were part of the ritual of the late afternoons of the long days from May to September. It was on the high ground in Upper Roxborough, in Mana-

tawna, to be exact, reached by Paper Mill Lane from the
Valley of the Wissahickon, that we could look off and see
the Schuylkill Hills, and beyond them the Stone Hills, and
beyond them again the blue and level line of the South
Mountain this side of Reading.

Those hills about Valley Forge suggested talk by mother
of the Chester County hills beyond them among which she
was born. That blue line of the South Mountain suggested
to father his boyhood's visits to his old aunties in Easton,
and the Blue Mountain to the northward on the way to
which from Easton, at Tatamay, his people lived after their
first settlement in Germantown.

Though I was reared a suburbanite, Germantown was
almost as much a country town as a suburb of Philadelphia
in my youngest years. There was a store at Main Street and
Washington Lane in which you could buy everything from
pepper to plows. There were "aborigines" of six generations'
standing who lived in ancestral houses and seldom went to
town, besides the newer comers from city and upstate and
across the Atlantic. There had already begun that drift from
country to town that was to lead to so many abandoned
farms and dwindled villages through all our mountain land.
We were always, in fact, we Americans, a migratory people.
My great-great-great-grandfather had come from the Rhine
Valley to Germantown in 1736. He moved to the Lehigh
Hills in his old age and lies buried at Schoeneck, just short
of the Wind Gap in the Blue Mountains. His son moved
in to Easton, which my grandfather, that son's grandson,
left to come to Philadelphia in 1820. There were four generations of us, Cornelius the immigrant, Jacob, Cornelius
Nolen, and Thomas Jefferson, that lived, for a part of their
lives or all of them, in the Blue Hills. That accounted for
my father's visits there, to his folks still resident in and

around Easton, and his much talk of Bluebergers and their ways.

So it is with most Pennsylvanians. The cityites among us have country cousins, the countrymen have suburbanite daughters and sons, and even in one lifetime a man may rightly claim all three statuses of countryman, cityman, and suburbanite. Trade has taken one of us upstate; a profession has brought another of us to town. He who makes his way in the city seeks a suburban home. Most of the city folk among us, whether of Pittsburgh or Scranton, Erie or Philadelphia, have roots in country places, know their way about in certain remote sections of the state.

It was not until automobiles brought us good roads, though, that I, personally, really got to know all quarters of Pennsylvania. Chester County and the Red Hills of Pennsylvania Dutchland I came to know in boyhood through family connections. Father used to take us on annual trips to the Switch Back above Mauch Chunk to see the mountains in their autumnal reds and yellows. There was my first going far afield up the valley of the Susquehanna and on to Niagara when I was seven. I spent a week at the Delaware Water Gap at fourteen. There were visits to the Juniata in 1887 and 1888, one of them involving a drive across country from Lebanon to Port Royal. I went with Uncle Jim to Gettysburg for the reunion of his regiment on the twenty-fifth anniversary of the battle. There were upstate assignments in my newspaper years and visits to alumni gatherings and teachers' institutes from the beginnings of my teaching years. I got to Bradford and to Erie, indeed to most parts of the state, save its southwestern corner, to which some of my people had emigrated from the Forks of the Delaware just after the War of the Revolution. Researches by the genealogist of the family had given me some knowledge of them and of their descendants and of the background of their lives.

If your family goes back, as do the Morgans of my ancestry, to seventeenth century days, you feel your roots are deep in the state's soil. If your family had the experiences of the frontier, as the Weygandts had, through contacts with Indians, chiefly friendly contacts as members of Moravian missions, you have associations with this place and that they visited in pioneer days. If your people were in the Revolutionary Army, you have a sense of proprietorship in state and country that no newcomers, no matter how devoted and loyal they are, can possibly have.

Old family letters, too, sent from backwoods places by your grandfather as he traveled about by canal and on horseback, make places unvisited by you only less familiar than places you traveled to and put up in of nights in years long ago. The dispersal of your cousinage, too, throughout the state, in Scranton, in Pittsburgh, in Harrisburg, keeps you from being merely local in your interests and sympathies. Pennsylvania has always been to me much more than the hinterland to Philadelphia. I am just listing another credential in saying this, not arrogating any particular virtue to myself. Folks upstate, many of them, do not expect the Philadelphian to know where Punxsutawney is, or Sunbury, or Somerset. Boy after boy, in talk in my office at college, has been surprised that I not only knew where such places were, but had visited them. The reason that more of us do not know what our state is, is that before the development of good roads there was no definite urge to drive city men to remote parts of the state unassociated with their own origins.

There is no so famed place for sightseeing in Pennsylvania as Niagara Falls, or the White Mountains. Though our

various healing waters took people in early days to Yellow
Springs in Chester County, and to York Springs and to
Cresson and Bedford, these places hardly rivaled as health
resorts Saratoga, or Poland Spring, or the many Virginia
springs. Mountain Pennsylvania, too, with its high table-
lands and many lakes, was slow to lure people to summer
there. Pennsylvanians had acquired the seaside habit. The
Upper Delaware and the Poconos, Montrose and Eaglesmere, might, indeed, be as attractive in every way as Mo-
honk and Minnewaska, or the Catskills and the Berkshire
Hills, but they were not different enough from the home
places to attract as did these outland places and the Adiron-
dacks and Green Mountains. They had not been written
about or painted as often as places to the eastward. We of
the Pennsylvania cities did not until recently learn much of
our state through visits to its summer hotels. It was not until
the development of true homes about these hotels that many
people became aware of the beauty of our Pennsylvania
highlands.

To the Pennsylvanian Pennsylvania has, of course, the
appeal of home. There is many a man from elsewhere in
the States, though, who finds a like appeal in Pennsylvania.
None too eager to receive strangers without credentials, we
are cordiality itself to people we know well enough to trust.
Philadelphia is accepted everywhere as the city of homes,
and it is as true of the whole state that it is a state of homes.
Even though we live in apartments we are loath to lay aside
or to sell any of the inherited treasures that are so generally
possessed by those of us of the old stocks. Heirlooms give a
family standing no matter what its social status. We are
proud of heirlooms. We do not believe an inherited com-
petence is tainted money. We are proud of such a com-
petence, as we are of all sorts of property. We and our for-

bears have worked for what we have, worked as hard as any people in the world, and we believe we have a right to keep the rewards of our labors. We believe that providence is one of the first virtues, and sweat of brow and body, and the will to save. We can sacrifice present pleasure for future security; we can deny ourselves luxuries to lay up provision against a rainy day; we can practice every frugality compatible with healthful living. Yet with all our powers of restraint we live well and value good food and comforts and well-appointed houses, and we have the gift of getting what we value. We are generous to the unfortunate, but we have a deep-rooted conviction that in nine cases out of ten the lack of fortune is the unfortunate man's fault. There is nowhere in the world more plenty and more independence and more "rugged individualism" than in Pennsylvania.

The Pennsylvania farmhouse of stone, with stone ended barn and stone offices, smokehouse, outside oven, ground cellar, carriage house and the like, with lilacs and fruit trees in the dooryard, is known of all the States as a symbol of well-being. There are those who have written us down "corrupt and contented." We shrug our shoulders and do not take the trouble to deny the half of the saying that is false. We are not, as a people, hypocrites. We are a downright folk who accept the world as it is, and find it good.

You know where a Pennsylvanian stands. He is dependable, and stable. He has been used to an inheritance of good things from the past. Generation after generation carries on traditions established in the family in colonial days. Cultivation continued from Old World origins and preserved here through the trying conditions of pioneer days is a possession of thousands of families.

Objects of art and household gear and silver brought across the Atlantic two hundred years ago or more are to be found in many homes. Chippendale furniture of late eighteenth century America is widespread through the state, and family portraits from a hundred years ago are surprisingly plentiful. Peales and Sullys and Eichholtzes are found in towns and in country houses, and the humbler paintings of nameless local painters are legion. Interest in the arts is never far to seek. This is a family with the gift of catching a likeness and a flair for color. That is a family of music lovers, of singers, of members of church orchestras or choirs, or of town bands.

The organ builder was an institution, and no village of any size but had its maker of woodwind instruments. This grandfather had a pleasant knack of turning verses, in the manner of Pope, or Burns, or Wordsworth, as you would have it. That grandfather could do prodigies with the quill pen, in deed, or album, or birth certificate. Artisanry in woodworking and in pottery and in glass blowing was some of it almost art. Home life was in home after home enriched by other interests than successful farming or trading or professional work. Beautiful coverlets were quilted or woven in all the homes of the better sort. Inventories of old sales and book cases and libraries handed down to to-day show books from early times a treasured possession. Folks were cultivated enough to be very critical of ministers and doctors and lawmakers. Collections of this or that, Indian relics, and bird skins, and minerals, were common. Young ladies made herbaria in the seminaries. They did painting on velvet, and needlepoint, too. Philosophical apparatus such as Dr. Franklin experimented with was widely distributed in the country places as well as in town. You find glass drums for such mechanisms in the detritus at Wistarburg. "Chinee" baskets from eastern Asia found their way even into inland homes and Nankeen and Canton and other Chinese wares are still to be picked up along tidewater. Stone china and soft paste were made for us in the English pottery towns, spatter for southeastern Pennsylvania and gaudy Dutch for the Susquehanna Valley.

Seven cultures were established in Pennsylvania, of Hollander, and of Swede, and of British Quaker; of German from the Rhine Valley and Switzerland, and of Scotch-Irish; of Connecticut Yankee, and of Virginian: a more varied congeries than any other state may boast. A lifetime spent in studying our peoples and their effect on their environment but scratches the surface of the subject. There is no end to the research necessary to find out about and to understand the divergences of these cultures, their varying picturesquenesses that have even to to-day resisted the leveling influences of American life. The past is still with us in more manifestations than in any other state. There is a charm in the details of these cultures for every sort and condition of man. Whatever your interest in life there is an appeal for you in some phase or other of our seven cultures.

And what beauty of landscape is background to all these varying facets of our cultures!

Sometimes, as you are following westward some city street, not far from the river front, at sunset say, there unrolls before you, as it were on a film, scene after scene witnessed by you in old years and memorable in one way or another. In the very forefront of all may be a night scene, indoors, on the top floor of the Academy of Natural Sciences. Bird lovers, members of the Delaware Valley Ornithological Club, are gathered about a table, listening intently, one and all, to Dick Harlow describing the finding of a raven's nest in Centre County. The March woods, with their low drifts of snow along the banks of green laurel, a bright sun flashing over all, he pictures in sharp and incisive phrases. You see the cliff he scrambles down, the nest on the ledge, with its eggs deep olive-green, brown daubed and brown streaked, against their background of white hair from the bellies of deer, rounded into a wide frame of sticks. He passes on to you the delight in treasure trove he had in coming on them, and the further and more abiding delight that beauty brings as his eyes drank in the warm snugness and the satisfying contrasts of color. Young faces and old about the room kindle at his enthusiasm. He makes us sharers in his discovery. We rejoice in the discovery for itself, and as a symbol of life triumphant over the rigors of wildness and cold.

It is not every state has such riches as ravens' eggs, or as the acre of fringed gentians that rises before me as I think of Nockamixon Swamp, its log houses and primitive industries, its potteries and coopers' shops and rows of beehives of straw. One year the sloping hayfield in the clearing above the swimming hole will be a sheet of dispersed blue shuttling back and forth under the October wind, and next year there will be no gentians at all, only the rough swamp grass and red top cuffed about under the intermittent northwester. When the stand of gentian is at its best you have a sense of largess of blue, blue on earth that you can handle and cherish, a loved and familiar blue, not just those wide and alien reaches of blue heaven no man may wander through.

As my thoughts swing in the track of the westering sun they fall on that third story flat in Downingtown that looks out westward past the gables of a log house, broad and low and steep pitched of roof. It is not that flat's family portraits on panels of mahogany I think of first, or of the Chippendale chairs or Hepplewhite table or old silver, but of that cup of milk glass so gay with the red and yellow and green dear to the Teutonic heart. With legend in German on it and the date 1744, it brings the Old World before me with a rush, the Upper Rhine Valley and the Switzerland that gave of their best to the New World two hundred years ago. It might chance that mug was Wistarburg, but I who have followed the plow over those sandy acres near Alloway have there come upon no piece of glass its like. There are few other of the old seaboard states can show treasures made by man comparable to this tankard of proportions that are a challenge to drinkers of the greatest prowess.

There swims up out of the sun dazzle on the city streets that quizzical and foxy face under grizzled hair of Abe Buzzard, a true poker face, first beheld by me as I was being piloted through West Chester jail at a very early age, that face I was to see later as Abe lolled at his ease in the sun against the timbers of a dugout on the Welsh Mountain. It is not every state can boast of an outlaw evangelist such as he.

Bridges of all sorts have long appealed to me, covered bridges because of old associations, and bridges of stone arches because of their beauty. One of these latter that has a way of heaving itself up into the sky before my vision is by Juniata, just short of Pfoutz's Valley. Back from the river it carries a country road over a tributary stream. It is high, sharp arched, narrow, mounting up more suddenly than any Scottish brig of them all, and bringing me, for all the familiar colors of its whitey yellow and whitey brown stonework, an instant sense that the Old World is immanent in the New.

If your errand takes you to the highest floor of a great office building you may catch a glimpse of the coppery disc of the sun behind the hills of Valley Forge. Out further west by south, you remember, are those equally fabled hills about Gettysburg, with the South Mountain not far away. There are not many states that possess two such places of military moment. At Valley Forge Washington's army steeled itself for the long war ahead, and at Gettysburg the Confederacy went down in disaster in its mad attempt to raid the North. You have made pilgrimage often to Gettysburg, but you have never been able to bring before your inward vision the hosts of battling men on the broad acres of fruitful farmland and among the woods crowning the heights that roll up in parallel ridges as far as eye can reach. All is peace here now. This May evening you wonder are the mockingbirds singing on the slopes of Seminary Ridge? They are greatly loved by the little lady in gray silk that lives here. She can wax ecstatic in her talk of their rain of notes falling through the dimness and through the chill luminousness of those later hours when the moon silvers her lawn. She has been able to pick out, through their constant return to chosen singing stations, seven mockingbirds one after the other joining in a mad medley.

It is against the afterglow you see, in your mind's eye, that mossed oil derrick toward the Ohio line. It loses its sharp lines as the night falls, and takes on some far semblance, on its bare background, to a gallows on a no man's land at the meeting of tracks across a Tweedside moor. It is long ago you passed it first and were told by its patient attendant that "She pumps thirty dollars worth of crude a day." It is so long deserted now there is no tang of oil on the air. You smell grape as you visualize the scene, for the last time you passed by on the Butler Plank Road the air was drenched with its stimulant sweetness. By the roadside are drifts of laurel white in the dusk, and hylas shrilling from the ditches as the cool of evening falls, and whippoorwills on soft wings beating by your car and crying from boulders and stumps and low limbs.

Nights and noons, dawns and days' ends, a thousand and one at least that were good to live and that are good to recall, come to mind. Moments of happiness indoors and out crowd one after another into recollection, folks it was good to know, talks that were racy, scenes that composed of themselves and cried aloud to be painted. Hours on high places return, hours in which it was good to stretch and bask in the warmth of the sun in the lee of some rock; and walks across country through stands of virgin hemlock with no underbrush to trip you save the hobblebush. There were wadings in trout streams overarched with rhododendron bloom. There were stumblings on little ponds over whose lilied waters wood duck steered their broods. There were fiddlings, and ballad singing, seances, funerals, auctions, camp meetings, gossips in country stores and taverns, hunting expeditions—should you live to be a hundred you would not have time to tell half the goodness of it all!

CONTENTS

ILLUSTRATIONS

THE BLUE HILLS

for Herbert H. Beck

IT is a gray eve of December, just at sundown, on the shore of Lake Erie. The wind is driving in mercilessly from the northwest, tossing the surface of the water into white-caps out beyond the shore ice. The last glow of sunset, a narrow band of winter yellow widespread over the gray mirk, serves only to make colder the aspect of the darkening stretches of ice and tumbling waves. The road runs so near the water there is no foreground of shore line to the picture. I note the ice; the bobbing ducks in their hundreds just beyond, with gulls dropping down among them; the white gleams of breaking water a little further away; the gray off-shore; the starless gloom of clouds low and dark settling down with the encompassing night over all the desolate scene.

The glass windows of the closed car cannot turn the cold the wind is carrying in. All they manage to do is to deflect the actual buffets of the volleying blasts. The body heat of the four men in the car and the warmth of its engine count for little. Such a cold wind is unescapable, penetrating, fraught with intimations of that final fate of our earth when it spins an icy cinder down "some frore arctic of the aerial ways."

The men in the car are of one mind in deciding to turn tail and to flee back to the protection of the nearby city. The city, though, was hardly a refuge from that north-wester, the clubhouse where we sheltered was cold, with its

1

members who were physicians writing prescriptions for the laity that body and soul might be kept together. Outside were piles of snow in street and sidewalk, relics of the last storm, much reduced, we were told, by the thaw that had preceded the cold snap we were experiencing. Late at night gritty snow sharp as sand began to nick the window panes. I could not but think of all the broad state southeast of us, with range on range of hills that on my passage west had hung blue in the distance, turning white now under the implacably advancing snow.

There had been no real warmth in that clubhouse all evening long save close to a fire of logs in one of its sitting rooms. There, after the formal banquet and following lecture, I fell into discussion with a man who had worked summers in his youth on the lake boats. He was full of chanties, some of them with snatches of Canadian French, and he gave me a sense of Erie in old days as a port of clearance for westward traffic that I had not had before. A stout upholder of yesterday, he was equally at home in to-day, with more than his share of that optimism nothing can keep down. Even if the West was filled up, with as little opportunity left there as in the East, was not there all To-morrow into which to jump off? To-morrow was as surely a new world as any virgin and unexploited prairie or sierra. And Erie, he thought, was as good for jumping off into To-morrow as the next place.

The whites and blacks and grays of the waterscape, of the birds and breaking waves and creeping ice, its low skies and its menace of night and winter, are clear in my memory now after fifteen years. What comfort comes to me from my memories is that picture of cold beauty, that sense of the warm life in gulls and ducks outriding the night in wintry waters, and that realization that our state is a bridge between the sea and the lakes. Ocean steamers from world-end places dock at our wharves in Philadelphia all the year round, and a varied commerce is carried from Erie on the Great Lakes all months but these of winter.

One whose concern is with the beauty of landscape of his state, with the harmony of its homes and their environment, with the richness of culture those homes housed, would rather consider the Marcus Hook of yesterday than the Marcus Hook of to-day. Here, at its southeastern corner, Pennsylvania abuts on the State of Delaware and on the upper reaches of the great tidal estuary of Delaware Bay. As I remember Marcus Hook forty years ago, there was still picturesqueness about it. It was not even then the "pleasant village, surrounded by apple orchards" of the gazetteer of 1831, the village whose cider was "of high repute." Forty years ago, though, its stretches of river front are now lined with oil refineries and blighted by their fumes and refuse, had patches of swamp shrubs with lush stands of reeds extending out into the shallows of the river.

Here I had come as a reporter on a pathetic story of kukluxing run-out folks of the old stock, a man and his woman of Swedish ancestry so poor all the toys they had for their two-year-old child was a rattle made of a beer bottle quarter filled with pebbles. There were then about enough houses of old brick, with outside offices, and other evidences of a prosperous past, to give the place, though obviously past its heyday, a certain atmosphere of colonial times. There were then tree-lined lanes down which one caught glimpses of broad waters, with here a schooner forging northward under her own sail, and there a tug puffing toward Philadelphia, brigantine or square-rigged ship in tow.

The reeds just off shore were then bird haunted; shad then still ran in large schools up stream to the spawning grounds; and rail shooters then found good hunting at the right time of the year. Then the breeze from the east was pine scented from blowing over leagues of Jersey; the swamps were rumorous with the wind in the reeds; the domes of muskrat houses thick-studded the shallows; the pastures ran so close to the shore line that cows at cud found the hours less heavy to pass through gazing at the tramp steamers outward bound to ports about all the seven seas.

It was through these waters that in later years our steamship plowed its way on the long trail to Liverpool. It was these lowlands, still open country with old houses snuggling under their dooryard trees, that greeted us on our return from Europe with their sense of well-being and hominess and plenty, their smack of our so long known and so loved Pennsylvania.

Now, on this morning of early April of 1933, there is little to recall memories of the Hollanders and Swedes and Finns who settled here before there came those English Quakers, those Swiss and Palatines, those Scotch-Irishmen, who made Pennsylvania the Keystone State. At Marcus Hook now the evident activity in mills and refineries in these hard times is all that is heartening in the town. The picturesqueness of shore line, the earnest of romance there is always about wharfs and jutting piers, the voices of the wind and of the birds in the reeds, are all but vanished. There was here a plum tree in full blow of greeny white in a backyard; there was there an old box bush by a home falling into ruin; and in a third place a river-front garden with clumps of bamboo but slightly winter blasted, about the red walls of what looked like a sea captain's home. These, and these only, in the town, are left to suggest old loveliness.

A little further to the north, at Painter, we found, between the shore line and the open water of the river, a narrow belt of reeds, through which waded and pushed his way a man brandishing a sharp-pointed rod. It was apparently a carp he carried in his left hand as he jabbed down in the reedy pools with his stick, a kind of fishing as primitive as any I ever came upon. It was poor sport compared to that which Peter Kalm records in his *Travels* was that of his compatriot Swedes, two hundred and more years ago. At one draw of a net, he says, the old folks told him, they would secure enough fish to load a horse; and at one shot twenty-three ducks had been known to fall.

The prelude to the man-stricken shore line of the Delaware at Marcus Hook had been good, sweet with the sharp and bleak sweetness of early April. The red maples were in full blow of scarlet in the swales; the willows were green by each spring hole and creek side; the high postwoods of beech were a glow of gray-white in the flashes of sunlight; the groups of old houses, white walled, about the mill villages on Ridley and Chester Creeks, were eloquent of that yesterday in which little manufactories were a human touch and not a blight upon the landscape; an apricot was a cloud of delicate pink against a sharply-sloping lawn of richest green; peepers were lifting their voices from marshes and wet meadows, mistaking the overcast morning for day's end and the hour of ecstasy. One needed all these memories of the countryside back from the Delaware to keep up one's heart in the oil-laden atmosphere. To-morrow there will be, of course, a river-front drive between greenery and clean water all the way from Philadelphia to New Castle—New Castle, whose old beauty of architecture and planting makes it the choicest little town in all this long valley of the Delaware. To-day, though, one must escape into the past, to have any large content in the shore line north from Naaman's Creek to Marcus Hook Creek.

Let us see a Sabbath morning in the early eighteenth century, with canoe loads of towheads paddling up-stream to the old log church on Tinicum Island, with V's of wild geese above them, and the waters about them breaking into spray as the sturgeon in their files drive northward. Let the somber strains of the slow movement, the second, of the Sibelius concerto in D minor for violin and orchestra, sound in our ears. If we do, we will have a proper accompaniment to the Indian-like progress of the Swedes in their canoes northward, under gray skies, with bursts of sunlight breaking through the low clouds now and then. We will be in the mood to know northernness and primitiveness and the sweet bleakness of old Aprils.

It is mid-June on Ginger Hill in the highlands of southwestern Pennsylvania. I am on pilgrimage to a countryside to which migrated men of my family a century and a half ago. Weygandts left the Forks of the Delaware in 1784 by wagon train for the hill country beyond the Monongahela. Either with them or shortly after them came neighbors, Stechers and Yohes, and now members of all three families lie in parallel rows with tombstones of carved and lettered marble above them, in the graveyard of the high-perched church. The low building of brick, like a thousand other churches in Pennsylvania, is of meeting-house type, with no offending steeple, and with the label of "Zion Evangelical Lutherian Church" on the wooden panel above its front door. I find my own name in full on a tombstone, and experience again that sense of mortality I had for the first time so many years ago at Schoeneck in Northampton County, when I saw "Cornelius Weygandt" on the flat slab of marble that, Moravian fashion, lay flush with the ground.

It is a churchyard with worn sod on Ginger Hill, and with sparse trees with leaves thinned by insufficiency of nourishment in the lean soil and by constant thrashing of the hill-top winds. The earth of the graveyard is pitted everywhere with holes two inches wide, maybe, and three or four inches deep, the work of skunks that have apparently here found rich treasure of grubs for all the shaley turf. Roses are everywhere, by tombstones and by the few graves that have no tombstones, and by walls and paths. They are not the trimmed bushes, low and many stemmed, of dooryard borders, but bushes of few stems that rise as high as your head. Most of the long stems are studded for half their length with clusters of pink flowers, so heavy all together that they bend the stems to curves that give them a wreath-like look. · I can distinguish that old standby of all Pennsylvania dooryards and graveyards, the seven sisters rose, and the damask rose, and several varieties of moss rose. There is also a rose whose name I do not know, of small buds of pink-edged white gathered in groups of three along the stems.

It is only after we have made the round of the graveyard that we look into the church through its long side windows. The wooden benches there are as worn as the sod without. The pulpit is low and simple, and you feel that here the minister must be, in the homely country fashion, wholly one with his little flock. Everything indoors and out has that suggestion of friendliness that only loving use through long years may bring about.

Pictures of that trek of my cousins from the Bushkill country to this tumbled highland above Dry Run rose before me as I looked at the graves of these descendants of the pioneers. We had not the time to look up the graveyard where lay those pioneers themselves, who were buried by the site of the old log church a mile or so away. I could see without half trying the Conestoga wagons with their great horses, and hear as if within earshot the clear-toned bells carried above the hames of their collars. I could see the following cattle, brown cows and oxen with wide horns, and I could hear their lowing. I could see the oldsters in knee breeches and broad hats, and their women folk ample skirted and bonneted, and I could hear their high-pitched and friendly "Dutch," now no more spoken on these hills. I could see the wagons and cattle and neighborly people stopped for the night; I could smell the woodsmoke, and the sweet grass the cattle cropped; and I could hear the pleasant sound of horses munching oats. The three hundred miles our pioneers had been twenty days in overcoming we had traversed in a short day, but how much more they had learned of Pennsylvania in their leisure than we had who had hurried almost all the way across the state in nine hours!

As we looked across country, cleared save for postwoods on all the high land, but treed along the creek bottoms, deeply sunken between the hills, we began to talk about the massacres of early settlers by the Indians and about the Whisky Insurrection. We have no family tradition as to what fate our kin suffered in any of the clashes, for these Weygandts were not our ancestors. We descend from Jacob, the son of Cornelius the immigrant, and these Washington County Weygandts from Jacob's younger brother Cornelius. The Whisky Insurrection is more instant to us than any of the Indian forays, because we have read that this hill on which we are is called Ginger Hill on account of an incident in that insurrection. Government troops sent out to arrest leaders of the insurrection put up at the inn just below us on the old Glades Road, by which we had climbed from Monongahela City, Parkinson's Ferry when our folks crossed it by flatboat. The inn-keeper sympathized with the insurrectionists. Why should not honest farmers turn their corn into whiskey without government license when they were too far from market to dispose of that corn to advantage bagged as grain? So the inn-keeper put ginger into the grog of the officers of the little force, which doctored grog is said to have put those hardy chaps sound asleep for hours, for more than long enough to enable mine host to warn the sought men so that they could get a good start on the law.

It is a pretty enough story in itself, and it affords a plausible explanation for the name of the hill, but I cannot help wondering if that name was not given the hill for a much simpler reason, the color of its soil. That soil is ginger-brown in every one of the cultivated fields about us, and names of hills for the color or quality of their soil are common enough. Red Hill in Montgomery County is Red Hill because of its Triassic red sandstone soil, and Barren Hill in the same county Barren Hill because its white sandstone soil yields scant crops. It is true, of course, that wars little or great often fasten names on hills, as in the instances of Militia Hill and Fort Hill just across from Barren Hill. Militia Hill and Fort Hill retain, after a hundred and fifty years, these names given them in the War of the Revolution. It may be, after all, that Ginger Hill is Ginger Hill for the reason given in the old story.

There were comfortable homes in plenty along the Glades Road and its tributary hill-roads, houses very like those of the eastern Pennsylvania from which this countryside was so largely settled. The land was laid out and farmed very much as Northampton County was farmed, and Lehigh and Berks. The church and its graveyard were about 1840, but of the very order of hundreds of their fellows, older and younger, further eastward and northeastward.

Yet the look of the countryside was not Eastern. Nothing was taken care of as it is in the longer settled districts. Dooryards were infrequent, and where there were dooryards there was not the wealth of flowers and shrubs in them characteristic of the home counties east of the Blue Mountain. The contours of the hills were different. Everywhere they crowded close together, near and far. There were not the snug little valleys of limestone that delight the Dutchman's heart. There was less tillage and more grassland than in the east. There was more greenery everywhere, in uncut fields of hay, in pastures, in brushland and in the more prevalent woodlots.

Far hills were all but wanting to the landscape. It was for the most part foreground and middle distance, with only occasional glimpses of those long lines of blue ridges so universal in the Appalachian highlands and in the Appalachian seaward slopes. It was late afternoon, with night near at hand. There came on us the feeling of being strangers in a strange land that has visited all of us at nightfall far from home. "We must move on," we said, the two of us almost in unison, "and get settled for the night."

As we moved toward our car a killdeer came winging by, laboring along more slowly than any killdeer of my previous acquaintance, but with that so distinctive method of flight. His crying, his way of beating by, his so warm and familiar grays and whites and red-browns, made all the hilltop homey in a trice. Known and loved places where we had met killdeer came back to mind—the flat valley far up Pickering Creek, the Whitemarsh Valley below Lancasterville, the little slough under Lederach. The flying and crying of that bird, his so harmoniously piebald feathering rejoiced in since childhood, was the touch of nature needed to make this strange place kind. With such an introduction we found "Little Washington" a hospitable and friendly town, martin-haunted and mellowed by its long adherence to old learning.

It is October, the seventh of October, 1932, but the valley

is as loud with the voice of waters as if it were spring. Its streams are in full spate; all its roads are crossed with runnels; and every hill-pasture and meadow is glittering with trickles and little pools turned gold under a sun high in the heavens. It is October the seventh in the Starucca Valley, famed in the days just after the Civil War through a painting by Jasper F. Cropsey (1823-1900) done in 1865. This painting was lithographed by William Dresser for "T. Sinclair Chromo Lith. Phila." as "American Autumn, Starucca Valley, Erie R. Road." It was, the last line under the title relates, "Printed exclusively for Members of the Crosby Opera House Art Association." It is not a rare print, I am told, and I have myself come on two copies of it other than the one I own. One of these, like mine, I found in Philadelphia, and the other, elaborately framed like this second one discovered, I came on at an antique dealer's in a remote byroad of Brookfield just south of the Ossipees in New Hampshire.

It was this lithograph that took us to the extreme northeastern corner of Pennsylvania at the height of autumn color to see how closely the print would approximate to the valley that inspired Cropsey. We were lucky to come without effort on the very point of view from which the artist had painted. The likeness of what was before our eyes to the lithograph was startling indeed. It must be that the lithograph most faithfully reproduces the original painting. Never before had I seen anything in nature so exactly like its transmutation into art—if I be permitted to speak of a lithograph as art.

Cropsey had evidently had to eliminate little from what he saw. Nature, in this instance, had done her selection for herself, and, stranger still, had preserved a countryside unchanged for sixty-seven years. Save for the two men and the dog on the rock in the left central foreground, all framed in for us by trees on either side and mountains in the background was just like the reproduction of Cropsey's painting. The bridge for the road in the middle distance was there, the two viaducts for the railroad were there, and there was a train crossing the lower viaduct and headed south like that in the picture. The colors were as those in the picture: the burnt orange and deep red and all the other tones of red; the wetness of the water; the green of the valley grass; the thin blue of the distance; and the light white clouds that here and there trailed across the promontories mapled red and the shadowy blue recesses of the mountain in the background far across the Susquehanna.

When we had slid into the valley of the Starucca almost unawares it had been strange, in this so amber light of autumn and with a richness of multicolored red on all the hills, to find the dominant note the loud voice of the waters. It had been stranger still to find a man's conception in 1865 of the lower valley, at its place of debouchment on to the Susquehanna, repeated before our eyes in the landscape of 1932.

The upper valley of the Starucca had been as much a surprise and delight to us as the lower stretch just above the Susquehanna. We had followed, for several miles, the stream that gives the valley its name before we reached a crossroads store with folks about of whom to ask questions. There we had learned that the followed stream was the Starucca of our search and that the stream it here met was the Shadagee. The hills about us for those three miles or so had crowded close, most of them cleared, but all of them set here and there with groups of sugar maples or solid woods of sugar maples of every gradation of color from burnt-umber through orange to clear scarlet. As we had crested the hill

leading into the valley a ruffed grouse had thrown itself into
the air from the hillside to our left and, describing a wide
curve, planed across the road and rounded to a wood's edge
far below us. That sight of rusty brown and buff and black
feathers, blended to a warm ruddiness in the full sunlight,
had given the countryside a sense of wildness and a completeness of autumn feeling that was lacking to it before. There
was abroad the scent of fields after rain, the slashing rain
of the night before. In our nostrils was the tannined smack
of fallen leaves. The mountain air was sharp. It is high here,
but so general is the elevation throughout all the neighborhood that you do not realize what look to be only hills are
ridges of over two thousand feet.

There is a northernness to all the region, a northernness
that manifests itself in several ways. You see no fields of
grain and few orchards, you catch sight of steepling spruces
against the blue distances, the wind pushes by with the wail of
winter in it. The names of the people on the rural free de-
livery boxes are New Englandish. The towns betray the
Connecticut plantation by their "Corners" and "Centers."
There are Preston Centre and Preston and West Preston,
and Scott Centre, and Herrick Centre, and Ferrell Corners
and Gardiner's Corners and Salem Corners. It was brushing
up, too, as so much of New England is, and where there were
still high hill pastures they had the austerity about them of
Vermont and New Hampshire.

The stone fences, too, took you north, though these were
not of glacial boulders, but of a flat stone, grayish green,
and easy to build into frost-resisting barriers. They were
high walls, and they climbed the close-crowding hills for
perhaps a quarter of a mile on either side of the valley road
that followed the Starucca. A coping of stone, laid at an angle
of forty-five degrees with their tops, finished them off in a

most shipshape fashion. This country was opened up by settlers before the Revolution, but its back valleys are of later
occupancy. Most of the clearings along the Starucca, judging by their houses, date from a hundred years ago, though,
it may be, there were log houses preceding these present
houses of clapboards. Its first-growth timber was most of it
cut, I take it, by 1880. The farms are small, with buildings
of only moderate size, and they have the look of being
occupied by folks that are farming on sufferance. Dairying
appeared to be what was most profitable.

Early afternoon though it was, as we had passed down the
valley the cows had been homing. They had stood by the
bars along the roadside, most of them, but a few had feared
to ford the sluicing stream and were nervously cropping the
lush grass of the water meadows on its far side, and looking
longingly at their fellows safely across that fifteen-foot
breadth of wild water.

We had noted cellar holes by the old road we had followed, but in most places the lilac bushes had disappeared
from their sides and we saw few stands of those low roses
of Provence and those chimney pinks that the Connecticut
folk carried with them wherever they went. You could not
escape the feeling that this countryside had had a fuller life
in old times than it was having to-day. Its people, though,
had probably never lived so well as those of the Great Valley,
or of southeastern Pennsylvania, or as those even of the
Alleghanian plateaus. You could not think long, though,
of yesterday, in the presence of the glory of sugar maples of
to-day. Such pageantry of red and gold as was this countryside's would not tolerate more than momentarily any thought
in its beholders other than of its own incomparable richness
and intensity of color. Before this autumn splendor, and with
this rumor and roar of water in your ears, you could be

aware only of the here and now. Floods we know, we of Pennsylvania, and the glory of October maples, so there was nothing alien to us here by the Starucca. It is only a riot of water not to be expected at this time of year and a greater intensity of autumn coloring we have to adjust ourselves to. That we can do quickly, but with no diminution of wonder at the wildness and beauty of the forgotten valley. It is safe in memory against the years, that tapestry of amber and burnt orange, of clear yellow and saffron, of scarlet and gold, all suffused with the glow of a sun just past meridian, and glittering in the reflections from a myriad pools and runnels of new-fallen water.

The four corners of Pennsylvania I have described serve as samples of the differing sorts of countryside in the broad extent of our state. They serve, too, in a way, to delimit Pennsylvania, to cut it off from Ohio in the northwest, Delaware in the southeast, West Virginia in the southwest and New York State in the northeast. The reminders of New England in Wayne County, in and about the Starucca Valley; and that suggestion of the South, in whitewash and mules and negro farmhands along Mason and Dixon's Line from Marcus Hook to Waynesboro and in the atmosphere of leisure that invests Bedford Springs, tend to emphasize how medial is the position of Pennsylvania. Pennsylvania is in a very real sense the Keystone State. It ties North and South together, this Pennsylvania of ours, as it ties together the Great Lakes and the sea, and as in old years it tied together East and West. Delaware and Susquehanna flow into the Atlantic Ocean, Alleghany and Monongahela into the Gulf of Mexico through the Ohio and Mississippi. For years the Alleghany Mountains were the Great Divide, and they even yet mark the frontier of the East, though now it is only the mid-central section of our country from which they separate us and not from an Indian West.

A deal of history unrolls before you as you motor from Philadelphia westward across the state, say to "Little Washington." You first pass through that part of Pennsylvania that was once Quaker Pennsylvania, a countryside settled principally by Friends from England and Wales and Ireland. Quaker Pennsylvania ends at "The Stone Hills." Outstanding landmarks of this broken range are Haycock Mountain in Bucks County, Rockhill in Bucks, "The Stone Hills" proper in Montgomery, the Welsh Mountain in Chester County and the York Barrens in southeastern York.

The German immigrants, when they could, settled on limestone. Their first center, however, was Germantown, on a barren stretch of gneiss in the very heart of the Quaker district. From there they migrated past "The Stone Hills" and settled the country between that ridge and the South Mountain. They passed over the South Mountain into the Kittatinny Valley, which sweeps southwestward from the Delaware above Easton to Harrisburg, and, as the Cumberland Valley, reaches on past Carlisle to Chambersburg and the Maryland line. You will find the Pennsylvania Dutch west of the ridge called Cove Mountain to the south and Tuscarora Mountain further north, and past the Alleghanies for that matter, and on to and beyond the Ohio line. There are Amishmen in Beaver County and familiar Lutheran names from Northampton, as we have seen, in Washington County. The Dutch have been the dominant people, however, only here and there beyond the Blue Mountain.

There were Scotch-Irishmen, many of them, in Quaker Pennsylvania, and Quakers, for that matter, who penetrated through Dutchland to the frontier. It was on the frontier the Scotch-Irish were most at home. They were instinctive

Indian fighters, restless, aggressive folk, desirous of the
elbow room and independence that could be theirs beyond
the longer-settled and tamer and more-governed districts
in the southeastern part of the state. They have given color to
the life of most of Pennsylvania to the west and north of the
Alleghany Mountain, though there were many New Englanders on our northern border and Virginians in the southwestern corner of the state. All three of these peoples,
British Quaker, Pennsylvania Dutch and Scotch-Irish, I
shall consider narrowly in the next chapter. I speak of them
here to give their distribution throughout our many mountained land.

All my life, and I am now well past threescore, I have
been trapsing hither and yon in Pennsylvania. There were
excursions in childhood to many places east of the Blue
Mountain: to Chester County, my mother's birthplace; to
Northampton County, to which my father's people had
moved after their first settlement in Germantown; to
Lebanon with Aunt Rachel, a trip marked by my first sight
of a straw-roofed barn, burning slowly by the side of the
railroad; to Mauch Chunk in Carbon County; and to the
Water Gap in Monroe. There were two expeditions, each of
a fortnight, to Juniata County, with Uncle Seal, who lived
in Lebanon. There was a trip with Uncle Jim to Gettysburg
in 1888.

I had made many walking trips in my teens, the most considerable of them from Mauch Chunk to Port Jervis. Most of
these, however, were in the general neighborhood of Philadelphia, up all the tide creeks from Crum Creek to the
Tohickon, for instance, but there were others in Chester
County and Lebanon and Juniata. I have driven by team
from Lebanon to Port Royal and back again from Port Royal
to Lebanon. I have bicycled over all the home counties round

about Philadelphia. I have summered in the Poconos for several years and tramped and driven by team over a good deal of Monroe and Pike Counties and some miles of Wayne County. From 1900 to 1920 there were many trips to this place and that on University business, lectures, talks before Pennsylvania alumni and the like. Wherever I went I was taken around and shown the famed and beautiful places, now at Bradford, now at Erie, now at York. Since the advent of the automobile there have been excursions to all parts of the state. Add to all this junketing about, hundreds of talks with boys at college about all that was delectable in their home neighborhoods, and thousands of compositions read about "Indian Maidens' Leaps," "The Last Panther of Lycoming," "Buffalo Swamp in Elk County," "Maple Sugaring in Monroe," "Trout Fishing in Tioga," "The Coalfields of Clearfield" and the like, and you will realize that nearly all place names in Pennsylvania sound familiar to my ears. Clear visualizations of places rise many times before my inward eye at mention of valleys or towns, rivers or mountains.

A great deal that made Pennsylvania picturesque has passed in my lifetime. I have seen both Delaware and Susquehanna full of rafts of logs. I have listened to the tinkling bells of the mules that pulled canal boats and rejoiced in the sight of them rounding a bend of the river. I have met Conestoga wagons almost daily on Main Street in Germantown. I have gone by stage from Philadelphia to Newtown Square and from Waterford to Port Royal. I have met thatchers of straw roofs; men who lived by gunning, both of game for market and of bird skins for women's hats; collectors of herbs for medicines and flavors; tin peddlers; turkey drovers; wandering glass blowers; vendors of homemade baskets; itinerant clock repairers; German bands on the tramp; and Savoyards with brown bears so well trained they could drink beer like men. I have seen, in the Poconos, flocks of hawks that were all day passing; our Delaware alive with great runs of shad; torchlight processions after political victories; village streets lined with solid houses of gray sandstone that had stood unchanged a full century; and a whole mountain ridge dappled yellow with chestnut bloom.

All these so good things I had come on in the share of Pennsylvania that I knew. There were parts of the state, though, I had never visited. That part of our trans-Alleghanian country on the Maryland line was to me long *terra incognita*. I had heard talk, since childhood, of the seven ranges of our Appalachian mountain system, but it was not until 1932 that I came to know the sixth and seventh ridges: Laurel Hill and Chestnut Ridge, and the great plateau that begins west of Bedford and extends almost to Laughlintown. To restrict our ranges of mountains to these seven is rather arbitrary, but there is, after all, something distinctive about each one of these seven, "Stone Hills," South Mountain, Blue Mountain, Tuscarora Mountain, Alleghany Mountain, Laurel Hill and Chestnut Ridge. The Tuscarora Mountain was singled out as a landmark, for instance, by the layers out of the pike from Downingtown to Harrisburg and the west, by way of Ephrata. The milestones on that pike read, so many miles "to P," that is, Philadelphia, and so many miles "to T," that is, the Tuscarora Mountain. That "T" gives those who like to joke at the expense of such of us as are Pennsylvania Dutch their little innings. They tell the story of the Dutchman of Hinkletown who was asked what the "to T" meant.

"To Towningtown, of course!" he replied.

The loyal son of Bedford will stand out for another seven ridges in his county alone, Scrub Ridge, Sideling Hill, Ray's

Hill, Clear Ridge, Tussey's Mountain, Dunning's Mountain and Will's Mountain, but it can hardly be contended that these so many elevations have the individuality of the seven major ridges that have been celebrated from old time. Call our ridges seven, or seventeen, or twenty-seven if you will—and you could claim even the highest number for purposes of argument—they one and all are "blue hills." From Poconos, from the Nescopeck Mountain above the Vale of Wyoming, from Bald Eagle Mountain just out of Bellefonte, from Grand View above Schellsburg, as well as from the points of view from which I have described landscapes in the four corners of the state, and from a hundred places else, I have seen hills hanging blue in the distance. Most of them have been ridges, level-topped, with few breaks in them other than the gaps of rivers, but more of them than are commonly known knobs and isolated peaks. Of this latter sort are Pocono Knob, a seven of cone-like tops above the Nittany Valley, and a good few round about McConnellsburg.

The blue of our "blue hills" is, of course, only the blue of distance, but blue the hills are nearly always, if of changing hues, from dawn to day's end, and during all months of the year. Far hills and far mountains are blue whether their trees are leafed or bare of leaves, whether their slopes are green with fern and laurel or under snow. They may rarely be old rose in the sunrise or purple in the evening light, but nine days out of ten all the year round, between dawn and sunset, they are one or another shade of blue.

In my earliest memory of our blue hills, as we looked at them, from the highest point of Paper Mill Lane, they were a dark blue, a blue that was almost slaty. To sit there in the phaeton, in Upper Roxborough, and to see the South Mountain forty miles away was to me to realize romance. I had, indeed, visited the South Mountain, but I knew nothing of its recesses and their many beauties, both natural and man-made. I had not then come on its trout-creeks tumbling down through blue swathes of forgetmenots or on its farm buildings warm-roofed with red tiles. In the distance the South Mountain was no real place, but the haunt of dreams. As I looked at it I heard horns calling, cool calls of horns rising from its bloom of blue. I was enchanted with such feelings as came to me years afterwards as I listened to the Pilgrims' Chorus from *Tannhäuser* or to the Alpine calls in the brass toward the close of the *Symphony No. 1, in C Minor,* of Brahms. I had been reading Scott, and it was perhaps *Anne of Geierstein* that had filled my inner consciousness with sounds and sights associated with mountain places. Those mountains in the offing were mole hills compared to the Alps, but mountains were mountains, resorts of all kinds of far-off, romantic, impossible things. I had not yet come upon Old World stories given a new habitation in these mountains; stories of dragons and pots of gold; of fools of gigantic strength and childlike innocence, and of a figure black cloaked riding a white horse with thunderous hoofs; of charcoal burners come face to face with the devil himself and of cattle that could talk on Christmas Eve.

We could not stay long on this high hill up Paper Mill Lane, for there was always a wind astir on the height, and we were afraid Nellie would take cold. It was a pull up from the Wissahickon Valley, and in these summer days the old mare was always in a sweat by the time we reached the top. The few occasions on which we drove there in the morning it was always winter, as I remember it, or at least after leaf-fall. Then the hills were of the deepest blue, as rich a color as any impressionist of them all has dared to put on canvas.

Deep blue these far hills of the South Mountain loomed up ahead of us one morning of recent years, as we motored, the sun behind us, up the Ridge Road to Jeffersonville, and from Jeffersonville to Phoenixville, and from Phoenixville to Bucktown, and then westward across Black Horse Hill to my mother's home country just east of the Brandywine. At a good few of the hilltops we rose to, the Blue Mountain was visible, not the full line of it, but just such bits of it as were revealed through the gaps and over the low places of the South Mountain. Other hills we crossed were of this blue or that, according as the slants of light fell on them, or according as the shadows of clouds on their slopes were deep or thinly dispersed. One and all they were hills of blue, these hills above the Perkiomen and the Schuylkill, these hills above the French Creek and the Brandywine.

So, too, hills farther and farther from home have hung blue in the offing, those other days not a few we went west to Lancaster and Columbia, York and Gettysburg. The Chester Valley hills are blue, and blue the Strasburg hills. The Susquehanna hills are blue, this shade and that as you look south or north, crossing the bridge from Columbia to Wrightsville. Blue, too, is the South Mountain, misty blue in the receding distance before us, as we journey from York to Gettysburg. All this is so familiar territory that its varying aspects unfold with no surprises, but with the deepening of pleasure we have in a countryside known to us all our days.

The hills crowd closer once we are over the Blue Mountain. Near at hand, in the full light of noon, they are green, a curiously dull green, but at other times of day, on other trips, all these low mountains that confront us between Chambersburg and McConnellsburg have taken on the blue of distance. In earlier years I have seen them, in May across the pink bloom of apple orchards, in November across the rosy ash of leafless second growth. There are old associations for me in all the ridges east of the Alleghanies, and I had the Alleghanies themselves on the horizon in summers long ago.

I have penetrated the ridges west of Bedford now, but for years even before I saw them certain scenes of our history enacted there made me feel I knew these places really strange to me. Their backgrounds I had visualized, almost since I had first heard or read of them, and I have had associations with Laurel Hill and Chestnut Ridge these many years. The great plateau west of Schellsburg was the only true surprise of my first trip from Bedford to Greensburg. That plateau's open country, its miles of grassland, its mountain-top air, its suggestion of a past of pastoral plenty, were a revelation to me. I did not know we had anywhere in Pennsylvania a stretch of country twenty miles long, all but all of it of an altitude of over two thousand feet, and those parts of it that fell short of two thousand feet no more than a hundred feet short. It was a real thrill to see at one place by the roadside a sign recording that the altitude was 2908 above tidewater.

The hills nearest home, "The Stone Hills," have naturally given me the most associations. So many little wonders of out-of-doors have been revealed to me here, so many small objects of art typical of our earlier days have I gathered here, so many hours of good comradeship have I spent here that I hardly know on what incident or treasure to seize as most typical of this neighborhood. I think of a rare morning of spring, and arbutus in its pink loveliness on gorges breaking down to the Susquehanna, where York County reaches close to the Maryland border. I think of the eagles that were the pride of Peach Bottom in my youth. I think of the thrill that was mine when I first looked on the Welsh Mountain from Honeybrook and realized that here was the home of Abe Buzzard, the last of the outlaws of eastern Pennsylvania. I think of Warwick Furnace on the south branch of French Creek. There the first Franklin stoves were made, and, before the Franklin stoves, early plates of Biblical themes for the old five- and ten-plate jamb stoves, the stoves that were put in the wall at the back of a fireplace and that carried the warmth of the burning wood of that fireplace into the room next to that into which the fireplace opened. The great box of iron filled from the heat of the crumbled logs kept that adjoining room even snugger, we are told, than that in which the fireplace itself was. I think of all the bustle and activity of industrialism there was once in this valley, now so quiet and pastoral.

I think, too, of all the *fractur*, or illuminated lettering and drawing, that was quilled and brushed in with color in the shadow of "The Stone Hills," in *haus segen, geburtsschein* and *taufschein*. These house mottoes to hang, framed, on the wall; and these birth and baptismal certificates to display in the same fashion, or to lay away in Bibles, or in the secret drawers of bridal chests: are plentier round about these hills than anywhere else in Pennsylvania. Of the scores of these that I treasure, I choose a house motto as a sample of the handicraft in old times of this countryside of trapdykes and sterile ridges of sandstone, of lush cedars and clay the best for redware in all Dutchland.

It is twelve inches long by seven and a half inches high, this *fractur*, a thing of beauty balanced in design, harmonious in colors, distinguished in lettering and in the detail of decoration. Its blacks and golds and old blues, with their slight touches of yellow and green and soft red, blend into a unity of effect with its firm-handed and exquisite quillwork and with the sprightly birds at its lower corners. It prays that

"Jesus dwell in my house and go from it nevermore, dwell there in grace or I shall be lost," a goodly saying, "written in January, 1824." The legend is of more pleasing sound and aspect in the German than in any English I can put on it, full-throated there, easy and complete in expression. There is a chant in the German, from "Jesu Wohne" to "verlassen bin." It is in rhyme, but if I print it so the perfect balance of the lettering is lost. Only a reproduction in color, with the flushed ivory of its old paper exactly caught, would do this house-saying full justice. The effect of the whole, humble in intention as it all is, is as truly beautiful as any piece of illuminated manuscript that I know.

From the countryside under the South Mountain I might select as typical the Conestoga wagon, or the printing at Ephrata, or the laborious art of the gunsmith, or the perfection of silversmithing in buckles worn on instep and kneecap on occasions of high ceremony. I should like to insist that the artisanry or art, call it which you will, of these various objects, runs in its appeal the whole gamut of the social structure from what contents the lowliest in the community to what contents folk of dignity and authority.

There is a rarer beauty, though, in that example of domestic art that forces itself upon me as the illustration that must be taken of the culture of the country round about the South Mountain. Up at Elizabeth Furnace, in northern Lancaster County, by a pass in the South Mountain, Stiegel began his manufacture of glass. There he failed, it is said, to attain to those effects of precious jewels reached by his best glass made at Manheim. Manheim, however, is always aware of the South Mountain a short distance to the northward. Whatever is of Manheim has in it a suggestion of the South Mountain, but nothing else I know of seems to me as intimately associated with those changing colors of the low ridge as a baptismal font of Stiegel I am fortunate enough to possess. It is of blue glass, of this blue now and of that blue the moment after, according as the light falls on it, but always blue. So it is with the South Mountain most hours of the day. From just after sunrise to just before sunset that mountain is always blue, gray-blue, misty blue, slaty blue, mountain blue, but blue. Even its old rose at dawn and its peacock purples at sunset have in them underdepths of blue.

The baptismal font is of changing blues, but it is always blue in daylight and in the white light of mantle lamps that burn oil and in electric light. Unillumed, it is a dark blue, but with light behind it, it comes to life like a great jewel. It is four inches across at its mouth, and four inches high from rim to bottom of foot. That foot is two inches in diameter and three-quarters of an inch high. The font is of diamond pattern on the swell outward above its foot, and ribbed above that to the rim. It is deepest colored toward the foot, possibly because its glass is thickest there, but it is of that lustrously jeweled effect everywhere, that effect that Stiegel glass and its kind alone possess among all the many experiments of the American glass makers. The font glows with crystalline effects in all lights, but I like it most, I think, at night, when, all the blues of out-of-doors whelmed by the darkness, it seems immeasureably precious as I twirl it this way and that under the lamp. A lucky child that, who was baptized from this bowl. Deep blue in glass in prophylactic against whooping-cough and a charm against the evil eye and all witchcraft.

I cannot disassociate the Blue Mountain from the Moravians and their music. On the road to the Wind Gap, at Schoeneck in Northampton County, where my father's people are buried, I have made pilgrimage many times. From the belfry of that little church, a belfry that looks off toward

Wind Gap and Water Gap, I have heard the trombones on the air of a golden morning of October, and within the walls of the church below I have heard the little orchestra of seventeen playing Bach, and Bach, and Bach, and Beethoven, and Bach. What better association can one have with these level ridges of blue, gap-broken, than that of the best of the Fatherland's music played in the churches of our own mountain land, with whose glooms and shadows and triumphant bursts of light and organ-voiced winds that music is in such harmony and accord.

Think of an Easter morning in Nazareth, or Bethlehem, just to the southward, and the procession, trombone headed, marching to the cemetery at sunrise. Think of the makers of violins and woodwind instruments in their shops among the foothills. Think of a whole community to whom music, in a near yesterday, was as large a part of life as it was only last night to the Welsh slate quarriers of Bangor so close by.

What I know best about the Tuscarora Mountain I learned from two fortnights of youth, one spent on the Tuscarora Creek, three miles or so out of Port Royal, and the other further up stream at Waterford. There are memories in abundance of both places, but not different in kind, most of them, from memories of other mountain places in Pennsylvania. There was my first acquaintance with the barking cries and demoniac screams of the great horned owl; nights loud with the concerted chorus of bullfrogs of thunderous voices; the running of a vixen, rabbit in mouth, through the firelight of our great holocaust of walnut logs, to her hole in the creek cliff; and the back talk and banter caused by Uncle Seal's charcoal sketch of log cabin and coon, with its defiance to all Democrats, flaunted so prominently above our tents. There are memories of bread baked in an out-of-door oven, of fish taken off in early morning from outlines set out all night; of a coon hunt; and of stories of all parts of the States from the inexhaustible experiences of Uncle Seal's wandering life.

There was nothing so distinctive of a remote countryside that retained much of yesterday, however, as the game of townball still played in the valley. They did not thank us for trying to introduce baseball at Waterford; they preferred the older game, with a home-made ball wrapped and sewed by the local saddler, and a paddle of white oak made by the old shingle-maker with the young wife and full quiver of children. The pitcher was called "giver" and the catcher "taker." The ball was to be "given" so it could be hit. "Over the fence is out" was a rule of the game, and a home run had to be made by fast running on a ball hit within the limits of the playing field. A man was out anywhere in the diamond if the ball was thrown across before him as he ran for a base. Two sides of any number were chosen, all the side not at bat, save the "taker," going into the field. It was pretty hard to hit a fly ball safe when the whole village turned out to play. A side was not out until every one on that side had been put out. You could be caught out on a fly ball back of the home plate, but fouls were not counted. There were no basemen, since a player was never out through a play at a base.

The temptation to me is strong to speak of the loons found breeding on certain of the lakes along our northern border, as an example of the wild life still holding its own in our Alleghanian regions. So many of us associate its "sad and wolfish call" only with Maine or New Hampshire, the Adirondack or Canadian lakes, that one would like to stress the fact that the loon belongs to us, too, as a summer bird. You cannot cite Loon Lake in Luzerne County as proof of the bird's summering in Pennsylvania, for that might have been named for a single migrant bird shot or seen there, in autumn or April. There are authentic records, though, of the breeding of the loon on Lake Como in Wayne County and on Hermit Lake in northern Sullivan, and these are records of very recent years. There are not so many large ponds or lakes in the Southern Alleghanies as in their continuation northward across the Susquehanna, but loons have found their way in spring and fall to the great Quemahoning Reservoir, and we may yet have a breeding record from there.

An old print of "Head Waters of the Juniata, Alleghany Mountains, Pennsylvania" is of a scene more typical of this part of our mountain land than that conjured up by the so vehement bird. You are not likely to forget the few times you have run across a loon on a pond small enough for you to get a good look at him. Gunmetal color, he is, and white, a very projectile of a bird, that can dive in a flash, and swim under water as fast, so it is said, as he can hurtle himself through the air. He rises clumsily enough from the water, disgorging sometimes quite a mess of fish if he is scared by a sudden surprise as you burst out of the rhododendrons on to the shore of his pond. All the wild is certainly in his voice, the loneliness of these barren ridges of the Alleghanies, and the greater loneliness of the skyey spaces above their miles on miles of rock ledge and forest.

That old print of Thomas Cole must be from a painting made way west in Bedford County. The river, divided by a great rock, rushes wildly down in the foreground. Just above the tumult of the waters is a double Indian bridge, a log thrown from the left bank to the rock in mid-stream, and a log thrown from the right bank to this same natural pier. A hand rail on either log makes the crossing easier for the fisherman with rod and basket, white trousers and jaunty hat of sporting type. His dog is already almost at the right bank, just short of which the beast pauses, sniffing the air. In the middle distance, beyond wind-tossed forest, a conical peak looms. The background is a gray sky of thin clouds, through which a line of seven birds is driving. L. Kimberly is the engraver. I do not know when the print was made, but I have little doubt it was in the lifetime of Cole, whose dates are 1801-1848. The china plate made from Cole's painting by W. Adams and Sons, of Tunstall, one of the Five Towns of Staffordshire, bears a signature of theirs that was used from 1820 to 1860. That does not help much, but the pink and white of the ware and its likeness to that of the "View near Conway, N. H." and to that of Shannondale Springs, Virginia, would indicate that it belongs to the eighteen-thirties or forties. Cole would not have had to swerve very far from the stage road that brought him from his Ohio home to the East to have come on the headwaters of the Juniata.

It is generally assumed that we have always neglected the natural beauty of Pennsylvania, but it was not until after the Civil War that this neglect began. Half the beauty of the state was not known until automobile days, but wonders along highways and railroads were long familiar. Our grandparents and great-grandparents demanded scenes from our Pennsylvania mountains in their magazines and in the books they bought, in woodcut and copperplate, in steel engraving and in lithograph, and they got them. Potters way across the sea in Staffordshire found it profitable, as we have seen, to make a plate of a scene in the Alleghanies. There are other plates representing the Columbia Bridge over the Susquehanna, Gilpin's Mills on the Brandywine, and the Delaware Water Gap. There were three Pittsburgh plates, two of steamboats and one of the penitentiary in Alleghany. There was another plate of the Capitol at Harrisburg, still another of Perry's Victory on Lake Erie, the victory that brought forth "We have met the enemy and they are ours," words as famous as any spoken within the confines of Pennsylvania save Lincoln's at Gettysburg.

As we go westward from the Alleghanies, in the southern part of the watershed our mountains make between the Atlantic and the Gulf of Mexico, the height of the ridges falls away. Laurel Hill, though, rises to above twenty-six hundred feet where you cross it on the Lincoln Highway at Biglow Heights beyond Jennertown. It is wild country hereabouts, wild enough to have harbored the last wolves known to have survived in Pennsylvania. Or if not survivors of our old packs, then free wolves that have roamed north-eastward from the mountains of West Virginia. Evidence collected by Samuel N. Rhoads and printed in his *Mammals of Pennsylvania* (1903) seems to show that as late as 1898, and perhaps until 1902, there certainly were timber wolves near Laughlintown. There are those, indeed, who believe there are still wolves in this part of the state. Certainly if the old belief is true that wolves will always be where there are deer in plenty there should be wolves in several parts of the state. There are deer in greater numbers in Pennsylvania to-day than for a full century.

The way westward that I have followed has avoided for the most part the areas of our state blasted by industrialism. What ugliness we have seen has been chiefly in gas stations, eating stands, and bungalows. The outskirts of the cities have deteriorated, and even the little clusters of houses at the junctions of country cross-roads with the pike have been invaded by red and yellow monstrosities. There is still, however, so much more countryside than city and suburbs that we can ignore this ugliness. We have evaded the regions stricken with cement dust, the mountains denuded of trees and piled high with slate and culm from the mines in the hard coal districts, and rivers and streams sullied by refuse from mills and factories and forges. Good judgment has not been used in some instances in widening the highway we are following. It is better, generally, to parallel the old pike with a new ribbon of cement than to broaden the pike at the expense of the century-old growth of trees along its sides.

There remain, however, all the way across the seven ridges, a remarkable number of old farmhouses and village homes of a quiet and dignified beauty. This way west is still picturesque for the most part, though it is no longer picturesque in almost every detail as it was a hundred years ago. The farmhouses of the Chester Valley are most of them set in oases of peace, and very many of them are beautiful. Of gray schist, or blue-gray limestone, or of a stucco of old yellow, and of woodwork painted white, they compose admirably, with their white fences and white outbuildings, against the background of green fields in the low places and against tree-clad hills of darker green on the Valley Hills behind them. North Valley Hill and South Valley Hill—I simply must repeat their names for the sake of the hundreds of memories they recall. After you pass into Lancaster County the effects of the countryside are less intimate, the valleys are broader, but there are still old houses of great beauty all the way to the Susquehanna. And beyond it, too, through York and Adams. Red sandstone dulls to a subdued warmness of tone with the years and adds a richness to the landscape, through the many houses built of it. Brick loses its rawness under sun and weather and enlivens the countryside through its frequent use in houses of later date than the eighteenth century ones of red sandstone and blue-gray limestone.

There are old trees before or around or beside many of the houses, a great white pine on either side of the front door, Lombardy poplars on a farm lane, or Norway spruces set all about the dooryard, these last about the houses of 1840. There are blackbird colonies wherever there are pines or spruces, the orchards are oriole haunted, and robins are busy about every home yard and fencerow. If you stop your car you hear quail bobwhiting from the fields about. Always there are turkey buzzards loafing aloft with motionless wings, buoyant and comfortable, you feel, with their backs well-warmed by the sun.

The dooryards are everywhere gay with flowers, roses predominant among them all now at the height of June. There are literally miles of them planted along the highways' fences all across the state. A friend of mine likes to believe that there are more red roses in Lancaster County and more white roses in York, but it is my observation that there are comparatively few pure white roses anywhere, that most of the roses are red or white and red.

If I had crossed the state a little to the northward of the Lincoln Highway, making my way to Greensburg via Huntingdon, Altoona, Ebensburg and Johnstown, I had sooner come on the districts with which the iron and soft coal industries have had their will. I saw enough of stricken countryside, as it was, in the Monongahela Valley. The day will come, of course, when such ravages will be much more concealed than they are now; that which was considered yesterday to be refuse found of use; the great slashes in the hills planted out; and streams again running trout clear to the sea. One can have no quarrel with what was inevitable, but one can look forward with hope to the healing of the still open wounds of a gashed countryside.

A boy of this countryside, born at Belsano under Laurel Hill, has been so hurt by what man has made of this so lovely mountain land that, come to manhood, he has broken

out in indignant verse to try to salve his hurt. That verse is
as true a symbol of the sixth main ridge of our mountain
system as the wolves about Laughlintown. They are a symbol
of the wildness of one portion of it; the verse of Malcolm
Cowley is a symbol of the beauty of which man has ravaged
another portion. You will find in *Blue Juniata* (1929) some
fifteen sets of verses about the life of the country about the
more northerly part of Laurel Hill. It is angry verse, a good
deal of it. We would know, even if he had not told us so
explicitly, that he had "loved fiercely" beauty and perfection.
This verse of his is largely his disappointment in his failure
to find what he would of these in his loved land. He gives
his protagonists Scotch-Irish names chiefly, but there are folks
of German names, too, among them. They are a forthright
and stark folk evidently, who know what they want and go
after it without much regard for their fellows. For all their
passionateness their lives have been bare and frustrated.
They work exhausted farms, lumber a little, labor in forges
or mines. There is the very smack of the devastated countryside in

> *the blackened slope above the mine,*
> *Where coke-oven fumes draft heavily by day*
> *And creeping fires by night*

and in

> *They scoured the hill with steel and living brooms*
> *Of fire, that nothing living might persist.*

It is a pity Mr. Cowley did not more often find beauty in his
homeland. There is beauty there and he has shown that he
can catch and imprison it. He perhaps explains why he does
not more often find beauty, in a note to the second sheaf of
verses in his book. "We had come to erect the sordid into a

kind of religion." What there is of beauty in his verses is to be found in his images, in his grotesquerie, in his warped love of his homeland. The close of "The Hill above the Mine" lifts with the "white bones" of its untombed dead "drifting like herons across the moon." The picturesqueness of stage-coach days is recalled in "Chestnut Ridge." There is the lament of old songs in "Blue Juniata." There is an unsentimental love for stunted lives in "Empty Barn, Dead Farm," a love so fierce it kindles the hard story to a dull glow. In his own twisty way Mr. Cowley has been loyal to the life of his countryside. He has presented the man-stricken districts of west central Pennsylvania more essentially than any one else.

It was under Chestnut Ridge, the seventh and last of our seven distinctive ridges, that General Braddock was buried, near Uniontown, after that disastrous defeat at Turtle Creek on the Monongahela below Pittsburgh. His men carried him south for three days until he died, along the road they had cut for the advance of his little army. The old legend that Braddock lost this battle with the French and Indians because he would not allow his men to fight Indian fashion from behind trees is apparently still accepted as historic fact. It was at Turtle Creek that Washington proved his efficiency in retreat with defeated troops, as, in later years, at the other end of Pennsylvania, he was to prove his powers of reorganization of dispirited and underfed men. It must have been a brave sight, indeed, here on the western side of Chestnut Ridge, as brave as that just before the battle at Turtle Creek, the march north of the British regulars in their full and famous redcoated uniform, of the picturesquely accoutered Colonials in homespun or buckskin, of the Indian guides and irregulars a throng in motley, all of them advancing as if on parade, and the artillery and the two hundred Conestoga wagons following.

It is a curious fact that the place of Braddock's interment near Uniontown is far more a place of pilgrimage than the scene of his defeat. The battlefield north of Turtle Creek is so shadowed with the steel mills of Braddock now that there is little there to remind you of this picturesque tragedy of long ago.

There is an unquestioned picturesqueness, under certain conditions, to the smoke-lacquered skies above the Pittsburgh district and to the smoke-filled valleys round about it. The Monongahela Valley may be a seething cauldron of vapors of all colors at sunset. On gray days its clouds of soft coal smoke may gather and swirl about and be blown away as spectacularly as any broken fogbank along the coast. The river hills take on shades of color that distance and mist and cloud shadows could never give them. They, too, are at times blue hills, but not unstricken of man as are the blue hills that I love.

We must have all realized by now, I think, that there are few places in Pennsylvania where you are out of sight of mountains, and next to no places where you are out of sight of hills. There is a roll to the country even in the southeastern corner of the state once you are out of the marshy flats along the Delaware. There is a roll to the country just back from the shoreline of Lake Erie. There are mountains in the northeast corner of the state, as we have seen, and hills in the southwest corner that would be mountains were not the general level of the countryside so high. Visit any of the famed places of the state and you are in uplands or mountains. It is very high country about Montrose and Silver Lake; it is high country about Harvey's Lake, and about Eaglesmere. It is high country above the Sinnemahon-

ing and the Conneaut. It is high country about Cresson
Springs and about Bedford Springs. There is a roll to the
tobacco lands of Lancaster, and a roll to the high tableland
that supports the virgin white pines and hemlocks of Cook
National Forest, up where meet the three counties of Clarion
and Forest and Jefferson. There is high tableland in Clearfield and Centre Counties, high tableland with a roll to it,
as you pass through places of such unforgettable names as
Drain Lick and Moshannon, Snow Shoe and Gum Stump.
This is comparable to the Pocono plateau around Tobyhanna,
and only less exhilarating than the Alleghanian plateau in
Somerset County.

A large part of our state's riches of every sort come from
our hill land and mountain land. What buckwheat we still
produce is hill-raised, a large share of our wheat and oats,
and no inconsiderable part of our corn. There, too, are large
districts good for grass, and rich in dairy farms. Most of our
apple orchards are on mountain sides. From our mountain
barrens come our huckleberries, a once abundant crop growing less now it is not safe to burn over, for their flourishing,
ground that calls to be reforested. Such forests as are left
are, too, most of them in our highlands, and there, or in their
valleys, are the richest stores of limestone for cement, and
of natural gas and oil. Hard coal and soft coal are alike
largely mountain mined. The tremendous head of water
poured seaward through Delaware and Susquehanna, Alleghany and Monongahela, is husbanded by mountain woodland, second growth and third, but still acting as a great
sponge for the retention and gradual discharge of this so
prodigal and priceless supply.

It is the rough countryside of our hundreds of mountain
ridges that retains for us our plenitude of wild life, our deer
and bear, our otter and bobcats, our wild turkeys and ruffed

grouse, and those lordly birds now fast disappearing, the duckhawk and goshawk. It is our miles on miles of wooded mountains and wooded hills that make our west winds so tannin scented, so charged with ozone, so rife with healing and heartsease. It is these wild lands that give us, on outcrops of stone and in clearings, our great drifts of laurel, rosy white in waxen stiffness, and that shelter our impenetrable thickets of rhododendron, whose great flowerheads of flushed white are the distinctive beauty of our woods in just begun July, as the humbler laurel is of those of our mid-June. Laurels are they both in our native speech, "laurel" the sun-seeking shrub, and "deer tongue laurel" its kin that loves the hemlock shade.

A few inches above the leaf mold of the woods' floor of our hills and mountains ladyslippers lift their moccasin-shaped flowers of pink, and exhale their heady fragrance, oversweet, on May eves. From the low branches of our woodland oaks and maples, the thrushes chant through the scented half-light, wood thrushes in the lower lands, wood thrushes and veeries on the higher hills, and wood thrushes and veeries and hermit thrushes all three in fortunate places like Buckhill of the Poconos. From Mason and Dixon's Line to our northern boundary, from the Delaware to the Ohio line, warblers of our three faunas, Carolinian, Alleghanian and Canadian, flash day long, from May to October, their varied hues, blues and yellows, blacks and reds, greens and oranges.

Go where you will in Pennsylvania, there are always blue hills in the distance. Under your feet the soil may be red or white or ginger-brown, but always in the offing the hills hang blue. Their effect is nearly always soothing, restful, refreshing, freeing. Of whatever stock the peoples bred in their shadows, Quaker, Dutch or Scotch-Irish, they have

loved these hills of blue. These people have been some of
them gypsy hearted and some of them stay-at-home. There
have been some of them to whom came the call "over the
hills and far away;" and others of them that felt that this
hill-sheltered home was a goodly heritage to be held fast to.
Few have not felt, with Masefield, that "The skyline is a
promise, not a bound." Those hills on the horizon could always be crossed, broken past, left behind, had one a mind to.

The blue hills of Pennsylvania bring you no suggestion of
the tribulations of their early settlers, or of Indian forays,
and the carrying away of men and women and children. This
landscape characteristically so far reaching and quiet broods
in the sunlight as if it had never known anything but peace.
There are, in the aggregate, despite all the coal mines and
factories, the oil wells and cement mills, the lumbering and
the foundries, fewer devastated districts than you would
expect. Take your way outside of the cities, anywhere
throughout the state, and nine places out of ten you pass
have their share of well-being and beauty.

There are nooks and corners everywhere to delight the
heart, both in wild land and farm land. I remember an old
shack of clapboards, perhaps a toll house in its prime, with
a Lombardy popular at its gable end, and purple veronica
in great swathes luxuriating in the barren soil of iron-stained
sandstone. I remember it particularly because past it rolled
up in the distance the blue hills of Franklin. I remember
the open glade of Cook Forest, through which the road runs.
There, with the wind murmurous through those old hemlocks and white pines, sprung with scanty tops one hundred
and fifty feet and more in air, a mocking bird had the temer-
ity to be singing, where among hermit thrushes and veeries,
magnolia warblers and golden-crowned kinglets, a mocking
bird had no business to be. He was as much out of place, as

much too far to the north, as if he had been singing at
Harvey's Lake or by the ice ponds of Tobyhanna. The hills
here were close crowded on either side of the road, too near
to have the blue of horizon hills, but with glooms of a curious blue-green in the forest just back from the narrow highway.

I remember a log house just to the north of Brookville,
not a very old log house, I take it, with blue hills beyond its
walls of silvery gray. It stood in a littered yard, but it was
so drenched, with all its neighborhood, in so sweet a scent
of the bloom of wild grape, a scent of such intensity that it
went to your head like wine, that I am likely to remember
it as long as I live. I remember a great house of gray limestone to the northward of Bellefonte, with carved lintels of
wood above its windows. Three stories high, it stood amid
tall trees in a yard that was mowed like a hayfield, a yard
without a rosebush or any other scrub. Past its tree-shadowed
gauntness I saw the blue of Bald Eagle Mountain.

I remember the hundreds of berry pickers in the alluvial
flats along the Susquehanna, men, women and children
crouching close to the ground and flanked by a long barn of
gray stone with two tiers of slatted windows. The scent of
strawberries melting in the sun was ambrosial there. Above
all brooded quietly the river hills, low mountains really,
comparatively near at hand but blue because of the mists
rising from the great flow of water down the valley.

I remember lines on lines of blue hills from this place
and that all over the state, seen past all sorts of foreground:
a steeply pitched field of red clover; a catalpa tree in full
whiteness of bloom; an oil derrick so old its timbers were
mossed green; a telegraph pole with a wood-pecker in red
and white and black bobbing up it; an Amishman's house of
pale pink and thin blue; a stretch of red soil, thorntree

whitened, that was the debris of an old ore pit; a high church of yellow stucco with rows of white stones close by.

There have been a thousand hills, no doubt, that I have passed or crossed, or seen in the offing, in my trips about Pennsylvania, hundreds of them long known and scores of them storied. There have been a scant few that took on a paradisal air, a bloom as of a better land, through some strange slant of light, or under the rainbow on a passing storm. The persistent and recurring memory, though, is of long and level lines of blue hills, dim in the distance, or cloud shadowed, and broken at wide intervals by sharp gaps river worn in old time, blue hills that spelled, nine out of ten of them, rest and healing, freedom and lift of the heart.

WHITETHORN AND WILD CRAB

for Elsie Singmaster

WHITETHORN is not one of the shrubs known to all our countrymen. It has been in cultivation, it is true, certain varieties of it, for two hundred years and more, and in Europe, as well as in America. One variety of it, under the name of Washington thorn, that came from south of Mason and Dixon's Line, was used largely in southern Pennsylvania, particularly in Chester County, as a hedge plant in the first and second quarters of last country. In the State of Delaware, the New Castle thorn, or cockspur thorn, still remained as a dominant hedge plant until the days of my youth. There are still extant great rows of it in places, many of them the worse for wear, but I have seen or heard of no plantings of it in recent years. From 1850 on, osage orange began to displace the choicer thorns in hedges, even in the districts where the thorns had long been widely planted.

So now, to me, in our Pennsylvania countryside, the thorn bushes and thorn trees are associated with waste places, or with pastures not too well brushed out, or with woodsedges, or with stream banks, and the like. I have seen thorns, this May of 1931, along the line of the Allentown trolley north of Lansdale; on the ore dumps of Warwick Furnace in Chester County; and along the Harrisburg-Ephrata Turnpike from the Welsh Mountain south to Downingtown. These bushes and little trees were, I take it, *crataegus coccinea,* or whitethorn proper. They vary greatly in size, but specimens taller than fifteen feet are rare in my experience. They begin to bloom when they are three feet tall, disposing their corymbs of white flowers dispersedly over their thorny branches. They assume all sorts of shapes, according to the exigencies of their situations.

The one I have liked best is a fencerow tree. Its lower branches have been cut off, so that the tree is shaped very like a dogwood. It has four stout stems twisting up close together and holding aloft, in late May, a dense head of closely clustered white bloom. Often there are green leaves in plenty on thorns, but in this little tree the bloom is so prodigal it conceals, from a distance, the unfolding leaves. Its sharp relief of white bloom against a background of dark cedars, its luxuriant bloom triumphing over its gnarled age, its isolation from others of its kind, its low crouching, as it were, under the gray skies threatening rain, give it a distinction in the landscape that the specimens of all sizes dotting a woodside can never attain to.

A pasture I know has whitethorns of aspects very varying, but all picturesque. Three of them, despite their thorns, have been trimmed by cattle into shapes like those of gigantic toadstools. They spread out wide tops of white over a narrow column of greenery rising from the ground and concealing the tortuous gray trunks. A stone's throw from these three, two thorn trees growing together have been eaten out by cattle, as high as their browsing lips will reach, into a veritable bower. There is an opening at least ten feet wide between the two supporting columns of greenery, and fully twenty feet of white bloom in the interweaving tops. These tops make a table-like slab of bloom that at the roadside face of the double bush ends flush with one of its pillars of greenery. At the further end a flat shelf of white bloom extends out like a half toadstool to the north. The twin bushes are at least ten feet wide, so the cattle have a bower, ten by ten, under which to shelter from the midsummer sun. To-day, with the temperature at fifty and a spanking north-wester driving in, the cattle are glad to be out in the sun.

Other whitethorns that content me are those dotted over the red ore banks of Warwick Furnace. They are of every conceivable shape. Some of them are narrow pillars of white five to eight feet high. Others show fans of white on handles of greenery. Still others are umbrellas of white, and others yet again greenery relieved here and there by corymbs of white flowers.

One May eve, on a traveled pike, we ran into a hollow full of fragrance. The wind was east. I looked in that direction for the source of the scent, but I did not discover it. Finally, two thorn bushes, just venturing out a few blooms directed my gaze to a woodsedge in low ground. They did not hold my eyes long, for my glance quickly lifted to a pink swathe of bloom ten feet above the thorn bushes. "Whoa!" I cried, and the car came to a stop. I thought that pinkiness bloom of wild crab, but I was not sure till we made our way back to the angle of waste land in which grew the pink trees between the cornfield and pasture. There were thirty of them, perhaps, in this triangle jutting from the woodsedge, stout and upward grown trees fifteen to twenty feet tall, standing just out of touch of each other. In instances, those sprays of pink bloom at once rich and tender in color did touch, perhaps because of the heavy rain of the day before. That pink cannot be described, but to each one of us who has seen it even once it will always remain "wild crab." That fragrance, so individual and equally indescribable with that shade of pink, filled all the little swale. It is a fragrance allied to that of our cultivated apples, but there are in it suggestions of the scent of violets, and of raspberries, and even of pogonia. Just as colors can vary in one light and another, so can fragrances of this shrub and that. If the fragrance of wild crab comes to you in concentrated wafts it is of one character, if in dispersed wafts it is of another. So, too, the fragrance differs if the crab blossoms are in sun or shade, dry or dew-drenched, or heavy with rain.

Our wild crab is a rare tree to me. Once I came upon it in western Lancaster County, and once under the Blue Mountain in Monroe County. This Chester County stand of crab was therefore a double delight to me, and more than a double delight. I had delight in its beauty, and in its rarity, and in its propinquity to a place associated with my people, for, nearby, at Milford Mills, my mother was born. I was still further delighted to find a specimen tree of it in a dooryard a quarter of a mile further on, close to the pikeside. Somebody, long ago, had dug up a little tree of it, perhaps from this same stand, and had tended it carefully. It was now larger than any of the trees we had just seen, fully twenty-five feet tall, and well-covered with bloom. Three times I have tried to establish the wild crab in our homeyard, with nursery specimens, but each time the tree died before it was large enough to flower.

Our height of blow of cultivated apple trees was three weeks gone when, on May 22, I came on this stand of wild crab in blow. It was a little beyond its height of blow when we discovered it, but there were still a few buds to open. The whitethorn cannot vie with the wild crab in fragrance, though the blowing whitethorn has not that repellent acridity of scent that handicaps the popularity of so many of the thorns. Nor can any of the thorns, this whitethorn that blows in May, or the cockspur thorn and the Washington thorn that blow in June, give the delight of color and form that makes the wild crab so grateful to the eye, in vase on mantel or in bowl on dining room table. To-night, our living room is decked, as it was never decked before, so far as I know, with these more than inch wide flowers of softest pink. To-night it is scented, as it has never been scented before, at least in our time, with this so rare and individual odor of wild crab. Perhaps, in old days, when this house was new-built, wild crab flourished, despite our hungry soil, in some of the little valleys of our Wissahickon Hills. It may well be it did, and that the flower-loving German folk who built this house with their own hands gathered *pyrus coronaria* in Mays of antebellum years, and had delight, as we to-night, in its color and scent, in this old room with its walls of enduring stone.

ENOS KEYL'S COW

for Levi E. Yoder

SOME time back there was a man named Enos Keyl lived near the top of Haycock Mountain. It is now ten square miles of second growth timberland, with little patches of open land about its little houses of stone and wood. It was about half farmland and half wilderness in the time of Enos, its scattered houses as often log as stone, with some few bits of first growth forest towards its highest ridges, nine hundred feet above sea level.

One year Enos cleared a new piece for a cow pasture. He fenced it in with a worm fence. It came up to good grass, grass fit to content any cow. He kept two cows there, a red one and a black one. Though they never cropped the piece close, or the half of it, the black one would break out. He got tired of hunting for her all over the mountain. He told his wife he would fix the heifer so she would stay in. He took his gun with him that morning when he drove the two to pasture, and watched to see when the black one would break out. He didn't have to wait long. The black cow went right up to the fence and began to lift a top rail with her horns. She wasn't well started when Keyl fired his gun in her direction. The shot came close by her and scared her properly. She never broke out again.

More than that, always afterwards, when she heard guns going off in the hunting season in the fall, that cow would go over to the fence, and, picking up on her horns any rail she found fallen off, would put it back carefully on the top of the fence. If the firing kept up she would make the whole round of the field, leaving the fence piled as even as even, every panel of it.

QUAKERS, DUTCH AND SCOTCH-IRISH

I. M.
Hattie Brunner

HE who puts this disquisition before you was taught in his youth that environment had as much to do as heredity with making men what they are. He still holds to that contention. He is not, therefore, worrying about the future of America. He does not believe we shall go to the dogs should the old stock peter out. That it will peter out, though, he has never feared for a moment. He holds that the States, with their opportunities for "getting on," for bettering a man's fortunes in all departments of life, and their hot summers and cold winters, will temper the newer comers from Europe, as these conditions have tempered the old stock who came here in the eighteenth century.

His prejudices may incline him to British and Germans and Scandinavians, but his experience with hundreds of boys of Italian and Polish and Russian Jewish extraction proves to him that the American environment will have its will of them as it has had of the peoples from the northwest of Europe. He happens to be wholly of the old stock himself, his ancestor most recently come to the country having been a Hessian officer in the English Army who stayed on in America after the War of the Revolution. He is, naturally, more interested in the old stock than in the newer stocks, but he strives not to allow his predilections to get the better of his judgment, and he has, he trusts, the tolerance that has been Pennsylvania's outstanding characteristic from the time of its foundation.

He believes the people of the old stock have made Pennsylvania what it is even to these so changing times, and he hopes that the standards and values that have been given us by the seven peoples of this stock shall continue to control, in large measure, our ways of life. He is in full sympathy with all these seven peoples: British Quakers; German sectarians and Lutherans; Scotch-Irish Presbyterians; Virginians unforgetful of Merry England; New England Puritans working westward from Connecticut; the Swedes and Finns who left us the old church of Gloria Dei; and the Hollanders, disappeared almost entirely save for an old house or two down the river toward Marcus Hook. He has no quarrel with men of other races and creeds than those from which he is sprung.

He is himself a composite American. The valley of the Rhine and the hills of South Wales have given him most of his blood; but he has in his veins, too, Scotch-Irish blood from County Down, and Irish Irish blood from the midlands of Ireland; Devonian English blood, and Yorkshire English blood by way of seventeenth century New England. There is possibly even a modicum of French blood in him, a New Testament in French that has come down in the family with the name of Maret in it coming possibly from the Maritzes of his authenticated German ancestry and pointing to a French origin of that name.

He does not forget St. Bartholomew's Eve, or, at the same time, that a Catholic ancestry in an older era is indicated for him by a silver-set rhinestone with a cross cut into its back that has come down in the family along with the Protestant testament. The wear on the rhinestone would seem to show that it had been worn, generation on generation, as an amulet around the neck. Time was, of course, when all the people from whom he came were in the old church. He does not forget the pre-Christian past still so often revealed in our folklore and in certain of our common practices. Scratch the Christian and find the Pagan is as true as "Scratch the Russian and find the Tartar."

His life-long preoccupation with English literature has been the greatest influence in his life outside of his family inheritance of traditions and culture and charts to steer by, and his fellowship with hundreds on hundreds of folks of all sorts and conditions. He has met and neighbored with very many of his kind. Irish folklore and yarning through the daily foregathering in his young years with an old Irish gardener from County Wexford, laid the foundation, with the reading of his Grandfather Thomas's two volumes of *Ossian*, for a deep concern with all things Celtic. The mountain folk of the Tuscaroras and of the Poconos, whom he knew in boyhood and young manhood, have had something to do with making him what he is, and so have the New Hampshiremen among whom he has spent twenty summers. There were teachers out of New England in school and college who, perhaps, inclined his thoughts toward Maine and Massachusetts and Connecticut, but they did not extend influences comparable to those of a Scotch-Irishman who said the "p" in his name of Thompson stood for Presbyterian. Perhaps because of the very diversity of his blood he has lived in comparative peace with all men.

This personal statement has been made to prove his right to dig out of himself many of the characteristics of the peoples of the old stock about whom he here writes. His name proves forbears from Germany. They were Lutheran, Reformed and Moravian. His mother's father's name of Morgan Jones Thomas gives him the right to say what he will of Taffy. The Thomases, so far as he can trace them, were Baptists. The Morgans were Quakers. His mother's mother was a Presbyterian Reed, and his father's great-grandmother one Catherine Nolan, whose silhouette with tip-tilted nose and high cheek bones and saucy uplifted chin points to her being a daughter of a more southerly part of Ireland.

He is concerned here with but the three peoples who were most largely contributory to making Pennsylvania the Pennsylvania we know, the British Quakers, the German sectarians and Lutherans, and the Scotch-Irish Presbyterians. There are books old and new about the four other peoples and there is much to be gleaned about them that has not yet found its way into books. No collector of antiques, and no one interested in folk history, but has come across some local color due to Dutch, and Swedes, and Virginians, and New Englanders. All in all, though, they had little to do with giving us of Pennsylvania our virtues and our weaknesses.

I pick up an old Bible in Hollandish now and then, or a bottle of clear glass enameled in colors with a Low Dutch legend, that indicate that there were outposts of New Amsterdam on the Delaware. A name or so, like fyke for the conical net of a fish trap, and kill for creek, tell of the one-time presence here of Hollanders.

One finds very little anywhere in the Delaware or Schuylkill Valleys to tell of their occupation by the Swedes. Kalm's *Travels* proves how widespread their settlements were in the mid-eighteenth century, but to-day we have only a few family names, a building here and there, a piece of old silver and the Rambo apple to remind us of their early prevalence on Delaware and Schuylkill.

There is a southern look to certain of the loghouses along our southern border, in the counties over against Maryland

and West Virginia; a southern touch to the fields and hedge-
rows, their negroes and teams of mules; a southern look to
old prints of watering places, Bedford Springs for one. It is,
though, in such a book as *Notes on the Settlement and Indian
Wars*, by the Rev. Dr. Joseph Doddridge, published at
Wellsburgh, West Virginia, in 1824, that the fullest testi-
mony is borne to the contribution of Virginia to our Pennsylvania culture. An England very different from that of the
Puritans is here revealed, an England as merry as that of
Herrick. Read the chapters entitled "The Wedding" and
"Sports" if you would know much of the Old World sur-
vived in the New.

There are indications of settlement from New England
in many of our counties along or close to the New York
State line. There are "centers" and "corners" in plenty
among the place names of Wayne County; farmhouses at
one with those of Connecticut and New Hampshire in the
valley of the North Branch of the Susquehanna; the very
roses and chimney pinks of Down East dooryards all the way
cross country to Erie.

There is still, too, some aftermath of the old feud as to
whether northeastern Pennsylvania should belong to Pennsylvania or to Connecticut. A governor of our state wished
to appoint a certain noted lawyer to an important judgeship.
There was nothing against the man, apparently, and very
much in his favor. The governor anticipated no opposition
from any source. When, however, the state boss heard of
the suggested appointment, he shook his head, saying: "No!
Blank will never do. He comes from those damned Connecticut Yankees who tried to steal a part of the state from us."

All such incidents, however, are no more than waifs and
strays from yesterday. Pennsylvania was made by the three
peoples aforesaid, British Quakers, German sectarians and

Lutherans, and Scotch-Irish Presbyterians, three peoples
that have blended into one of the most hard-working and
energetic and generally capable sorts of Americans. I would
make what I have to say of these peoples objective as well
as subjective. In all three groups, from their beginnings in
America, there have been people of every condition of life
from the humblest to the most spacious. I could tell stories
to the detriment of all three peoples, and stories to their
praise. I would not hesitate to tell stories of the former sort,
were they fully revelatory of any of the peoples, for all three
could stand such stories. It is my belief, though, that, in the
end, in life as in art, that what counts in a man is the best
of him. So, too, it seems to me, it is with a people. Laugh at
them, each one of them, I shall, of course, and they can
stand it. There is never a day passes I do not laugh at myself. A laughing mother, of whom nearly everybody said,
when he first met her: "She's Irish, isn't she! God bless
her!"—a laughing mother brought me up to laugh at everything. She held, in her mid-Victorian way, that there were
some things too sacred to be laughed at, but in practice she
laughed at everything. So her son shall not hesitate to laugh,
if he will, at certain characteristics of the old stocks behind
him, as he laughs at those characteristics when he discovers
them in himself.

The Pennsylvania Quakers of British ancestry and the
Pennsylvania Dutch are more alike than either people is like
the Scotch-Irish. There were, indeed, some Germans who
went over to the Friends. We find Tysons, for instance,
who were Tiesens, Friends in later years, many of them, but
others who have held to their ancestral Mennonite faith.
Dutch and Quakers have blent largely during their years in
southeastern Pennsylvania, until they are one in about
seventy-five per cent of their characteristics. The common

denominator between either group and the Scotch-Irish, large too, but not quite so large, might be written down at something more than fifty per cent.

We are, all three peoples, alike in essentials. We all have the will to work; we are all frugal; we are all lovers of simplicity; we are all willing to face the facts of life as they are; we are all staunch individualists save a few come-outer Quakers; and we are all conservative. On the whole, the Quakers and Dutch have been noncombative and tolerant, and, on the whole, the Scotch-Irish have been intolerant and contentious. The Scotch-Irish hold to what they believe so vehemently that they can hardly be tolerant. They would many of them feel themselves hypocrites were they tolerant. They have taken their Calvinism, for instance, much harder than have the Pennsylvania Dutch Calvinists of the various branches of the Reformed Church.

The militancy of the Scotch-Irish has been of the greatest service to the less combative Dutch and Quakers. The Scotch-Irish made themselves a bulwark in colonial days between the Quakers and Dutch and the Indians, a bulwark that the Indians sometimes broke through. There have been "Fighting Quakers," from the War of the Revolution to the World War, and it is proverbial that it is easy to get one's "Dutch up," but Quakers and Dutch have seldom loved fighting as Orangemen love it. There was a great deal of Orange intensity in the Scotch-Irish who settled the backwoods of Pennsylvania.

There is much more, too, that is rebellious in the Scotch-Irish than in Dutch or Quakers. For all their conservatism the Scotch-Irish are impatient of authority, at odds with outside interference in local affairs, touchy always, at the same time dour and kindly, high spirited and severe. It was the Scotch-Irish who were responsible for the Paxtang Boys and the Whisky Insurrection. They are more imaginative, too, than the more Teutonic people. There is a Teutonic heaviness of Saxon sort about the Quakers as there is a Teutonic heaviness of Hoch-Deutsch quality about the Pennsylvania Dutch. The Scotch-Irish are wittier and more malevolent, with quicker changes of mood and purpose than their more even-tempered neighbors.

You are very much more sure of what a Quaker or a Dutchman will do in any given set of circumstances than of what a Scotch-Irishman will do. All of which is to say there is a Celtic element in the Scotch-Irishman. It isn't hard to see a John Hielandman of long ago back of many a douce deacon, a John Hielandman, dirk in mouth, creeping into the window of some lonely castle keep, in the black dark, to drive that weapon home, with a sure hand, to his enemy's heart. Thence, too, come the Scotch-Irishman's love of plaintive and desolate airs, his clannishness, his play-acting, his love of wild nature, his ready forgiveness for wildness of blood, in a Robbie Burns he worships, or in a neighbor who has a quarrel with the law.

The Scotch-Irish have not the love of the soil that distinguishes the Dutchman and the Quaker. The Scotch-Irish like trade, and occupations that have to do with mechanics. They have largely disappeared from the farms throughout the state. They went in, almost from the time of settlement, for the professions and politics, work in forge and mine, and, as soon as it was available, for railroading. They loved the plow no more than did their darling Robbie Burns. The Pennsylvania Dutch had been displacing the Scotch-Irish on the farms from the last years of the eighteenth century on to the time of the Civil War, after which you found most of the Scotch-Irish in the country towns and the cities. It was not until a hundred years later, about 1890, that the

Dutch began to turn in large numbers to factory and city trades.

The Quakers are a forward-looking group. They are fresh-spirited, not at all tired with life or weary in well doing. They believe the world can be quickly made better than it is. Meanwhile they are satisfied with their own lot, but not satisfied with the lot of their less fortunate neighbors. There is, of course, danger of smugness in such an attitude, and there are Quakers who do not escape smugness. They like good things for all and sundry. They have, on the whole, well-appointed houses, well-shrubberied lawns, good living and all country contentments. They are always, by choice, countrymen. They are fond of out-of-doors, and of sports, field sports and country club games. They gave the Philadelphia district many of its best cricketers. Reform in forms of government, as in political conditions, is really a sort of sport to them, the game they are often most ready to play. They are rather sure of their ability to put the world to rights, and they have certainly tidied up many of its odd corners. They did good work abroad during the World War in organizing and carrying out relief to the needy, and in anti-slavery days they were foremost in seeking the freedom of the negro. Unless they restrain themselves, they can, like all reformers, become "Meddlesome Matties."

The journal of John Woolman symbolizes the Quakers at their best, as we know them in the busy affairs of life and in their moments of leisure and of contemplation. It is full of quiet light, it is warm and sunny, cheerful as robin song, and a bit prosaic.

Old World types recur with surprising frequency among the Quakers of to-day. This Quaker schoolmaster looks like an English sporting squire. This occupant of the High Bench in meeting would need no make up to enact John Bull in a pageant. This hotel keeper, ready with "thee" and "thy," is the proverbial "mine host" of old prints. This professor of mathematics, lean and yellow as ever Yankee was, was as quick with the answer as any keeper of a crossroads store, and one of our country's best after-dinner speakers. This ironmaster, who wore high boots under his trousers until he was almost the last of the kind, could swap with any man of his generation, give a talk on radium, write verses on a coal scuttle, or drench a sick horse. He, too, personified in himself Big Business in his time. This Davy Crockett of a museum expert and dealer in old books was a backwoodsman who could take a rift, no matter how "foul," in Delaware or Oregon, hold an audience spellbound with his humor, and so write of a robin that you could see the bird before you with head cocked for the fated earthworm.

All of which types, John Bullish and Yankee, go to show how difficult it is to generalize about a people. Yet after all we can generalize, and generalize profitably about the Friends a little more than we have. The Quakers are a moderate people, despite their possibilities for fanaticism in economics as well as religion, a temperate people, a restrained people, a quiet people, and lovers of peace. Their very principles make against their consideration of tact as a virtue, but I have never seen a more tactful treatment of a scene at a religious service than the handling of a distraught woman who insisted in speaking from the floor of the meeting. She had clothed herself in scarlet, perhaps the more to attract attention. She rose in the quiet of the meeting on First Day morning and began to mouth wildly. He who sat at the head of the meeting was equal to the occasion. He rose and said: "Let us all rise and recite in unison the Lord's Prayer!" In the confusion attendant upon the large meeting getting to its feet, and in the subsequent thunderous recitation the distraught sister was led out.

The severity of the Quaker rule varied greatly among Friends all in good standing at meeting. I say "varied" because the severity is over now. There is dancing to-day even in the school houses on meeting house grounds, and plays and pageants use the meeting house itself as stage settings. Kerchiefs with borders of lace were worn yesterday with shun-the-cross bonnets as well as plain bordered kerchiefs with scoops and coal scuttles. One old Friend in Germantown, almost the last to wear a coat without a turnover to its collar, was said to forbid his daughters to wear edging of any sort on their garments, even in places where it would not show and indicate vanity to a censorious world.

In the home of this Friend there were no pictures on the walls, for all art was vanity as well as all lace and furbelows, and all icing on cake and fancy molds for ice cream. On a mantelpiece of imitation onyx reposed several white conch shells placed so as to conceal the worldly pink of their interiors, and above the conch shells hung a hornet's nest of soft gray. There were pieces of coral, too, alarmingly red, on the parlor table along with *No Cross No Crown* and Barclay's *Apology*. That redness of coral was tolerated because, after all, it was made by God, and it was not an illustration of man-made lust of the eyes for gaudy colors. There were the gray nests of red-eyed vireos resting above the conch shells on the mantelpiece, and Venetian blinds in the windows. Inside the pier table, a pier table that no doubt had once had a mirror above it, were old decanters, to show that certain ancestors had had a taste for spirits. The decanters were empty when I knew the room. They were tolerated, perhaps, because they were of clear glass, blown by that man of God, Caspar Wistar, over at Alloway in New Jersey.

The furniture was Empire, but a restrained Empire, heavy and without carving, and covered with black haircloth. Two great house-leeks, nearly a century old, stood each in a French window that opened out on the porch. The infrequency with which the leeks were covered with little stars of pale pink endeared the plants to this straight old Friend, as did a like infrequency of bloom on the pittosporums in the dining room on the other side of the front door. There must have been some detail of the finish of this mansard-roofed house that troubled old William W. Certain it was that a conservatory opening out of the living room of the house of a Friend around the corner troubled him. There was too much brilliancy in its camellias and saffron lilies, its chorizemas and strelitzias. What he thought of the gaily colored needlepoint of the wallets of his father's generation I never learned, but they no doubt, too, were vanities to him. William W., however, was rather unusual even in those days after the Civil War for his concern over brilliant colors. Most Friends had no quarrel with them in flowers or in the tints of autumn foliage.

Friend William did not even delight in good horse flesh, a weakness of most Friends yesterday, as brightly shining automobiles are to-day. He kept no team, living near enough to the railroad station and to meeting not to need one for his daily convenience. He always walked to meeting at the head of a procession consisting of his wife and their six daughters. He was a self-contained man, but his humanitarianism led him once to an exhibition of anger for which he never forgave himself. He all but struck another Friend at the door of the meeting house, because that Friend had killed with his cane an innocent garter snake that had been sunning itself on the flagstones leading from road to meeting house.

As you looked at his house there was not a chintz or lace curtain in the windows. There were Venetian blinds on the first floor and window shades of a green the color of the blinds on the second floor. Similar shades blinkered the windows of the third floor. The front lawn was broken by no flower beds, but a belt of bronze coleuses gloomed in a narrow bed against the porch. The side yard was planted to fruit trees, pears chiefly, since apples did not do particularly well hereabouts, but with a pie cherry, too, and several peach trees. The trees were planted in straight rows with military precision, a fact that one of his worldly neighbors did not let him forget. There was a grape arbor, about whose produce he was also teased by this bearded veteran. As a matter of fact the grapes did not bear most years. The arbor's situation against the northwest side of the house was too shaded, and its chief utility was to afford a cool place for the women of the house to sit in the hot days of summer.

How the men who married Friend William's daughters did their wooing I do not know. All six of the girls went off one after the other as each reached twenty-one. That wooing must have been managed during their visiting round at aunts and uncles of less rigid rule, or during the two weeks of summer, when, in successive duos, they escaped to Beach Haven, where certain kindly cousins had a cottage.

It was an often-repeated legend in the Roberts family, that story, I mean, of the trek on horseback in 1716 of Edward and Mary and their babe to the Great Swamp below Quakertown, of their spending of their first winter there in a shack, of Mary's contraction of smallpox from the Indians, and of their long life there together, he dying at eighty-two and she at ninety-six. Descendants of Edward and Mary, in the sixth and seventh generations from them, accompanied by the chronicler, husband and father of the said Roberts descendants, visited the site of the old settlement some two hundred years later. The face of the country was changed materially from what it was as described in the old warrant. Beaver Run was still there, but it was arable land about it now, all the two hundred and fifty acres, and not the "Savannas, Swamps, Cripples," etc., of the original deed. There was not in sight much game such as the gentle Quaker preacher was given the right to "hawk, hunt, fish, and fowle," all for an "English silver half crown," paid every year at Pennsbury.

There was, however, one discovery made by the visitors that seemed to confirm the family legend and that brought up the past with startling instancy. Back of the stone house, now the home of the farm, was a summer kitchen. On entering this one-roomed building we found that it was of logs on three sides, under its clapboards, and that the fourth side was three-by-four construction, clapboarded. Was this not the "leanto" of the original settlement of 1716? Such three-sided structures of logs, with bark roofs, with a fire just beyond the open side that was never allowed to die out night or day, housed settlers in backwoods places in Pennsylvania as late as the eighteen-fifties.

An old man up in the Poconos told me in 1905 that he had gone down to New York when he was young to get a wife off an immigrant ship, that he had secured a stout girl, a German with wooden shoes, and an "underpinning above them" that seemed to show she could stand hard work, and that they had passed a comfortable winter in a three-sided log shack, "with a fire for the fourth side."

In the Roberts legend there is great stress laid on bark as a material for the shack, but this means, I take it, only that it had a bark roof, and that if, as the legend is, the

After Koellner

A HILLMAN'S HOME

shack was anchored to a white oak tree, that was to give the structure stability in whatsoever great gales should blow. It is said that a second house here, supposedly a log one, was replaced in 1729 by a substantial stone house, part of which, with a leaded glass window in the attic and a date stone in the gable end with the inscription "E. & M.R., 1729," persisted until 1868.

The third house that I would describe as typical of Quaker building preserves to this day all the four kinds of construction that are to be found in Pennsylvania farm houses. It is situated to the north of Jericho Mountain, in the same county of Bucks in the western part of which is the Roberts log leanto just described. This Jericho Mountain house presents on its first floor a room with walls of logs, the lower part of the original house on the site, built presumably before 1700, for the grant of land goes back to the sixteen-nineties. Next to this first section of log construction and on one level with it, is a section of stone construction. Next to this, and a step down, is a timbered room, of barn construction. And next to this, and several steps below its level, is the kitchen of three-by-four construction, clapboarded. A second story, over all four rooms, is of more recent origin.

Under old maples, and at the foot of the orcharded slope of Jericho, it is as picturesque a home as I know. White painted, long and low, it composes perfectly into its tumbled countryside with the blue hills of the Delaware in the background. Here I have gone often for apples, in November generally, for Grimes Goldens and Stayman Winesaps, and for Belleflowers and other old-timers, too.

This house under Jericho, when I knew it best, in its occupancy by Thed Pershing's folks, was as interesting indoors as out. Furniture, largely mahogany, and house fur-

nishings were alike antiques, collected some of them from
this countryside, but some from up Shamokin way and others
from as far away as Newmarket in New Hampshire. Here,
too, I have come in blossom-time to see all this northern
side of Jericho pink with bloom, and to note Duroc Red
hogs, and Bourbon Red turkeys about the barnyards, and
an old screech owl, in the red plumage, dreaming away in
the sun at the entrance to the hollow in the maple back of
the house.

The Whitemarsh countryside is rich in manorial houses, a
good many of them built by Quakers. Samuel Morris built
in 1723 "The Wentz House," as it was always called in my
youth, on the Bethlehem Pike above Fort Hill, and Anthony
Morris built "The Sheaff House" in 1796, just off the
Skippack Pike. It will be noticed that both of these great
houses passed from people of Quaker stock to people of
Dutch stock. So it has been with many other great houses
between the Blue Mountain and the Delaware. It is given to
the Pennsylvania Dutch, in a very literal sense, to inherit the
earth.

I know a great country house near Gap in Lancaster
County built by a Scotch-Irishman that only about thirty
years ago passed over to "The House Amish." The people
of this sect meet first in this man's house and then in that
man's. The Amishman that bought this house cut out all the
partitions between the rooms on the first floor, putting in
round iron pillars to support the upper stories of the house.
To take the place of these walls he put in sliding doors that
would roll back and give one large room capable of seating a
hundred people. I remember, years back, when certain poorer
members of "The House Amish" had to have the meeting,
when it was their turn, they had to resort to the barn. It is
a matter of pride with such an Amishman, however, to have

a house large enough to house all the little flock to which he belongs.

Both Quakers and Scotch-Irish have a tendency to work their way to town, the Scotch-Irish almost to a man, and the Quakers three out of four. The Quakers do not, however, stay in the city, if they can help it. It was only about 1890, as I have said, that the "Dutch," in any large numbers, began to desert the countryside. They still, however, the large majority of them, stay in the country, and areas of Chester County and Lancaster County that were Scotch-Irish or Quaker are now Pennsylvania Dutch. All the way down the Brandywine Valley to Embreeville you will find now the Lancaster Dutch, and you may hear an auction in northern Chester County, say at Honeybrook, conducted in Swabian where thirty years ago nothing but English would be spoken.

"The Sheaff House" I never saw in its glory. When I visited it, it was dismantled, the furnishings still in it, but gathered, most of them, in the great hall and in the other rooms of the first floor preparatory to being sent off to auction. I remember how sumptuous but in what good taste those furnishings were. An extension table, in three parts, of a bright wood, cherry I think, was what I coveted most. It was Hepplewhite, my best-liked of eighteenth century styles, and it consisted of one central table with square-ended drop leaves, and of two end tables, each with a square-ended leaf and a rounded leaf.

What pleased me most in all the house was the spaciousness of the hall into which you entered up those broad stone steps of easy tread and banistered with delicately wrought ironwork, and the just proportions of the rooms on either side of the hall. The great staircase in the cross hall was imposing, too, with a wide window on its landing between the second and third floors, a window Palladian arched and facing the west. I remember, too, the great brass radiator in the hall floor, and being told that the system of hot-air heating here installed was one of the first in any country house round about Philadelphia.

It was by the merest chance, years after my visit to "The Sheaff House" that I picked up a pitcher of Jersey glass that had been one of its treasures. I had known the pitcher for years as one of the show pieces of an antique shop. It had been bought at too high a price to sell at the advanced price on what he paid for it that the dealer thought his due. He never happened to tell me its history, though I am so keen on having a pedigree for each item I buy I sometimes wonder do I compel the dealers to invent a story now and then to content me. After 1928 the pitcher began to drop in price, but it was not until the fall of 1932 it came to the figure I had set as my price for it. When he was wrapping it up for me the dealer said: "I bought that years ago at the Sheaff sale, of the stuff from that big house way above Chestnut Hill." It chances, too, that I have a memento of "The Wentz House." Seventy-five years ago, an aunt, then a girl, dug up a root of ivy from "The Wentz House" while she was visiting there, and took it back to the old "Roberts House" at Branchtown. There it flourished, and one day in 1900, the granddaughter of that house whom I had married, and I, dug up several roots from "The Roberts House" and planted them on the north wall of our cottage on the Wissahickon Hills in Germantown. There it has grown to the tops of the second story windows and shelters nests of English sparrows and robins. It is a small-leafed ivy of the hardiest sort.

The façade of "The Sheaff House" is imposing as you climb the little hill before it. It is of dressed gray stone, overlaid with two great pilasters of whitish stone that rise to the low triangle of the front gable. Lifting between the two windows on either side of the portico over the front door they balance pleasantly and give the Grecian touch that is so great a delight to all brought up in the true tradition.

The outbuildings and walled gardens of "The Sheaff House" were a marvel in their time. The orangeries and the greenhouse between them are gone now. The tall stable between the house and the road, with its three bridges to second, third and fourth floors, is rearranged now. It no longer houses, either, those long wagons with their roomy beds, wagons in which the Sheaffs drove to Saratoga in the heyday of that famous resort.

Quiet persistence is one of the Quaker qualities. Such persistence is not only that of the individual but that of a meeting or of a community. It is a persistence hard to combat. So found out Aunt Elizabeth. She lived on in the Chester County countryside after her sister moved to the city with her family. Her sister's daughter, who had married a Friend, died after the birth of her first child, in the early eighteen-forties. She was buried in the graveyard of Lionville Meeting. Her family, though themselves at least twenty-five per cent Quaker, with a militantly Friendly grandmother, put up a tombstone a little higher than the fifteen-inch stone conventionally proper.

Aunt Elizabeth, visiting Lionville from her home four miles away, found that the high stone, foundation and all, had been sunk in the earth until its top was at the height above the turf of its neighboring stones. Such a treatment was too much for the quick blood that was Aunt Elizabeth's inheritance from her Scotch-Irish and Welsh ancestors. An early morning visit of hers to Lionville restored the offending stone to its original position. Shortly afterwards she moved to Lionville, where she could keep tabs on the stone. It was soon found sunk again. Aunt Elizabeth restored it to the height she thought proper. Unfortunately there was no cement in those days or she might have circumvented the tight-lipped Friends. The battle went on without a word spoken on either side for as long as Aunt Elizabeth lived. After her death the stone reposed sunk to the orthodox height. Now there is no meeting at Lionville. The meeting house became a schoolhouse. Nobody cares how high or how low are the stones in the graveyard.

The good lady had been bedridden several years. It had been said, by unkind neighbors, that she could have gotten up for an hour or so daily if she had wished. If that had been true, which I doubt, early in her illness, it was not true any longer. In her family connection a woman of a later generation did so manage affairs, winning by her assumed invalidism a great deal of sympathy for herself and many kindnesses to her daughters because friends were sorry for the mother. Lydia Ann was really bedridden. She looked gentle and long suffering, meek and mild, as she lay there in bed in the room so scrupulously neat, and smiled sweetly on those who called upon her. There were always flowers on the table, and she could see the changing pageant of the seasons on the Chester County countryside from her position of vantage as she lay propped up in bed. She had not lost her interest in things at all. Worldly as it was, she had still joy in food. She was avid of neighborhood gossip, dominant in her household, and though she never could go to meeting she was sought for advice by "the powers that be" of that organization.

Though she had been taking a rest cure for several years, her family thought maybe a regularly prescribed regimen as laid down by Dr. S. Weir Mitchell might help her. It was a trip in those old pre-motor days from Philadelphia to that corner of the Brandywine Hills where she lived. Finally they brought the great physician to her bedside, on the early afternoon of an autumn day. She was just topping off her midday meal with an "after clap" of black walnuts. The doctor's eyes were riveted on the rich nuts. "What is this you are eating?" were his first words to her.

"Black walnuts," she replied with spirit.

"Well," he countered, "I always did hear that nothing could kill a Chester County Hickory Quaker."

It is perhaps unnecessary to add, after so inauspicious an opening of his first visit, that it remained the last, and that Lydia Ann did not profit by his advice and suggested regimen.

Mary Grew had many stories of Friends, as you might expect in one who lived on Franklin Square when that was a center of Quakerdom. She attributed most of these stories to the long memory of a descendant of William Penn, Guglielma Maria, in whose house she was a paying guest. Guglielma had known everybody worth knowing in the Philadelphia of the mid-years of the nineteenth century. One of her acquaintances was an old lady of unswerving purpose in regulation of all in any way related to her. She was particularly vigilant with daughters-in-law. There was small fault to be found with the housekeeping of the wives of five of her six sons. The wife of one son was, however, a little lax in this, to the old lady, the virtue next to godliness.

There was occupation for mother-in-law for each day of the week from Second Day through Seventh Day. First Day, almost a feast day, saw, theoretically, all the sons and daughters-in-law and grandchildren with the old folks for dinner. And it was so far from a fast day that filled decanters were on the dinner table. Each Second Day, however, saw the old lady on the trot, calling on one of her daughters-in-law, and each Third Day saw her calling on another, and so on throughout the week. She had no regular sequence of calls. All that was certain was that each daughter-in-law would be called upon by her mother-in-law one day in the week. It was a part of the unescapable cussedness of things, complained the daughter-in-law, not so good a housekeeper as she might have been, that the old lady so often happened in on her when things were not in apple pie order. She had a large brood of children, all boys again, as in her mother-in-law's family, normally destructive urchins, trackers-in of mud, displacers of household gods, who left toys where old ladies might trip over them, and secreted bread and jam sandwiches in wing and fireside chairs and hid sticky raisins and stickier figs in the recesses of hair-cloth-covered sofas.

Mother-in-law, of course, thought that all these lapses of her grandchildren were their mother's fault. What put her out though, more than any other of the manifestations of the presence of children where children ought not to be allowed to roam, was dust. There was no dust to speak of, she maintained, where furnace coal was properly cleaned and children were prevented from playing. And yet, she held, everything should be dusted every day whether there was dust or not. The very thought of dust was enough to distract her. That enough help should be kept to see the house dusted every day from garret to cellar was taken for granted.

Eleanor Coal-Scuttle Bonnet had lectured her daughter-in-law Helen Scoop Bonnet until she was tired. Her campaign to make her daughter-in-law aware of the wickedness of dust had begun by insinuations; it had progressed to hints; and in the end it had resulted in a militant out-in-the-open declaration that no woman could be called a good housekeeper on whose mahogany parlor table you could write

your name in the dust. That open declaration had been followed by many of the sort, but none of them did any good.
Poor Helen Scoop Bonnet could not help it. She had not
either the will or the strength to cope with dust. Her mother-
in-law came to the conclusion that only rigorous methods
could prevail to bring about a cure in her erring daughter-
in-law.

So, one day, when her hostess was called off by so violent
a demonstration from the boys that she hurried to the nursery, arnica bottle in hand, to anoint the hurts that must be
the cause of that demonstration, the old lady stole down-
stairs into the parlor, and wrote "slut" with her finger in the
dust on the top of the mahogany table just inside the hall
door. Lest the old lady be too severely judged by a generation that, while plain spoken to a fault, has lost the vigor of
our American speech of the eighteen-forties, I should explain
that that dread word was only a synonym of slattern in that
old day. And slatternly, I am afraid, it must be confessed
the daughter-in-law was. She was also a lady of spirit. She
showed her husband the writing in the dust when he came
home. She told the children and the servants that they must
not rub it out. She decreed this in tones so emphatic that no
one dared to tamper with the writing. It was to remain there,
she said, until her mother-in-law dusted it out. And dust it
off the nonplused old lady did on her next call, but not
before the report of the writing had spread abroad through
Philadelphia to the greater discontent of the old lady than
of the young lady. The old lady regarded herself thereafter
as shamed by the brazenness of her daughter-in-law. The
triumph of Eleanor Coal-Scuttle Bonnet had been her defeat.

The Pennsylvania Dutch are well aware that it is an old
world in which we live, a hard world in which men must

labor to live, but none the less a good world. They doubt it can be made into a better world. They are a kindly people, God-fearing and religious but with a large forgiveness for both sinners and sin. Church is still one of the institutions in all the Dutch countrysides, but it is the social side of church they most care for. Once in a while you find a Sunday School superintendent who tells you he wishes to be told of his faults and shortcomings by the minister, but for the most part we take seriously our church obligations of attendance at services, contributions, and the looking after our less provident neighbors, and leave vexed problems of belief to the clergy.

The Pennsylvania Dutch have a full delight in all the senses and no quarrel with the natural instincts. They work so hard they have little time left for any of the higher arts but music. They retain their folk arts of household sort longer than any of the old stocks in America. They have, like the Quakers, a love for scientific investigation. They hold to property and to the patriarchal system in the family. Labor leaders find the instinct of the young people who work in silk and hosiery mills and cigar factories to do what their parents tell them to do a decided impediment to organizing those young folks into unions. The old folks counsel conservatism and the not joining of any new-fangled organizations.

The Pennsylvania Dutch are little envious of their neighbors and more prone to accept their lot without rebelliousness than most Americans. They can get along and save money under discouraging conditions. They are slow to change their politics or religion or traditional ways. They take life easier, in the sense that they accept what comes with less question, than most people, but they want to be let alone to live life as they see fit. Their gods of the second order are the family, property, food and church, but their great god is work. They delight in work for its own sake as well as for what money and possessions it brings them. They make the best of farmers and mechanics. They make good doctors and good ministers, good ironmasters and good engineers. They father whole countrysides as country storekeepers and grow well-to-do in doing it. They are devoted collectors of this and that, but since they have given up the reading of religious books in German they are not so interested in "literature" as are the Quakers and Scotch-Irish. They are curious about all creatures great and small. They love to sit out of summer evenings after heavy labor and to identify this insect and that tree toad and the bird over yonder by their voices. They love the thistle bird so much that, good farmers that they are, they will leave a patch of thistles for him here and there. He comes to their garden lettuce in the evening light, and chatters to them in friendly fashion as he feeds. Distelfink and Dutchman are alike busy, mellow, kindly, keenly cognizant of the night that follows these late hours of the far-spent day.

There are, of course, Dutchmen and Dutchmen. There are old fellows who look like the profiles on medieval German prints, old Amishmen with three-pointed beards that seem to have stepped straight out of Dürer. There are hearty young fellows in bakeries and tailoring shops that you could hardly distinguish from other young Americans of the old stocks. And yet, when you get to know them, even the average and prosaic country storekeeper, say, will be found to have reserves of folk interests unusual in Quaker or Scotch-Irishmen. This blond and chunky boy comes of a family that for two generations had conducted a musical academy in a remote village, where nearly all the musical instruments were taught, and a number of sound instrumentalists and singers were turned out. This old man who gets drunk every

Saturday evening can make a wheelbarrow that will last a lifetime. He will use oak lumber he has cut himself and seasoned, adzed and planed, fashioned into wheel and frame, bottom boards and front boards and side boards. He will have done the wheelwright work of it at his own little forge, and painted it the traditional red and black.

This college professor who looks like an aristocratic old club man fond of his port wine can talk a bird out of a bush with his mimicry of its mate's notes. He rides to the hounds and gets his brace of woodcock, no more, every year. He knows more of wild swans than any of his fellows, and can talk of them so that hardened old sportsmen and museum workers hang on his words.

"Persimmon Jake" loved the wild as much as the college professor, and made his living out of it too. He roamed Rockhill in Upper Bucks and Montgomery a generation ago. Bringing his finds to the country stores of an evening, dandelion greens and poke in spring, berries later on, and wild teas and persimmons in the autumn, he would dance for the crowd there if they bought him out. They delighted in his hoe-downs, so they frequently took all his five-cent bunches and boxes of this and that, and set him, literally, dancing with joy at his successful salesmanship. When he was feeling particularly amiable, he would take certain small boys home with him for the privilege of looking at his coffin, which, made for years, he kept under his bed. It was a memorable occasion, indeed, when he would pull it out and lie down in it, to show the little crowd how well it fit.

We reached the sawmill where old Ezra Moyer was working by a quarter of a mile of corduroy road. Not only was there no depression for him, he told us—our visit was in 1933—but for sixty years he had lumbered in his neighborhood with a like crew of five, and that not more than

DELAWARE WATER GAP

fifty miles from Philadelphia. That seemed most remarkable to me. The lumbering had been mostly in hardwoods, from which he got out barn timbers and bridge planking, mine props and mine ties principally, but many other sorts of lumber, too.

The minister of the plain clothes sect wore a regalia that looked almost that of some ritualistic church, but he was just folks for all his get up. He was at an auction out of his bailiwick, and he was thirsty. He had tried some of the soft drinks peddled round among the crowd. They gave him no relief. It was in prohibition days, but he was in Dutchland. So he did not hesitate to make known his wants to the soft drink boy. "Is it possible," he said, "there is no good ale in this town? Bring me two bottles of good ale, ale that will lay my thirst!" The ale was forthcoming; the thirst was allayed, the minister took on a new lease of life, and fell to bidding so boldly that the afternoon session of that auction became a success.

The old boy who lived in the slab house covered with building paper put his finger to the side of his nose and winked. "You wouldn't believe what I have in there," he said, and winked long and hard, holding one eye shut as much as a minute. My guide to his corner of the hills had told me the oldster was not so bad when he was sober, but "resolute and bold" when he was drunk. Fortunately he was sober now, but living in this out-of-the-way place because he could not get along with neighbors. He had just sold the old log house on the place, which, for all its picturesqueness, he liked much less than the black-papered monstrosity in which he lived. I was not listening to the colloquy very intently, for I had just picked a swamp flower unknown to me, and, which, as yet, I have failed to identify in the botany books. It had foxglove, or pentstemon-shaped flowers, of a clear vermilion, as brightly and excitingly colored as those of the cardinal flower itself. However, I soon found what he had in there. There was a Gottschall clock made over in New Britain, a pottery sugar bowl with laid-on decorations, and a little drinking cup in glass not referable to Wistars or Stiegel or any other of the old blowers. All three he valued far above the prices of 1933.

Cyrus was a joiner. He was said to have thirteen grips, and he belonged to so many organizations of one sort or another that he could get you out of any scrape you got into in all that countryside. State policemen and justices of the peace gave you godspeed as soon as you got him to work in your behalf. He was most abstemious in both food and drink, lively, full of good stories, a jack of all trades and a masterly farmer. He knew where you could find anything you wanted in all a broad area, for he knew every man that lived in that mountain valley, a district twenty miles long and five broad. He knew, too, many other men in other parts of the country. He was a power in politics, but he had never run for office. He was a spruce bachelor, devoted to his old mother. Ask him about this hex or that powwow man, this basket maker or that deserted forge, where to find fox grapes or trout, and he supplied you at once with the information that you were after. He had ready speech and the facial control and power of mimicry of the trained actor. He had knocked about the world a good deal before he settled down on the ancestral farm, but wherever chance had thrown him he had fallen on his feet. He had backslid as a church attendant, but he contributed to the neighborhood church and he attended all its social functions. He was witty, a tease, interested in everything, warmhearted, generous both of his time and money, the best of company. He was the most tolerant man I ever met, tolerant of everything save sins of omission.

If you ask me in what particular way this man was distinctively Dutch, I shall answer in his tolerance, his appetite for work, his innate conservatism, his instinct for sticking to the farm when he was more interested in city life. In our natural desire to differentiate between things and people we are more apt to lay stress on their dissimilarities than on their likenesses. So it has come about that we distinguish sharply between the Pennsylvania Dutch on the one hand and the Pennsylvania Quakers and the Pennsylvania Scotch-Irish on the other by calling attention to the contrasts between the folk art and racial qualities and habits of life that came from Germany, and the folk art and racial qualities and habits of life that came from the British Isles. When we so do, we often forget that the Pennsylvania Dutch have, in addition to their distinctive domestic arts, nearly all the domestic arts, too, of the British Quakers and Scotch-Irish. Other arts, too, are common to all three peoples. From the time of their coming all three peoples built their houses of logs, as had, indeed, the Hollanders and Swedes before them, and as did the English who came to New England, and the English who came to Virginia.

The first stone houses of Pennsylvania did not, however, grow out only of local conditions, as did the log houses. They were definitely an adaptation to local conditions of English architecture. The typical Pennsylvania farmhouse, of micaschist, or limestone, or red sandstone, was English in all its details of moldings and hardware and stone dressing. Only a church now and then, and the covered wooden bridges and the barns were after Continental originals. Our barns are Swiss, of course, and the term "Swiss barns" is in as general use as the term "Bank barns" to designate them. These barns are built, most of them, into a bank, as are so many in Switzerland, with the hay driven in over a "bridge" into the second floor of the barn, and the cattle kept below in the basement, if so the portion on the lower level may be called. The covered wooden bridges, too, come directly from the valleys of the Rhine and the Aar.

Built-in cupboards and furniture are, too, in nine instances out of ten after English originals. Works of clocks from the Palatinate or Switzerland are to be found occasionally, but in nearly every instance the clock case is after an English model. Beds and chests of drawers, highboys and lowboys, chairs and light stands, are likewise nearly always Chippendale, Hepplewhite and Sheraton. Tables are sometimes after German originals, and dower chests almost always. Ironwork in floor candlesticks, lamps, trammels, andirons and the like in Pennsylvania Dutch houses is similar to those in Pennsylvania Quaker homes and Pennsylvania Scotch-Irish homes. Many linens and quilts and carpetings are alike in all three sorts of homes, but there were, of course, definitely Dutch ways of decorating such articles. In Dutch homes you find undecorated articles, like the undecorated articles in the homes of the other stocks, and decorated articles be-tuliped, be-pomegranated, be-peacocked, or be-doved. Oftentimes, too, the domestic arts of the Dutch influenced the domestic arts of their neighbors. Samplers done in Pennsylvania show, nearly all of them, Dutch detail. Pottery made by the Quaker Vickerses in Chester County was very like that made by Nases and Leidys in Dutchest Montgomery.

There is an engaging just folksness about the Pennsylvania Dutch. The hillman in the log cabin up on the bench of the South Mountain calls the well-to-do farmer at the mountain's foot by his first name. The Lady Bountiful of a neighborhood is "Hattie" to all, men, women and children, to whom she brings most substantial aid. They buy red meat for the minister when he comes to dinner, but he is "Charlie" to more than half his congregation. They are not afraid of humor in a sermon, or in a charge to a minister just being installed in a new position. The Rev. H. M. Mühlenberg, patriarch of the Lutheran Church in Pennsylvania, was asked to welcome five young missionaries of the German Reformed Church to America way back in 1752. He began his greeting with the words: "Behold, I send you forth as sheep in the midst of wolves; be ye therefore wise as serpents and harmless as doves." Realization of this as a jolly of both congregations and pastors of a rival church, in no way lessens it as proof of a very human attitude in church affairs. There are many country churches that for over a hundred years have sheltered congregations of both Lutherans and Reformed: the one denomination will meet one Sunday in the morning and the next Sunday in the afternoon; the other will occupy the church afternoon and morning on those same Sundays; and so on throughout the year, with very seldom any breach of perfect amity. It is one of the oldest jokes of the countryside to play on the word "Reformed." As we were passing a farm one winter afternoon our hostess pointed out a man loading manure in his barnyard, saying, "That man's a Lutheran with a Reformed wife."

The Scotch-Irish of yesterday were not more concerned with religion than the Quakers and Dutch of their time, but they were much more concerned over Heaven and Hell. They had a livelier sense of the actualities of either place than the more phlegmatic and less imaginative peoples. Their Presbyterianism took harder hold of them than Quakerism of the Quakers or Lutheranism or Calvinism of the Lutherans or the German Reformed. Only the perfervid quietism of certain of the Dutch sects wrought on those folks as Presbyterianism on the Scotch-Irish. The Scotch-Irish awaited judgment, knowing they deserved little of their Lord. They had a certain satisfaction in the surety of their damnation. They rejoiced in all abominations of desolation. They have changed their beliefs, changed in all ways more than the Quakers and the Dutch. The Scotch-Irish are less forthright now, less severe, less belligerent, but they are still forthright and severe and belligerent. They are vigorous, energetic, full of two-fisted determination.

The Scotch-Irish have been our political leaders, for better or for worse, as you may chance to think. They have been the developers of our regions of Pennsylvania beyond the Alleghanies. They have taught us the delights of wild nature, the beauty of wild things, the appeal there is in thrush song, and in the whistling of woodcock during their aerial vagaries in the moonlight. They have carried Macpherson with them as well as Burns, and they have demanded the reprinting of *Ossian* in Harrisburg and Carlisle as well as in Philadelphia.

The Scotch-Irish, of all our Pennsylvania stocks, were the most anti-British in the Revolution. There were plenty of German patriots like General J. P. Mühlenberg and fighting Quakers like Timothy Matlack, but so many Germans belonged to pacifist sects, sects from which the non-resistant Quakers sprung, that these two peoples were in considerable numbers neutral and a good few pro-English. There was an exodus of Germans from Pennsylvania to Canada after the War of the Revolution, and there are sections near Toronto that to this day have barns and houses, spring houses and caves, that are very like those in certain sections of Bucks and Berks.

There was an inheritance of anti-English feeling among

the Scotch-Irish who came to America. Remote ancestors of theirs had fought as Scots against the English, in their native land, before they were planted in Ireland. That the Anglican Church was the state recognized church of Ireland was resented by the Presbyterians. It is to be remembered that the kin of our Scotch-Irish who remained in Ireland were the leaders of the rebellion of 1798. Added to their patriotism, their chip-on-the-shoulder temperament and their impatience of governmental restraint and their love of a fight for its own sake, the inherited anti-English attitude left few Scotch-Irish in America who were not against England. To-day, the Scotch-Irish of Colonial American ancestry, whether or not they are conscious of themselves as Scotch-Irish, are in sympathy with things English, as are most of the old stock of whatever origin, without ceasing to believe that all things English are the better for the sea change that came over them in the passage to America.

There are many Scotch-Irish types from the quiet and pawky to the dour and wild. There was the storekeeper from Blair County, filled with satisfaction when he had made a deal for huckleberries at a cent less a quart than he feared he would have to pay. There was Andrew Maclehose, in stock, flowered vest and tailed coat, rubicund and blue-eyed, with a great shock of white hair. He was a front and nothing more, for all that he was a member of the state legislature. There was a Red Campbell, the very picture of a Highland reiver, with red beard and pig's eyes, but the kindliest of men and the best of neighbors, who thought funerals were merrymakings and the appropriate backgrounds for jokes about the departed. There was the old merchant out of Butler who would never take off his hat, taciturn, high cheekboned and shy, who grew rich by his ability to look wise and say nothing. Also he always knew none but helpful people, who let him in on the inside in all sorts of profitable undertakings.

There was Dr. Buchanan, a D.D., who nearly lost his orthodoxy, in his own estimation, by coming to believe that such a non-churchgoer as myself would not go to hell. I was a great trouble to him, but I was able to make it up to him in a measure, by taking him early one September morning to a field where he picked the first full mess of mushrooms he had found since he was a boy. He was a passionate, keenly intellectual man, who wore himself out by the intensity with which he felt things. He was banished to a country parish, largely because of his militant orthodoxy, where he made himself many warm friends and a warm enemy or two, by the vigor with which he threw himself into affairs temporal as well as spiritual. He was disgusted with the lack of intellectual interests among the younger ministers of his faith. "Muscular Christians," he would say, "are all well and good, but they need to be spiritual and intellectual first." It was really intellectual he wanted them to be. He had an eager, questing mind, and a fanatical hatred of all that was low and mean. He would have been more unhappy than he was had he not kept himself too dog-tired with work to be able to worry over things as he wanted to do.

There was Mrs. Moore, that heroic old lady of eighty who would not have people worrying over her even when she was in a critical condition. She hated to be fussed over, to be taken care of, to be the center of concern because she was ill. She would make her folks laugh at any cost. I never knew a human being of higher spirit, one whom I admired more, and I write down what I have to relate of her in all respect and as a tribute to her indomitable heart. Her husband told me the story of her that I tell, when he was an old man of eighty, told it with tears in his eyes.

"Aye! Umph, Corney, did you hear about Mrs. Moore coming out of ether after she had her eye out? She was restless, poor old body, and not able to get her mind clear quickly. She was moaning there, and tossing as much as she had the strength for. The nurse said to me: 'Try your hand, now, Mr. Moore, and see would she know your touch and be quieted.' The nurse had been rubbing her poor old legs ever so gently, pipe stems now that had been so shapely when she swung on the gate, and me passing, when she was a big girl. I put my hand on the one nearest me, and she seemed eased a bit. The nurse said: 'Do you know what's happening to you now, Mrs. Moore?' And what do you suppose she said? The spirit was in her! She said—aye! umph! It's just what she said: 'My leg's being stroked, and by a man, too!'

"Aye! Umph!" he repeated, and hit me on the back in the excess of his emotion and pride.

The Scotch-Irish lost none of their ancestral pawkiness in their transfer from the Old World to the New. Scotch as Scotch may be is the quiet battle between the session of the Presbyterian Church at Middle Spring, in the Cumberland Valley, and one "J. P." The brother was "cited" to the Session for taking venison from an Indian and giving him Meal and Butter for it on the Sabbath Day. This happened in 1746. It is copied from the church records by the Rev. Alfred Nevin, author of *Churches of the Valley*, a book of antiquarian interest published in Philadelphia in 1852. The entry runs thus:

"J. P. appeared, and acknowledged that being at home one Sabbath Day, he heard a gun go off twice quickly after each other, and said he would go out and see who it was; his wife dissuading him, he said he would go and see if he could hear the Horse-bell: having gone a little way he saw an Indian, who had just killed a Fawn and dressed it: the

Indian coming towards the house with him, to get some victuals, having, he said, eat nothing that morning, he saw a Deer, and shot it, and charg'd and shot again at another, which ran away; said P. stood by the Indian until he skin'd the Deer; when he had done, he told said P. he might take it in if he wou'd, for he would take no more with him, upon which, said P. and W. K., who then had come to them, took it up, and carry'd it in; when he had given the Indian his Breakfast, said Indian ask'd if he had any Meal; he said he had, and gave him some; then the Indian ask'd for Butter, and asking his wife about it, he gave the Indian some; but he denies that he gave these things as a Reward for the Venison, inasmuch as they made no Bargain about it."

Despite this ingenious, not to say ingenuous, explanation, the Session judged "that J. P. do acknowledge his Breach of Sabbath in this Matter, and be rebuk'd before the Session for his Sin." There was no getting away from a Session of a community where there were Killoughs and McKees, Finleys and McCombs, Maclays and Andersons. I wish I could establish the identity of J. P., for I think his descendants should be proud of such a pleader, but the Rev. Mr. Nevin used only the initials, afraid lest the descendants of 1852 of the condemned man would be ashamed of such worldliness.

John McKenna was a good Sabbatarian. In fact he was in every way a true son of the Kirk. He would countenance no playacting and he was not to be seduced into going to *Lucia* on the specious plea of his nephews that there was no such wickedness in a performance of that work of Donizetti because opera singers could not act. "They have the intention to act," he countered, "and everything is in the intention." *Lucia* was Scotch, his nephews told him, and there was

Scotch blood in Melba, and maybe after all there was some truth in the old story that the Italian composer was no Italian at all, but an honest Donald Izett, from "Edinboro' awa' " that had somehow expatriated himself. "And if he did," said Uncle John, "it was probably for no good purpose."

Uncle John lived in the hinterland of Pittsburgh, with his widowed sister and her two long boys. Both the boys were over six feet, and he a good six feet six, a fine upstanding bachelor of forty-five. His nephews were in college and he came on to Philadelphia now and then to see them and to hear a good concert. He had heard Melba in concert, in which she sang operatic arias as well as old Scotch songs. Like another of his stock I knew he liked "apples, chess and old Scotch songs." He was not above the fleshpots, either, for all his Puritanism, and it was his love of the fleshpots that was in the end his undoing.

One holiday time when his nephews were home, their mother had gone into Pittsburgh to do some Christmas shopping. Word came home that she had been knocked down by an automobile and taken to a hospital. That word came to them after eleven o'clock Saturday night, after they had had several hours' worry over her non-return by train. They hired an automobile and set out for Pittsburgh. They were still eight miles from the hospital when it came midnight. Uncle John had been waiting for that hour, flashlight on watch. He made them stop the car. He got out, saying, "I'll walk the rest of the way. You both know it's wrong to ride in any vehicle on the Sabbath." The boys kept on in the car and found their mother suffering chiefly from the shock of the accident. Uncle John was at the hospital at two A.M. He was a four mile an hour walker and proud of it, as he was proud that he had vindicated his Sabbatarianism. "The Lord," said Uncle John, "has taken care of his own.

He always will, lads, mind that, if you put your trust in Him."

It was a Sabbath morning shortly afterwards that he fell. The rule of the house was there could be no cooking or no taking in of food on the Sabbath Day. Such practices were unnecessary labor and forbidden by the Lord. So the two quarts of milk the family received daily were delivered late Saturday night that the law might not be broken. They kept no servant, though Uncle John was far from penurious. So the boys, one or another, when they were home, saved steps for their Uncle by going out just before Saturday midnight for the milk. Had it been left on the front steps it might have been stolen, all the folks in town not being so godly as Uncle John. Alec said to John II, when he brought the milk in:

"The milkman left two quarts of cream instead of two quarts of milk. What shall we do about it?"

"Do nothing," replied John the younger. "Leave it to Uncle John."

The oatmeal, steel-cut, had been put to simmer on Saturday just after the evening meal, so it was done to a turn by breakfast time Sunday. The fire could have no more coal on it after midnight Saturday, but its retention of heat throughout the night was an act of God, and not due to the sinful contrivance of man. The boys bulldozed their mother into putting the pitcher of cream where the pitcher of milk usually stood and into silence about the milkman's mistake. Uncle John always drank a glass of whole milk as well as disposing of that he put on his oatmeal.

"The milk is good the day," said Uncle John as he washed down his porridge with the glass of cream.

"Milk," said Alec the Bold. "That's no milk, but cream!

The milkman must have made a mistake in the dark and left us two quarts of cream."

"Was it that now?" Words tumbled from Uncle John's lips too quickly for his judgment to suppress them. Or was it that his sense of humor got the better of him. "It's as I've always told you, lads!" he said. "The Lord has taken care of his own."

"You don't mean to say," Alec broke in, "that we're not to pay for the cream."

"Of course we're to pay for the cream." Uncle John was quick witted enough to reply, but the boys had seen the gleam in his eye as he had rejoiced at the way the Lord had taken care of his own, and Uncle John knew they had noted that gleam in his eye and the satisfaction in his tones. He was uneasy and hemmed and hawed a bit.

"I'm afraid now, lads," he said, "that those words of mine might be misconstrued. If you'll no make mention of them to others I'd be much obliged."

He was getting himself in deeper and deeper. He hesitated a moment, and then took the final plunge:

"I could find, maybe, a dollar or so for you lads now and then to take in a concert, a respectable concert such as I went to with you there at the Academy of Music."

The Lord had delivered him into their hands, and he knew it. Their life was freer from that Sabbath, and fewer searching questions were asked by Uncle John thenceforth, about their comings and goings.

There may be a log cabin in Pennsylvania of Scotch-Irish origin more famous than Stony Batter, but if there is I have not heard of it. It was in this house that James Buchanan was born, in a wild gorge of the Cove Mountain, northwest of Mercersburg. It has been brought now into Chambersburg, where it houses an antique shop. "Stony batter" was a name given to a sharp ascent on a road whose loose ana rolling cobbles made footing difficult for man and beast, and the pull up for Conestoga wagons of the utmost difficulty. In New England "hard scrabble" is applied to a road in a very similar condition.

There are Scotch-Irish manor houses in several of the Pennsylvania counties, in Philadelphia, in Lancaster, in Cumberland, and in Blair. Late though it is there is none more palatial than the Baker Mansion near Hollidayburg, which now houses the Blair County Historical Society.

It is the churches, though, rather than the houses, that are the finest flower of the Scotch-Irish civilization in Pennsylvania. The Norriton Presbyterian Church, near Fairview in Montgomery County, is one of these that has not been spoiled by reconstruction, but you must go to the Cumberland Valley to see the finest of them all, the most beautiful meeting house of any description that there is anywhere in Pennsylvania. It was a gurly day of mid-March that we visited it. We had driven all morning from Germantown with an easterly storm at our backs, and now, at noon, we were at Rocky Spring, amid the slate hills that rise above the limestone of the Cumberland Valley, and make the tumbled approach to the Blue Mountain. The Scotch-Irish chose slate land for settlement almost as universally as the Dutch chose limestone. There was surface water on slate, and areas of unwooded land, and it was more quickly brought under cultivation than the more heavily forested limestone.

This Presbyterian Church was established here in 1738 when all its countryside was frontier, little cleared, and subject day and night, from spring to fall, to Indian raids. It is quiet enough here now, save for the fifing wind out of the northeast, the falling of the waters that burst out of the spring, the chorusing of the swamp blackbirds newcome after a long absence to the meadows about, the lamentations of the just-dropped lambs in the fold across the way. It is isolated, lonely, and deserted of men, this church and its graveyard on the oak knoll. Since 1794 it has stood here, with the old-time congregation of Indian fighters and subduers of the wilderness long dust in their graves in its shadow.

They were a hardy race, these McCalmonts and McConnells, these Beards and Culbertsons, who built the first church here so early in the eighteenth century, a log church, of course. They had gone, almost to a man, with their second pastor, the Rev. John Craighead, to the Revolutionary War, and long is the list of battles they suffered and, for the most, so luckily survived. Their children fared well enough, in worldly success and cultivation, to be able to build this church, with Walter Beatty, designer of the old courthouse at Chambersburg, as its architect.

Warm it was in its varying hues of red on this day of east wind and low clouds and dull light. Foursquare it stood and sturdy, unharmed by time, but mellowed to so soft hues of old red and soft red, of apricot and saffron, that you could not but take it to your heart as you would some swale of the foothills burned rich color before the neighboring slopes had felt the touch of fall.

The bump of limestone from which pours the spring that gives the church its name, is set sparsely with trees, a large oak, a couple of hackberries, and a half dozen cedars, thin-plumed and spindling, chief among them. The situation of the church on the knoll, close by the road, which runs between it and the spring, and above the quarried bluff of limestone where there were limekilns through a long yesterday, is prominent indeed, but there is hardly enough business in the countryside or enough interest in it to tourists, to bring many this way nowadays. The church can be seen from many points about the neighborhood, but it draws few visitors save in summer. Then, descendants of the original members of the congregation, scattered from the Atlantic to the Pacific, come here on pious pilgrimage to the tombs of their ancestors, and members of patriotic organizations, like the Daughters of the Revolution, who have put a bronze tablet on the walls of the church, gather here for meetings and celebrations. There had not, however, been services in the church for more than a year before we visited it on Sunday, March 19, 1933.

It is in the best of upkeep inside and out. Never did brickwork wear better than this, though the bricks are obviously not of the hardest burning. There are black-headers among those of reddish cast, a number of them being used to outline "1794" in the north gable. The foundations are of the blue limestone of the neighborhood. Any sheds for horses and teams that may once have been here, and the log leanto we hear about in early descriptions, are gone now. The church itself had long ago been rebuilt like its neighbors at Middle Spring (Shippensburg) and Big Spring (Newville) had the Scotch-Irish who founded the church not moved out of the neighborhood, to have their place taken by the Pennsylvania Dutch of other faiths. A few Dutch did find their way into the graveyard at any rate, Boeshores and Lightners conspicuously among them. When the Rev. Alfred Nevin did his *Churches of the Valley* in 1852 he wrote down the congregation as diminishing, and the Rev. W. A. West had to record it near its end in his *Centennial Memorial Presbytery of Carlisle* in 1889.

All the detail of the interior of the church is exactly as it should be, the paneling of the doors and of the ends of the pews, the balusters of the handrail to the pulpit, the pulpit itself and the sounding board and canopy, and the trim of the window back of the pulpit. Mr. Beatty was a good architect, a firm servant of tradition. The pulpit and its surroundings, with the reading desk below it, are still painted the dark oxcart blue they have always been painted. The pews are still unpainted, showing the beautiful grain of the big sticks of bull pine from which they were cut. What else is painted of the interior than the pulpit is painted white, as are the trims of the windows outside and the shutters. The floors of the aisles are paved with brick. There is a rickety ladder leading to the loft above, into which the pipes from the two old cast stoves are apparently allowed to pour their smoke, to find its way out by the ventilator in the south gable.

All in the neighborhood, like the church itself, inside and out, speaks of yesterday, all but the newly installed macadam road by its door. The rigor of its wooden pews, with their straight backs and top moldings that catch you in the back of the neck, is of that era that thought discomfort a necessary accompaniment of religion. Its two ten-plate stoves could have no more than tempered the cold of its interior in wintry weather. There is no organ loft or singing gallery. It was the psalms, doubtless, that they sang here, perhaps with no other precentor than the preacher, and, it is likely, as they are found in the Bible, without setting over into verse.

The neighborhood is no newer looking than the church. All is of a hundred years ago, the mill race from the little dam below the spring; the log sheep-fold that must have been once of thatched roof in the farmyard across the road; the fallen limekilns; and the snake fences zigzagging up the hills.

The thoughts that were uppermost in our minds as we drove home into the pelting northeaster were that backwardness is more often the preserver of beauty than is progress, and that beauty had been cared for in old years by these so hard Puritans, the Scotch-Irish Presbyterians. If they had not cared for beauty they had not chosen Beatty to design their church; and ironically, if they had not been so restless and had not moved on out of this neighborhood, less tasteful descendants of theirs living here had, in the mid-nineteenth century, certainly rebuilt the beautiful old meeting house into a church of comfortable ugliness. It was being left stranded that preserved the Rocky Spring Church, one of the thousand and one proofs that cry aloud the truth, that our forbears were closer to beauty than we are. Education may give back to us a taste we have lost by breaking with tradition, but it can never give us a better taste than that of these people who knew and loved the roll of the rhythm of the King James Bible, and Milton, and *Ossian*, and Robbie Burns.

SWALLOW HOLES

for Horace Mather Lippincott

TIME was when every other barn I knew in Pennsylvania had a swallow hole in each gable. They were there, of course, to encourage the swallows to people the barn, a peopling long held to be proper and to make for good luck. The feeling in the old days was that a barn without swallows was hardly a barn at all. Barn swallows were even more necessary to the barn than martins to the holes in the house eaves or to the little porticoed villas on the dooryard poles. Pewees under the porch roof, chipping sparrows in the doorside honeysuckle, robins in the lilacs, blackbirds high in the pines or spruces, song sparrows in the dwarf box, a pair of orioles in elm or locust or giant buttonball by the ground cellar, kingbirds in the orchard trees just outside the dooryard—without this complement of nesting birds a country house was without its necessary "avian addenda."

It did not necessarily follow that those barns without swallows holes had no swallows. That oldest type of English barn with ventilating slits in its stone ends could admit swallows by these, though the birds had virtually to creep in through the apertures only three inches wide. The swallow holes, up in the peak of the gable, averaged some eight inches in diameter, and the birds could enter by closing their wings tight to the body when they were just short of the holes and let themselves drive through with the impetus of their flight. Often, when the swallow hole proper was lacking, there was a window in the barn peak from which it was easy to remove a pane of glass so that the birds could go in and out. In barns with little windows of heavy fixed slats in the gable ends you sometimes notice that a slat is missing. Such an occurrence bespeaks, I think, most often, a slat deliberately pried out to let in the swallows rather than the wear and tear of the years. If there is a swallow hole in the peak above such slatted windows you will seldom note a missing slat in any one of them.

Even if there was no opening of any sort in the barn ends, you might still have swallows in the barn. If the birds had a fancy for some barn in a particular location they would adjust themselves, in some instances, to the opening and closing of the barn doors, even though that adjustment meant their imprisoning from six to six. Entering such a barn early in the morning I have been greeted by a little tumult of glad cries from the birds as they circled around and then dashed out into the sunlight and bright reaches of air. I have seen mother birds in great distress when the early closing of the barn doors has caught them out foraging and prevented their return to feed the nestlings and to hover them for the night. I doubt, though, unless the squabs were very young, that such an exclusion of the mother would result in tragedy. Perhaps the father, in such cases, would rise to the emergency, but, even if he did not, the feather-lined cup of mud up in the peak was snug and warm, and out of the way of most marauders. No rat could climb there, and barn owls, despite their name, are none too plenty in barns, at least in my experience and what hearsay has come my way.

The swallow hole that I have noticed oftenest in frame gables is a diamond, or uptilted square, to each of whose points is attached a little triangle, apex inward. Why the diamond or square unelaborated with the triangles is not so

usual I cannot pretend to say. The circular hole, too, is a
common form of swallow hole in wooden gables, and in
stone gables, too, possibly because it is easily made in either
sort. The date stone sometimes accounts for the absence of
the swallow hole in the stone-gabled barns, as the customary
place to recess it is the very peak, the customary place as
well for the swallow hole. When I have noted both date
stone and swallow hole together there are signs that the
question of adjusting them has been a grave one. In one
barn the relation of the two was nicely balanced by putting
the date stone in the peak and using two swallow holes
instead of one, one to either side and below the centered
marble slab. In another barn this date stone, which is
usually square, was lengthened out from a square to a par-
allelogram two feet long and lowered a little from the peak
so that the rounded swallow hole might be centered above
it. The square hole in a wall of masonry is rarer. It is commonest in the brick-walled barns of Butter Valley, where it
is sometimes the center of a decoration of apertures, a brick
end in width and a brick's thickness high, extending out in
the shape of a great X.

Other swallow holes not uncommon in barns with wooden
gables are arms of inward-pointing triangles making a cross,
with three to five triangles to an arm; a single triangle; a
star, generally five pointed; the conventionalized tulip of
six petals, so often, like the star, found as a barn symbol and
on gravestones; and the heart that, in glorified form, is so
constant on baptismal certificates and painted chests. Rare
shapes of swallow holes, but hardly, I think, local or personal, are a single crescent with points down; and two cres-
cents facing each other with points turned in. A star above
with the two crescent moons below, their points turned in-

ward and upward toward the star, is the only swallow hole design of which I have come upon but the one example.

The position of the swallow hole is pretty constant on all barns, well up toward the peak so that the birds can pass in and out even if the barn is nearly full of hay. Full it is not likely to be in late April when the barn swallows return, but if the swallow hole were lower than the peak the birds would have trouble tending their late broods in August. The swallow hole is sometimes so small that the birds cannot drive through in the manner described above, but must alight on its face, edge themselves through and drop off into the loft. So, too, I have seen the birds drop out of the narrow fixed slats that flank either side of a window and that arch flatly over its top, when a sash of the window or a pane of its glass has not been left open for them.

If peak windows may be regarded as swallow holes as well as ventilators, they are the largest swallow holes, larger even than the half circular openings in stone gables in upper Chester County or the jig-saw swallow holes of Cherry Valley and the Poconos. The jig-saw circles were probably of as great an area as any peak window, but their cut-out shapes were so narrow the swallows would have had difficulty getting in and out by them had there not been a circular cut-out space of four-inch diameter in their centers. The Pocono jig-saw circle was eventually opened up somewhat more by the well-directed pebbles of passing small boys who could not resist so tempting a target.

Convention dominates the making of swallow holes as it does that of barn symbols or weather vanes. Almost all the swallow holes of Pennsylvania are of the be-triangled diamond, the cross of triangles, the little circle, or the larger half circle. One and all the shapes are fewer year by year, even in wooden gables where they are so easy to saw out.

It may be that the modern farmer has hardened his heart against having swallows in the barn, as the modern house-wife has hardened her heart against martins in the eaves. He does not perhaps adhere to the belief of his fathers that there is luck in swallows. He has been educated out of the old-time faith that certain shapes of swallow holes are efficacious against fire as are those same shapes as barn symbols. You must go now to back country places to find even every third barn with a swallow hole, or to some old settled community that has resisted change, to the Poconos for one place and to northern Chester County for another.

There are old swallow holes still to be found in plenty along the Ridge Road from Morgantown to Phoenixville. This is a long-settled country, finding its outlet by a pike that has been much traveled from old time. Along the Ridge Road, for miles on miles, centered the life of the country-side it tapped, the countryside between the French Creek and the Schuylkill. Here were not only farms, but ore pits and forges, mills and lime-kilns, cotton factories and tan-neries, inns and country stores, smithies and the shops of cabinet makers and tinkers, churches and graveyards. Just off the Ridge Road were the mines of French Creek and Warwick Furnace.

There are huge barns and houses of colonial feeling along this road, with great oaks and great willows nearby, old apple and pear trees, box bushes and kindred signs of old-time prosperity and love of homeyard and garden. In certain of these great barns, with ends of red sandstone or blue-hued limestone, are some of the most pretentious swallow holes I have seen. And lest "pretentious" seem a large word for a detail of such humble office, let me hurry to say that some of these swallow holes are fully two feet long, and of an arched top a foot high in the center. They have some of them a brick trim. Through these great holes the swallows can forge in full tilt and with wings widespread. There are circular swallow holes, too, in some of these great gable ends, little fellows of six-inch diameter. There are certain squarish ones made by a stone taken out as the course close to the peak was being laid and the opening it left lapped by a wide stone on the laying of the next course.

There were no swallows about, not even martins, that first day of April on which I last came home to Germantown this way from "The Three Earls" and Ephrata. The Kloster had been good this wintry day of spring, its gray walls and gray tombstones, above and about which blackbirds veered and meadowlarks shuttled in hesitating flight, calling and whistling after their kind. Churchtown, on its hilltop, had been good, too, with its centuried quietude, its quick lifting lanes, its box bushes and its robins score on score. The abandoned ore pits at Warwick were a rich red ocher in the evening light. The sun, rapidly sinking behind us, warmed all the bare woods to a red as kindling as that of the blossoming maples. The hills right and left were plushed with a bloom of soft purple. The shadow of the car lay right ahead of us on the narrow road, mile after mile. The plowed fields were deserted of men; the teams of horses were housed for the night; the barnyards that had teemed with jostling cows on our way out at noon had to content themselves with the straw stacks red gold in the level light, the stock all now in stall; all the chickens were to roost; the ducks only of all the farm creatures were busy out of doors, hunting peepers perhaps in the flooded swamps. The red sandstone of the old barn gables was ruddy against the fast-dropping sun. It will be a month, though, before the barn swallows welcome the sight of those gables with glad gurglings as they home northward after their eight months of absence. Good as this evening is, with all its wild radiance, that evening will be better. In that warmer time there will be white blow of cherries wreathing the woodsides, plum blow and peach blow in the dooryards, and all the watered lowland lustily green with quick-growing grass. Then there will be the twittering swallows weaving their graceful flight about the ruddy gables and passing through the swallow holes into the friendly gloom of the great lofts. May all those who hear the birds so come to rest, their sleepy sounds and semi-quiet, know a joy in home equal to that of the swallows. Their good-nights are content itself.

GALLESDAG

for M. Grace Stone

FAR away as are the Alps, they cast their shadows now
and then across the uplands of Pennsylvania. When these
shadows darken our landscape we may hear, if we have
ears to hear, the horns of old romance calling by prosaic
postwoods or in tannin-scented gap of the hills; we may be
carried, if we submit to their suggestion, across the broad
Atlantic to mountain pastures where brown cattle graze and
tan-colored goats, and where all the flowered grass is rever-
berant with the hum of bees. It may be high noon there, as
in the vision just recorded; or day's end with depths on
depths of purple gathering in the great gulfs of the Säntis;
or a rapt night whose spangled skies are those our forefathers knew in their years under the snow peaks and gla-
ciers.

It is a little thing may open up the far vista through
which such shadows fall. It may be the rhododendron clusters of "Alpine roses" carved on some butter mold, brought
maybe from Switzerland to the valley of the Conestoga. It
may be a little cabinet in which to hang your watch by
night, a little cabinet of cherry and curly maple that passed
year on year on the wall of an old house east of Haycock
Mountain. It may be straw beehives, row on row, under the
thatched sheds narrow and squat, that shelter them from the
northwesters of winter on the Perkiomen hills. It may be
the note of cowbells on bare slopes above the Susquehanna,
clear-toned cowbells cast from bell metal, and not the thin

affairs of sheet iron that tinkle as if half-muted. It may be the tin horns, long and flaring of mouth, with which, a generation ago, the farmers and farmhands of York and Adams Counties were called in to dinner. All these, butter molds, watch cabinets, beehives, cowbells and tin horns have originals in Switzerland, whence came so many of the ancestors of our Lancaster folks, and of not a few of those of us from the other "Dutch" counties.

None of these things, though, have taken me to old years so remote as has a chance phrase heard one day of mid-October on a hilltop above Blooming Glen. Our host was telling me of apple picking. "My wife says that it is the thirteenth of October is Gallesdag, but my father always says it is the seventeenth of October."

"Gallesdag?" I queried. "What is Gallesdag?"

"It is apple-picking day. It is the day all the old folks say is the day you should begin picking winter apples."

"And who is Galles?" I asked, thinking of course of some saint of the church, not a few of whom still control our goings and comings in German Pennsylvania, stout Protestants though most of us be. Neither man nor wife could tell me. I looked up the St. Gall I had heard of most often, that companion of Columban who came out of the murk of the Irish coast to Switzerland, and gave his name to monastery and town and canton. I could not find what was his day, however, in the books to hand. I appealed to my friend the last of the polymaths, and heard that the day of that Gallus who is best known as St. Gall was October the sixteenth.

Investigation discloses no particular association of St. Gall with apples. Apple-picking day is Gallesdag just because it falls almost coincidently with the saint's day in mid-October, when winter apples should be gathered from the trees and stored away safe from the freezing weather which may thereafter be expected. What is remarkable is that German Pennsylvania should retain in 1932, some thirteen hundred years after his death, the name of this old notability of the late sixth and early seventh centuries who is else little known save among churchmen and scholars. It seems to me a preservation more to be wondered at than that of any urn of earthenware in Indian mounds hereabouts, and as thrilling as the discovery of a Viking battle-ax in wild earth in Minnesota.

The joy of coming on this old name for apple-picking day has been with me all this golden end of October that has succeeded my hearing of it. Gallesdag will be always associated in my mind with the deep orange and with the reds of coal-like glows on massed sassafrases that I drove past on my way home from Blooming Glen, with the tender green of just sprung winter grain on the rolling fields, with wheeling buzzards high in the thin blue of the sky, and with the scent of apples over rain-washed roads. And yet always, above, beyond, afar, tower, half the world away, those snowpeaks of St. Gall by Lake Constance, casting their shadows on this rich and mellow countryside with presage of oncoming night. The lights of the purring car have a darkness out of old time in the Alps to pierce as well as the darkness of nightfall in Bucks County in October of 1932.

VALLEY FORGE AND GETTYSBURG

for William A. Thomas

THERE are contrasts, sharp and dividing, between the two places in Pennsylvania that marked the turning points of the Revolution and the Civil War. When you think of Valley Forge you think of winter. When you think of Gettysburg you think of summer. When you think of Valley Forge you think of a time when all but all of America was backwoods. When you think of Gettysburg you think of a time when America was settled from Atlantic to Pacific and the frontier was fast disappearing. When you think of Valley Forge you think of snow falling, whiteness in the air, and wind in bare trees, or of blue shadows on snow long fallen. You think of men under dire privation, poorly clothed and lacking stout shoes, with stiff lips and a spirit of do or die in their hearts. You see, whether in accordance with historical fact or not, Washington on his knees in prayer, his white horse close by and a few officers about him, in a narrow valley between huddled hills, tree clad and deep with snow. The many pictures of Valley Forge have had their will of you, as have what you were taught in school and what you have read in history. If you are of the neighborhood, as are we who were born and brought up in the environs of Philadelphia, you have heard stories handed down the generations that confirm your childhood's teaching and your reading.

No story of that winter of 1777-1778 is more persistent and more widely spread round about than one of the scantiness of clothing for the men housed in the log huts of the encampment. These buildings, of which there were a thousand to shelter the eleven thousand men of the army, were made of logs, eighteen feet long and sixteen feet wide. The interior measurements of the huts must have been about sixteen by fourteen. Those that housed the men had, as a rule, no windows and no fireplace, and only one door. They were filled deep with straw and held twelve men. The fires by which the men cooked their food were outside, opposite the door. When a fire before the log cabin died low, the local story goes, the man whose chore it was to replenish it was given the warmest clothes the twelve possessed. No one of the group would have a complete outfit. One man would lend the fireman a sound pair of boots, a second a pair of pants without holes, a third an extra coat, and a fourth a fur cap with ear tippets.

Such an episode was truer, I take it, of the first month of the encampment than of its later months. Moving in on December 19, 1777, the army had to live in tents, or in commandeered quarters in the neighboring farmhouses, until the log cabins were completed. The orderly books and journals of officers indicate that the necessary huts were completed by mid-January of 1778. In your mind's eye, you can see at bitter nightfall, and the wind rising, the rows of log cabins that sheltered those sorely tried men. There are a thousand cores of fire before the rows on rows of huts, but the huts themselves, save the officers', have no window glows indicating warmth within, for there are no windows. There are no men anywhere to be seen, save the sentries on the trenches about the camp, and those about the generals' quarters. You see the stone house of the Potts that sheltered Washington down where the Valley Creek falls into the Schuylkill. It is there to-day, in all its old-time beauty of simplicity, after more than a century and a half of time and change.

Despite all the rumor of the camp from reveille to tattoo, Valley Forge made its teeming life manifest by few sounds that penetrated far beyond its borders. Songs and shuffles there must have been, for all the low moments in the early days of the encampment. Where there was so much youth there must have been a great deal of the merriment and jollity Ensign Ewing speaks of in his journal, and merriment and jollity have always an accompaniment of noise. The boys must have longed for the warmth of dance halls and chimney corners in Philadelphia, over which even in those ill-lighted days there must have hung a low glow of reflected light. The recurrent sounds that come to us over the years from Valley Forge are, though, the whistle and moan of the wind through the leaves that hung on the low oaks of its hills and about the low eaves of its log cabins. All who have painted scenes of the life of the encampment and all who have written of it in verse or story or play have heard that plaint and have allowed it to haunt them as they used brush or pen.

The winter and spring that Washington's army spent at Valley Forge have been painted in too dark colors. There was suffering enough in the forced marches his troops made before they went into winter quarters there. There was a lack of shoes for the men until the saving and curing of the hides of the creatures killed for beef had become the regular procedure. The men were cold and wet before the log huts were built, but that period of tenting was for hardly more than three weeks. Ensign George Ewing, whose journal of his service with the Continental Army was published in 1928, tells us under the caption of January, 1778, that "about the tenth of this month We got into our huts." They were, he writes, "built in three lines, each line four deep five yards asunder." Their size was "eighteen by sixteen feet long, six feet to the eves." They were covered with staves, the chimneys in the east end. These with the chimneys were probably the huts of the officers. The door was apparently not opposite the chimney, but in "the south side." The officers' huts were in the rear of the men's, twelve men in each hut and two "cores" of officers.

Only a month after a letter of Washington to Governor Clinton noting the privations of the army the troops were fit enough to be up to high jinks. Theodore W. Bean tells of the incident in his *Washington at Valley Forge* (1876). He cites no authority for it, but it is doubtless one of the many stories handed down in the neighborhood. That such a yarn is more credible than the average folk tale seems to be indicated by the authentic records of the May-day frolic that followed six weeks after these brave doings on St. Patrick's day. As Bean has it, some Pennsylvania Dutchmen made a figure of a Paddy and set it up close by the huts of a contingent of New Englanders. The Irishmen camped nearby were as quick on the trigger as Irishmen always are, and threatened to mob the New Englanders, believing it was they who fashioned the image. It was only the intervention of Washington that avoided a serious fracas. He asked the Irishmen to point out the men guilty of the Paddy. They could not. So Washington said that the whole army would celebrate St. Patrick's day. He ordered the commissary to dispense a whiskey ration to every man in the encampment, and what had threatened serious trouble ended in jollity.

From General George Weedon's *Valley Forge Orderly Book*, published in 1902, you get primarily only the official side of things, orders, payrolls, supplies, forage, drills, parades, care of the camp, use of wagons and horses, court martials, desertions, gaming, disposition of prisoners, illness, inoculation against smallpox, hospital regimen and the like. Yet underlying it all you become aware, from this entry and that, not only of the daily routine of it all, but of the spectacle it was. You realize the rows of log cabins, more than a thousand of them, for the eleven thousand men encamped on the rolling slopes and in the hilltops of second growth. There is picturesqueness in what is conjured up by the record of February 8, 1778: "In future the reveille to beat at daybreak, the troop at eight in the morning, the retreat at sunset, and tattoo at nine in the evening. To render this duty uniform, the drummers' call to beat at the right of the first line and [to be] answered throughout that line, then through the second and corps of artillery beginning at the left. The reserve shall follow the second line. Immediately upon this three rolls to begin and [to be] run through in the manner as the call. Then all the drums of the army at the heads of their respective corps shall go through the regular beats, ceasing upon the right, which will be a sign for the whole to cease."

I have supplied no words here not in the orders save the two "to be's" absolutely necessary to make the meaning clear. Those drum beats sounding from hill to hill of the camp and re-echoing along all the river hills must have been a memory unforgettable to all who heard them, the men of the army and all the folks on the farms round about.

It must never be forgotten, as Weedon's *Orderly Book* tells us so explicitly on March 1, 1778, that the country that fed the Continental Army was a country well stocked with provisions. "Thank Heaven," the record runs, "our country abounds with provisions, and, with prudent management, we need not apprehend want for any length of time. Defects in the commissaries' department, contingencies of weather and other temporary empediments have subjected and may again subject us to deficiencies on a few days."

Before the foraging of both armies began to denude it of supplies this countryside in Chester and Montgomery counties was literally a land flowing with milk and honey. In the Great Valley were homestead farms of Welsh Quakers two generations old, in deep soiled limestone land. Across Schuylkill were the most southerly parts of Pennsylvania Dutchland, with every farm stocked to the full, both house and barn, with food for beast and man. There were manor houses about like the Vaux-Audubon-Wetherill house on the Perkiomen, an estate of three hundred acres with great house and barns and outbuildings that had cost its builder $18,000.

There is no doubt at all but that the army was well supplied with food for the most part of its entrenchment at Valley Forge. It could not have been welded into the weapon it was after it broke camp there had the physique and mobility of the men not been built up during that winter and spring of 1777-1778. All Baron Steuben's genius of organization would have gone for little had not the army been well fed and warm and well accoutered in its camp. Things were not running smoothly, perhaps, until February, but after that time they improved rapidly, and it was a well-trained and hardy army that took the field after mid-June of 1778.

It is true that the orderly book does imply in one reading of a famous passage an army "in rags." This is the whole passage: "Nothing does, nor nothing can, contribute more to the health of soldiers, than a clean camp, clean clothes, and victuals well dressed. These, however deeply involved in rags an army may be, are to be affected by attention in the officers. The General therefore calls upon every officer from the Major Generals to the corporals inclusively, for their exertions: hoping thereby, with the blessings of God, to prevent such number of deaths which unfortunately have taken place since we came to this ground."

Smallpox and pneumonia were the causes of most of the deaths, but the inoculation finally carried to the last man ended the scourge that smallpox was, and the coming of spring, by allowing the men to spend most of their time outdoors, much diminished the losses by pneumonia.

Nor does it seem that the adjuration to the men always to shave the beard and to "appear with clean hands and face" would have been made had they not had hot water and soap. "Want of uniformity in the soldiers' clothing," runs the order, "and its indifferent quality, so far from excusing slovenliness, and unsoldierly neglect in other respects, ought rather to excite each man to compensate those blemishes by redoubled attention to the means he has in his power."

It was in the times before the Continental Army went into winter quarters that the Ensign Ewing aforesaid found the gloomiest hours. "Were I to describe," he writes in his journal, "the hardships and difficulties we underwent from this time [September 12, 1777] until the fourth of October no person but those who were with us would credit my relation. Therefore I chuse to pass it over in silence rather than those who should see this work should think me guilty of an hyperbole."

Ensign Ewing obtained a furlough on February 4, 1778, and went home to Cohansey in South Jersey. He did not return to Valley Forge until March 20.

On April 7 "some roguish chaps tied a sheaf of straw to the tail of Joseph Anderson's, brigade quarter-master's . . . horse, and set it on fire and let him run, which very much offended him, and he set out to the General to enter a complaint."

On April 15 the Ensign tried to attend a play in the Bakehouse, but the house was so full he could not get in. "Then," he writes, "a number of gentlemen went to Major Parker's hut in the fourth where we spent the evening very merrily." On April 16 he has to make entry: "My head ached very badly this morning occassioned by my last night's frolic."

It was May 1 brought the most surprising entry of all in Ensign Ewing's journal. "Last evening," he writes, "May poles were erected in every regiment in the camp, and at the reveille I was awoke by three cheers in honor of King Tamany. The day was spent in mirth and jollity, the soldiers parading, marching with fife and drum, and huzzaing as they passed the poles, their hats adorned with white blossoms. The following was the procession of the Third Jersey Regiment on the aforesaid day. First, one sergeant drest in an Indian habit representing King Tamany. Second thirteen sergeants drest in white each with a bow in his left hand and thirteen arrows in his right. Thirdly thirteen drums and fifes. Fourthly the privates in thirteen platoons thirteen men each. The non-commissioned officers and soldiers being drawn up in the aforesaid manner on the regimental parade gave three cheers at their own pole and then marched off to headquarters to do honor to his Excellency but just as they were descending the hill to the house an aid met them and informed them that the General was indisposed and desired them to retire, which they did with the greatest decency and regularity."

There is mention of "cruel oppressors" in Weedon, of British incitements to American soldiers to desert, and a "scandalous performance," an advertisement in the *Philadelphia Evening Post* declaring that all who enlist in the

Continental Army are to be held for the duration of the war. On the whole, however, the enemy when mentioned are not referred to in bitter or unparliamentary terms. That there was hobnobbing between men of the two armies, as there was in the Civil War and in the World War there is no evidence, but a story told by an English Friend about the neighborhood of Valley Forge sets one to wondering. Robert Sutcliff in *Travels in Some Parts of North America* (1812) tells of a visit to relatives who lived on what is now commonly known as the Audubon-Wetherill estate. During the occupation of Valley Forge the Vauxes lived there. It was "in full view of the great American encampment at Valley Forge, and on the opposite side of the river Schuylkill." While Mr. Vaux resided there, Sutcliff says "he had frequently the company of General Howe, and the other British Commanders. One day it happened that he had Howe to breakfast and Washington to tea."

The intelligence department of the American army must have known of Howe's visits. Why, then, did they not try to take him prisoner? Did they regard him as a friend, as gossip has it he was, and so allow him to come and go? Perhaps they would rather have had him in Philadelphia than a general who would be more eager to dislodge them from Valley Forge. There were brushes, of course, between British and American troops, between scouting and foraging parties, but no engagements of moment during the six months December 19, 1777, and June 18, 1778.

The Morgans of my own ancestry lived not many miles from Valley Forge, on Pickering Creek. That there should have come down to us certain household treasures from them proves that there was not serious pillaging in their direction. Fence rails the men would steal for their fires, and food, but there seems to have been little lifting of household gear.

The army would requisition horses and cattle at times, with payment for them, of course, but not in the gold the British in Philadelphia could pay. It was hardly to be wondered at, under such conditions, that such farmers as were neutral or pro-British in their sympathies would rather sell to the British than to the Continentals.

The scars of the occupation of the hills of Valley Forge healed rather quickly. Robert Sutcliff, from whose *Travels* I have quoted above, visited Valley Forge on "Sixth Month, 8th 1806" in the afternoon on a drive from the Chester Valley to his "cousin W. B.'s" on the Perkiomen. "We passed over," he writes, "the ground occupied by the American Army under General Washington, as an entrenched camp during the war. The remains of the entrenchments are still visible, although the site is again become a thick wood; so rapid is vegetation in this part of the world."

Another Friend, Henry Woodman, contributed a history of Valley Forge to the *Doylestown Intelligencer* in a series of articles in 1854. Meanwhile the story of Valley Forge had found its way into the histories and school books. These articles by Woodman, however, were written by one who was thoroughly familiar with Valley Forge. His father had been a soldier encamped there. He was born and brought up nearby, and herded his grandfather's cattle from pastures where once had stood the huts of the encampment. His book preserves a great deal of the local lore about those six so critical months in our history.

That Valley Forge was a place of pilgrimage in the early years of the nineteenth century we have Sutcliff's record to prove. Earlier than that, though, many of those that had wintered there returned to look over their old camping ground, Washington among them. Woodman tells us that his father met his old commander-in-chief there in the late summer of 1796. It was as the elder Woodman was plowing the Front Line Hill. Washington was on horseback, and accompanied by a black servant.

One living as near to Valley Forge as I have all my days has inevitably made pilgrimage there time after time. I have gone there by train, and picked up seedling rhododendrons that had slipped down the railroad cut because of the gradual undermining of the wood's floor at its top. Those rhododendrons, carried home in my pockets, are now full grown, eight feet tall and crowned with blossoms of pinky white June after June. I have carried home picture on picture of the place. I can recall a flight of great blue herons over Schuylkill, the kingfisher I have seldom failed to find on Valley Creek, the blue jays that are to be seen and heard racketing around on Mount Joy. I have deplored the tearing out of the old fencerows on the farms of the camping ground, the cutting down of the old orchards, the demolition of the old houses. The hills of Valley Forge were far more beautiful in my youth than they are to-day. Then there was no intrusion of a Gothic church, of an architecture alien to eighteenth century America; and then the countryside was still a typical stretch of Pennsylvania farm country. Now large portions of the park look like a cemetery without graves. Gettysburg has been preserved as Pennsylvania farm country. Valley Forge has suffered the indignity of being turned into a "park." With the tradition of leaving old houses in a "park" established in Fairmount Park in Philadelphia, it is strange that a similar policy should not have been followed here.

There is still much of beauty here at Valley Forge. Fencerows and houses can be easily destroyed, but not the contours of the hills. The dogwood trees that are one of the glories of our Pennsylvania May have been cherished. There is nowhere they do better, or are found in greater plenty. The people turn out in thousands to see them, reducing the progress of a car to the pace one must follow in a crowded city street. If you would enjoy the dogwoods of Valley Forge arrange to arrive there at daybreak.

I like best to recall the hills as they were in the long ago, before the days of automobiles and when shanks' mare was dependable for miles on miles. I remember our tramp from the railroad station up toward the Pickering Creek, the baker's wagon we met on crossing the North Valley Hill, and the delectable quality youth and hunger gave to the Dutch bread we secured from him. I remember the eight-sided schoolhouse, and the goslings in the overflow from a roadside spring, and the glad light of late April over all. I remember my passing by Valley Forge on a long day's tramp from Germantown to the Eagle, breakfast in Norristown, lunch at Valley Forge, supper very late at the Eagle. That in mid-September, and the next morning the fields white with frost. I remember walking to Valley Forge from Bryn Mawr, and a white-crowned sparrow, one of no more than a dozen I have seen, singing at the roadside, by a drift of late left snow. I remember the gentleman from Louisiana I piloted here, and how agitated he was, so agitated he could hardly sign the visitors' book in Washington's headquarters for the trembling of his hand. A great-grandfather from Virginia had wintered here with Washington, and his descendant had never been at Valley Forge before.

I recall a trip by automobile here early in November, on a day when I had awakened to rain falling and freezing on the trees. The rime was gone by afternoon, but the landscape was gray all the hours until the fall of night. Even the brown of the oak leaves and the red-brown of mazzard leaves were dimmed by the gray mist that thinned up from

VALLEY FORGE FROM THE GULPH ROAD

the fields. There was no old rose this day in the buds of the oaks. The woods were winter gray. The cedars were a dimmed bronze or a frosted purple. The only warmth was in the red top of the fields, reddish even under the gray skies spitting snow.

Along Valley Creek the greens and grays were so near they were unaffected by the fog. The laurels and hemlocks were bright green and shining with the drip of condensed mist, the rocks were gray with water-filled lichens, the woods floor was brown and purplish ash. The kingfisher at the dam breast was a loud blue and white, a vivifying flash of color in the dull day.

It was another gray day we went to Valley Forge on December 17, 1933, with mist shutting off all the distances. You could barely see Mt. Misery from Mt. Joy, narrow as is the creek cleft between. No Schuylkill River was visible from that hilltop where the Gulph Road drops towards Washington's headquarters. What you could see of the country was vacant, bare, sodden with rain and lifeless for the most part. There were crows stalking about here and there, but without success, while we watched them, in finding any food. Now and then a whirl of starlings tossed out of the mist and on into the mist. The trees stood gaunt and leafless, with crows' nests and squirrels' summer dormitories of leaves, making black blurs in their tops here and there.

As we walked down to a bake oven we ran across a scatter of feathers from a hen ringneck, the work of a fox, perhaps, or of a great horned owl. The ground-hog holes sunk in a mound whose one time service was difficult to guess were filled with mats of wet leaves. Not a squirrel scolded us, not a mouse squeaked away as we plowed through the deep leaves of the woods floor. There was no little brown creeper, or nuthatch, or downy woodpecker busy on the straight trunks. No golden-crowned kinglets drifted through the low hemlocks; no sparrows rose from the roadside; no hawk hovered above the fields of bleached brown. The woods were deader than the open country to the eastward, where we had seen the crows and the starlings.

There were only monotones everywhere, the dim grays of the wooded hills, the bleached browns of the open spaces, the muddy white of the mist. Even the laurels and hemlocks native to these stony hills were without their characteristic green glitter, dulled by the mist that lurked about their stands. Bittersweet, winding up the scrub about the reproduced log hospital, almost alone brought any vivid hue into the scene, but its opened seed pods were at best but points of reddish yellow. The very red top was winter killed to strawy white.

Two of the seven cultures of Pennsylvania have been dominant since the days of its settlement in the country about Valley Forge, the cultures of the Quakers, Welsh and English, and of the various Germanic elements from which are sprung the Pennsylvania Dutch. The Swedes were at Swedesford on Schuylkill not many miles below Valley Forge, and there were Hollanders in Germantown and Norristown. There were Scotch-Irish round about, too. Only New Englanders and Virginians of the seven members of the old stock in Pennsylvania had not come in numbers to this neighborhood. As a matter of fact certain Virginians, like Henry Woodman's father, married into families in the neighborhood, and there were similar alliances between New Englanders and long-established Pennsylvania families.

All the culture of Pennsylvania was summed up in the countrysides about Valley Forge and Gettysburg. And by culture as distinguished from cultures I mean ways of settlement, styles of houses and barns and outbuildings, conditions of hunting and lumbering and farming, the conduct of crafts and professions, the habits of daily life, the traditions of church and education and play and interior decoration and domestic art that distinguish Pennsylvania. Pennsylvania has been for more than two hundred years now of the center and of the province, Augustan and frontier, East and West, tidewater and backwoods, European and Yankee. Valley Forge and its neighborhood are typical Pennsylvania hill country. Gettysburg and its neighborhood are typical Pennsylvania hill country, but nearer the mountains than Valley Forge. There are Pennsylvania Dutch about Gettysburg, and Scotch-Irish in numbers, with but few Quakers or Hollanders.

When you think of Gettysburg you think of our Pennsylvania countryside at its best, a countryside swept by the full tide of summer, heavy with the increase of the earth; wheat fields ready for the cradle; peach orchards full set with fruit; the low and wooded hills full bannered with leaves at their lustiest; ledges of gray rock reflecting the heat in quivering and vibrating waves; turnpikes gleaming white in the sun; farmhouses dozing in the moon amid acres of corn; barns whose open doors reveal them close-packed with hay; cattle knee deep in the shallow fords of slow-moving streams, content in the shadows of covered bridges. On this pastoral scene, so quiet and remote, with mountains hanging blue in the distance, breaks suddenly all the fury and tumult and loud horror of war. There was little sound, as I have said, all winter long and in the spring and young summer, at Valley Forge. There was little quiet for three days of early July about Gettysburg, save in the ears of the men to whom death had brought silence forever.

I had been to Gettysburg but once in the horse and buggy days. That visit had been for me, however, a momentous one. I had gone there for the twenty-fifth anniversary of the battle, on July 3, 1888, with my uncle who had fought there on the Northern side. It was not only the great movements of troops, the maneuvering that interested me, and the identifying of this place as Culp's Hill and that as Round Top, this ridge as Seminary Ridge and that lowland as the Peach Orchard, but the little incident that this man recorded as having happened here and that little incident that had happened there. Two men of my uncle's regiment got into an altercation as to where the one of them lost his leg. He said it was by this fence panel. The man who carried him back said it was by one five panels away. The one-legged man brandished his crutch about the head of his rescuer and they might have come to blows had their comrades not laughed them out of their tempers. Here on Culp's Hill had been enacted the very story I was to meet afterwards in Kipling's "Mutiny of the Mavericks." They pricked a reluctant fighter with their bayonets and compelled him to lead a charge. He went berserk, performed prodigies of valor, and then went back to his old trick of shirking the next day.

It is forty-seven years as I write since those days at Gettysburg with Uncle Jim. I was never so hot in my life as on those nights we slept under the roof of the two-storied house in that valley town. Yet every morning I was fresh for the adventures of the day. The guide that took us over the battlefield was a survivor of the battle. A piece of his skull had been shot away and the silver plate that replaced it had slipped a little so you could, as he said, "see his brains pulsating with the hard thinking he was doing to make the battle clear."

Of all the buildings of the battlefield I remember best an old barn with a straw roof that came through the battle unscathed. If I remember rightly, it had been used as a

GENERAL MEADE'S HEADQUARTERS AT GETTYSBURG

hospital. It was called by a characteristically Dutch name, Shealer's barn, or Shearer's was it? It is so long ago I heard the name I am not sure of it. It was of the wide weather-boarding that is so sure a sign of antiquity in any building in Pennsylvania. Its roof was of very steep pitch, like that of the Kloster in Ephrata, giving a suggestion of the Old World to the place where was tried a principle of the New. When I saw that barn, the great battlefield on which it stood was still farming country of yesterday, an unspoiled stretch of rolling valley and noble hills. You could follow the plow then across the path of Pickett's charge and pick minié balls and eagled buttons and strange gear else from the unfolding furrow. There were still the bullets unprobed for in the oak timber of Shealer's barn, which, after its last wounded were gone, slipped back into its old ways of peace as easily as the many farmers that had fought on the field that brought it renown. Its daily use, and the presence there always of the farm folk, preserved it fairly well down the years from the relic seeker.

Like Valley Forge, Gettysburg has been a shrine to visit from the day it acquired fame. Thither my grandfather went, the father of Uncle Jim, on the second anniversary of the battle, on July 3, 1865. The "Adjutant" he refers to is Uncle Jim. The "Lucy" to whom the letter is written is my mother. Grandfather and his fellow pilgrims to Gettysburg had to be ferried over the Susquehanna because the Columbia-Wrightsville bridge had been burned in the scare caused by the Confederate raid into Pennsylvania.

"Gettysburg July 4th, 1865

Dear Lucy,

I scarcely know in what vein or form of expression a letter should be written on this the nation's day and from this place of historic fame, embracing so much of sorrowful and cheering memories. Only two years ago you may recollect we were called upon by the police on a quiet though agitating Sabbath day, to aid in erecting fortification in the environs of Philada. to defend it against an anticipated rebel assault!!

My reply was—'Philadelphia must be defended on the line of the Susquehanna'—and at this place three days thereafter commenced the conflict which continued for three days with fearful uncertainty but culminated in the defeat and retreat of the rebel forces and the relief of the timid souls in our city who apprehended its capture, and the disappointment of the traitors in our midst who desired it. The sacrifices of those 3 days of national agony are now being commemorated.

I have just returned from a walk, before breakfast, to 'Cemetery hill,' and a glance from it over the battlefield and various positions where men fought and bravely died that our country might live. If the 'Adjutant' had been along to give explanations it would have been much more satisfactory—indeed I had some hopes of descrying him among the numerous blue-coats and straps in the streets and hotels but have thus far been disappointed.

Yesterday was and to-day bids fair to be a glorious day, so far as nature can be desired to co-operate with man's arrangements for enjoyment whether he be farmer, gathering his crops of hay and wheat—traveler, or pleasure seeker.

I left Oakland on the Philada. 8 o'clock train for Columbia where we arrived at 12 o'clock and a large party crossed the Susquehanna on a little locomotive-power Steamboat which landed us in Wrightsville where we were detained an hour waiting for the cars to York and when carried to the latter place were detained another hour waiting for the cars from Harrisburg to Baltimore by which we were conveyed to 'Hanover Junction.' At this latter place we were detained an hour and a half waiting for the Gettysburg train to perfect its arrangements for carrying the crowd which now amounted to 9 or 10 carloads and the road being apparently a 'poor' one was poorly supplied with accommodations. We did however get started, and after numerous stoppages and delays and much grumbling, with a full quantum of swearing among some of the more irascible passengers we arrived in this celebrated town at 7 o'clock distant from Wrightsville by R.R. 54 miles and by turnpike about 34.

Next mystery to be solved was that of board and lodging and after three or four trials I turned in at an impromptu boarding house where there is a great abundance of eatables and better lodging than I expected to be able to secure on such an occasion.

I have as yet seen but three persons whom I know—James M'Clure of Brandywine, Col. W. B. Thomas of the City and Mr. Saml. Shearer, one of the acquaintances of early life who married a sister of Dr. Isaac V. Wm. Davis. The town was in commotion last night to a late hour with new arrivals. A vendor of *pyrotechnics* had a stand in the square and from the continuous explosion of rockets, roman candles and crackers and the gyrations of Catherine and pin wheels I presume his venture proved a decided success. An excellent band was playing at intervals and towards midnight the notables were serenaded and called out to address the crowd, Govr. Curtin, Genl. Howard, etc., responding. The night air was soft and balmy; the moonlight all that tender lovers could desire, consequently all Gettysburg was in the streets in its most attractive garb in addition to the influx of thousands of strangers many of whom probably did not retire from the street during the night—as I heard that large numbers made the pavements their resting place for the night which was one of the briefest for by 4 o'clock this morning the bells commenced to ring forth a merry peal and were followed by the firing of the national salute. Vehicles have been coming in in a continuous stream since sunrise bringing in the people of the surrounding country, and the cry is 'Still they come.'

The services and ceremonies of the day are to commence at 9 o'clock (meaning 10, I suppose) and the hour is approaching so I shall have to drop the pen presenting and resort to the 'Hill' to see and hear the notables who are expected to constitute the attraction of the day. Many were expecting the President—but it is understood that he is not here—Genl. Grant is reported gone to Albany so we must be content with Gov. Curtin, Genl. Meade, Howard, Geary, Doubleday and such others as may be on hand.

12½ o'clock.

I have been out with the procession which moved at 10½ o'clock but I soon tired in the attempt to look at and listen to the performances and wandered over 'the hill' listening to the various enquiries and observations on the subject of the battle and its consequences. You know my dislike to mingling with or being wedged in by crowds particularly under a broiling sun. Genl. Geary Acting Prov. Mar. for the occasion issued a Military Order forbidding the sale of intoxicating drinks between 4 o'clock P.M. of the 3d and 6 P.M. to-day which order was sanctioned by the Burgess and I think must have been observed as I scarcely have seen a drunken man to-day. The farmers could ill afford a holiday as it now seems likely to produce a rain this afternoon and there is a large amount of hay and grain cut, and all requires immediate attention, but they and nearly all the other visiters will leave in the course of the afternoon and I shall not stay long behind them as Gettysburg has but few attractions to induce a prolonged stay. '*And where to next?*' will doubtless be your enquiry but really I have scarcely yet decided but will endeavor to inform some of you soon.

I should like to hear from home but scarcely expect to do so while moving from point to point, and must hope that all are well and that Theora and her young brood are doing as well as the hot weather will permit. I should like to know whether 'Jim' (so he persists in signing himself) is still at Washington or has been discharged as well as several other things which I suppose I will not get to know before reaching home.

I asked our landlady this morning whether eggs were scarce in this country (a gentle hint) to which she replied that they were, the traders having bought them all up and they rose in consequence of the approach of this celebration to 40 cents per doz. which I thought rather singular if none of the houses of entertainment used more of them than she did.

Among the pedlars, showmen, Charlatans and dispensers of notions we have in our house a blind man who has an electric magnetic box and just now has the house full of women upon whom he is practicing for amusement and I am overpowered by their screams and anctics—he I think is slightly drunk and they immensely noisy so I shall have to give up my writing and mail my letter, leaving it to the newspapers to eulogize the performances of the day and give you Genl. Howard's speech and other details, as I think I am writing in a rambling manner without much coherency.

Love to all

Yours affectionately

M. J. THOMAS"

Automobiles have made many trips to Gettysburg possible to me of recent years. I have been there in the spring when there are as many dogwood trees in bloom as at Valley Forge, and a great many Judas trees to mingle their magentaish pink with the white blossoms of the dogwood. I have been there in June when all the countryside was deep drowsed in summer. I have been there in winter and driven home through a hundred miles of wild northeaster that almost held back the car. There were times when, headed into it directly, we could hardly see the road a car's length before us. I have been there in October, both early and late. A trip that revealed our Pennsylvania at its most striking was that of Sunday, October 28, 1933. It was a day of full fall, with crows in the air and soaring buzzards.

There were still a good many leaves on the oak trees, but they had been browned by frost the most of them and they sounded very wintry as they whispered ceaselessly in the light wind that was abroad. The part of the field that appealed to me most for its natural beauty was the section below Little Round Top and the Devil's Den. It was a tumble of gray rocks from among which sprung chestnut oaks in a dispersed stand.

The guide made Pickett's charge very clear to us as we stood by the wall where it ended. It would seem that it was suicidal to send these men across against the Union lines, but if they had broken through the men further to the left on the Union front would have been flanked.

All of the battlefield, except those parts in which there are monuments or graveyards, is preserved as farmland, that is, almost all. If it is not preserved as farmland, it is preserved as woodland. There is no intrusion of park-like places on any part of the battlefield. What was open in the time of the battle is for the most part open still. What was second

THE BATTLE OF GETTYSBURG

growth at the time of the battle is second growth still, even
if many of the trees that were there in 1863 are now cut
down. We got a very clear idea of Cemetery Hill to the
east and Seminary Ridge to the west. We got a very clear
idea of the three days' battle. The Southern army won the
first day and drove us back on the town, through it, and on
to Cemetery Hill. Our right flank was just outside the
town and our left flank was on Round Top. We got our
troops in the latter part of this line on the heights just
about twenty minutes before the Confederates in the rush
of the two armies for this vantage point. When the Confederates found us in occupation there, they had to fall back.
In the second day's battle things were more even, although
there were more successes on the Union side than on the
Confederate side. On the third day the climax came with
Pickett's charge in which the flower of the Southern army,
that part which had not been in action before, tried to charge
with bayonets under a heavy artillery barrage for almost a
mile from the Confederate position on Seminary Ridge to
the Union position on Cemetery Hill. It is almost where
Lincoln made his address in the fall following the battle
that Pickett's charge reached its furthest point, was broken,
and hurled back.

It is not so much the specific items of information that
under cultivation that were once under cultivation, most of
the field is, as I have said, still farmland. Fences like the
old fences, walls like the old walls, roads in the main following the course of the old roads, and farm buildings that
came scathless through the battle are still here to bring back
an almost accurate picture of what conditions were in 1863.

It is not so much the specific items of information that
we acquired that I treasure as memories of the day. It is
rather the clarification of what took place during the three

days of the battle, a realization of how important it was in preventing the Confederates from breaking through to Buffalo or Philadelphia and so dividing the North, and the sense of the benign fruition of fall that remain with me now the visit is years in retrospect.

It is not, though, moments of these more recent visits that recur to me oftenest when Gettysburg reasserts itself in memory, but moments of that visit of 1888, when the battle was but twenty-five years in the past. There were many men in blue then. They are all but gone now. Gone, too, are those old days of leisure and of varied work and of varied and leisured living that the processes of modern civilization are blotting out. Valley Forge and Gettysburg, though eighty-five years apart, are much nearer together, they and their backgrounds of ways of living, than Gettysburg and to-day, only seventy-three years apart. Our country never gave so much to men as in the eighteen-eighties. Those days of summer we spent on the battlefield were in old times that were truly good. The stars we saw above us those nights so hot we would not sleep were still fighting in their courses for America. The freedom won for us by the men of Valley Forge and preserved for us by the men of Gettysburg was unchallenged in 1888.

GOATS: A CONCERN

for David Lawrence Vaughan

For long years the goat seemed to me alien to our American landscape. To be sure, I knew him a full half century ago, between the shafts of a cart, as a part of "the suburban scene." I envied certain of my friends his possession, and the glory of driving folks off the sidewalk as you bore down on them, chariot-wise, behind his formidable horns and determined sense of right of way. I envied the lads that herded the nannies of "Irishtown," thinking "the poor man's cow" much more interesting than any Alderney or Jersey in paddock or pasture.

As my years increased, the ranks of the goats lessened, and I felt more and more justified in my feeling that there was something foreign about them, that they were not a part of our farm life as horses were, and cows, and sheep. They were just pets for children, like the donkey, or, in their long horned and lop-eared varieties, surprising adjuncts to the landscape, like white peacocks or swans. So, when I noted goats so often as centers of interest in representations of mountain scenery, I began to wonder did they have a right to be there, or were they there as elves and goblins are in American stories for children or skylarks and nightingales in American verse, in sheer imitation of Old World art. The question of goats in American pictures grew finally to be a matter of "concern" to me, as the question of driving to meeting in a surrey might have been to a Friend of the days after the Civil War.

The craze over Angora goats was coincident with my child-hood, in the seventies. That craze brought up talk of the preceding craze over Cashmere goats, of the fifties, and of that still earlier craze, of the thirties, over Merino sheep. All the waning years of the century, however, goats grew fewer and fewer, in goat carts, on corner lots, or tethered on front lawns. Even the belief that goats' milk was particu-larly invigorating to people of weak constitution could not stay the depletion of their numbers. The goats had almost disappeared, by the late nineties, from the suburbia in which I lived. The last "private" goat cart I knew in Germantown lingered on until the days of the World War, when even the Philadelphia Zoological Garden gave up that time-honored institution, which held rank, in the affections of the children, with the donkeys and donkey carts so long a feature of the place.

There came a revival of goat keeping after the World War. A number of breeds, perhaps known before but not much exploited, took place, one after another, in rural econ-omy, but gradually faded away again, Saanen after Toggen-berg, as Nubian after Maltese before them. The goat is again a comparatively rare beast in most parts of eastern America. Here and there are regions, one in North Caro-lina and another in northeastern Pennsylvania, where there are quite a few goats, but except for a herd here used in the making of vaccine and another there for the production of kids for Passover, they are thinly distributed throughout the country that was once the thirteen colonies. On the whole only the Italian and Greek peasants used to goats' milk in Mediterranean lands and the valetudinarians who fancy that milk beneficial for their digestive ailments are still faith-ful to goats. Everywhere throughout the East sheep are coming back, but not yet the goats.

If we can attribute verisimilitude to the old prints, or take them as a fairly representative cross-section of American life, there were many more goats, relative to the population, in the second quarter of the nineteenth century than there are in the second quarter of the twentieth century. There are five illustrations by W. H. Bartlett to *American Scenery* with goats in the foreground. Though its two volumes are dated 1852, some of the plates are of 1838, and they may be all taken as inspired by the look of our countryside as it was in the thirties and forties. Lithographs by Nathan Currier with goats in them are perhaps a little later in date, but neither "Our Pasture" nor "Fording the River" would seem to picture a countryside of later than the forties.

It is only after persistent questioning of those who know our country's yesterdays and by much reading of old books and agriculture papers that I have come to wonder if, after all, the presence of goats in these old pictures is something else than a convention. I used to think the goats were there because Theocritus established goatherds and their charges as a part of pastoral landscape; because French countrysides of eighteenth century delineation delighted in goats; because goats, as a sign of the zodiac, bounded blithely in the woodcuts of old almanacs; and because visitors to Apennines and Alps and Pyrenees had been charmed by goats against these mountain backgrounds, and demanded replicas of goats in all souvenirs to take home to America. Such a souvenir might be a chamois of metal mounted on a crystal of quartz or an ibex of great horns that was so upstanding and tense you owned his whittler an artist. Another such souvenir that fascinated me in childhood was a chromo of a high pasture dotted regularly with blue goats and tufts of that ruddy pink rhododendron that is called Alpine rose.

The goats with the sheep in "Our Pasture" of Nathan

Currier are, too, blue coated, but not so deep a blue that they cannot pass for gray or black if you wish so to consider the color. Unmistakably gray is the goat in wax that trots before the lady with the rake in my paper and wax group under glass. My plaster-of-Paris goat of Mephistophelian expression is portly and piebald brown and white. Both this fellow and his kin of wax were probably brought to the door by peddlers of post-Civil War days.

In my childhood goats were considered "wonderfully health-giving animals." It was *de rigueur* to keep a goat in a racing stable for the benefit of the string of horses there, and few livery stables or car-barns were without a bearded billy. There was supposed to be a great virtue in the strong odor disseminated by *capra hircus*. Up in northwestern Pennsylvania, in Erie County, as recently as a generation ago, you often found at least one goat with a flock of sheep, "for the sake of the sheep's health." This custom may have been a survival from that earlier day when goats offered sheep a very necessary protection against wolves. Goats are high-hearted creatures, and many stories are told of their presenting a wall of tossing horns as they surrounded and shielded their own kids or a parcel of ewes and lambs.

In Sullivan County, in a long-established Quaker community along the Loyalsock, there were so many goats in old days that letters still preserved refer to certain men of the neighborhood as "goatherds." This in 1825, or thereabouts. In New England, too, I come across rumors of goats being more common a century ago than to-day. My neighbors in Sandwich have half memories of old folks telling them that goats could eke out a living in winters would starve a cow. The goats could thrive on next to nothing. Ethan Allan Crawford is quoted in *The History of the White Mountains* (1846), by his wife Lucy, as saying that goats would do well in the Notch, but that they would be

GOATS IN AN EIGHTEENTH CENTURY CUT-OUT

too much trouble. Whether this "trouble" has reference to their propensity to stray I do not know, but I do know that a bunch of goats put in an old pasture in Tamworth not so long ago to keep down the brush escaped now and then and ate whatever they met even to the bark of trees and the lichens on ledges.

It may well be, then, that the landscapists who put goats into scenes in Crawford's Notch and Centre Harbor, Little Falls in New York, and the Shenandoah Valley in Virginia, and into "Our Pasture" and "Fording the River," wherever those scenes may be in Middle States or New England, have been painting with eye on the object.

Goats are certainly picturesque creatures. They compose into landscape as well as geese do, or cows. Their habit of striking attitudes on places of vantage, even if those places of vantage are no more romantic than the rock faces of old quarries, seems to show their appreciation of an art of life. Goats can freeze into a grave immobility, and hold their positions almost indefinitely. They are also capable, as an old encyclopedia says, of "an admirable celerity," and are very graceful in their capers from rock to rock. They suggest far-off places and old time. Even in youth they have the look of a most venerable race of beasts. They carry you back to the earliest days. They may well be, as certain of the old commentators declare, a means by which man climbed from savagery to civilization. They fit into primeval forest and bare mountain slopes as naturally as do deer. It would not seem in consonance with the narrow road in the shadow of the White Mountains for Bartlett to put sheep into his picture of that road's passing of Pulpit Rock. Sheep must have cleared hill pastures to thrive, but the hardy goats may be trusted to do well, as Crawford suggests, on the scant grass and the browse of the barren Notch.

THE SEVEN RULES OF WISDOM

I. M.

Henry C. Mercer

It is by the merest chance my most interesting bit of *fractur* was preserved. Levi Yoder was visiting a house where in a day or two there was going to be a sale. The folks were moving out and wished to be rid of all their old stuff. Levi asked them if they had any old books with painting in them, or other pieces of old painting such as they had seen him buy at sales. They said they had not. He asked again and again, as opportunity offered when they showed him this or that. Finally, the woman of the house remembered that she had thrown "two pieces of colored paper with German on them" into a bureau drawer, hoping "whoever bought the bureau would take them along with it." She did not want, she said, "to be to the trouble of burning them." She was not easy when she had a bonfire. She was surprised when Levi gave her money for them. One of these "pieces of colored paper with German" represented Adam and Eve with no clothes on, in great blobs of pink paint, and with exquisite lettering about them.

The one that came to me is "Die Sieben Regeln Der Weisheit." It, like its paradisal fellow, fills every scrimption of space on the twelve-and-a-half-inch by eight-inch page of an old copy or account book. Fortunately for its preservation, the page the fractured page was joined to was left attached to it. The *fractur* had thus a backing that, no doubt, was responsible, along with the paint's covering of

132

cherry gum, for its freshness of color after a hundred years of handling and neglect. Across the bottom of the page, to balance "The Seven Rules of Wisdom" at the top, is "Written in the Year of Our Lord 1834."

Between top and bottom are thirty-five squares, twenty-nine with both words and designs in them, and six with designs only. The squares are arranged in seven rows of five each. As with nine out of ten objects of household art done in Pennsylvania Dutchland the dominant colors are red and yellow. Two red bands with a yellow band between them box in the whole *fractur*. The lettering is chiefly in black, but all the capitals are in red and yellow, or in red and green, or in red and yellow and green. The linen paper has mellowed to a clear cream, of parchment-like texture. There are touches of blue in many of the designs. The blue tones smoothly with the gold into which the covering of cherry gum has turned the yellow.

There are seven birds on the *fractur*, birds in yellow and black and red. They are distelfinks, with only the red to vary their color from that of nature. Maybe memories of the goldfinch of Germany, with red in its plumage, carried across the Atlantic and affected the coloring the limner used in depicting the thistlebird so familiar in roadside and door-yard. The necks of two of the birds are extended to swan-like length. A butterfly-like design, with the butterfly very highly conventionalized, is that most often repeated on this *haus segen*, for as such it must have been made. There is no sign, though, it was ever framed. Its early years were, perhaps, spent in the family Biblia, and then, as those who had been proud of its possession passed on and successors without a love of traditional things took their places, "The Seven Rules" was relegated to some old chest in the garret until such time as even that last stronghold of antiquities was cleaned out preparatory to the dismantling of the home.

Sprays of flowers are next most numerous to the conventionalized butterflies among the designs in the squares. There is, curiously, only one tulip. Conventionalized pomegranates are found, but most of the sprays had best be dismissed as "just flowers," their formalization being carried to the extreme. There are a number of scrolls, most firmly executed. From them, in instances, a floral spray sprouts out. Every detail is masterly, and the thirty-five blocks, with bands at top and bottom, build up, despite the divergence of detail, into such a consonance of color as is comparable only to that in Persian rugs of many items but of unity of effect.

How to read the legends concealed here had been too much for Levi, and it proved too much for me, too. Brought home the *fractur* was turned over to the younger generation. Ann quickly found it was not a rebus or an acrostic. She discovered word one in column one was to be read as the first word in a sentence completed by all the words in column two, reading down; plus the first word in column three; plus all the words in column four, reading down; plus the first word in column five. So reading we translated our first rule: (1) "Do not do all you can do for that is officious." Reading the second word in column one with all the words in column two; plus the second word in column three; plus all the words in column four; plus the second word in column five, we had: (2) "Do not question all you do not know for that is unwise." Continuing this same method of reading we found the remaining adages to be: (3) "Do not believe all you hear for that is to be credulous"; (4) "Do not give all you possess for that is prodigal"; (5) "Do not tell all you know for that is foolish"; (6) "Do not sit in judgment on all that comes before you for that is presumptuous"; and

THE SEVEN RULES OF WISDOM

(7) "Do not desire everything under the sun for that is absurd."

One saying of the seven recalls a proverb of Solomon; and another a maxim of Benjamin Franklin. All of them have parallels in the folklore of many countries. What is remarkable is to find seven such aphorisms together, and presented with such artistry of pen and brush. The motive underlying the presentation may be very like that which inspires a worker of needle-point to blazon forth: "What is Home without a Mother?" but the result in one case is art, and in the other something less than art.

As people motor through this rolling country of Bucks, few of them have a sense that every other home still houses treasures of household art largely different from any to be found elsewhere in America. I have delicate work of silversmiths and of cabinet makers from hereabouts; quaint basketwork and warm-toned pottery; ironwork of rare skill and leather tooling worthy of Cordova; but the best of the folk culture is in the local stories and in the *fractur*. Of outsiders only he who is accepted locally as sympathetic to all that is native will ever find either. The Mennonites, among whom *fractur* work is most general, do not like a "noten buch" or a "gesang buch" or a "haus segen" to pass to strangers. Family pride demands these treasures be kept by the descendants of those for whom they were made. As for the stories, those who know them keep mum about them except in rare bursts of confidence. City folks would find the country stories too simple and too child-like, so they think who live in Rockhill and Haycock and Nockamixon.

Would this countryside not have an added appeal if those who travel it by Easton Road or Bethlehem Pike could visualize in the houses of the old stock such treasure as I have described? The folks that own the treasures split about half and half, as folks do on most issues, on caring and not caring for old art and artisanry. There the treasures are, though, many of them, this one cherished in the treasure box, that one discarded to a horse-hair trunk in the garret. I have as much joy in thinking of these things as I motor along a highway or byway as I do in thinking of the flowers and birds and beasts hidden close by in swamps, and on cliffs, and by woodsides. There is fringed gentian here, swathes of it about a deep pool; a duckhawk is plucking a pigeon there; seven deer are sniffing the wind in a third place. In this centuried mansion of stone there is a Stiegel pitcher as full of light as a sapphire; in that 1870 house of brick is a chest on chest of crotch walnut with a patina as glowing as that of a rifle stock; in that little shack, clapboarded over logs, is a local history in which is folded *fractur* in blue and gold as rich in tone as the illuminated manuscripts of monastery libraries of the Old World.

RE RACCOONS AND HUNTERS' MOONS

for Irvin Anthony

THERE was no story I coaxed Aunt Rachel to tell me oftener than that of Uncle Pline's raccoons. All her many tales of her girlhood's home in Chester County were dear to me at four, but this lifted my heart higher than any other of them all. It brought the wild life of the hill farm into the tameness of my suburban home. In the vividness of her recital of its details it almost compensated me for the absence of the pet raccoon I longed for but never possessed. The affectionate ways of the little creatures, their nuzzling with dog-like noses and their patting by black paws, so diminutive and so like human hands, were an unending delight as the old countrywoman recounted them to me in those years more than a half century ago.

Uncle Pline had stayed on in Uwchlan with his grandmother when, in 1847, his father and mother and brothers and sisters moved to Philadelphia. He could not tear himself away from his country familiars, barn and grist mill, covered wooden bridge and ford, race and dam, uplands where the cattle grazed and valley with its sounds of sluicing and falling water, the Dominiques that he had raised and the two raccoon cubs he had caught and tamed. When he did come to Philadelphia a year after the rest of the family were settled there, he brought his raccoons with him. The folks lived west of Broad Street, where there were still bits of woods and truck patches. The boy tried to persuade himself his pets would be happy there. Whether happy or not

137

they flourished there. They did too well, in fact. For all that they were fed all that was good for them at home, they foraged round about. They liked best what they found for themselves.

Folks in the neighborhood began to talk of stolen sweets. Bowls of applesauce set on bracketed boards outside of kitchen windows were found empty. Even crabs left in deep baskets in backyards were missing, hidden though they had been by a mat of seaweed. The climax came when a dozen jars of preserved peaches stood out to cool on a back step were cleaned out to the last drop of juice. The despoiled housewife, while she had no evidence, accused the raccoons. City people were near enough the farm, in those days, to have had handed on to them stories of the thieving of raccoons. The pets were adjudged guilty by an aroused neighborhood and were condemned by the family council of Thomases to be taken out to the Falls of Schuylkill and released. Uncle Pline had admitted that his raccoons were sleepy and distended as to their paunches immediately after the preserved peaches disappeared, though, he maintained, in their defense, that not a drop of peach juice was found on paws and fur. With the neatness characteristic of them the raccoons might well have washed up and slicked themselves after their indulgence. Uncle Pline was, of course, deeply troubled by the sentence meted out to them, fearing that, after a year and a half of semi-captivity, they would not know how to fend for themselves.

I have wondered at their fate. Did they work up the river to the Wissahickon and become the ancestors of the raccoons that have lived all my life about Mom Rinker's Rock? The Falls of Schuylkill is not far, after all, from the cliffs above the bridge at Walnut Lane. Perhaps the family of four youngsters trapped at the old place across the road

from us were their descendants of the twentieth generation
or so. There would be as many generations of raccoons as
that, would there not, from 1848 to 1908? These four
youngsters, with their parents, had been preying upon our
neighbor's corn. They were caught crowded about the box
trap that had tempted into it their mother. Two had escaped
up neighboring pear trees when the gardener visited the
trap. They were hurt in being shaken down.

One of these two, brought over to our place in a cage and
exhibited by its proud possessor, gave our venerable Maltese
tomcat, William Shakespeare, the scare of his life. Seeing
a box put down in the lane, and noting, no doubt, a strange
scent, William approached the box gingerly, on tiptoe. The
little raccoon caught sight of the cat, and, fearing an enemy,
made a half spring toward him. He couldn't do more in the
confines of that box. William jumped backward and up-
wards in one wild bound, and continued to jump backward,
in lower and lower bounds, until his strength for such an
unusual progress was exhausted. Then he turned tail, and
made for the back door as fast as he was able.

The first raccoon I had really gotten to know well belonged to Charlie Backus. That was when I was a very small
boy. It was held captive by a long chain that permitted it
to descend from its box in a tree and play about in the yard.
There it was on good terms enough with the dogs until they
got too rough in their play. Then the raccoon would resort to
its claws. Not getting enough exercise in its circumscribed
orbit, it grew exceedingly obese, but it never forgot to keep
itself perfectly groomed.

It was in Waterford, far up the Tuscarora, that I first
came on the coon hunt as a gala occasion in country life.
In most places beyond the home counties around Philadelphia fox hunting is hardly more than a sordid business of

securing furs. That is all it was in Juniata County. There, however, in 1888, coon hunting was the sport of sports. Bear and deer were "big game," it is true, but their pursuit had a relation to the larder, whereas coon hunts were sport for sport's sake. The very youths who were worn out by the baseball we tried to substitute for the older game of town ball still in vogue there, were tireless in the rough going through rhododendron thickets and slash that completely used up the city boys. Those youths, twenty miles and more back from the railroad, thought there was no joy comparable to that of felling the tree to which the dogs had driven the coon and of seeing the black and tan fellows pile in to the kill.

It was after the summer in Waterford that I, now aware of coon sign in stones pawed out of the creek beds in search of crawfish, in the worn bark on the upper side of slightly leaning trees with large hollows high above the ground, and in footprints on the muddy banks of Wissahickon, began to realize how many of the creatures there were near home. Walking in the fields above the creek valley with my Irish terrier, I noticed him, far ahead of me, take to rolling with unusual gusto in high red top. Arrived at the scene of his ecstasy I found that a raccoon, reduced to skin and bone but still of active odor, was the cause of it all. Later I was to find the hand-like impress of raccoon feet in light snows, but though they were evidently much about the woodpile and hen runs I never saw one on our acre, as I did an opossum now and then.

As we went out to look at the raccoons at Levi Yoder's, the woodsedge facing us was a wonder of delight. It was late afternoon, with the sun at our backs, and reflected from the dogwoods and gums, the sassafras and red maples, the hickories and tulip poplars of the postwoods to the eastward.

That woodsedge was a tapestried wall of reds and yellows, warm browns and burnt orange. The raccoons did not understand why we were there unless to feed them. The two old ladies climbed each the wire front of her cage, and gazed expectantly, and put out black paws strangely human. One climbed so she was directly across the great cartwheel of the rising moon, pale silver in the eastern skies. Father coon, in a low run back of the ladies, rushed up and down excitedly. The last of the eight children, we were told, had just been sent away to a regimenter of raccoons, to be disciplined into good behavior. He had been spoiled by too much attention and too much handling and too many privileges. They had taken him out of the cage to show to visitors, and had allowed him to climb the orchard trees, he looked so cute peering around the great branches with that so knowing and sharp-snouted face of his.

Last time we had visited the Yoder raccoons the old man had been given a cherry pie. This he had carefully untopped, clearing off the crust flake by flake, and washing each cherry separately in his water pan. Maybe, like myself, he did not like the cornstarch that had been put into the cherries to take up their juice, and to prevent the syrup running out when the baked pie was cut.

That was plowing to wonder at and remember, that which extended eastward from the raccoon runs. Absolutely parallel, and all of an even height, the furrows extended away for a quarter of a mile showing not a bit of the soy beans just plowed under for a fertilizer. All the freshly upturned earth was warmly tinted in the rays of the low sun streaming in from the west. The sun itself stood jug-shaped on the horizon's rim, a deep red and glowing, of a liquid intensity that you would say, but for its coolness, was of the fiery flux of red-hot iron.

As we left the raccoon runs Levi pointed out to us the killdeer by the duck pond. There they had been all summer,
twenty strong, crying intermittently all day and almost constantly all night. Would they rise now and wing away, a
waving line, against the rising moon? No, they contented
themselves with running along the shore of the pond, tilting
themselves, in prime feather and as neat as pins despite the
mud through which they teetered.

The killdeer lived in peace and plenty, as did everything
on this farm. From wandering guinea hens gently buck-
wheating to wing-waving geese strident voiced, from twelve
cats motherly bunched on old farm gear by the barn to seven
fat bullocks in the barnyard, every living thing was in well-
being. Lofts were full to the roof with hay; cornstacks
crowded together about the hen houses; the yield of dent
corn of deepest yellow had overflowed from the cribs to the
overhead in this little office and that. The root cellars were
full of beets and potatoes, pumpkins and cabbage. Happiness,
slightly apprehensive over the very plenitude of harvestings,
was in the hearts of the Yoders. Happiness in their happiness
was in the hearts of us who were visiting them.

The fatness and sleekness of the raccoons was but a part
of the general well-being of the farm. No wonder they were
fastidious about their food when they had the choicest tid-
bits of all the sweets and staples the place afforded. Here
they were thought arch and knowing because of that fas-
tidiousness. In other places I have known them outlawed as
food because of their insistence on washing their food. Indian half breeds in northern New Hampshire write them off
the possible contents of the larder because of that habit.
The family that so disapproved of the roast raccoon their
neighbors prized lived near a mud hole with green scum
upon it. Having no access to the family well, the only clear

water roundabout, the raccoons would wash their food in the scummed water, bringing the food clean to the washing and fouling it by the washing in that water. This same family ate skunk with gusto, holding it rivaled breast of chicken. They skinned the piebald fellows under water, removing the scent sack without disaster in the process.

So far as I know New Hampshire it does not particularly prize raccoons as food. I hear of woodchuck in the pot, and of lumberjacks taking to hedgehog when fresh meat is scarce, but very little of eating coon. The little brother to the bear is not, perhaps, so common there as further south, though in certain seasons he has taken toll of our sweet corn. Being inclined to sympathize with the contention of our neighbor that raccoons, like black rats, "had their right to a living same as another," we bore with their raids on the corn patch. One year, however, their depredations threatened wholesale destruction of the crop. Loath to do it, we set a trap baited with salt cod, and caught a raccoon in good fur, though it was only September. He was held by a hind leg, badly smashed in the powerful jaws of the fox trap. There was nothing to do but kill him. If we had let him go he would probably not have come back again, but he might well have died of his wound. I went to the barn for an ax. When I came back he sensed what was coming and put his front paws over his head as if to protect it. One blow put him out of his misery, but those paws over his head and the look in his eyes haunt me now years afterwards.

I had had no experience in skinning a creature and curing its skin since boyhood days when I trapped muskrats, but the raccoon fur was so fine a one I put my repugnance and sentimentality in my pocket and essayed making a fur of the coon's coat. I did the job more successfully than I had anticipated, and made a presentable coonskin. I was dis-

trustful, though, of its keeping, and took it to Dave Mc-
Cadden at the Academy of Natural Sciences, as soon as we
got home. That was perhaps a fortnight after I had skinned
the beast. Dave looked it over, and ejaculated: "My God,
the tail!" I had neglected to take the bone and gristle out
of it. He smelt of it, and said, "I guess it's all right." A
moment's manipulation with a knife, and it was discovered
mortification had not set in. Dan made a pliable fur of it.
It is in our camphor chest along with a muskrat skin of nearly
thirty years earlier. The one fur of either beast was not
enough to make up into anything to wear, and I have trapped
no creature since the marauding raccoon of 1918.

In the nineteen-twenties coonskin coats were the rage
with college boys. As furs go, coonskins are, of course, of
no great rarity or choiceness, and the general roughness of
their effect in a long ulster was considered very masculine
and manly. The comparative paucity of the long hairs makes
coonskins look a bit moth eaten and the markings on them,
the black stripe down the back and the dabs of black on
cheeks and ears, give a certain quaintness of effect that tends
toward grotesquerie.

The mask of the coon is rare alike in stuffed specimens,
as a motive in decoration, and in illustration. There is a
whiskey uses the mask, "Coon Hollow Bourbon Whiskey,"
a brand that derives its name, perhaps, from the old refrain:

> *Possum in de gum tree,*
> *Coonie in de hollow.*

The face of the raccoon appears both on the paper label and
as an imprint on the glass of the flatly curved flask. It is a
very white-cheeked and bright-faced raccoon that, head
rested on paws cherubwise, looks out of the hollow of the
tree on the label. It is the same visage that is molded on

the glass, but necessarily less sharp in detail and lacking the verisimilitude of color of that of the label.

So far as I have read, there is no complete and satisfactory explanation of the raccoon on the log cabin of the Harrison campaign of 1840. The log cabin itself was a symbol of the backwoods Indiana where General Harrison lived, and a glorification of all backwoods places and people. That was good politics then, when there were so many backwoods places in all the States, as the glorification of "the forgotten man" was in 1932, when the relation in numbers of nobodies to the general population had so greatly increased. The cider barrel, too, is easily understood, as the beer barrel would have been had it been used in the Hoover-Roosevelt campaign. But why was the raccoon chosen as symbol and rallying emblem of the rural democracy that was to be won to the support of the hero of Tippecanoe? The raccoon is clever, resourceful in escaping pursuit, a game fighter when cornered, bright faced, engaging in manner, companionable. And all backwoods folks knew these traits of his. Did folk sentiment, in a moment of illumined vision, establish him as a symbol of homespun democracy, as folk sentiment, through slow ages, established the fox as Reynard, the one keen in counsel, the very symbol of the knowing and tricky leaders of the people in their contest with church and law and feudal lord? Do we see another beast epic, at once allegorical and realistic, in the course of creation? Perhaps, but I am far from sure.

Certain it is that there has never again been such a glorification of the backwoods era of American life as there was in this Harrison campagin. Though William Henry Harrison came of a family long and favorably known in American life, he was hailed for political purposes as an Indiana backwoodsman sprung of the soil. His house at Great Bend was assumed to be a log cabin. The truth seems to be that there had been a log cabin on the site of one of the ells of that house. That is the way it was often with an American house not only on the frontier of 1840 but in the earliest settlements along the Atlantic seaboard. The log house went up with the first clearing. Sometimes the second building was an ell of plank, larger generally than the original log house. Other times this second building was an ell of barn construction, clapboarded, and other times again it was of stone. In many instances the log ell remained, in others it was replaced by some other of the familiar later sorts of house. The log cabin, in other instances, stood at a distance, across the road say, from the second building, and was used as summer kitchen, or corn barn, or woodshed, or black-smith shop, or coach house. A surprising number of these old cabins remain, often plastered over so you cannot see the logs, often just whitewashed, but of so many coats with the years that all unevenness between logs and the stones and mud in the interstices of the logs are completely hidden. Often, too, the logs are closed in by clapboards. No more than one out of ten log houses surviving reveals itself at first glance as a log house.

It is from the Harrison campaign date the log-cabin ink-wells in glass, certain of the log-cabin whiskey flasks, the log-cabin banks in pottery, the log-cabin lithographs on campaign songs, and the score other flauntings of the back-woods origin and affiliations of the Whig candidate.

Many of the associations with "Tippecanoe and Tyler, Too," log cabins and coons and the rest of the old symbols, bobbed up again in the campaign of William Henry's grand-son, Benjamin Harrison, in 1888. In that year, my uncle, a staunch Republican, remembered his old art of stage-coach painting, revamped it, adapted it to campaign purposes, and

RACCOON BANKS OF THE HARRISON CAMPAIGN

drew on a sheet, in charcoal, a sketch of a log cabin, a coon and a cider barrel, and hung it by the roadside in front of our camp above the Tuscarora. When we broke camp we draped the sheet on the rear of the wagon in which we drove back from outside Port Royal to Lebanon, to the cheers and jeers, as chance was, of loyal Republicans or dyed-in-the-wool Democrats.

So it was, when I came on, years afterwards, two banks of earthenware representing a log cabin, with cider barrel at either end, and coon on roof, I could not resist them. They are made to imitate Bennington, in brown and yellow, but they are, I think, of the blue clay from which redware is burned. They are so covered with yellow slip that not a suspicion of the basic material shows anywhere. There is not a chip to reveal redware beneath. The detail is carefully done. In either end below the slabbed-in gable is a door and a window, and by either door the cider barrel. There is a window, also of nine panes, on either side of the cabin. Long shingles cover the roof, three tiers of them sufficing to stretch from eaves to ridgepole. There is a chimney at either end. All out of proportion to the house, a raccoon, modeled by some one more familiar with a rat, sprawls along the ridgepole between the chimneys, his nose touching the one and the root of his tail the other. If that space is judged to be twenty feet the raccoon must be larger than a panther. A rat-like tail, instead of the bushy brush of the raccoon, trails two-thirds of the way down the roof. The cabins, three and a half inches long and three inches wide, rest on bases five inches by four. They are five inches high from base to chimney top. Touches of green, from copperas no doubt, give the banks affiliations, along with the yellow slip and the brown of ferro-manganese, to the colors of ceremonial platters. They were made right in Philadelphia, though, and not by a Dutch, but by an Irish potter, one Peter Kelley. He has signed his name on the bottom of each cabin.

The songs of the first Harrison campaign are legion. Only Foster, the various settings of verse by Tom Moore, the Hon. Mrs. Norton, Thomas Haines Bayly, and Mrs. Hemans, and the operatic selections from Rossini, Donizetti, and Bellini, are more prevalent in the old collections of music.

One of these old songs called "Old Tippecanoe, a Patriotic Song, to be sung at Baltimore during the Young Men's Whig Convention, and most respectfully inscribed to the Young Ladies of the Monumental City by a Pennsylvanian," was issued by L. Meignen & Co., at 217 Chestnut Street, Philadelphia. It is entered in Washington "in the Year 1840." It is a lithograph with Harrison's picture in stock and open-bosomed vest with coat of high rolled collar, a picture against a background of flags and surmounted by an eagle poised on the top point of a five-winged star. Under the General's portrait in the center is the famous log cabin with the cider barrel at one side. This log cabin has no coon on the roof. It has a chimney off center, but not at the end, and its corners are of notched logs. It has three windows on each side both first and second story, and door and two windows in the front end. You see in the background tall pointed trees, but whether the spruces of the forest or the Lombardy poplars of planted estates, it would be impossible to tell from their delineation. I suspect, of course, that they are spruces.

A covered wagon is passing out of sight on the road that runs to the left of the log cabin, and an ox cart, properly two wheeled and escorted by a man with goad over shoulder, is passing in the foreground to the left. Below are cannon

on either side, and soldiers in a snowy landscape with covered wagon and sleigh. Under this is the legend, "Ensign
Harrison 19 years of age." Four ovals mount on either side,
making themselves, with the cannon at the bottom, a great
oval until they come to the picture of the General at the
top. To the left these read first, "Governor Harrison at the
Council of Vincennes with Tecumseh." Above that we see
the General on horseback in 1812 at the head of seven thousand troops. Above that we see "General Harrison & his
Army going into winter quarters at the Maumee Rapids in
1812." Top left we find "Harrison's Victory at Tippecanoe."
Reading down on the right the four ovals are "Harrison's
Victory at the Thames," "General Harrison hastening at
night to the assistance of General Winchester," "General
Harrison making a treaty with the Sacks & Fox Indians,"
and lowest right, "Lieut. Harrison at the Maumee Rapids."
The designs are done on stone by R. J. Queen and the litho-
graphing is by P. S. Duval.

"Old Tippecanoe," which bears a sub-title, "A Patriotic
Whig Song," has apparently never been proofread. It is full
of misprints, some of them difficult to guess right. For
sample of it I quote:

> *Ye Vanites of wide Pennsylvany,*
> *Of ev're old state and each new;*
> *Take warning, come out with the many,*
> *And vote for old Tippecanoe;*

> ### Chorus

> *And vote for old Tippecanoe;*
> *And vote for old Tippecanoe;*
> *Take warning, come out with the many,*
> *And vote for old Tippecanoe.*

There are twelve sets of verses altogether, each worse than the others.

Another lithograph by Sinclair of Philadelphia is called "Arouse My Gallant Freemen! a Whig Song by Thomas F. Adams, Esqr." The music is arranged by Thomas C. Carr and it is published by Osbourn's Music Saloon, 30 South Fourth Street, Philadelphia. The lithograph in this cut shows General Harrison on horseback galloping toward the White House past the cider barrel and log cabin and flapping eagle of the skies. On the right of that White House you see a coach and four and the Kinderhook Hotel. There is a plaza in the center. The skies are heavy with clouds. The words are what you would expect in such a composition.

A third Harrison song is called "The Harrison Song." On the cover of this is a lithograph "drawn on stone by W. Sharp and lithographed by Thayer, successor to Moore of Boston." It is by Thomas Power, Esq., and published by Parker and Ditson at Boston in 1840. It shows you General Harrison at the battle of Tippecanoe. You see him on horseback, one of four officers between a line of troops marching plumb into the Indians and discharging their guns at fellows brandishing tomahawks at very close quarters. The troops back of the four men on horseback are marching into battle as if on parade. The song reaches its acme in stanza four. I quote that and the chorus:

> From stately hall and cabin wall
> Let paeans loud arise;
> The people's choice is HARRISON!
> The dauntless and the wise.
> O'er every hill be echoed still
> The watchword of the brave,—
> A knell to every tyrant ear,—
> THE HERO COMES TO SAVE!

Chorus—With heart and voice we'll gaily sing,
And tell Columbia's foe
Of the days when he went soldiering,
A long time ago,—
Of the days, &c.

The music of "The Harrison Song" is by Sporle.

At the Ohio Whig Convention at Columbus on Washington's birthday, 1840, there were twenty thousand men in the procession in Harrison's honor. McMaster describes it in his *History of the People of the United States:*

". . . Some walked, some rode, whole delegations arrived in canoes or log cabins or boats, mounted on wheels and drawn by six or eight horses, and decorated with banners and mottoes. On one banner was the American Cincinnatus with his hand on the plow. On another he stood at his cabin door dealing out hard cider to canal laborers. A delegation from the Maumee brought, on wheels, a model of Fort Meigs. A company of Mad River trappers came in a log cabin decorated with coonskins; the men from Cleveland had a square-rigged brig; a party on foot shouldered cornshuck brooms; on the roof of some of the log cabins as they rolled along sat 'merry fellows eating johnnycake, and drinking hard cider and singing patriotic songs.' The great procession was on the second day of the convention. With eight men marching abreast, and the cabins, canoes, and boats in line, it was two miles long."

The raccoon, though, was celebrated, sometimes, for himself as well as a symbol of the backwoods or the democracy of Harrison. A strange and not altogether understandable song is to be found in a portfolio of music of one Louise T. Chamberlain. There is no date on the song but as its fellows in the portfolio are dated from 1835 to 1843 I suppose it is approximately of a vintage circa 1840. It is called: "Settin' on a Rail or Raccoon Hunt." It runs thus:

As I walk'd out by de light ob de moon,
So merrily singing dis same tune,
I cum across a big raccoon,
A sittin on a rail, sittin on a rail,
   sittin on a rail, sittin on a rail,
Sleepin werry sound.

I at de raccoon take a peep,
An den so softly to him creep,
I foun de raccoon fast asleep,
   ||:An pull him off de rail,:||
An fling him on de ground.

De raccoon gan to scratch an bite,
I hit him once wid all my might,
I bung he eye an spile he sight,
   ||:O I'm dat child to fight,:||
An beat de banjo too.

I tell de raccoon gin to pray,
While on de ground de raccoon lay,
But he jump up an run away,
   ||:An soon he out ob sight,:||
Sitting on a rail.

My ole massa dead an gone,
A dose ob poison help him on,
De Debil say he funeral song,
   ||:O bress him let him go,:||
An joy go wid him too.

De raccoon hunt, do werry quare,
Am no touch to kill de deer,
Becase you kotch him widout fear,
   ||:Sittin on a rail,:||
Sleepin werry sound.

Ob all de songs dat eber I sung
De raccoon hunt's de greatest one,
It always pleases old and young,
   ||:An den dey cry encore,:||
An den I cum again.

Banal you say, but it is no more banal than the songs crooned to us to-day. What is, perhaps, most remarkable about it is the impossibility of its patter as negro dialect.

Nor has the raccoon had justice done him in literature of the better order. Thoreau does not make much of him, nor, as I recall it, does Burroughs. He has not a place in *Uncle Remus* commensurate with his worth. Only *A Little Brother to the Bear* deals with him as he deserves. There is knowledge of the raccoon, and sympathy with him, and good writing in *A Little Brother to the Bear.* "A keen face, yet very innocent, in which dog intelligence and fox cunning and bear drollery mingled perfectly"—that is as close to a "placing" of the coon among his kind as I have come upon.

So often did I hear in youth mid-autumn nights of full moon spoken of by Aunt Rachel as "coon hunting nights" that it is of coon hunting I think to-night when I see the full moon standing almost directly in the zenith and throwing the shadows of the sassafrases directly beneath them on the frost-bitten grass. Let who will think of *Tristan und Isolde* and descant on a *liebesnacht.* What the high moon and white brings back most insistently to me is Aunt Rachel's stories of Seal and Cos and the neighboring boys off across the hills to the Brandywine, the haunt of raccoons innumerable. Of those nights, too, Uncle Seal used to speak when rain drove us into our tents in the walnut grove above the Tuscarora. Coon hunting was the sport that proved the hardihood of country boys, a democratic sport. The squires might have their fox hunts, the hillmen their rabbit snares. Coon hunting was the farm boys' sport, the Brandywine Hills their paradise. "There was never anything better in life," Uncle Seal would declare, "than good coon dogs giving tongue on a hot scent, unless it was the riot broke out from them when they treed the varmint, or the crash and scramble and fight when the tree fell. When those things happened, as I remember it, there was always a hunter's moon in the sky, white frost on the meadows, and boys and dogs so happy they didn't know what to do with themselves."

The association of my mother, who was only nine when they moved away from Milford Mills, with the hunter's moon, was with election time, though, and Whittier's poem, "The Eve of Election," which she used to quote as her father had before her:

> From gold to gray
> Our mild sweet day
> Of Indian summer fades too soon;
> But tenderly
> Above the sea
> Hangs, white and calm, the hunter's moon.

There is with me, though, no association of sea and hunter's moon. It is most times with our Wissahickon Hills, with oaks full leaved and murmurous, that I associate the hunter's moon, for it is here I have lived more than half my years, and never from 1900 to 1935 missed a hunter's moon.

It is a night to-night with the hunter's moon riding in the furthest depths of the sky, this night of the twentieth of October. The moon is all but full, this moon of late October, a night or two only from perfect roundness. Where there is hoar frost on fallen leaves there are little mirrors of brightness; where there are spiders' webs on box bush and tubbed pittosporums there are blobs of soft light as if flakes of the moon itself had spalled off and fallen and been enmeshed and held captive. The whirls of pear blossom, the second blowing of a spent tree, after a drenched summer and the onset of autumn, are as distinct in the moonlight as they were twelve hours earlier in morning light. Even the blossoms of the pink shell azalea, set individually and far apart on their sparse stems, and close crowded each single flower by its ambient leaves, are distinct dabs of brightness as they stir in the wind and cup and spill the moonlight in their corner of the heath bed.

The pit-pats I hear in its recesses, under laurels and rhododendrons, may be of rabbits or of a nosing opossum. Whatever beast it is it refuses to identify itself by coming out on the lawn. I am wondering which of the two would be the more silvery. The opossum, I take it, for the rabbits I have flushed so often in the moonlight have shown but a streak of silver in the cotton tail bobbing out of sight. The opossum's white, soot dusted, would be, I should think, pure silver in the full downpour of moonlight from the great disc unfathomably far and lonely in the vault above. Clear and unbroken as its shafts fall on lawn and shrubberies, they are splintered and disseminated into moon mist in the hollow across the road, moon mist so dense one wonders is it of the skies or the smoke from burning leaves. The tang of tannin is on the air, but all the other earth scents have been smothered out by the frost. Even the seed pod on the shrub bush

has to be crushed before it releases that fresh scent that has
fascinated me from childhood. Then we knotted the red-
brown flowers in a corner of a handkerchief, as we did a
stone for that rough sport of London Lou.

That scent takes me back to earliest childhood, to a memory of myself pulling myself to my feet in a crib and wondering at the white round swimming like a great jelly fish
through the skies. I cannot be sure it was the hunter's moon
I beheld on that occasion, but I can remember that it was
cold standing there holding to the crib end, and that I soon
crawled back under the bed clothes, content to watch the
moon from that less advantageous point of view. I remember, too, that much later night I turned from my own small
boy in his crib and caught four owls black against the pale
yellow disc as it westered beyond the thinning sassafras, the
four snuggled so close together on a bare limb that their
outlines melted together and I had to guess what they were.

The hunter's moon is the last of the season to preside over
white nights loud with the pull of wind in the leaves of the
great oaks above our house. By October's end the trees are
pretty well stripped, and what flow of wind there is to be
heard is that through the mazzards that hold their foliage
until November and snowfall. The varying reds of their
leaves often make warm spots on the first white carpet.
There are no pines or spruces or hemlocks about our house
to make the nights murmurous with wind in the trees the
whole winter through. It is only on the wildest nights that
the bare limbs of the black oaks and sassafrases add their
quota of creakings and groanings to the caseless fifing and
complaining of the wind about the eaves, and through the
palings of the balustrade about the second story porch, and
in the cracks between the roof shingles. After the hunter's
moon of late October we hear no more in full that soothing

voice of the wind in the leaves until late April brings the next crop to their spring lushness of slushing flow.

It was in the hunter's moon in old times that deer shooting began, in those years that dogs could be put on their trail. In middle New Hampshire there was freezing weather of nights and early mornings and late afternoons from mid-October, and vension could be trusted to take care of itself in creatures properly trussed and hung high from poles slung between trees. On white nights of the hunter's moon the runways of our south woods were well watched, and enough deer for the winter's larder fell to the rifles of wood-wise men. What a sight it was, on such a night of flooding moonlight in Ossipee, to see the white buck that was as great a marvel in this countryside as any white hind out of old romance, of Charlemagne or Arthur or Red Branch knights! There were no silver bullets poured in Ossipee, and it is believed that the white buck of Lovell's Pond came to a natural death after being a wonder for a full quarter century.

As one well past sixty lets his memory unroll before his inward eye the long film of sights of out-of-doors that have given him delight, what place do the hunters' moons occupy? There must have been fifty of them at least he knew as such, and noted. He is no hunter. Since he heard, in boyhood, the scream of a cottontail struck by a bullet from his chum's rifle, he has had no joy in the kill and next to none in the chase. There have been in his life necessary killings of copperheads and woodchucks and hedgehogs. There have been times when the depredations of deer on his garden have put murder into his heart, but he knows so little of hunting he has no more than an association or two of it with the hunter's moon.

What there is of dramatic instinct in him, what there is in him that allows him not only to see things from the point of view of another and very different person, but to be that other person in personality and character, in that other person's point of view, permits him, though, to realize what this moon has been to thousands and thousands in whom the hunting instinct is still strong. This November moon so high in heaven to-night is lighting home men of all sorts and conditions from clerks and bakers to financiers and clergymen with bags of squirrels and rabbits, pheasants and quail. This same moon in the years gone, before there were restrictions on the hunting season for this or that game, has lighted all sorts and conditions of men to their lonely stations by runways for deer and elk. This moon has made possible coon hunts innumerable, hundreds of thousands of coon hunts, since the States were colonies. And on how many lovers has it looked down, and on how many mourners, this hunter's moon, so high and cold and aloof from the little lives of men? It has looked down, with its austere indifference, on hot hates and petty ironies, on hearts worn with the monotony of life, on illness and on crime, on hunted men as on hunted beasts. One thinks of husbands and fathers in old years following by its light wives and children being carried away toward Canada by Indians, footsore men of our Continental armies on forced marches—all the far-flung panorama of our country's past.

The world and all that in it is, tattered trees and frosted fields and glittering roofs, white roads and all the cloudless and empty skies, the million living people near at hand but out of sight one and all—the world and all that in it is seems incredibly old and beautiful and inconsequential. There is that in moonlight that brings a chill to the heart. There is that, though, in this particular moon, the hunter's moon, that after it has brought a chill, quickens, arouses, sets the blood to marching steps. There wake somewhere within us ancestral memories. What has happened to our forbears on nights such as this stirs in us and all but comes to consciousness. We are alert, expectant, ready for wonders. The old Adam, the untamedness of man, his predatoriness, has us by the throat. Our centuries of civilization cannot down the elemental Nimrod deep-seated in us. Americans of the old stock are backwoodsmen all.

NEWTOWN PIPPINS

I. M.
James B. Thomas

IT was the Spitzenburg I was brought up to believe the finest apple, and, after it, the Northern Spy. Both were often on the table and I could not but acknowledge that they were good, very good indeed. It was my father so taught me, pointing out the excellences of the one or the other as he pared or ate of it in that expansive mood that comes in orgies late at night, just before going to bed. He liked a crisp and juicy and aromatic apple. Aunt Rachel, who kept me posted on all the fruits they had on the farm in Uwchlan, talked most of the Rambos she had liked as a child. A tree of them grew close to the house, just beyond the Sheldon pear tree at its gable. Now, in her age, she liked best the Sheepsnoses because she could scoop out their meat with a spoon, and swallow it without the necessity of chewing. The Sheepsnoses were in the orchard, up hill from the house at Milford Mills.

It was not until Uncle Jim was an old man that I heard talk to remember of the Newtown Pippins of this nook in the Chester County hills. It was difficult to find Christmas presents he really could take some pleasure in after he was eighty. I had given him one year a five-eighths basket of Sheldon pears because of the tree of that variety by the garret window of his boyhood's home, that tree in which the Dominiques roosted. I had bought another year a map of Chester County of 1847, with the names of all the owners of farms upon it. I was at my wits' ends to find something that would bring back the old place to him when he told me he would very much like to taste Newtown Pippins again. It was the real old Newtown Pippins he wanted, not the modern fruit, so called, that came from Albemarle County, Virginia, and was really an Albemarle Pippin. It was a long chase before I ran down a basket of them at the Twelfth Street Market in Philadelphia, not ripened yet to the golden color with cheek of old rose of the perfected fruit.

That was the last basket of Newtown Pippins I came on until, ten years later, we were motoring in Montgomery County. It was a day of March in 1931, and we were progressing slowly through Evansburg, between Skippack and Perkiomen. Halfway by the village we saw a stand of apples at the roadside. Some of them were obviously Stayman Winesaps, very red-cheeked from the long drought of the previous summer and fall. Those six months without rain to speak of brought the richest color to all fruit that I have ever known in this neighborhood. In the midst of the Winesaps was a basket of yellow apples flushed on one side a deep rose. They were labeled "Newtown Pippins," and their looks bore out the label. They were average samples of such specimens of the variety I have come upon in late winter. They were a little shriveled, but that was to be expected on a March 21. I was afraid to buy the basketful lest they go bad before we could use them. The Winesaps were in perfect condition, so I bought a basket of them. I bought, too, a carrier of the Newtowns for "auld lang syne." Home, and the Newtowns sampled, I was sorry I had not bought the whole basket. The very first pippin I ate brought back my youth to me with that taste between vinous and musky. I had forgotten it, but at the first bite I knew it as that of an apple that had been on our table in my childhood days. The taste was as distinct as that of a Belleflower, or a Smokehouse, or a Grimes' Golden, and it was altogether delightful. That first pippin was a little dry, and so proved, too, its fellows, eaten one each the next day, and the next. That dryness was perhaps because of the lateness of the season, or because the apples were grown on an old tree in a farm orchard, and not, like the Winesaps, from a commercial orchard, with modern storage facilities.

It was pleasant to learn that the Newtown Pippins came from over at Arcola, not far from Audubon's home on the Perkiomen. It was apples of this variety that John Bartram had chosen, as America's finest, to ship to Benjamin Franklin in London way back in 1758, and that had so delighted Jefferson that he gave them a place in his orchard at Monticello. It was Jefferson who set Alexander Wilson to search out what bird sang that most beautiful song of all birds of our American forests. Jefferson took Wilson to where the song could be heard and Wilson identified the singer as the Wood Thrush, or Wood Robin, as we call him throughout Pennsylvania. So Jefferson, too, has a place among early American naturalists along with Bartram and Audubon.

All the fruit books of nearly two hundred years praise the Newtown Pippin, English as well as American. Lindley lists them with favorable comment, but it is the American editor of the New York edition of 1833 who adds: "The Newtown Pippin, when perfectly matured, is undoubtedly the richest flavoured and finest apple known." In my Downing's *Selected Fruits* (1871) it is averred: "The Newton Pippin stands at the head of all Apples, and is, when in perfection, acknowledged to be unrivalled in all the qualities which constitute a high-flavored dessert apple, to which it combines the quality of long keeping without the least shrivelling, retaining its high flavor to the last. It commands the highest price in Covent Garden Market, London."

You will find such praise only in the eighteenth and nineteenth century books, however, the modern pomologists relegating the Newtown Pippin to the background because it can be successfully grown, they say, only throughout a restricted range. The true Newtown Pippin, they maintain, does well only in the Long Island of its origin and in the lower Hudson Valley. Such is not the belief of Arthur Browne, Esq., Fellow of Trinity College, Dublin. In his *Miscellaneous Sketches*, Vol. II (1798), he writes it down "the product of the Jerseys." He knows American conditions, for he spent here his years from five to seventeen (1756-1773), in Newport, Rhode Island, and in Cambridge, Massachusetts. It is in his essay on America that he pays particular attention to our "most exquisite fruits," among which he picks out for especial mention "the so famous Newtown Pippin."

Famous as the Newtown Pippin is, there is uncertainty as to the exact place of its origin in western Long Island. The first tree of the variety is said to have grown on the estate of Gershom Moore, near a swamp in Newtown, county of Queens, and to date from early in the eighteenth century. All that neighborhood is now built up solidly. The first tree died in 1805, having carried the name of the place of its nativity literally around the world. Princes of Flushing "featured" the Newtown Pippin, but even before the day of these pioneer nurserymen it had made its way to many parts of the Colonies. It was carried into Virginia as early as 1755, giving rise there to the sub-variety known later as the Albemarle Pippin. Through the Princes the Newtown Pippin went north and west, to establish the fact it was not an apple for all soils and all exposures.

From round about Philadelphia and New York, however, great quantities of Newtown Pippins were shipped to Eng land, their good traveling and keeping qualities helping to establish them in favor there even before the Revolution. From that early day down through the middle years of the nineteenth century the Newtown Pippin was popular in England, Queen Victoria cherishing it always as her favorite apple.

Its day has passed now, and it is only here and there that the original form of the Newtown Pippin will be come upon, the northern flattened form that yellows evenly from maturity and takes on the characteristic flush of old rose. In Virginia they still make much of the southern form, a less flattened apple and of slightly larger proportions. In our Pennsylvania hill country, however, where it was once generally grown, it is only in an old tree here and there, like the one at Arcola, that the Newtown Pippin persists. Nor is it easy to buy, should you wish to set out a tree or two. The commercial nurserymen, like the commercial orchardists, have eschewed it. It is still the apple, though, that it always has been, distinctive in flattened form and axis askew, and in yellowish flesh and madeira-like flavor.

THE MASTER OF US ALL

for B. F. Fackenthal

THERE were few nights of my years from seven to seventeen but knew the skies to the northwest red with the glow from iron furnaces. That way Conshohocken lay. I saw the skies light up when the chimney lids were lifted, and fade out again as the lids were let down. I saw this spectacle from backyard, from back porch, from Aunt Rachel's window in her second story back room, and from the window on the stair landing as I climbed to my third story room. That room faced southeast, so no glow in the skies northwest of us could delight me from its windows.

From the time of our coming to Tulpehocken Street father had taken me to the cupola on nights of storm so that I might know the beauty of lightning and of the rolling masses of thunder clouds. I was seven when these visits to the cupola began; and often during the ten years we lived in this house, a square box of plastered walls, strawberry roan and cream in color, such visits were repeated. I kept certain treasures up there, birds' eggs, butterflies impaled on pins, and the like. As the years went on few besides myself ever climbed the narrow stairs to this eyrie. There were the wasps, of course, that somehow managed to get in and to imprison themselves there and that I released if I came upon them before they starved or beat themselves to death against the glass. None of the treasures within were so good, though, as the lightning and thunderheads without. All told, those moments of delight in storm could not have totaled at a great number,

165

many as were the thunder storms of summer evenings, because a small boy's activities take him out of the house and hither and yon at all hours between daylight and dark. He missed, maybe, two storms out of three. The skies lighted by lightning were almost rare experiences, the skies lighted by the Conshohocken stacks almost a nightly experience.

If the subject of iron furnaces came up in conversation when Aunt Rachel was about she would speak of Warwick Furnace, on the south branch of French Creek, in northern Chester County, only seven miles away from her childhood home in Uwchlan, and still in full operation in the second quarter of last century. She knew more of Warwick than she did of Greenwood, her grandfather, Isaac Thomas's, furnace near Pottsville.

Now all that remains of Warwick Furnace, beside the home of the ironmaster, is the stack and a slag bank. The old furnace, a charcoal furnace, was opened in 1737 and it was in blast off and on until 1867. Here, or at Coventry just below, the first Franklin stoves were cast, and cannon and shot for Washington's army in Revolutionary days. The slag from the furnace is still a boon to the neighborhood. Hauled from the great bank, and spread on the valley roads, it keeps wheels out of the mud when frost is coming from the ground in spring and in periods of wet weather at other seasons. All is secluded and pastoral here now, with turkey buzzards so unafraid of man they refuse to leave a chicken they are picking clean when his car passes no more than fifty feet away. The valley is lush grassed, with full-flooded streams, mint-lined and tufted with water cress. Here there are calls of cool-voiced orioles even at high noon, and a wind that turns over all the leaves and reveals their undersides of silver. You are out of the world at Warwick Furnace now, in remotest country quiet, where once were all the noise and bustle of a furnace, the rumble of charcoal-laden carts, the groaning of the shoes and chains that braked the wagons bringing ore down from the Warwick pits, the churr and slither of water wheels and the loud babble of busy men.

"Warck Fornace" and "Jahn Pot," you find oftenest on the five-plate stoves that were made here in the eighteenth century. So were the ironmaster of British origin, John Potts, and his furnace, "Dutched" by his Palatinate workmen, who carved the wooden molds and poured the iron into the sand castings made from those molds. These plates are be-tuliped, of course, and illustrative, most of them, of this or that passage in Old Testament or New. Many of the plates are direct transfers to wooden molds of the wood cuts of the Nürnberg Bible of 1736.

The ironwork of grandfather's grist mill at Milford Mills was perhaps largely from Warwick Furnace, the nearest place where they could get castings made. Wrought iron was pounded out a little further down French Creek from Warwick, where the south branch meets, just above Coventryville, the north branch from the falls. Here stood the old Redding Forge. I have often wondered did the wrought iron of my most treasured item of ironwork come from Coventryville. This stand was picked up in Lionville, a few miles to the eastward of the forge. I am not sure whether the stand is for a flatiron or to set in the coals of a wood fire to hold a little saucepan. It is a light and airy affair, eight inches long at its feet and seven inches at its top. Its sides and feet are one piece, very like the mahogany sides of an ottoman, but flatter. These sides support two openwork scrolls, each of a large scroll and three smaller ones, the two scrolls set with large ends diagonally opposite each other. Perhaps it would be better to say that the scrolls are reversed, so that a large scroll and a small scroll make the

outer ends of the openwork and four little scrolls come together in the middle of the stand. No description can more
than suggest the clean-cut delicacy and the easy balance of
the little stand. It is good down to the slightest detail, such
as the curves of the feet, the notching of the undersides and
the riveting of sides and scrolls. It is at once dainty and
hardy, the most heartwarming and solacing bit of wrought
iron I have met in a lifetime of collecting.

Another bit of wrought iron I like much is the twisted
piece with a ring at the end that once supported the spout
of a wooden pump and held it tight into the main body of
the pump. It is fifteen inches long and most dextrously
fashioned.

Our set of so-called "fireside utensils" in iron came from
the neighborhood of Boyertown, and their metal, perhaps,
from the Furnace nearby, Colebrookedale, at one time like
Warwick under the management of the Pottses of Pottstown.
It is the proportions of these utensils and the designs cut in
their handles that win me. They are fork and "cake turner"
and ladle and strainer. Their handles, thirteen to fifteen
inches long, all bear one design, a linked chain with half-
links at either side of it. This chain design flowers into a
tulip at either end. The nineteen-inch ladle is, I think, the
best proportioned of the four. It, like all its fellows, has a
hook at the upper end. Then comes eight inches of handle,
three-quarters of an inch wide and an eighth of an inch thick,
tapering towards a round of iron four inches long. At the
end of the round there are two inches more of flat decorated
as is the upper handle. To this flat is attached the bowl of
the ladle, five inches in diameter and rounding down to a
greatest depth in the center of an inch and a half.

The strainer is a very replica of the ladle, save that its
bowl is perforated all over with holes of the diameter of a

small pea. The fork, too, is very similar save for its two tines. The "cake turner" is shorter, only thirteen inches to its flat of four inches by two to two and a half. This flat springs from the handle with rounding edges which spread out into the shape of a reversed spade when the round is two-thirds full circle.

All these implements were, I think, primarily intended for use in sausage making, one of the great occasions of the year in Pennsylvania Dutchland. The cake-turner, while it may have been used for reversing buckwheat cakes on the griddle, was originally employed in pressing sausage into the stuffer. It could have done service, too, in smoothing off scrapple in the pan. I have no doubt the fork was used for toasting bread over the fire, but its first function was in handling the pieces of pork and beef that went into the grinder.

A little trivet in the form of a snake is one of my treasures in iron. The antique dealer from whom I bought it knew nothing of its original habitat. The broad flat head of the rattlesnake and its neck make up the handle. The creature's eyes are raised, holes having been bored into the under part of the head and the thin iron remaining on the upper side gouged up into the protuberant bumps. A diamond design is outlined on its head, with lines paralleling and intersecting it. The body coils in from a half-inch diameter to a very thin tail, unlike that of any poisonous snake I know. The trivet is not quite four inches across and it is two inches high. It is of much rougher workmanship than sausage implements and iron-holder, but it has about it the appeal of primitive handwork.

The snake is none too common a motive in ornamentation of any kind in Pennsylvania. Snakes rise against each other, heads in, in wavy U-shaped designs on the little boxes that snuggle under the sides of Conestoga wagons. I have seen a snake of burned clay, coiled and lifting its head to strike, in a decorative panel intended to hang on the wall. Blown into shape in the thinnest of glass and coiled while the glass was still pliable, snakes were a rather common product of the South Jersey factories, and often peddled by the glass-blowers on the streets of Philadelphia. I am told there are snake designs sometimes on the bent over arm that holds a Betty lamp, but I have come on none such myself.

My lamp with a swinging cup came from the neighbor-hood of Hereford Furnace in southeastern Berks County. It is a simple and crude affair of good lines, seven and a half inches tall and with a heavy base five and a half inches in diameter. The support of the yoke from which the cup is swung is tooled with notches and rings, but restrainedly tooled. All is browned and roughened with age. No puff of wind or chance knock could upset this so solid and low lamp.

Of much later date, a hundred years later perhaps, are the two little plates, seven inches high and six broad, from a stove of the eighteen-seventies. The pair of these, which I found in Adams County below Gettysburg, show father and mother and small daughter in post-prandial ease in the sitting room. Father reads the paper; mother, book in hand, watches daughter as she offers some tidbit to the cat, whose kitten plays with a ball on the floor. Long curtains are draped in the high windows, in one of which is a hanging basket with a plant in it and in the other of which is a birdcage. An oil lamp with an elaborate shade rests on the rather heavy-legged table around which the family is gathered. It is the decade after the Civil War, that decade to the life.

I should like to think I possessed some memento of great-grandfather's furnace at Schuylkill Gap, in Sharp Mountain, Schuylkill County. Isaac Thomas gave up the attempt to carry on this furnace in 1807, after an eleven years' experience with it. If it is true that an eight-petaled flower in relief was a mark of this furnace, as I seem to remember set down somewhere, then perhaps my handled crock "with rose in relief" is from Greenwood. This handled crock is a direct reproduction in cast iron of the three-pint handled crocks in redware turned out by so many potteries.

There hangs in my backyard, from the greening apple tree in front of the barn, a half-gallon iron pot, three legged, painted in white and green. It is there because Solomon Diehl thought a place so like in many ways as ours to his grandfather's on Lehigh Mountain, ought to be like that place in having a pot hung from an apple tree. His grandfather's three-legged pot was painted red and black, but ours, Sol thought, would be more in keeping with its surroundings if it were white and green. So the bands that circle our two-quart fellow are white and green. His grandfather would never tell them why he hung the pot from the apple tree. If pressed for a reason as to why he had it there he would say: "For the birds to drink out of."

I have asked many questions as to why such pots should be swung from apple trees. Everybody admits they are to be found so swung all over Dutch Pennsylvania, but I have had no illuminating answers to my question as to "Why? Why? Why?" We all know that iron is lucky; that iron nails driven into a fruit tree cause it to bear freely; that "iron, cold iron, is master of us all." There is some more definite reason, though, that eludes me, why iron pots are swung in apple trees. Perhaps some day, unexpectedly, the reason for such a custom will be revealed to me. Meanwhile, I have a little delight of the eyes in this half-gallon fellow in my backyard, with "Pocasset" cast just below its rim, as it hangs, spruce in green and white, from a low limb of the greening. There is water in the pot for any length of time only after heavy rains. That water evaporates quickly. There are few days in which the birds could there find enough to assuage even the mildest sort of thirst.

In all these objects of iron that I have been writing about the utilitarian element is dominant, though most of them have decorative features as well. In a pair of colonial shoe buckles that I have, utility is not neglected, but iron and brass and silver all blend in the service of the highest artisanry. The arched frames, four inches and three-eighths from end to end, three inches wide, and one and three-eighths inches high as they rest on the table, are of brass, silver mounted. The silver is not plated on the brass. It is a thin veneer soldered on. There are twelve half-moon openings, every other one reversed, on both sides of the frame, and four on each of the frame's ends, the inner half moons facing up, the outer down. There is simple but captivating chasing on the silver.

The delicacy and proportions of the wrought iron frame and tongue within the outer frame of brass and silver have an appreciable part in the appeal of the buckles. They are of the lightest construction, but wholly serviceable, and with charm of outline and sharpness of craftsmanship. They have rusted very little in their eightscore years of existence. They have been treasured, cared for, held of high worth. A most workmanlike mend on the side of one of the frames proves that beyond doubt. Whoever repaired this break was admonished, and most successfully, to make a neat job of it. A bit of iron is riveted across the break, on the inside, where it does not show. This bit of iron gives a strength to the arch of brass as great as it had originally.

Buckles for low shoes though they be, there is pomp and circumstance about their effects of iron and brass and silver. Where there is silver there is a sense of richness, just as surely as where there is brass there is a sense of sunlight and radiancy. Those were occasions of ceremony when these buckles graced some dignitary's shoes. They suggest proud clothes and regalia, medals on breast and ribbons of honor, inaugurations and state balls, gentlemen and ladies stately in a minuet. They speak pomp and circumstance as do trumpets and shawms. They speak also a finished craftsmanship, a perfection of artisanry that approaches very close to art.

The buckles were found in Rockhill, in upper Bucks County just west of Haycock Mountain, a countryside from which splendors of blood and state are long since departed and where high artisanry is far to seek to-day. Here the buckles had been for more than a century and a half, relics of that old time when there was much of the essential culture and of the proved craftsmanship of America in this lonely hill land, when what was of the center was also of the remotest corner of the provinces. In more places, far from tidewater as well as at tidewater, than we are wont to believe possible in colonial America, and on down through the early years of last century, there was an art of life that was of the fine arts. It was none the less an art in those instances in which it was a simple life, the life of an artisan on a far hill farm, provided always it was lived in accordance with a considered code, a code handed down the generations. Out of the perfected craftsmanship of this kind of life could come such an object of art as these buckles. In the more patent art of life lived in manorial places such buckles were in more frequent use, no doubt, but they were no more a part of that life than of the life of the artisan who made them. We have come to regard such mementos of the past as these buckles as sign and symbol of the days of those who lived in a richly furnished homestead, where there were family portraits, an old library, grounds laid out with pleasances, orangeries and box-gardens, fish ponds, great stables and a race track. They are no more essentially symbol and sign of such days, though, than of the days and backyard shop of the artisan who made them, an artisan who was the inheritor of the craftsmanship of the ages, and the familiar of all patterns of beauty that the mind of man has devised.

THE LION'S SHARE

for Hattie Klapp Brunner and Ray Brunner

THE lion's share is, as you would expect, a large one among the decorations and symbols of early American art and artisanry. It is not, however, so large a share as you would expect it to be. As an outpost of England the colonies from Maine to Georgia held stoutly for years to the emblems that spelt home to their folk. The lion was on the arms of Great Britain several times repeated. It was rampant to the dexter, over against the unicorn rampant to the sinister, and, in little, rampant thrice on one of the quarterings. On another quartering of the shield was the royal lion of Scotland rampant, and there was still another lion, in this instance passant, as the crest that crowned the whole coat of arms.

In the second and third quarters of the eighteenth century, when so much of colonial art came into being, the lion was far better known in America than any other animal as a decorative device, and even as well known as dove or peacock or thistlebird, as tulip or pomegranate or pink. The eagle, of course, had not come into its own as yet. It was just another bird, scarcely more familiar on armorial bearings than merlotte or pelican or heron. In Pennsylvania Dutchland the eagle was familiar, in his double or two-headed form, from the arms of the German Empire; and it may well be that the German imperial eagle is the original of our national emblem. It is hardly likely that the bird as the colonists knew it, the stealer of fish from the osprey, or a ravager of lambs and poultry, was its original.

175

The lion was, of course, in all the A. B. C. books as the picture beast of L, whether that "L" stood for "Lion" or "Löwe"; and in the almanacs, where among the signs of the zodiac, it stands as the symbol of July. The lion is not infrequent, too, with the unicorn, on bridal chests. It is on stove plates, however, that we find it oftenest, especially in pre-Revolutionary days.

The first lion on a stove plate that I came upon was that at the Kloster at Ephrata. This plate shows Samson's killing of the lion, as related in *Judges*, 4, 5. The plate is marked Jacob Huber, who was the founder of Elizabeth Furnace, in Lancaster County, the place famous, in later years, as the site of Baron Stiegel's first experiments in the making of glass. This picture of lion killing closely reproduces the woodcut in the Nürnberg Bible (1736).

In the great collection of stove plates and firebacks in the Doylestown Museum, gathered together by Henry C. Mercer, are several other plates from five- or six-plate stoves that are decorated with lions, most of them depicting Samson's feat. An unusual one, a fireback, and obviously post-Revolutionary, bears the legend "Pro Patria" at the top. It shows a lion rampant, making off to the left, while prodding him on is a lady of matronly proportions, perhaps a Miss Columbia as imagined by a designer more familiar with Britannia than with younger ladies. This lion grasps in one lifted forepaw a sheaf of fourteen arrows like those we all have seen grasped in the feet of our American eagle. A stove plate of this Doylestown collection that reproduces the lion and the unicorn in all the detail of the British coat of arms is from across the Delaware in New Jersey. It is marked "Oxford 1746," and comes, of course, from that Warren County furnace which flourished from 1742 until 1882.

The lions on inns in pre-Revolutionary days must have

been legion, judging by the number that survived, under their old names, down to the days of prohibition. The Blue Lion Inn in Philadelphia is long gone, and the Golden Lion of Waterford, New York, on the Hudson above Albany. Lionville, in Chester County, Pennsylvania, still holds to the name it had from its inn sign, and Red Lion in York County. Stockbridge in Massachusetts rebuilt its famous Red Lion Inn when it burned down. Until 1930 a red lion swung in the great frame of the Red Lion Inn on the Bristol Pike, just to the northward of the Poquessing Creek, which here is the separating line between Philadelphia and Bucks Counties.

It was a shock to find this old landmark gone when on May 28, 1931, I made pilgrimage to Torrésdale to visit the old inn. For two hundred years exactly, from 1730 to 1930, some sort of lion had welcomed passersby to this hostelry. Its doors bore placards declaring it "closed and padlocked," another of the thousand and one old inns the victims of prohibition. Inquiry of neighbors disclosed the sale of the sign to the Doylestown Museum "last summer." We lost no time in making off across country on its trail. Early in the year as it was, the day was full summer. On the previous Friday, May 22, I had gone all the way to the Susquehanna by back roads, and found all the countryside still quick with spring. The day had been made memorable by the coming upon wild crab in blow, a bloom unequivocally of the spring. There was no languor in the air then, but now, six days later, in this rolling country by the Delaware, it was full summer. There was the scent of locust blossom on the air, but no wind to thin it out. It came to us in heavy wafts, languorous as the haze that lay over woods and meadows and tillage. The grass stood thigh high, all but ready for the mowers. The corn was a hand's span above ground, and under cultivation, with horse teams slowly harrowing here, there and everywhere, nine of

them to every shuffling tractor. Every other team was on a
hill-top, against the sky. Horse chestnuts spiked up their long
heads of bloom about the homesteads, white horse chestnuts,
the most of them, with a pink fellow about this place or that
which approached the manorial. Red-winged blackbirds rose
from the tussocked hollows as we passed, meadow-larks
clattered up from the grassfields, a turkey buzzard or two
lazed through the sun-steeped air. Grackles followed in the
wake of the harrows, no more put out by the chugging trac-
tors than by the stout Dobbins. There needed only cricket
song, a week away perhaps, to make the day one deep in summer. With the hearing of that song fall is all but upon us;
after we hear it, we are aware of the brevity of summer. Summer is, indeed, the briefest season. Spring lingers on into June
in upland places, and, in the hours of early morning, even in
such lowlands as these. In June, hay harvest, like the crickets,
brings the suggestion of autumn and of the fruitage of the
year.

Arrived in Doylestown, we were quickly in the presence
of the lion that had so long lorded it over the inn yard at
Torresdale. It was a good-sized fellow, more than four feet
long and at least three high. It was of a red-brown color on
the side of the sign we first saw, and of red-brown streaked
with green on the other side. Over it, as it stood with head
turned at right angles to its body, and with tail waving in the
air, was a broken arch like that of a cupboard top, with a pig
for crest. So on one side. On the other a cat replaced the pig.
Both aspects of the lion revealed it as a friendly fellow,
almost benevolent in fact, with an expression that was little
short of benign.

The lion on Pennsylvania Dutch objects of art other than
stove plates and chests and inn signs is rather unusual. The
writers of *fractur* use it now and then, but in all my hundred

bits of the illuminated writing I have only two lions, and the pair of them on the one *geburtsschein*. It is so crude an affair altogether that most who see it put it down as a child's effort. I am not so sure. Many of our back-country folk in the third or fourth generation from Germany lost a good deal of the Old World culture through the rigors of a life that left little time for the amenities and even for the lesser arts. They had few opportunities, before the development of the public school system, to win back, through education, something of the culture that they had lost. These two lions of the Melinger birth certificate are of a lemon yellow rather than of the correct tawny. Three inches long and two inches high they front us, heads towards each other and twisted tails waving defiantly towards the right and left margins of the certificate. The beasts have long, lugubrious faces, outlined in lead pencil, apparently, before the yellow was washed in.

I suppose the only lions that these good folks of Manor Township in Lancaster County knew were those in the A. B. C. books and in the almanacs and in the Nürnberg Bible. They never had the opportunity to get the start from a lion in a traveling circus that I received one July day along the Waullenpaupack. We were driving northward, with surrey and pair of grays. We were just surmounting a sharp rise. At the moment we topped it I saw a lion against the sky, couchant, with no visible means of support. Another moment and I saw that it was roped to the top of a circus van pulled by four horses. It was perhaps drugged, too, for it looked sleepy and it took no interest in the cows in a field nearby. The circus was passing westward along a road at right angles to ours. They had the lion ready, I suppose, for the next town in which they were to show. It was beautiful there on the tawdry wagon of red and gilt, all its warm tawniness brought to a glow by the full sunlight. Your second thought was that it was likely a toothless old fellow come almost to the end of its tether, but no second thought could destroy the first sight you had of it in its glow of yellow against blue sky and high piled white clouds. Our horses smelled it and were restive, but I had great joy in it in the brief time while it was passing out of sight. I could not help wondering had any one before us ever seen a great cat in this neighborhood since the last panther was shot here a half century before.

Panthers our early German backwoodsmen, of course, knew, but it was not after panthers they drew the lions of *fractur* and painted chests and stove plates but after the little fellows so familiar on the woodcuts of the primers and almanacs. A lion rampant, with open mouth and tongue extended, adorns a fold-over picture I have. It must be a part of some old A. B. C. book or the like, for E. F. G. H. I. J. K. cross the top of the picture you see when you fold back the two halves of the lion. Despite a decided action with its paws as you see in some football linesmen who play high, the beast is kindly looking. The rhyme runs thus:

> *A Lion rousing from his Den,*
> *On purpose for to range*
> *Is soon turn'd to another Shape:*
> *Lift up and see how strange.*

Folding back the upper half of the picture, you have that eagle's head and wings that, with the lion's body and hindquarters, make up a Griffin. The legend runs:

> *A Griffin here you may behold,*
> *Half Beast, half Fowl to be,*
> *Once more do but the Leaf downfold*
> *And a frightful Sight you'll see.*

The next verse explains what we see:

> *Behold within the Eagle's Claws*
> *An infant there doth lie!*
> *Which he hath taken as a Prey*
> *With Wings prepared to fly.*

In *The Instructive Alphabet,* an A. B. C. book of 1808, published by Samuel Wood of No. 362 Pearl Street, New York, "L" is symbolized by "Lion," as in a hundred others of its ilk. It is a rolling-eyed fellow, with tail twitched aloft, but its appearance belies the "literature" about it. A rhyme tells us:

> *The Lion ranges through the wood,*
> *And makes the lesser beasts his food;*
> *So tyrants on their subjects prey,*
> *And rule with arbitrary sway.*

Which is not only instructive but properly democratic. This rhyme subjoins the little woodcut of the lion. On the opposite page, two inches wide by four long, there is this description of the king of beasts: "The Lion stands at the head of the feline race, being at once the most dignified, the strongest, and the most generous of the family. He has a large head, short round ears, a shaggy mane, strong limbs and a long tail, tufted at the extremity. His general colour is tawny, which in the belly inclines to white. From the nose to the insertion of the tail, a full grown Lion will measure eight feet. The Lioness is smaller and destitute of a mane. Under the scorching sun of the interior of Africa, his courage is so sublimed, as to be the terror of all other quadrupeds. But the Lions of mount Atlas, whose top is covered with perpetual snows, have neither the strength nor the courage of those of Bildulgerid or Zaara. Here they are most numerous, and unconscious of any superiority in man; and a single Lion of the desert will rush upon a whole caravan, as if insensible of fear, to the last gasp."

Information in natural history was merely incidental to the primers. There were other little pamphlets devoted solely to beasts. One of these, two inches by four, I picked up in an auction at North Conway, New Hampshire, where I could look off to Mt. Washington, when I tired of the crying and the crowd. It was printed at Concord, by Robert Sherburne & Co. in 1830. Its account of the lion runs thus: "The lion is a native of Africa, and the hottest parts of Asia. The largest lion is 5 feet high, and 13 feet from the nose to the end of his tail. His form and gait is majestic. His head is large, ears rounded, his eye-balls round and fiery; his chest shaggy, his tail bushy at the end, and a yellowish brown mane 2 feet long on the side of his head & neck—his color is a pale-tawny. He is the model of majesty, strength and activity. When he roars, he puts his mouth to the ground, and is heard to a great distance.

"His habitation is in the darkest forest: on the approach of night he quits his den and prowls about for prey, roaring hideously. His favorite flesh is the Hottentot, the Horse, the Elephant, and the Camel. When he seizes his victim, it is with one vast bound, he knocks it down and gives the mortal blow with a tremendous roar.

"The lion's flesh is eaten, and his skin is used for a mantle or bed, by the African negroes."

This account, like *The History of Beasts* in which it appears, is obviously intended for school children, though its rhetoric and punctuation would doubtless trouble a scrupulously conscientious teacher.

True Stories Related, like *The Instructive Alphabet*, is a publication of Samuel Wood of New York, but without a date. It, too, came from that North Conway auction. Its preface reveals that the tales in the book are to serve as an antidote to romantic farragoes. So the compiler sets down for children, the story of Jonah and the whale and of Daniel in the lion's den, among others of more recent origin. The book is illustrated with little woodcuts. The two showing Daniel unharmed, among the lions, and his false accusers attacked by the beasts, have much more detail and much more action than the lion in *The History of Beasts*. In the picture of Daniel in the den, a great lion crouches quietly by Daniel, who, with face uplifted, is thanking the Lord for his safety. In the picture of the false accusers two big beasts are putting their paws upon the villains, preparatory, it is to be supposed, to devouring them.

In the *Union Primer* for 1837, printed in Philadelphia, there is a lion as much like those in the Zoological Gardens as you find in any sort of cut. Its whiskers are in evidence and its tail expresses considerable feeling, twitching nervously. The red ink in which all this book is printed gives the beast more verisimilitude than most of those printed in black possess. Like so many A. B. C. books it compromises between Old and New World birds and beasts and scenes. The robin and tortoise are certainly New World, the ibex and kite certainly Old World. Lesson XVIII presents us with a picture of a thatched cottage. Lesson X asks "Do you know how hard the beaver works?" Again, England and America called up.

It is the story of Daniel, and the story of Samson, of course, that brings the lions to the forefront in any illustrated Bible. In the Nürnberg Bible the prophet is twice depicted in safety with three beasts about him. The scene is first introduced as background in the upper right of a full-page plate of Johann Friedrich the First, Duke of Saxony. Three lions, maned, sit and lie placidly about Daniel, who, with hands pressed together in prayer, awaits what will be. Again the den is depicted, in the proper place in the *Book of Daniel*. Here, the prophet, in agony, lifts his face in supplication to the heavens, though neither of the two lions nor the lioness makes any hostile move. The lion that Samson masters is so obscured by the hero as he pulls its jaws apart you get little notion of its power or majesty. The lion in *Kings* is charging like a dog alongside of Solomon, while the wise Queen of Sheba proves the king with questions. Children, no doubt, have held this beast a dear, for there is a marker here, and the book opens to the woodcut. The lion seems thoroughly domesticated, a very housecat of a lion. My Nürnberg Bible belonged to folks who lived near Trumbauersville in Bucks County. It was brought by their ancestors, I take it, from the Old World, as were certain other heirlooms of prosperous people. It is all in good condition, wooden boards a half inch through, leather covers, leather straps with brass clasps, paper and many prints. Its cuts are not in every instance as distinct as they might be, but that is because the blocks were too often printed from, I think, and not from the thumbing of curious readers.

Historiae Naturalis De Quadrupedibus Libri is an engaging folio printed in Amsterdam in 1657. It is by Johannes Jonstonus, "Medicinae Doctor." It is a very leonine book, or perhaps it would be better to say "liony." A lion skin figures on its title page, being held aloft by two centaurs, between whose legs another lion, a crown on its head, peers out cautiously. Copper plate L shows two lions, one trottant, the other couchant. Both are heavily maned and quiet looking, the lower one almost pensive in aspect. Those on the next page are very different in appearance, both lioness above and lion and lioness below snarling to their hearts' delight. The creatures on the next page are crosses of the lion with other beasts. Leucurcuta is half lion, half horse, and Martigora, a creature with human face, lion's mane and body and a forked snake-like tail. I know nothing of the history of this book, but it has been long enough in America for several generations of children to have cut butterflies and beasts from it for their scrap books, if clippings and this kind of writing and that tell a tale accurately.

Clay lions generally come in pairs. Yet no one of the four I have is a mate of another, though two were cast in molds of like design. A friend of mine found the middle-sized lion with its fellow in a junk shop window and bought the two of them, knowing I should be glad of one of the pair. This lion has been in the kiln twice. It was molded in halves, cemented together with clay and then burned. It was then slipped with green and brown slip and burned again. The slip makes it a unit. It is lying down, back paws tucked under it, and front paws extended before it. Its head is turned at right angles to its crouched body. Crouched though it is, it has no intention of springing. It is a sleepy old fellow, only the tail twitched up along its side showing any tendency towards nervousness. It is eight and a half inches long, four and a half inches high, and the base on which it lies two inches wide.

A smaller lion is, too, in redware. It is four inches long, two and a half inches high, and the base on which it rests an inch and three-quarters wide. It is crouching like its larger companion, but it is looking straight ahead of it. It would not "dress" a mantelpiece so well as the larger lion. The little fellow is more portly, too. I visited it now and then for several months before I got it at my price.

My largest clay lions are doorsteps. They rest on bases nine inches and a half long and four inches and a half wide.

They are great-headed fellows, rising four and a half inches above their bases. They are, I think, casts of old molds made for use in a pottery. Both are cast solid, instead of in the usual halves, but of what material I am not certain. Were it not that one has been glazed white with a tin glaze I should say there was cement with the white clay of their composition. Cement, though, I am sure, would not stand the kiln. Perhaps, after all, they are of a particularly heavy stoneware. Shoe buttons are used for the eyes of the fellow coated a deep brown. Save for the glaze and the eyes the two are very like. This pair of fellows, kept handy to the front door, would provide you with formidable weapons against unwelcome visitors.

I have a china lion, too, a fellow hardly larger than a Noah's Ark animal. It is in red-brown and pink. Its face and paws and hindquarters are pink. A great mane in red-brown covers all its head and neck and extends almost halfway down its back. It, too, is couchant, on a bed of green grass. There is not nearly so much modeling upon it as upon the lions in redware. It is three inches long, three inches high, counting its bed of grass, and an inch and a half wide. It is, I believe, Staffordshire, but it is far from the royal lion of England the best potters turned out.

A pair of Staffordshire lions that I know are larger than this little fellow which came to me as a Christmas present. They are five and a half inches long and three inches high. They are brown of mane and gray of body and they rest on bases of grass-green, with a gilt line running around the fronts of the bases. Their tails are curled up over their backs. They have black noses and open mouths of red. They are a pair, one facing at right angles to a body to the left, and the other facing at right angles to a body turned to the right.

A lion on a pitcher very like Wedgwood, white against a

background of blue, is shaking fiercely a dog it has caught by the back. It is one of a pack which has been pursuing the lion. It is a squat pitcher we find the lion adorning, a pitcher said to have been made by the Turners of Longton a century and a quarter ago.

The lion on the "Millennium" plate is submitting to the blandishments of an undraped figure, presumably the child that "shall lead them." The child stands between the lion and the cow, with a leopard at his feet. Close by are two horned creatures which look like goats, but one of which, I suppose, must be a lamb, that fabulous lamb that lay down so peacefully by the lion. It is an uglier plate than you could conceive possible for the mind of man to devise, yet it brings a fairly good price, despite the wretched pinks and browns and light blues in which you generally find it. It is less repellent in dark blue, but in my experience, it is as rare as the Richard Jordan plate in that color.

I have never seen a lion in our Pennsylvania Dutch chalk-ware, though the lion was common, in my youth, in the baskets of plaster objects peddled round by Italians. I have a lion in what is close kindred to chalkware, a plaster of Paris toy fastened to a base that roars discreetly when you press it. It came to me from Somerset County, along with a pig and cat and cedar bird, the last named attesting, I think, to the American origin of all four. This lion is closer to the proper tawny hue than any other in my menagerie. The color is in evidence everywhere save in those parts covered by its mane, which is of a purplish black. This lion sits bolt upright, front and hind paws together and tail wrapped round them. Its face is more doglike than catlike. It would certainly win its way to any child's heart.

Lions surmount two compote covers that, with their lower halves, were wedding presents to Daniel Atwood over fifty

years ago. Of cloudy glass, they gaze out quietly towards
Moultonboro, where, by the Whittier Highway, the imagination of man had long ago picked out a lion's head in a
bump of granite just west of East Sandwich. Time and road
widening have obliterated that head now, but it was just
as surely suggestive of the lion as the more famous head in
the Crawford Notch of the elephant, or of the Great Stone
Face in the Franconia Notch of Daniel Webster. Three lions'
faces closer to home are those on a glass goblet of mine. The
etching on its bell-shaped bowl indicates a German origin,
but the cloudy glass of its stem is very like that which Sandwich on Cape Cod handed on to a score of Pennsylvania and
Ohio factories.

The only lion I have in blown glass is a little fellow two
inches long and an inch and a half high. It is on a greenish
bottle, perhaps a scent or medicine bottle, three inches wide
and four inches high, and less than an inch from front to back.
There are scrolls above and below the panels the lion adorns,
and the familiar two tulip leaves nine times repeated on the
sides of the bottles. There are scrolls above and below an
empty panel on the back of the bottle. Or perhaps this I
call back is really front, and the empty panel once bore a label
telling us of the contents and their maker. There is a ground-
off pontil on the bottom of the bottle. Its neck, a little more
than an inch long, and a half inch in diameter, is set at
right angles to its shoulders. It is a very square bottle, crude
and of an uneven color, but with that pleasantness about it
that so often goes with primitiveness. It might be from Old
World Germany, or from some South Jersey factory, Medford or Glassboro or another, that inherited traditions from
Germany.

America has its share of marble lions. They date, most of
them, from that era of pretentious country places, the first

decades of last century. Two of these fellows spent long years on the tall pillared porticos of the Carpenter house on Germantown Road in Mt. Airy, seven miles northwest of Philadelphia. As much of the statuary at Philellena came from the estate of Joseph Bonaparte at Bordentown in New Jersey, it may well be that these lions were part of the purchase. Carpenter finished his great house in 1844, not so long after Bonaparte gave up Point Breeze and went back to Europe. These lions are about three feet long, fifteen inches wide and twenty inches tall. They are a little weathered, showing that they have been long out of doors. They are far from fierce, the one with its head on its paws being almost of gentle mien. The other one, that is gazing straight ahead of it, looks tired and bored, like the straitly-caged ones in a circus.

Almost a mate to this fellow is one of the lions that endeared themselves to passers in Frankford Road for long years from the front steps to Dr. Guernsey's office. They have moved with him to his present home back from the pike, and even here, on a street that boasts a cow grazing by its side, they attract a great deal of comment, for all they are so undemocratic beasts. I should not be at all surprised if these lions, too, did not come ultimately from Bonaparte's place at Bordentown.

Little lions in marble may sometimes be had for a song. I was offered a pair of them in a Philadelphia junkshop for a dollar and a half for both. They were replicas of the famous beast that rolls the world under its paw. They were not at all badly cut. One was perfect. The other had been mended, but its general contour was preserved so well you could not see a sign of its injuries from a distance.

A lion carved out of wood that came to me from Lebanon County may have wandered far from home. It has a Swiss look to me. Yet its wood, if not white pine, is so like white pine that only an expert could decide whether it was or not. This fellow looks as if it had been fashioned after a study of a coat-of-arms, rather than from life. It is lean and hungry looking, with a great head. Its open mouth discloses sharp teeth and its tail is curved angrily over its back. It is heavily maned. Many details are carefully executed, hollowed ribs, deeply-cut toes and tufts of hair on hocks. It is moving slowly on all fours, and roaring, I should say, judging from head upthrown and jaws widely extended. It is painted the dark brown common to clock ornaments and wall plaques. There is no sign, however, of its ever having been attached to anything. It may be it was, like its pottery brethren, just a mantelpiece ornament.

There is no lion on either of my more modern-looking springli boards, the two I think of as "made in America." The old and worn board that looks as if it were Old World German has, however, two lions, a large fellow on the front and a lesser one on the back. The lion on the front of the board is four and a half inches long and three inches tall. It is heavily maned. Tulips spring up from the grass under its feet. Calf and horse accompany it on one side of the board. On the other side you find the lion repeated in miniature, the only one of the beasts and birds so treated. Here, two inches long and an inch and a half tall, the lion foregathers with antlered stag, wolf, crane, boar, elephant, rabbit, goose and fox. Just why the lion should be so popular a design for the iced animals on cakes I cannot guess, but so it is. I know no use of the lion as decoration or motive in America that so emphasizes its importance as this doubling on the German springli board.

A lion carved on a rifle stock is one of the curiosities of Dillin's book, *The Kentucky Rifle* (1924). It shares place there with a double eagle, of German origin surely, and with an American Indian. Men whose ultimate origin was German were our first riflesmiths, and they may have taken pride in those two-headed eagles of their Old World allegiance. The presence of the British lion would appeal to English colonists, and the Indian to those of all stocks here long enough to have become completely Americanized. Business is business. It may be, of course, that the beast is not really a maned lion at all, but our Pennsylvania mountain lion. The panther was plenty hereabouts before the animal drives brought about its extermination. The panther was not admired enough in old days, though, to be made a motive in household art, or to be painted on an inn sign, or to be cast in pottery.

There may be more than a blazoning of the lion on the arms of England to account for its presence in statuary and in household art, and for its place in the regard of men. It may be, too, that the veneration of it as king of beasts will not account for all its celebrity unaccounted for by its presence on England's arms. It may be that the place the Persian lion had in decorative motives brought from the East into sixteenth-century Germany has affected such of us as are Pennsylvania Dutch in holding a brief for the lion. Tradition dies slowly among us. It may be that part of such prominence as the lion still has is due to its symbolism of July, in the signs of the zodiac, or to the dominance of the constellations of Leo and Leo Minor over the hearts of men. Those who would trace the outlines of the two great beasts in the midnight skies of May would like, perhaps, to have reminders of them in *fractur*, in etched plate on rifle, in clock ornaments, or in mantelpiece bric-a-brac. Liquor drunk at an inn with a tawny lion on its swinging sign would put greater heart in you than that drunk under a Turk's Head or a Blue

Boar. A horse hitched to a post with cast faces of lions about it would grow strong, surely, in wind and limb.

Almanacs and atlases of the heavens were pored over in old times in a way we can hardly realize now. So much depended on signs and seasons in those days when men had so much less to do with their destinies than they have to-day. There was in old days always something distinguished or spectacular about everything associated with the lion, from that Richard of England who was Lionheart to those showers of meteors, the leonids, which made a wonder of November skies round about the constellations Leo and Leo Minor.

One guesses wildly, with further and further reaches into the past, to account for the general interest in lions. One takes a long shot and asks can traditions of the cave lion of Europe have come down to historical times among our ancestors, if there was knowledge of the lion among the folk other than that which came from the coats-of-arms of kingdoms and empires, the chapbooks and travelers' tales. The Romans, perhaps, whose amphitheaters were the shambles where so many lions were slaughtered, may have brought stories of them to France and Germany and England. Caesar's legionaries, or the builders of villas from Kent to the Welsh marches, may have talked the cult of the lion on highways and in byways.

One wonders, and wonders, and wonders again, how early the constellations Leo and Leo Minor were so known to men, and how generally they were so known. Lying in our summer skies just below the Great Bear, they occupy a prominent place during those months when men most comfortably may scan the heavens. Those constellations would serve, too, to keep the noble beasts in mind. The lion has not, however, through any circumstance, tradition, legend, nobility of mien, or association, persisted as a dominant motive in

American art and artisanry. It had its heyday in America before the War for Independence; it held on until day before yesterday in the A. B. C. books; it has a certain place still in statuary. It has been largely displaced because it was associated with alien things. That it has survived in as many instances as it has, proves how innately appealing it is, and how appealing as a symbol of an aristocratic order none too well liked by the modern world.

WALLETS OF NEEDLEWORK

for Annie Hoopes Maris

IT was on trips to Chester County, with Aunt Rachel, fully fifty years back, that I first saw wallets and purses of long ago. It was as satisfying to me as any episode in a story book to watch a farmer come into the store at Cambria Station, take a deep leather pouch out of his pocket, unwind a leather thong from round about it, and dig out a handful of silver and copper and pay for some little purchase. It could not be for tobacco, for the storekeeper was not allowed by his crusading wife to keep smoking or chewing tobacco or snuff in his store. Bagged tobacco stems to put into the nests of chickens and pigeons he was allowed to buy, but to that lady, so concerned with her neighbors' morals, snuff and chewing and smoking tobacco were only less wicked than alcohol. And yet, late in her life, when she heard the coast-guards shooting at rum runners trying to slip into the inlet to a Jersey thoroughfare, she used to hope "Those dear men would get away." So can the years mellow even a Hickory Quaker with "reform" in the blood.

It amused me in those remote years to hear her old grandmother say that she could not see why Abigail objected so to tobacco. Didn't Abigail's great-great-grandmother, her own grandmother, smoke a pipe? She went into the great fireplace to smoke it, to be sure, so that the house would not be "scented up," and she would not let her menfolk smoke in any room save the kitchen, but it certainly made

194

folks less irritable if they had leave to smoke. This old lady, my great-grandmother, had her first child in 1800, so her grandmother's old age was probably in the years just after the War of the Revolution. Old women who certainly considered themselves ladies smoked on into later years than that, country cousins having told me that in their youth, in Mexican War days, it was no unusual sight to see old bodies in Quaker bonnets puffing away contentedly on long-stemmed pipes. That the taking of snuff lasted on later still is known by the personal observation of all of us over fifty.

There were tobacco pouches as well as money bags of soft leather. They seemed always to have enough fine cut in them, if you scraped about with pipe and pressing finger, to make another pipeful. There were bill-rolls and wallets and pocketbooks of leather. Now and then some old lady pulled out a cardcase or purse of bead-work, or conversation led to the unearthing of some old wallet in needlepoint from a drawer in a shaving stand or from a camphor chest. It is because they were so often just tucked away in the nearest drawer on disuse and not consigned to the camphor chest that so few of them done in wool survive, and that nearly all that do are so moth-eaten.

Both the folks at Cousin Abigail's and the folks at Cousin Ann's had much to say about needlepoint. It seemed to be held aristocratic for some reason or other, as bead-work was held aristocratic. All those who were old folks to me in youth said that those who were old folks to them in their youth agreed that wallets or braces in needlepoint were proper things for a girl to give her young man as an engagement present. My old folks did not always put it just that way. What the most of them said was that old gentlemen and old ladies had told them a pocketbook of needlework or suspender straps in needlework were considered, in the last years of the eighteenth century, or in the early years of the nineteenth century, a correct presentation from a lady to a gentleman on betrothal. It was good luck then, as it is now, to put an old copper penny or a shinplaster note for ten cents in the pocketbook.

It was the custom, in the days of my youth, never to send a guest away without some gift, but I never was given any of the old bill-rolls, or wallets, or pocketbooks I was interested in. Perhaps it was the sentiment associated with the old needlework as engagement gifts that prevented their bestowal. I was given sometimes old stamps, or old stamped envelopes, or letters, or a glass of jelly, or of preserves, and once a kettle of live fish to take home, but never a wallet. One of my city relatives who thought her country cousins had more of the family treasures than was their due used to ask them if they would not will her this or that when they died. If they said they would, she would write, underneath the seat of a chair, or on the back of a picture, "By will to Esther," and be on hand at the funeral to carry off the spoil.

I had not the courage for such tactics. All I asked of most of these country cousins was family genealogy or family history. I wrote all down they told me, even from young years, and so I came by a good deal of family history and many relationships that might otherwise never have been preserved. It would not now be known that a Penina of five or six generations back was clubfooted, or that a Reese of that same large family had fallen into a tub of scalding water and so come to his death, if I had not had so consuming a curiosity as a child. With such trivial items, however, I acquired a good deal of first-hand information of real importance about old times and a few family letters that might otherwise have been destroyed.

It was in comparatively recent years, perhaps ten years ago, that I acquired my first bit of needlepoint, a bill-roll cover six inches by twelve. I had resisted, a year or two before, a piece some fifteen inches by eighteen in mustard yellow and old red, in the frame of a mahogany fire screen. Whether it was of Martha Washington, or of some Old World saint or a self-portrait of the old lady who made it, I have no guess. My bill-roll cover was, too, dominantly in red and yellow, but there were in it, too, green and purple, and light blue and dark blue. The colors are laid on in sharp up and down angles like the pictures of the Andes and Sierra Nevadas we used to make in school for our exercises in geography. Some call this brightly colored sawtooth decoration "diamond-back rattlesnake design." It is not a bad name at all for it, as it suggests such snakeskin and as there are wallets and bill-rolls made out of snakeskin. My roll is lined with buckskin, and it is held together by a thong of buckskin fastened to one end of the needlepoint cover. Just what kind of knot was used, I do not know. There is no short thong at the other end of the needlepoint to which to tie the long thong. The needlepoint is done over that tough and open burlap-like material that is called "canvas," but that is far from any other canvas I have ever seen.

There is no name on this bill-roll. On a wallet of needlepoint, whose wool is now badly worm-eaten, is needled in the name "William Foulk" and the date "1800." The "William" is still distinct, but the moths have had a good meal on the "u" of the "Foulk," the last letter of which is on the second line of the lettering and numbering, just preceding the "18" of the "1800." The "k18" is to the left of the front of the wallet and the "00" to the right, separated by the highest jagged peaks of the needlepoint. The design and color of this needlepoint are very like those of the buckskin lined bill-roll. There is less red, however, in the needlepoint of the wallet, perhaps because the moths were most attracted by that color. They have pretty well cleaned it off its "canvas" base. The wallet is bound with red tape and lined with a glazed material of pink, chintz perhaps. This wallet has a tie tape corresponding to the tie thong of buckskin of the bill-roll. The wallet has two compartments, and it would hold approximately as much as the folding leather wallet of to-day. It is six by nine inches, four inches on each side of the wallet, and an inch lap that covers the "William Foulk 1800" on its front.

My needlepoint wallet of earliest date is, like its fellows, of Quaker origin. Its legend is "17 - H. L. - 84." Two cards within it are invitations to dinner in 1814 and 1816 to Hope Lippincott, who must be, I suppose, the "H. L." whose initials are worked upon it. Was Hope then an old lady, or a lady growing old, and how and when did she come to have her initials inscribed on this wallet of diamond rattlesnake covering? Did girls work their initials on needlepoint for wallets as they did on samplers, or is this "H. L." some other Lippincott than Hope, or is it just coincidence that these two invitations to Hope Lippincott should come in a wallet with the initials H. L.? One of the cards is printed, with Hope Lippincott's name written in. The other is wholly in longhand. The printed one reads:

PRISCILLA WILLS and ISAAC NICHOLSON present their respects to, and solicit the company of Hope Lippincott on Fifth-day, the 24th of the Third Month, 1814

The one in long-hand reads:

> *Jane Lippincott and Job*
> *Eldridge present their res-*
> *pects to and respectfully*
> *request the company of*
> *Hope Lippincott to dine*
> *at John Haines': on fifth*
> *day the 26 of the 3d mo 1816*

The colors of the wool used in this needlepoint work in order of their occurrence from top to bottom are purple, light purple, brown, orange, yellow, brown, light purple, red, yellow, brown, green, yellow, brown, light purple, purple, light purple, brown, orange, yellow, brown, light purple, red, yellow, brown, green, yellow, brown, purple, light purple, brown, orange, yellow, brown, light purple, red, yellow, brown and green. There are thirty-eight serrated lines altogether of seven different colors or shades of color, and so arranged that the general effect is bizarre and striking. The three compartments of the wallet are lined with glazed green chintz. It has been carefully preserved, and it is now nearer to its pristine colors than any other of these wallets. The wallet of Isaac Whitelock of Lancaster is the earliest in date I have seen or heard tell of. Its date is 1754. In the youth of that descendant of Quakers who owns it, it used always to be filled with Continental money. It had been evidently a family treasure rather than a thing of use, for years on years, perhaps for more than a century.

Far handsomer than these four diamond-backed pocketbooks of woolen needlepoint is a large two-pocketed wallet, with its pockets both opening in the one direction, so that it could have been hung on the wall to hold letters if not used as a pocketbook. It is seven inches by twelve and all of silk save the "canvas" base and pasteboard backing. Its decoration of ruddy strawberries, of the size of the wild fruit, in pink diamonds and against a background of green, is in needled silk. Its lining is of green silk that has held its own marvelously against the years. The wallet is made, so the whole family in conclave has decided, by weaving a needle carrying a silk thread again and again through the little openings in the "canvas." The needlework looks almost like crocheting at first glance.

It is the most beautiful thing of its kind I have ever seen, with each strawberry of red and pink centered in a squarish diamond of pale pink lines about a sixteenth of an inch broad. On the lower pocket, at the top, appears the name of "Henry Row 1794." This wallet came from a family of Williamsons, Quakers, in Chester County. The "Foulk" of the other wallet suggests a Quaker origin, too, but Bucks County. There have been many of that name in and about Quakertown since old times. This "Row" wallet is worn a bit on the outside, but it is surprisingly bright on the pocket fronts folded in.

I know similar contraptions in figured chintz, but these generally house sewing kits rather than notes and bills.

Of like feeling to the needlepoint work in wool are old embroidered straps for "gallowses." These straps are far from severe in color or design. I have a pair that are said to come from Germany. I doubt it, for they have the bastings still in them, and the many good housewives from the old country that I have known would one and all have finished up whatever they had put hand to before setting out on the long journey to America. These suspender straps are cross-stitched on canvas in black and green and red and pink. They date, according to the story that came with them, from

Civil War days. They were given to a veteran of those days, after he came home, and they are of a sort you associate with red-shirted firemen in the full regalia necessary to their parades. They were left all but finished, perhaps, by some old woman, and given to the veteran, maybe, as a memento of her after her death. They are two inches wide and twenty-four inches long. They are wedge-shaped at one end as if intended to be thrust through buckles.

Needlepoint in such narrow confines as those of suspender straps or wallet covers is more pleasing to me than needle-point framed for wall decoration or needlepoint on chair seat or top of footstool. Needlepoint is, nine times out of ten, bright and gaudy stuff, of which a little goes a great way. It is, however, very symptomatic of its period, of that period of highly colored decoration from Revolutionary times to the times of the Civil War. Such gaudiness, or richness of color, call it which you will, was needed to warm men's eyes, if not their flesh, in those days of cold houses on wind-smitten hill farms.

HELENA AND HER PETS

for Emily Godley

IT was just under the cliffs of the granite quarries of Redstone that we came on the silhouette of Helena. Before we saw that was her first name and Henkel her last we were attracted by that insouciant profile. It was not only that she looked unmindful of the worst the world could do to her. That was attractive in itself, but we would not have taken to her so strongly had she not looked, too, simple, childlike, naïve. In her armor of innocence she could afford to be careless. There was still more, though, to win us. Somehow she took us south from New Hampshire, clear across New England and New York, to the homey valleys under the Blue Mountain, shallow valleys white-piked and studded thickly with stone houses.

Her silhouette was passepartouted, an inappropriate treatment for a silhouette. By her hung another silhouette, also passepartouted, of Salomon Henkel, with long Teutonic nose and century old stock and cut of coat. The two of them belonged together, but they came so high for the light purses we had in pockets that we were forced to content ourselves with Helena. Carrying her home to Sandwich, we ensconced her in a proper frame of gilded metal, part of a large spoil of all sorts of frames acquired across country in Vermont. So friendly was Helena in aspect that we could not bear to be parted from her for three-quarters of the year. We took her south with us to Germantown.

She hangs on the wall in Ann's room over the cherry desk

from northern Bucks. Above her is a cool and dainty print
of a dancer by Currier and Ives, a print in which green and
white predominate. To her right is a steel engraving of
Washington Irving, to her left a lamp in a jar of redware,
brown glazed and shapely. Little brass candlesticks lend their
shining brightness to the desk top. On the flat of the desk,
extended by its sloped front turned down, are gathered the
pets, almost a Noah's ark of animals and birds.

There are a good many of them of pottery, our Pennsylvania redware. There is a big dog, six inches high, with the
shaggy head of a poodle. He is a child's bank. There is a deer
couchant, not more than three inches long, and hardly as
many inches tall, antlered, alert, but without restlessness.
There is a cow, an exceedingly bovine cow, a muley cow,
with a benevolent expression. She is a warm yellowy red
with spots of white. She is four inches long and something
more than two and a half inches high. There is a squirrel,
with startling white eyes, a squirrel that sits in the orthodox
fashion for squirrels, with tail curled over his back. He holds
in his paws a nut almost as large as his head, a butternut by
its shape. There are white bars on his tail and green stripes
on his shoulders. He sits on a redware slab one and a
quarter inches wide and one and three-quarter inches long.
He is two inches and a half high. The bird of this family
of three, cow, squirrel, and bird, is not a dove or peacock
or parrot. I am not sure what he is, but I incline to the belief
that he is intended for a thistlebird or goldfinch, with his
yellow plumage picked out with green and black on the
wingbows, with white and black on the head, and with
black on the tail. There are two lions in redware also among
these pottery figures, a dog couchant, and a dog and a bird
on the one base but at peace with each other.

The plaster beasts and birds are as numerous as those of

pottery. There is a goat, bearded and Machiavellian, with trimmings of brown. There is an owl larger than the goat, of a reddish cast, and amiable in expression. There are two portly rabbits, each with ear linings and lips of pinky red and a brown blob for a tail. There is a cockatoo in yellow and red, and two doves in white, with red dots on their breasts, billing on a stand. There is a white poodle, and a brown and yellow lion. There is a white lamb, and a red squirrel.

In years of search and of questioning all who know the birds and beasts in plaster, I have never been able to find where they were made, and where certain types of them are being made even to-day. I have never come across a mold used in their making. It is in the Dutch country that you find the most of them, but the Dutch antiquers generally deny them. "It was Italians from the city that peddled those birds and dogs and cats around, those cornucopias and baskets and vases of fruits," says the sage of Ephrata, "and there are none of them older than old people still living." So it may be. I do not know. I have myself come on no evidence the one way or the other, as to their being of country origin and Dutch, or as to their being of city origin and Italian. Other antiquers vociferously deny an Italian source for them.

I know as little of the origin of the wax figures under glass, though both the texture of that glass, and the costuming of the human figures under it, seem to indicate a foreign origin. I have been told they are Swiss, but I do not know on what authority. The figures in wax are of a vintage nearly synchronous, I think, with that of the "chalk" birds and beasts, and with that of the blown glass deer and coachdogs that one finds also under glass. These glass figures are, however, a great many of them, of American manufacture. The wax figures are all mounted on papier-mâché bases, by a

HELENA AND HER PETS

toothpick-like sliver of wood, or by glueing to a little block
of wood. Very often flowers made of linen accompany the
wax figures, those figures being considered not alluring
enough alone. I have only a few of them, a girl shepherding
a goat with a rake rather than a crook, and two men on horseback overshadowed by a brilliance of colored flowers that
rise above them in proportions large enough for oaks. Two
of the three sorts of flowers have so much of the colors and
contours of nature as to be identifiable as edelweiss and rose,
edelweiss of pure white and rose of old rose. The third
flower, of ten white petals purple tipped, I am not sufficient
of an alpinist to identify. The wax figures are of folks out
of Arcady. The girl with the goat wears tight bodice and full
skirt and broad-brimmed hat. A red ribbon is twisted round
the yellow hat, the bodice is brown and the short skirt white
with a green border. The horsemen have plumed hats, short
coats of brown and gray and trousers of blue. Their stockings of white and ankle-high shoes hardly seem the perfect
accouterment for riding. The youths seem to have been
seized while dancing on the green and thrust into the saddle.
The one horse is black and the other gray, but both alike
have saddle cloths of pinky red. Goat and horses, girl and
youths, are the most gaily caparisoned of Helena's charges,
a little ornate for the quieter creatures in redware and chalk
and glass.

Over them all, however, Helena presides with dignity, as
becomes a physician's daughter or clergyman's daughter of
the Valley of Virginia a hundred years and more ago. I am
not sure of her identity, but perhaps I have stumbled on it.
In the winter after we brought Helena down from New
Hampshire I sent to Indiana for *Two Centuries of American Mennonite Literature* (1929). When the book arrived
from Goshen I fell to conning it. On page 12 I found this

note about *Choral Music,* "the first Mennonite Musical Production," printed at Harrisonburg, Virginia, in 1816: "The
Nachricht states that many of the melodies are taken from
the Reformed Hymn Book, that Pastor Johannes Braun
wrote the Vorrede, and that Dr. Salomon Henkel bore a substantial share of the printing costs." It may be, of course,
that there were two or more Salomon Henkels, and if there
were only one, he may have been M.D. or D.D., but I think
I am justified in having a strong presumption that this Dr.
Salomon Henkel is Helena's Salomon. The proprietress of
the antique shop at Redstone came from Washington, and
she had done, so she told me, a good deal of her collecting
in the Valley of Virginia. I am more than sorry now I did
not return to that shop when I had a little more money
and squander a portion of it on Salomon. The man who
subsidized a hymn book would have had an interest in birds
and beasts made for the delight of children. His impressive
profile would have been in place looking down on this collection of Dutch toys.

"LET BOX NOW DOMINEER"

for G. Richard Nichols

WHERE a man plants box, there he means to live out his days, and there he plans his heirs shall be after him, year on year, for long years. Who plants box loves box; who loves it knows its ways, its growth so unnoticeable that it is an adage to say "as slow as box"; its growth so gradual that the lustiest bush will not outstrip a man's height in his lifetime, even if, by reason of strength, he shall last to fourscore. If he who plants box be a young man that planting writes large for who may read that already he is sure of the future, that the years will bring peace and plenty, that he will not have to change his abode, or want for what will maintain it. If he who plants be of middle years it is a sign he is certain of patriarchal age, or that his affairs are so fixed that here where he watched the box increase and the sand run low he may content himself with the hope that men of his stock will dwell after him.

But to-day there are not so many who do plant box, and there is not a little of it of old time that is done away with through the spreading out of the cities of our Eastern seaboard, its chief home in America. There are many, in truth, who are indifferent to box, and not a few who dislike it. The latter hold it of funeral aspect, associated with mortality. You will find it in churchyards in America, in Moravian cemeteries in the hill country of Pennsylvania, and at the head of graves of long dead Quaker folk in Rhode Island, but a churchyard shrub, particularly, it has never been with

207

us. A churchyard shrub the yew is in old countries, and since the yew is rare with us, and since the box, through its little change down the years, has come to be considered fellow to the yew, this suggestion of it as emblem of the grave has some justification. And yet, the hale greenness in old age of the box, and its tender leafing, many centuried though it be, spring after spring, make it rather emblem of lasting life. So, mostly, it seems to me, always when it stands alone, olive stem supporting green globe as sturdily as Atlas his world's burden. There is no other of our dooryard familiars, bush or tree, that is so certainly symbol of abidingness, not pine or cedar, cypress or holly, arbor vitae or yew, for all that one and all are in form or lasting leafage symbol of life to many people.

It is thus, standing by itself, that I love the box tree best. Not a single tree alone, but a pair, one on either side of the farmhouse door-stoop. So have I found it, again and again, in the long-settled river valleys and along the seaboard of the Atlantic, from Massachusetts to Virginia, these always and everywhere its largest specimens. Oldest, too, perhaps, but I am not sure. It may be that the little bushes of the hedge or border, dwarfed through clipping and crowding, are as old or older. Planted as I love it, one bush on either side of the home's front door, it has not the aristocratic suggestion of the box border. There is a distinction about a box-lined walk, even in the short walk one so often comes upon from old turnpike to country house that is scarcely back far enough to be out of the dust of the highway, a distinction something more than that which comes from the sense of permanence that box cannot but impart. In my experience it is not generally the oldest houses that boast such walks, but those of the early nineteenth century, houses that are, in Pennsylvania, often of Italianate architecture, houses in New

England often that pile up higher than the low-set buildings that have an unmistakable eighteenth-century air. Such box-approached homes, even though they have no more than an acre for lawn and garden, have about them a suggestion of the manor, but it is only the great country places where there is space for mazed paths and parterred garden that can gather to themselves the full distinction box may give. Such were Vaucluse just out of Newport, the DuBarry estate on the Wissahickon Hills, and such, fortunately, still is Mount Vernon by Potomac.

Visit any one of these, and ever afterward box will be to you truly a "shrub manorial." It was a sure instinct that led Galsworthy to put the scene of Harbinger's stormy love-making to Lady Barbara between the clipped box of the gardens of Sea-House. I refer to this episode, which I feel an intrusion of Old England into our greater New England, just because I always feel that things manorial, beautiful as they are, and justified though they be by our history, are, when all is said, a little dissonant to our American life. The gables of a square-built stone house whose lichened olive walls are cool under great sycamores, and beyond this corn-fields in tassel stretching acre on acre over fat level land along the placid river: this is America. And hill pastures with sheep above a silvered house of clapboard and moun-tains through their scattered spruces, this, too, is America; and a hundred other scenes of our countryside; but hardly the manor, hardly Mount Vernon, hardly the DuBarry place, hardly Vaucluse.

The comfortable home of 1830 with its box walk is more typical of our Atlantic seaboard life, but most typical the door-side pair of bushes. It is true, I think, for all my doubts, that these door-side boxes are the oldest of our box. It was costly, in the early days, to bring out the rooted cuttings from England, and all told those that were brought could not have been many. Nurseries before the Revolution were few, and most of them little plots existing only for the adornment of the place that cherished them, so it could have been generally possible only for the wealthy to plant box extensively. The "average man," on farm, or little lot of little town, must content himself with the door-side pair. If these are not, the Eastern seaboard over, older than those on the manorlands, they are certainly larger, as they are certainly older than those of the "comfortable" homes.

It was in such a "comfortable" home that I, at seven, fell under the fascination of box, or rather of box walk and box borders. Certainly that walk and those borders, when I came to know them in 1878, of bushes knee high and almost as wide as high, were not so beautiful as the great balls of the door-side boxes of the one-time farmhouse where I now live; but they were good to me then; and they bred in me a love of box that has grown with the years. Those bushes are gone now, along with the Norway spruces, blackbird haunted, that flanked them, and the old square house has been so remodeled that its circumambient trees, survivors of the generation of Norway spruces, could not recognize in it their coeval so bright-hued and Italianate. Now it is "colonial," pebbledashed colonial, yellow-pebbledashed colonial; then it was pink-roan of plaster for two stories and cream for the third, of flat roof far overhanging and bearing on its center glassed cupola much berodded against the lightning. The tin of this roof, out of sight, was modest-hued, but the concavely curved porch roof that extended across the front of the house had its tin bands alternately bright green and brighter yellow. The elaborate cast iron of the supports of this roof was of a duller green, almost blending with the green of the box that bordered the beds on either side of the door-step. Just outside these beds a red gravel path ran parallel to the grass-grown street, and at right angles the path, box bordered and red graveled, that was my childhood's delight, ran from porch steps to street steps. As you looked at the house from the street the effect was of lines parallel and at right angles, the lines of the heavy blue stones that topped the street wall, the line of porch roof, the line of house roof, the line of cupola roof; the fences, the squarely-trimmed box walk: only the spiring cones of the spruces disturbed the many squares the eye found in place and house, and even these trees rather added to than disturbed the formality of it all. So formal was all, indeed, that even the pink-roan plaster of the house could not affect the serenity of the place, and, as for the red gravel —well, I must own, gay though it was, and inharmonious with the pink-roan house, it set off the box as walk of gray slag or of ashes grown green with moss may not do.

It is with some such place as this that would be bizarre were it not formal that I not infrequently associate the box walk, in the valleys of Delaware and Hudson. Often again it is with a type of house that resembles a child's bank as children's banks were thirty years ago, partly Italianate, partly classical, with a third story that is no more than airspace, roof that ends flush with the wall, corbelated cornice, and little portico over the front door. Still again I associate box with the pillared type of house that approximates more or less the Greek temple. Box borders I have known, of course, by houses other than these, houses older and houses of more recent construction. They are usual by the long low white-washed houses of Germantown, such as Wyck, whose bushes a hundred years old are a hundred years younger than the house. They are to be found by that heavy-gabled house of gray micaschist, past whose gardens

I go daily to the train, a house on the whole inoffensive for the time its date stone tells us it was built, 1869.

With all these houses I refer to I have associations, but none so pleasant as those with the now vanished box walks and borders of that pink-roan Italianate house of happy memories. Those were good days I lived there, the days of seven to fifteen; there are none happier in life. One is sturdy enough by seven to "gang his ain gait" in little matters; one is too young at fifteen, if one's family is still between him and the world, to be troubled with problems. For me these days between seven and fifteen were days of unresting energy, energy that must find vent in those hours when other boys are not about, in finding employment for itself. Such employment I found, for part of the time, about the box hedges. It was more fun jumping them with other boys to jump with, but it was fun to jump them even when alone.

It was a never-failing amusement, too, to tease the spiders, gray fellows with backs red-beaded, that built funnel-shaped webs up from the depths of the boxes to spread out circular-wise on their green tops. How fiercely the spiders would rush out from their concealed lurking place when you agitated, howsoever gently, the outermost edges of their web, and how much more precipitately they would rush back when they found boy instead of fly or moth the agitator. The gardener thought these webs bad for the box, and broomed them off whenever he swept the paths, but inasmuch as his heart was with the vegetables far rearward in the place, he attacked the spiders too seldom to cause them to lose heart, and to spread their snares elsewhere. To offset what sweepings he made of their webs I fed them at times with what I thought would content them, flies, moths, mosquitoes—and now and again a burly rosebug, which gave them a good fight, or a bronze-green June bug that they fled from in terror.

In the red gravel between the box rows ants sunk their shafts, throwing up little hills of red powder that were of the exact hue of the sand in the hourglass by which father's eggs were cooked. I never counted the ants, however, among box insects, as their excursions were more often further afield than through the gloom of the box branches. Of the box rows, however, was the great wasp, two inches long, we called "locust killer," whose presence brought a spice of danger to the security of the box shelter. There was no rattlesnake or copperhead hereabout, or here in the box we should have found them as you find them in the great box hedges in the mountain valleys of central Virginia. And as such dangers were absent, and boyhood had no sense of tetanus germs lurking everywhere in the soil, local lore made the great wasp possessed of a deadly sting that our lives might not be without some savor of "the tempestuous loveliness of terror." We believed, or at least more than half believed, that if one of these vivid fellows of orange-red, black banded, stung us, we would soon be as the locusts they flew with so lumberingly to their holes under the box roots. Often I lay close by to watch them come home from hunting, and, as the days passed, I learned to know what meant that rasping sudden end of cicada song, for almost immediately after its ceasing would come the "locust killer," heavy flighted with the weight of prey, to alight on the gravel and drag the victim in after her into her shaft. Sometimes the wasp would drop the locust on the path and with angry buzzing would hover around, or drop onto the ground and, with wings jerking up and down, rush around in search of him. Tigerish in colors and tigerish in ways though she was, her goings and comings were as welcome to the spirit, tired of the too ordered beauty of the trim box, as are the lightning's zig-zags at eve across the too untroubled skies of long summer days of cicada song and unmoving air. It is on such days now I remember the "locust-killer," wondering why I so seldom see one and whether that is because of less heeding eyes and ears or of a real lessening of the clan.

On the larger places to right and left of us, and on the places to right and left of these again, were box walks and borders too. Of these four other gardens the most interesting to me was that next door eastward of us. Its borders were clipped so close they never reached more than six inches in height during the ten years they were familiar to me over the fence. As I remember those borders they seem to have been all summer long in fresh leaf, and it may well be that they were, for the old Alsatian gardener, Wilhelm Herrise, always rises before me, shears in hand, as he in the flesh so often rose from behind the hemlock hedge that surrounded the garden when I stole over there for the white grapes that grew so plump and luscious on the trellises within the box borders. I mention the grapes to prove that sometimes, at least, the box is maligned as a leecher-out from the ground of all sustenance for any other living thing about its stand. It may be that the grapes grew to such perfection because of the art of Wilhelm Herrise, or because the box was so closely clipped it made little root, but I have seen flowers of all sorts, many of them of tender sorts such as sweet peas and foxgloves, growing lushly cheek by jowl with box.

That they are benefited by it I would not for a moment maintain, though on my own acre ferns flourished for years under one great bally bush; and that it is avoided by birds, at least that the dwarf box is, I think, incontestable. Though a zealous egg collector for only a few years of boyhood, I have always had an eye open for nests as for box, and yet, despite my interest in the two I have never found them in conjunction but once. That is, I have but once found a bird's nest in dwarf box. That once was in the low box of the path-side of my boyhood's home, the roan-pink house, where the chipping sparrow that more usually preferred the extremity of a low spruce limb, or the *pyrus japonica,* or the vines of the porch, by some chance built. I cannot remember now if that effort was of happy fruition, but I well remember the morning when brushing against the low hedge, heavily drenched with dew, I flushed from it the bird I had seen again and again on the gravel walk, and, parting the dark green foliage, disclosed the four eggs, little, and of so in-tense a blue that the dark spots were bitten out against that background with a distinctness I have never again noticed. The cup in which they rested, lined with black hair, was no more than fifteen inches from the ground, so low that puss would not have had to climb to snatch the sitting mother in her mouth or to extract the young by insinuated paw.

Friends, wise in the lore of nests, to whom I have ap-pealed for their experience as to birds nesting in box, have in but one instance out of seven come upon more than one nest in a lifetime; and not one of these but has been on the prowl for birds from seven to seven times seven. It may be of course that, as one suggests, the conformation of the box bush with but slightly divided stems offers situation for no nests larger than a chipping sparrow's, but the fact that an-other man has found a catbird's nest as well as a chipping sparrow's and a song sparrow's partly explains away this theory. My own theory had been that it was the lowness of the bush and its dry bitter odor combined that alienated the birds. Certainly the tall tree-growing box with its more wide-spreading limbs does not confine its odor as does the tight-growing dwarf box, and certain also is it that this variety does harbor many more nests. In the tall box I have found nests of robin and wood robin and cardinal, as have several of the men to whom I appealed. That the odor is not wholly disagreeable or that the protection afforded by the conformation of the low box is an offset to it is proved by the fact that in winter birds are not at all averse from roosting in it. In my dooryard's largest box, a globe that was halved by the ice storm of 1902, snow birds roost on and off all winter through. And here, too, I have found as fellows to the snow bird winter wren and songsparrow seeking refuge from storm and cold.

Jealously guarded, no doubt, was that chipping sparrow's nest in the box walk hedge, like all other nests on the place, by the small boy that watched it, but not so other nests on other people's places. Forays were made, for instance, to Thomas's not five minutes away by the hurried procedure of boy on hunting bent. Here were woods where any adventures were possible, stream and pond where were roach and muskrat, and beyond these a lawn that sloped up between wood and pasture to banks of laurel and rhododendron against hollies and high hemlocks. A row of cedars and arbor vitae cut off the lawn from the pastures northward, a row famous for nests of robins, cedar birds, and cardinals; low "ornamental" shrubs of many sorts clustered here and there on the skirts of the lawn, harboring catbirds and brown thrashers; grackles were in the high hemlocks and Norway spruces beyond; wood robins and vireos, realizing that here they were protected, dwelt in the low limbs of woodstrees southward of the lawn. There was assuredly good hunting here, but it was as dangerous as it was good. It was not only forbidden ground, all Thomas's was that, but forbidden ground trespassing on which you were sure to be chased, as nine times out of ten you would not be chased from the forbidden ground on the town side of the brook. The little gardener, a swift runner and black-avised like a pirate, maintained his dignity and reputation for rigor by refusing to see or hear us if we kept our side of the brook and our voices below concert pitch. Once espying us out on the lawn, however, he came after us at a gait that made the gaining of the high boarded boundary fence of Thomas's seemingly impossible. Yet, somehow, that fence was always gained ahead of the gardener. Why, in those old days, I could never understand, for his reputation was such that I never doubted the sincerity of his intention to catch us. Catch us, however, he sometimes did, if we penetrated beyond the lawn top's laurels and rhododendrons. Further than that, past the tall quick-growing box trees of the "hidden walk," across the carriage road and through the gap in the hemlock hedge to the "box garden," no one was hardy enough to adventure. Even to-day as I walk through that overgrown path between the boxes and the laurel, or loiter a moment in the "box garden," on my way to the train, when all Thomas's is public park, I am sometimes seized with a sudden sense of peril, so ingrained in me is dread of that proximity, even to-day when all old adventures in Thomas's are buried under the weight of years. Yet little seems changed here. The woodstrees look as of old, the laurels little taller, the hedges of hemlock and box just about as they were. Of course, I was not in the old days too familiar with the hedges; I knew them then only from the fence-top on the road that ran along the garden's end opposite that I approached from the lawn slope; but I have found it often thus with places known in childhood. You were little then, and trees and bushes magnified themselves in your imagination, and, too, I think, even to your outward eye, and when you see them again after many years, when they are really greatly grown, they appear to you as no larger than they did to you of old.

The clipping that the box of this garden has been subjected to, year after year, has, I think, as a matter of fact, kept it down to about what it was when I knew it in the late seventies. It was planted at the time the creator of the place built his first house here in 1858. The house stood between garden and hidden walk on the lawn top, where its owner, greatly devoted to what he liked to call "the vegetable world," could overlook from one or another of its windows the progress of his protégés. There after ten years his wife died, and he shut up the house never to enter it again. In due time he was consoled in orthodox fashion by that "deceased wife's sister." A home they must have, so the new heavy-gabled house I have referred to with the date stone 1869 was built and the former home allowed to fall into decay, until it was little more than a ruin vine-overgrown and infested with English sparrows. It was torn down only a few years ago. The box in the garden remains much as it was when the house was abandoned. Indeed I doubt if it has had opportunity to heighten or broaden since then, for winter-killing as well as clipping has had its will of it.

A neighbor who remembers the box in his own garden since 1874 can see little change in it other than that brought about by the replanting where it was winter-killed or had died out in the long years since then. His mother, at nearly ninety, recalled that it was smaller when she first knew the place about 1850, but it seemed to her to grow with much less vigor than did the older box that was in the garden but that was done away with in "improvements" that were made in the seventies.

Such "improvements" are, as I have intimated above, all

too frequent. And even where the box falls in with the scheme of new landscape gardening it has been removed from many places simply because it has grown unkempt or straggling with age. It will recover from winter-killing, often, if given a chance, and careful wiring will restore a bush that has lost its heart. But the typical American of to-day finds it hard to wait. If anything in his garden fails at all, he must out with it and replace it with another specimen or something "equally as choice." If he would have box at its best he must take the trouble to keep heavy snow off it, but this he seldom will consent to do, thinking perhaps that what cannot protect itself should be left to its fate. So it is, I believe, that he so seldom fashions it into any sort of topiary work. It is too difficult to keep in form and vigor through our hard winters.

Oldest, least, most formal, of box gardens that I know is one some five miles as the crow flies from this of my neighbor's on the Wissahickon Hills. This trim little fellow is laid out in two contrasting halves just under the lea of a country parsonage whose aspect would tell you it was early eighteenth century even if the records did not state that it was built in 1713. When you step into this box garden from the piazza that has been added to the old stone house you have your choice of visiting first either the one half or the other. You may inspect the half before you or enter the broad arbor, grape covered and low, running halfway the garden's eastern side, that shuts out the sun dial and brick parterres of this nearer half, and ushers you out on the path that bisects the garden. Your impatience deciding in favor of the nearer half, you enter a path through box borders, between greenhouses and bricked parterres.

Already your glance has fallen on the sun dial set in this half's very center, fifty feet from either side of the garden and thirty-seven and a half feet from garden end and walk that divides the whole in two. So formal is all that the impulse is irresistible to pace off the distances. But first you note the four bally boxes attendant upon the sun dial, the curious shapes of the bricked-in parterres of snapdragons and verbenas, now in full bloom, of pink and roses whose bloom was gone with June, parterres of circles and balancing ells. You note, too, that the bally boxes about the sun dial in the center are balanced by equally bally fellows just within the outer borders that enclose long, narrow beds about the garden's confines.

These things noticed, your eye seeks the other half of the garden to find what there is there to balance the formalities that have just been delighting you. You note the vine-covered summer-house that balances the sun dial amid the bally boxes; the long, narrow outer beds that are a counterpart of those you first inspected; the box-lined diamonds that balance the two brick circles; and then the rose-grown trellis at the further end of the garden to delimit that half as the greenhouse wall does this. Throughout perfect balance of outline is maintained, though there is a feeling, because of the clustering of box in the further half, that these brick-lined segments about you, without shadows or darkness of color, lose something of effectiveness by the contrast. Had the two halves been reversed, the difference would have been more accentuated. As it is, you pass from the less interesting to the more interesting and so avoid any bathetic effect.

The English gardener, haitch-less, wizened, of red hair bleaching out, who presides over it, thinks it well enough for America, but a poor garden compared to those he knew in Bedfordshire in boyhood. With the greatest politeness he explains that you cannot expect much in box gardens in so young a country, a country only two hundred years old, and one with winters so severe. It was the snow and ice lying on these borders, he continues to explain, the two hard winters the place was tenantless, that killed out their centers here and there. Before that he had heard tell the borders were perfect for three generations. If the place goes back to 1713, he says, so may the garden, for the box would look to be two hundred years old. It has been clipped again and again, he says, and not often enough at that, but if he is right as to the age of the box its condition speaks good care, indeed, on the part of the Presbyterian parson whose home this was in old times.

Is it only my own associations with box, I wonder, that bring me such heartsease when I dwell upon it? I do not know, but I do know that the shaping of boxwood into flutes and oboes was for years the daily task of the old maker of woodwind instruments, my grandfather. His ear, correct as a tuning fork, is, alas, not mine, but other of his traits are, for better and for worse. May it not be, then, that the love with which he labored so to fashion the boxwood that it might voice rightly the Bach and Beethoven that were his adoration passed over in its entirety to the wood itself and so was passed on through his son to the third and even to the fourth generation of his descendants. That his concern for box was so great as to amount to liking, my boyhood's toys, the chessmen that he made of it, bear witness; and the stands for "the philosophical and magnetic apparatus," in the inventing of which he spent his years after threescore, and too many of those before threescore for the prosperity of his family. The box he used, was, of course, not our dwarf box, nor yet our tree box, plain or variegated, but the great tree box of the Eastern Mediterranean. This great tree box he never knew as "standing timber," nor does his grandson, save in such lesser specimens our country's climate and brief

age can afford. Now and then, however, from some source
explicable or inexplicable as may be there comes to me, as my
eye or my thought falls on box, not English parterres but
secret pleasaunces above the Bosphorus, terraces haunted by
dark deeds of assassins, close kin to those I first met in the
Arabian Nights. It was probably my father who told me of
the Turkish home of the box his father used, and for which,
he, too, had a liking. His desk ruler, jealously cherished,
was of box, and a paperweight, its companion, heavy enough
to hold down the rebellious pages of his strongbacked diary,
was an inch-thick cross section of a box-tree above five inches
in diameter, preserved bark and all through its long journey
over land and sea. Is it not likely, then, that my own love
of box is atavistic as well as individual, and that my small
daughter prefers it above other bushes of her dooryard acquaintance to sustain her doll's hammock, and to hide her
Chinese lantern, through some inheritance, as well as because of what she calls its coziness? Perhaps, perhaps not;
but so I often think as, station bound, I pass through the
box alley of Thomas's, where sings that bird whose "boxwood flute" is sweeter than that of any bulbul of Stamboul,
or of the English blackbirds Henley praised—the wood
robin, salving for the moments of my listening, with those
woodwind notes of his, all smart and wrong there is in the
world.

Long as box has been the familiar of man, I have not
found that it has gathered about it many sayings or that it
has been much used in any of the rites that mark high days
or holy days. I have known sprigs of it to be inserted in
mole runs to discourage those tunnelings, on the supposition
that its odor is distasteful to the sensitive noses of the bur-
rowers. Efficacious, however, it is not in my experience, any
more than is poke stem or cucumber or any other of the

fabled deterrents that gardeners' lore has imagined against such depredations. I have found it surer to watch for the moles on the hour and half hour, when, this same lore has it, they work.

Wreaths of box at Christmas time I have knowledge of, but it is rare in this use, though it would seem in old English practice that it was once the favorite green from Candlemas to Easter Day. So Herrick tells us, singing in "Candlemas Eve":

> *Down with the rosemary and bays,*
> *Down with the mistletoe;*
> *Instead of holly now upraise*
> *The greener box for show.*
>
> *The holly hitherto did sway;*
> *Let box now domineer,*
> *Until the dancing Easter-day*
> *On Easter's eve appear.*
>
> *Then youthful box, which now has grace*
> *Your houses to renew,*
> *Grown old, surrender must his place*
> *Unto the crisped yew.*

A blessed trinity of shrubs, surely, holly, box, and yew, and one hardly to be found together anywhere on our eastward seaboard from Alabama to Massachusetts, so infrequently indeed that you will find box alone of the three on at least twenty places to one where all appear. Holly, our American holly, that hardiest of shore trees of our sandy stretches along the Atlantic, will do well in some unnatural situations, though oftenest, transplanted, it dwindles out in a score of years. If you can carry English holly over the winter north of Baltimore you are doing well, indeed.

Neither of the varieties is a trustworthy tree in the average country dooryard, as box is, for all its frequent winter killing, as far north as Newport. Yew, either the spreading English yew, or the more upright Irish yew, is a rare tree indeed on our old lawns, and I can remember almost every specimen of any antiquity I have seen. Our native yew, beautiful as it is with its berries, deep red and cup-shaped, in our mountain woods, is no more than a groundling, and almost unknown in our dooryards. So it is that box alone of the three that Herrick sings, holly, box and yew, is in any real sense known and loved of Americans. Again I should say, Americans of our Atlantic seaboard, for although you will find old box in Ohio and Kentucky, and less plentifully in other parts of the Middle West, it is much less common there than in the country between the Appalachians and the sea. Even here in the more recently opened up and higher sections it is seldom come upon, as, for instance, in the valley of the upper Susquehanna in Pennsylvania or in the highlands of New Hampshire.

I would not for a moment claim the box a universal tree throughout the eastern United States, but I would claim it as the very symbol of long settled communities in the East that have been prosperous from old times. Apple tree and orange lily all the country born of the East will know, whether they come from plantation in Virginia or hill-farm in Maine, but when your man speaks of box he knew in boyhood then you know him one come of land long cleared, and, there are nine chances to one, lovingly tended for two centuries. Such a one will speak of box with a certain thoughtfulness, for, somehow, it is a bush that breeds thought. It may be that it takes his imagination, if he be a man traveled or read, to older countries, but even if he be neither read nor traveled, still he will grow thoughtful, if he has known box in youth, when you speak to him of it. It may drop out of his mind no more than the memory of his mother's touch, or of his first-born's smile, when mother is no more and child grown man. Why this is so I have hazarded guesses, but, except in citing the sense of permanence and dooryard domesticity there is about box, nothing more satisfying than guesses. So I must let the matter rest, in half wonderment at why it is, wholly content that so it is.

THE GRAY OF THE MORNING

for Ruth A. Firor

THERE is so much more to "the gray of the morning" than the color of the early hours. There is the sense of dawn yet to be, of the freshness of the world under dew, of the day ahead all too short for the joy that may be discovered by the mere seeking of it. They are themselves of the best of hours, these between cockcrow and daybreak. They are the hours of robin song, so essentially those that I never think of the phrase as applicable to the edge of daylight before the return of the birds in March. One robin will sometimes venture before the small hours turn from night to the gray before sunrise. Most of the robins wait, though, for the faint flush of light that spreads wanly up the east. Then they are quickly at it, one after another, until so many are singing you cannot count them all.

If you are roused out of bed by robin song, and lean on the window sill to watch the greening willows take form from the darkness, you will note one little wonder on another. A rabbit will flop slowly across the lawn. Another will flop after him. There will be a scuffle, and next you will see the two facing each other like fighting cocks. At the one instant they will rise against each other with thump of powerful hind paws against each other's ribs. Fur will fly, and they will be seen facing each other again, their positions reversed. The leaner fellow will be where the better cushioned fellow was, and the portly one crouched gravely in what was the station of his thinner rival.

226

The appearance of Lady Cottontail now effects a diver-
sion, and round and round they go in long loops, down the
opening in the shrubbery below the shadbush and up behind
the old fencerow and out on the lawn again by the sassafras tree. They move at a slow lope, but fast enough for
you not to be able to tell which is which. They are spaced
at rather regular intervals, so that it seems not so much a
love-chase as some grave sort of game, or some rabbit
ritual sacred to the spring. Round and round they go with
unfailing regularity and with no sign of fatigue. Their speed
is not great enough to make them dizzy, though you wonder
will you grow dizzy watching them. Of a sudden all three
bolt for the heath bed on the other side of the lawn. You
have heard no sound and seen no shadow of a threatening
wing. Something, however, has awakened fear in their timid
hearts and driven them to cover.

The gray of the morning is now past. It was past indeed
when the rabbit antics began. It was a time of sounds rather
than of sights. In the real gray of the morning you can see
no more of a rabbit than his way through the darkness made
known by that bobbing cotton tail. It was a time when, before robin song, the cocks were answering each other through
the thinning darkness, crowing drowsily and at intervals
rather than with the sudden challenge of midnight or the
bravado of daylight's reiterated sallies. It was a time when,
the robins and the cocks silent, the cooing of doves had a
chance to be heard, from near and far alike, and to soothe,
perhaps, even more quickly than robin song or cockcrow,
what hearts were awake to hear.

You will be aware, as you listen, back in bed, to the
sounds that presage daybreak, of the faraway clatter of
horse hoofs, the milkman's beast nearing as he and his
master make their so closely co-operative rounds. You will

hear from miles away the whistles of the valley trains, this one hoarse and that one mellow, but both at one with the gray of the hour. As hoofbeats and hollow whistling die away, cockcrow reasserts itself in diminuendos drowsier and drowsier, and the robin chorus lifts again, but seemingly from further away. You turn over with your face from the light, and sink away into oblivion of all things. You have known the gray of the morning at quarter to five on April 9, 1931.

PARROTS, PAROQUETS AND A CAGE
OF TIN

for LeRoy Smith, Jr.

IT is not always the proper association, that of parrots
and sailors from South American ports. As I sat in the auction room by the side of the inn at Line Lexington and
looked at what I thought a cage of block tin for a parrot,
associations of the contraption and of the bird with this or
that came into mind. Associations with old ladies and their
talking pets, of cursing cockatoos in the barrooms of yesterday, of green lovebirds in little cages of wood at Christmas-
time in pet shops and department stores flitted in and out of
thought.

I had never owned a parrot, nor had any of the family
connection, that is the bird in flesh and feathers. In China,
on a cup and saucer of spatterware, made in Staffordshire
for the Pennsylvania market, I had a parrot. He was resplendent in red and green, as many of the birds are in life.
The English potters would have hardly put his image on
goods to go over the sea if they had not thought we liked
parrots in Pennsylvania. True, the parrot is rather rare in
spatter. I could think at the moment of only two others
than my two on cup and saucer, the very replicas of them
on a cup and saucer that have been stowed away these ten
years in a kitchen cabinet close by Ephrata. I could think of
one on a pottery pie plate, the famous Andrew Headman
creation of 1808, now in the Pennsylvania Museum. I could
remember other parrots in *fractur*, on birth and baptismal

certificates I had picked up at odd times through the years.

The inn in whose shadow was the auction room had perhaps representations of parrots on painted tin or painted chests or jewel cases of wood. That inn had the Dutchest furnishings of any inn I knew, scenery mirrors gay and beautiful, *taufschein* and *geburtsschein* with heavily Teutonic angels, portly Windsor chairs and sets on sets of balloon-backs in original stenciling of alarming colors, and the largest cupboard of "Gaudy Dutch" china my eyes ever delighted in. Surely there must be parrots represented in some of the domestic art here assembled. I looked forward to finding them as curiously as I did to the food I anticipated at the inn, the dollar and a half chicken dinner for a dollar that the auctioneer advertised, that dinner that was to be as Dutch as dumplings. I did not find any parrots, though I poked about in so many corners I was afraid I would be suspected of being a prohibition agent. The dinner answered all expectations, save in one item. The noodles in the chicken soup with which we began had no saffron in them to color them the yellow that warms the heart. From coleslaw to snitz pie all else was as it should be, and so much of it all that the groaning table positively daunted the appetite. Pale noodles, though, are unforgivable. They are as disappointing as pepperpot without pepper. Noodles of deep yellow and painted parrots I missed in that inn's prodigality of Dutchiana. I was so lost in speculation over that parrot cage of tin I was not always aware of what bargains I was passing up, a shaving mirror, Sheraton, for seven fifty and a nicely cut-out salt box for a dollar and a half. I woke up to buy a three-tuliped plate in soft paste for seventy-five cents, but half the time I was wondering where that rounded bird cage was made and what was the story of its making. Now it associated itself in my mind with the first containers for a ball of twine I had seen in the stores of the seventies and eighties, the openings in its sides being spaced as were the openings in the twine containers. Now it seemed to resemble the central ball of such chandeliers or candelabra as you used to find in Lancaster County. That was why so many thought it was a lamp. I remembered—was it at Nathan Long's at Manheim?—a great hub somewhat like it, from which extended out arms with cups and bobêches.

It was a slightly elongated globe, this at Line Lexington, I guessed about eighteen inches high and fifteen in diameter. I was too generous in my estimate. When, at last, it having been passed over again and again as the next item to be put up, I asked if it were to be sold, and it was put up and I had bought it, I found it fourteen inches high and thirteen and a half inches in diameter. As a matter of fact it was a slightly depressed globe, not far from the shape of an Edam cheese. What made it look elongated was the two rings of tin, each an inch and three quarters wide, in which it terminated, top and bottom. The cage rested on the bottom ring, which enclosed its round floor. There was an eight-pointed star with circular center design, blocked out on this floor, and a large one, of like shape, blocked out on the roof of the cage. From the center of this roof rose a cone of tin, with a wire inserted in it, to attach it to the ring, three inches and five-eighths in diameter, and an inch and a quarter wide, that served as its handle. This ring, of a piece of tin with edges folded in, like those of the handle of a Paul Revere lantern, was separated from the cone below by a little dewdab of tin, a four-lobed pyramid with each of its sides depressed in the middle.

Twenty-five strips of tin, each folded in and each with a raised line near either edge, run from top ring to bottom ring, making the bars of the cage. These strips are set nearly an inch apart on the band of tin that runs around the greatest girth of the cage, midway between top ring and bottom ring, and they almost touch where they are soldered to these rings. A neatly made door would admit a medium sized parrot to its interior. The cage is in fairly good condition. There is just enough rust here and there in touches to show that my first guess that the cage was of block tin was a wrong guess. It is light to the heft and with a bird small enough to be comfortable in it, it would have been easy to move from place to place so that Pretty Poll might be all day in a sunny window. It has been occupied, the bird lime on the floor indicates unmistakably.

It is difficult to say why it appealed to me so strongly that I waited long into the afternoon to see it put up. It is not beautiful; its material forbids that. It is a good piece of craftsmanship, it is of balanced proportions, it is light and airy and suggestive of old times. It is the only one of its kind I ever saw. It it provocative. I cannot help speculating as to what sort of parrot it contained. Fourteen inches of height and thirteen and a half inches of width do not allow of a large bird. The perch, a tube of tin soldered to two opposite slats of tin, is only four inches above the floor. No long-tailed bird could have been comfortable on that perch. Perhaps it was a dove and not a parrot was housed in the cage. And yet, somehow, I lean to the conjecture that a parrot was the occupant. I should like to believe that it harbored one of the last of the Carolina paroquets that once visited Pennsylvania in large flocks. What we have missed by their disappearance was borne in upon me several years back by the joy I had in an escaped parrot that spent one summer and fall with us. Somehow or other, this green and red fellow, though larger than the thirteen-inch *carolinensis*, did not seem out of place among bluejays and flickers nad great-crested flycatchers. His calls were no more raucous than theirs and his brilliant hues did not brand him as exotic. A measurable pleasure went out of life with his disappearance in early winter.

The quill men and painters of *fractur* knew the Carolina paroquet, or a bird of colors almost identical with his. The proof of that is in the combined birth and baptismal certificate I have of Johan Philip Franck, who was born on March 9, 1786, in the sign of the "crab." It was in Washington County, Maryland, he was born, but that county, though south of Mason and Dixon's Line, is as much a part of Pennsylvania racially and culturally as if it were in the northern state. Hagerstown is very closely akin to Waynesboro and Mercersburg just to the north, and Salzberger Township, where Johan was born, has the authentic Dutch ring. There is a combination of printed outline with color filled in by hand and of freehand coloring in the certificate. All the six birds are printed on it in outline, the one parrot in the upper lefthand corner. Sandwiched in between a tulip in red and yellow and a pomegranate in red and yellow and green, he is red and yellow and green. Johan's parrot has a yellow head and neck with dabs of red on his forehead and a red band across his neck; his shoulders and breast and tail are green; and his wings are yellow, edged and streaked with red. Over against this I put the description of *Conuropsis carolininsis carolinensis* as Montague Chamberlain rephrased it from old Nuttall's *Manual* (1832): "Head and neck yellow; forehead and sides of head orange red; body and tail green, the belly tinged with yellow; wings green and yellow, the edges tinged with orange red."

There are two Joseph-coated parrots on the birth, baptismal, and confirmation certificate of Catgarina Trumbohr. It is a printed form filled in by hand. It was published by Jungmann and Gruber in Reading in 1794, which was, I suppose, the year in which it was filled in and decorated. Cat-garina was born in 1776 in "Frenconi" (Franconia) Township, "Montgomeri" County, and she was confirmed in the Reformed Church in 1793, when she was seventeen. Her parrots are big fellows, seven inches long and two broad, at upper left and right of the big printed heart that fills most of the *taufschein*. There are smaller hearts to the lower corners right and left. I cannot make out whether the man-faced suns below the big heart, the tulips and pomegranates about it, and the parrots, are outlines filled in or not. All are crudely done. The parrots are unique in that both are collared with a ruffled band, in mauve on the left-hand bird, and outlined in brown ink on the right-hand one. The heads of the birds are red, the necks and breasts yellow. The tails and wingbows are a pale green. The outer parts of the wings are bright red. Two black lines with black dots between them run down the middle of the wingbows.

There is not even so much verisimilitude in the other Dutch parrots I know. Two of these, secured in Bucks County, are of plaster, plump fellows mounted on a ball. Below the ball a circular round, molded like the base of a column, rests on a rectangular base two inches by three. The birds are a pair, one with its bill turned to the right and the other with its bill turned to the left. Each, of course, required a mold of its own. Both birds are yellow, with tails of red. The feet of the bird with bill turned right are red, the feet of its mate black. Both have black bills. They are seven inches long and three inches across the broad of the back. It is nine inches from the bases of their stands to the crown of their heads. They were, I suppose, ornaments to stand opposite each other on the ends of a mantelpiece.

As I had watched the parrot cage in the auction room at Line Lexington I had heard much comment on it. The two little pans at either end of the tubed roost had confirmed nearly all in the belief it was a lamp, and the bird lime on the floor had been mistaken for candle grease. "The candles they put in those shallow pans must have been broad and flat like those for night lamps," I heard from one woman. Another was wondering would it look well on the porch, with an electric bulb in its center. A third thought it might be used in a henhouse as a safe protection for an oil light if you hadn't electric light to lengthen out the hens' working day.

My own first wonderment was: Had it made its way from tidewater? Hardly; it looked like Pennsylvania Dutch tin-work. I tried to think of any parrot I had known anywhere in our tier of counties from Monroe to Bedford, but after long rumination all I could recall was one parrot in Lebanon. The thought of the Carolina paroquet was very slow coming into my mind. I tried to recall what birds there were in the A. B. C. books. "Adler, Distelfink, Gückel, Nacht-Eule, Pelican, Pfau, Uhrhan, Yelper" came readily enough to mind as there rose before me the little woodcuts on the inside of the front cover, but I could recall no parrot.

It was not until I was home and got out my Dutch books that I found "Psittacus—Papagey—Parrot" at the head of a page in the body of the text. I was surprised to find it; I hadn't remembered it at all. There, too, was the effigy of the bird, washed in with green color and standing on a stout branch of leaves and berries of red. An appropriate maxim is appended to the word about the bird, to the effect that there are many people who, like the parrot, chatter about what they do not understand:

> *Bey manchem es doch auch so geht,*
> *Er plaudert was er nicht versteht.*

Yes, we must have known the parrot in folklore and the paroquet in the woods, in our Pennsylvania hinterlands. There faded out the figure of the sailor, red handkerchief about neck, that had haunted me as I had watched the cage of tin on the auction table. There rose in its stead a schoolhouse by Deep Run, and the children bringing the master the paroquet they had just rescued from a pigeon hawk. "Can't we keep it?" they pleaded, and at their words a happy thought struck the old man. "We'll get Tinker Singer to make us a cage. A wicker cage wouldn't hold a fellow with a bill like that. We'll keep the paragey in the schoolhouse window until it is too cold for him overnight. Then I'll take him home and winter him. Perhaps he'll be well enough by spring to fly off south again. By the time I take him away we'll all know his colors so well we won't have any trouble remembering how to paint him in *fractur*."

THE ART OF HIRAM: VARIATIONS ON
BRASS, COPPER AND BELL-METAL

for Lillian and Harry Freiheiter

THE Bible puts rather a bad name on brass. There was
a splendor of brass, it is true, in the temple of Solomon,
with its twelve oxen of brass supporting the great sea of
brass, pomegranate encircled, and its pillars of brass and its
basins of brass. "Sounding brass," however, like a "tinkling
cymbal," is a figure for emptiness, or nothingness, in the
New Testament; and in the Old Testament a heaven of
brass is a punishment from God that shall blast as with
flame. The word "brass" does not recur, all told, enough
times in either of the testaments to lose its brilliance, its
sheen as of sunlight, its suggestion of a trumpet call. There
is a brightness and a blare inherent in the word, and all that
it connotes is lively, and showy, and warming. There comes
no sense of richness or of nobility at the mention of brass,
and brass-workers, many as they have been all over the
world from Benares to Birmingham, Rome to Rio, Oslo to
Annville, and in all ages, from prehistoric times until to-day,
have never made objects of art that all men have held
beyond price.

There has never been, so far as I have read, a more distinguished worker in brass than that Hiram whom King
Hiram of Tyre sent to King Solomon to help build his famous temple. This Hiram, "a worker in brass," was "filled
with wisdom, and understanding and cunning to work all
works in brass." Hiram went "to king Solomon and wrought

all his work." I read of this Hiram, and of the building of Solomon's temple, during dull hours of preaching suffered in childhood, dull hours endured none too patiently. The handsome pastor of pleasant voice could discover nothing more interesting to the child than that two and two make four. So the child was driven to explore the little biographies of hymn writers at the back of the hymnal, and to re-seek those passages of the Old Testament he had found engrossing from the chance acquaintance he had made with this book or that in Sunday School. There was no reading aloud of the Bible at his home, at meals or on Sundays, though phrases from many of its books were often on his parents' lips. His was not a religious family, even Aunt Rachel, who brought so many old traditions to the children, shying away a little from talk of godliness, as she did more decidedly from assumptions of sanctity or "unco gudeness."

As I have sat at country sales, both east and west of the Susquehanna, and watched spirited bidding for little lamps of the sort made by Peter Derr, of Upper Lebanon, I have often wondered had he taken to heart his "I Kings 7:13-51." Derr certainly wrought with a loving care and with a precision of workmanship that were all but the artist's. There have been, I suppose, many brass-workers from Hiram of Tyre to Peter of Upper Lebanon, more distinguished than our Pennsylvania lamp maker, but there is none other so interesting to those of us who are preoccupied with the crafts of Pennsylvania.

Peter Derr signed and dated a good many of the lamps he made from the eighteen-forties to the eighteen-sixties. These signed lamps have always eluded me, much as I have sought them as little masterpieces of casting and turning and brazing. I never chanced to be at an auction where a signed one was put up, those I left bids for never came my way, and those I ran on in antique shops were always priced too high for me. I have two lamps, unsigned, that I think he must have made. One is the very replica of a swinging lamp of his, signed, that has tempted me in Pottstown all my antiquing years, and the other has about it certain earmarks of his artisanry. The swinging lamp in the Derr tradition I bought from the back of a dealer's cart as it stood outside the door of another dealer's auction. It is a cup of brass with nine lines incised around it, swung in a yoke of copper. This copper holder is riveted to a rod and the rod fastened to a heavy base, so that the lamp cannot easily be knocked over. It so happened that when I brought this lamp home I found there, just come by the mail from a bookman of North Jersey, a package of books of all sorts. Among them was *Persia*, by Frederick Shobel, published in Philadelphia by John Grigg in 1828. Looking through it I came on this passage on page 146: "The Persians have no candles for lighting their houses. For this purpose they use brass cups, fixed upon rods of the same metal, which they fill with pure white tallow, having a cotton wick in the middle."

Here was that parallelism between things Persian and things Pennsylvania Dutch come upon for the nth time in my collecting experience. I have seen many Peter Derr lamps of brass that are variations in one way or another of the familiar Betty lamps in iron, but of these swinging lamps in brass only three or four other than my little treasure. Even in iron these swinging lamps are far to seek.

The bit of brass I like best of all the scores I have gathered in long years of collecting is a miniature lamp made in the shape of a tea kettle. It is four inches in diameter from the base of the arm from which it swings to the kettle snout from which the wick protrudes. It is four inches from the base of the kettle to the top of the arm. The hook fastened to the end of the arm is four inches long. It, like the wick-picker, is of iron. This lamp came from Christiana in Lancaster County. Its cover, relatively larger than the kettle lid, is nicely turned. It has a little hole in the very center. Swung from the mantelpiece of our living room, this lamp awakens curiosity in all beholders. It, too, may be from the hand of some early brass turner of North Lancaster or Upper Lebanon, possibly, like the cup lamp, from the hand of old Peter Derr.

It is in the blood, more than likely, my concern with brass. For generations my ancestors, when not preaching and writing, were turning wood, a preparation for the brass turning done by my grandfather, when, about the middle of last century, he developed his experimenting with electricity to a serious avocation. His thermopiles and the stands and cases he made for them are turned and tooled as admirably as any of the old candlesticks, and a good deal of their detail is even more carefully executed. I played with this turned brass as a child, and I collected brass buttons in a haphazard way, aided and abetted by an uncle in Lebanon who had gathered together a few in his pursuit of Dutch pipes in porcelain and of Dutch bridal chests.

Buttons of brass are most valued when they have historical associations, though they were common enough in old days on all sorts of suits from the fustian of farm laborers to the blue broadcloth of the dandies. The man who collects Civil War buttons gathers them together indiscriminately from the one side or the other, Confederate or Union. You note sharp bidding for buttons of brass, at low figures, of course, at certain auctions, and again years will pass without a pair put up. They are bright and cheery, but far from things of beauty, gewgaws at best, like beads made to trade with savages.

Uncle Seal gave me an old copper penny, too, now and then, and those gifts stimulated my search for such coins in all places likely and unlikely. I have dug up a silver spoon from a fencerow, and I have stood by as a signet ring was raked off the top of a just-spaded bed by Laurence the gardener, but I have never known the joy of finding an old penny. I have seen my neighbor spot one on his driveway, but although I have dug a good deal about old houses I have never picked up one of those much-desired copper rounds with Columbia's head and its aureole of thirteen stars. Boxes of junk acquired at auctions have been more productive, and I have gradually brought together a little collection of the great coppers. One that I own is the wheel of a pie-marker, with only the last figure of its date in the eighteen-fifties obliterated by the serrations in its edges. Another pie wheel, with a delicately cast iron handle, was probably also once a cent, but it has been so worked over all the old insignia are lost. I like these crude affairs better than the later ones of cast brass, with wheel at one end and crimper at the other. Best of all I like the fellows so great I sometimes think they must be pottery coggles. One of these has its revolving disc two inches in diameter. It is, I think, of bell metal. One side of the wheel is tooled with deep gouges and the other side with shallow gouges. The other, a wheel of brass an inch in diameter, makes exactly the coggle-mark I find on old pottery.

Our three pairs of brass andirons are all very good. The little pair thirteen inches high were in the old house at Milford Mills where my mother was born. From there they went with Aunt Ann to Honeybrook. There were no open fireplaces in the house there so mother was able to buy them back. They have candlestick turnings that vary from an inch to two inches in diameter, one of the larger rounds making the finial at the top. The next larger pair of andirons have only their finials of brass, urn finials not unlike those on the Eli Terry clocks. Below these three-inch tops is a little plate of iron two inches square. Below the plate each firedog presents a flat front of wrought iron like the urn back of an Empire chair. They came from Palmyra, in Lebanon County. The third pair were one of my first purchases. These are big and bold, wholly of brass, with heavy acorn finials. They are eighteen inches high. They had long done duty in the great fireplace of my study, but they are now features of the living-room fireplace, displacing there the Palmyra pair whose iron supports have burned out. The pair from Milford Mills lead an easy life in the dining room fireplace, where fires are few and far between.

Two little jam hooks, that slip into plates screwed to the mantel supports, are even daintier than these little firedogs. These jam hooks, from an old house across the Wissahickon from us, in Roxborough, match the handles of the most delicately turned shovel and tong handles I have come on in any excursions to country auctions and antique shops between the Appalachians and the sea. These hooks jut out three inches to the ends of their curved arms, at the ends of which rise sharply tooled finials like a miniature andiron top.

Two little round spoons hang from one of these jam hooks. They have bowls of brass and iron handles. The smaller spoon is six and three-quarter inches long from its hooked end to the further edge of its bowl. It is riveted to its carefully fashioned handle of iron by brass rivets. There is an inlay in brass and delicate chasing on this handle. The molding or turning of the handle is deftly done and the hook in which the handle ends is a thing of grace. The larger spoon of like sort is more crudely made. It is nine and three-quarter inches long, and its bowl, like that of the other, is two inches across. It is dated 1823 on the handle, which, looked at from above, is wedge-shaped. The decorations on the iron are roughly cut little circles and v's. The handle is riveted to the bowl by copper rivets. It belongs to another order of craftsmanship entirely from the first described spoon, which is masterly in every detail and in proportion and balance.

It was a rare May day of bird song and blown clouds that I bought and brought home the "cake-turner" of brass. Bought in North Lancaster it went with us all the way to Chickies and Columbia and back again to Blue Ball and Beartown, to Honeybrook and Downingtown, and shared with the sweet and blowzy bloom of wild apple the honors of that outing. White clouds and skies of clear blue above the greening woods, white pikes and great chimneyed houses whitewashed or weathered gray, orchards white and orchards pink and orchards pink and white, all were good, but best of all the little swale of wild apple blooth, soft and pink and fragrant, and the joy of this rare meeting, only the third of a long lifetime, with the prized flowers and their fragrance that takes the breath away. The cake-turner, that humble flat of brass, will, I think, never fail to bring back that day of days. It has about it, that cake-turner, the appeal of handwork and the appeal of a long-used and lived-with thing. It has a well-proportioned handle of iron, ten inches long, with a hook at the end, but with no chasing upon it. It is fastened to the flat of brass with two brass rivets. That flat, three inches by two and with corners cut off at the handle end, has two crosses graved upon it by a tool that makes the zigzagged lines of a coggle. Two zigzagged lines, a half inch long, are laid across each other at right angles, and each of these right angles is halved by another line, so that you have eight arms to the cross, each at an angle of forty-five degrees from its neighbor. These eight-armed crosses, or stars if such you choose to call them, are against the upper cut-off corners of the flat. Above the crosses, looping its inch wide upper edge, is another coggled line. And another coggled or waved line, a double line, crosses the paddle below the stars, making a design like the familiar wave motive on pie plates of redware, with the high place of one wave above the low place of the other. It is the simplest kind of decoration, but pleasantly balanced and in the Pennsylvania tradition. It stands out distinctly against a brass susceptible of the highest polish. The utensil is not, I suspect, a cake-turner at all, but one of the many pressing and smoothing tools necessary in the making of sausage and scrapple.

It is only a few years now that our house has had electric lighting. Before that we relied on oil lamps for reading and candles for illumination of the rooms. With twoscore, maybe, of candlesticks, with their candles all burning, the effect was one to be remembered. Folks who visited us when all the house was so illuminated never forgot the effect of the candlelight under the low ceilings and reflected from the ivoried walls. Candlesticks were among the first antiques we bought when we went to live here in 1900, and candlesticks were given us by others who felt their appropriateness to this house. I cannot begin to list all our pairs of tall candlesticks, or the saucer-shaped ones we picked up one by one, or were given us, always singly as it chanced. I remember the buying of one of the latter sort, of very red brass, at the Sisters' House in Bethlehem. I remember another that came with me from my parents' house, of bright yellow brass and below standard height. There is no family piece I can remember longer, not the Grandfather clock, or the secretary bookcase, not the two little volumes of Burns or the family Bible.

It is the short candlesticks of the narrow base sort that I like best. We have these of five and three-eights inches in height, of four and three-quarters inches in height, and of four inches in height, two pairs of the shortest kind. The pairs mentioned first and second both have round bases and are distinguished by their good proportions. The shortest fellows have, both pairs, eight-sided bases, one of the pairs having them cut off at the corners and the other pair with bases all of whose eight sides are of one length. One of these little pairs is so light you might think it stamped out instead of cast, but cast it is, like the heavier pair. The two larger candlesticks of the four pairs hold candles of ordinary size, but the other two pair were meant, I think, to hold the little wax candles so distinctive of Moravian services.

There is an infinite variety of forms revealed in these brass candlesticks. You are lucky if the so-called matched pairs you come upon are exact mates. They are not in half of the pairs you are offered. Some of these are larger than any we have, great fellows that once graced the ends of some old mantelpiece and held candles long enough to burn a winter's evening through. There are others small enough for a doll's house. Of late years our countryside has been "planted" everywhere with Russian candlesticks, seven-branched candelabra of poor shapes, and single candlesticks in trios, square based and square shouldered, of a coppery brass and of good lines.

It is the saucer candlesticks with which you have the closest associations. It was those with which you lighted yourself to bed in childhood. It is those you still use most in your summer home beyond the range of electric lights. A Hepple-white side table in the hall of a country house happily so situated, a cherry table with leaf up against the wall, and a dozen of these bubble-light and wide-panned candlesticks, waiting to be carried to this near sleeping room or that far attic, has brought a sense of cozy comfort to many a city-worn week-ender, unyoked for the nonce from the office treadmill.

Just when those crude candlesticks of heavy rolled brass were made has always bothered me. They may date to early eighteenth-century days, when most of the brass we used in candlesticks and household gear of all kinds came from England. Such candlesticks can hardly be the work of artisans trained in Old Country traditions. They seem rather the first experiments of an artisanry that was arising in the clearings, the work of handy men who had never served their time to the trade of brazier or coppersmith. One such, so heavy for its five-inch saucer and three-inch upright that you think it bell metal on a first meeting, seems to me to belong as definitely to the period of what I have long called "log cabin culture" as a be-animaled painting on glass I rate as my first primitive. The candlestick has its thumb-piece soldered on and a heavy round of brass where stick meets saucer.

This candlestick is, I think, gotten out by hand, without the help of machinery. Its saucer is not a perfect round as it would be if it were "spun" with a tool on a form clamped on a lathe. It must be that it was laboriously pounded out of heavy sheet brass by its maker. Though the candlestick has every appearance of age upon it, it may be only the crude work of an amateur in comparatively recent years. Verdigris forms quickly and indentations and scratches are easily ac-quired. Its shape, though, and the hammer marks upon it, seem to take it back to the days of the hammered kettles of brass, days before the coming of the lathe to back country places.

There are some good shapes even in the late stamped-out candlesticks and spirit lamps made from the thinnest of sheet brass, and weighted, many of them, with lead in their pedestals. This sort of work has, though, a tinniness about it that sets it apart from the old work in heavy rolled brass, whether "spun" or hammered out. In much of the later work soldering takes the place of the overlaying and "dove-tailing" and brazing of the colonial and early American periods.

We have three brass lamps, besides a number of brass lanterns, from a swinging night-light of small size to such a railroad lantern as the brakeman carries back at night to "flag" following trains. The most recently acquired of these lamps is of a solid brass cast and turned, with a heavy saucer base five inches in diameter and six inches tall. Its oil chamber approximates to acorn shape, but the two-tubed top it needs to complete its equipment as a spirit lamp is missing, as it is in another saucer lamp, of cylindrical reservoir, I have coveted often in a certain shop window. My saucer lamp is of very hard and heavy brass, and it could not have been very easy to handle.

Brass is always about you indoors and out. The door knob and the knocker on your front door may be brass, and the key with which you let yourself into your house each evening. The chain on the inside of the front door may be brass, the chain with one end fast to the jamb and the other to an end piece or bolt that runs in a slot screwed to the door itself. This device enables whoever answers the knock to see who is without before the door is opened. The bolt and chain is a safeguard against tramps in country places even to this day. The one on our front door I remember since 1878 when it was put on the front door of my father's house in Germantown. Tulpehocken Street was the last street in our part of the town and not far from sheltered valleys where tramps were wont to harbor. For more than thirty years now it has given a sense of security to our house, in a situation that was lonely when we settled here and is even now considered remote by city folks.

The catches on our windows are brass, and brass the card tray on the hall table. Brass, too, are the candle trimmers and their tray, and the sconces above them. There are brass candlesticks all about the living room, brass-handled shovel and tongs on the hearth, brass dipper and brass dripper on one jamb hook, brass andirons above alluded to in the fireplace, and a brass kettle with an azalea of soft pink in it in the north window. In my study there are bits of brass everywhere, candlesticks on the mantel, a box for communion wafers and a salt shaker just brought home, and on my writing table for me to play with until their novelty has worn off. Here, too, is an inkwell of brass, a big fellow five inches in diameter and three inches high with seven quill holes about the glass pot. Of brass, too, is the little traveling inkwell, four inches high and oval, an inch wide and a half inch through. It, too, belongs to the quill age, having two places for such pens, one on either side of its little container of glass. Of brass, too, are the clasps of many of my books from the great martyr book of Ephrata (1748-49) to the little collections of sacred songs gotten out by the Billmeyers of Germantown in the early nineteenth century. It brightens a room of a winter's day, brass on the mantelpiece, and about the fireplace, and in the stock and on the ramrod of the frontiersman's rifle standing in the corner. The old gun, a percussion cap fellow of more recent date than the flintlocks, is marked "S. Miller" on the barrel. The scrollwork in brass about the patch box is richly decorative. The patch box lid is brass, too, and delicately chased. That lid opens as you push down a brass thumbpiece in the shoulder round of the stock. On the side of the stock opposite to the scrollwork and patch box lid is a star in brass and a brass plate. Against the burled wood of dark red of which the stock is made the brass glows as if it were gold. On the mantel a flintlock pistol of brass shares interest with a little kettle of hammered brass, six inches across and four inches high. This kettle is one of the early ones with a wrought iron handle swung from a rim of wrought iron copper-riveted to the hammered brass. Here, on the mantel, I should have placed, had I succumbed to them at Levi Yoder's, a brass match box, copper trimmed, in the shape of a soldier's hat of Civil War times, and a pair of brass epaulettes red tasseled of those same times. The epaulettes were so precious there was a lock and key to fasten them to the shoulders of the uniform.

Here on the mantel, too, are my little locks of brass, tiny padlocks no larger than a wristwatch. They were used to fasten the little jewel boxes of painted wood and painted tin and the slightly larger medicine carriers, calfskin covered, or the letter boxes of stenciled tin in which love letters and wills were safe from prying eyes and prattle. One and all these little padlocks I have found have been keyless. Some are plain, but most of them are not only graved, but graved a good deal for such tiny objects. One, scarcely more than a half inch in diameter, and heart-shaped, has for decoration a double line of etching. One slightly larger has a conventionalized spray of drooping effect deeply cut on its face of very hard and very pale brass.

What strikes your eye first, if you are a stranger entering our dining room, is the great jug of brass to the left of the hearth. Seventeen inches tall, thirteen and a half inches in diameter and of five-gallon capacity, it was once, I believe, the receptacle into which "revival coffee" was poured from the great kettles of brass and copper and iron at upstate camp meetings. The kettles were swung on apple butter trammels or on chains from stout trunks of white oak laid in the forks of two trees about fifteen feet apart. The great brass jug was set on the ground at the fire's edge, a great funnel of heavy glass or brass two feet long was inserted in the jug's mouth, and the kettle tipped by a specially made device, which consisted of a round of wrought iron as big as a barrel hoop mounted on a long wooden handle. Slid up around the great kettle, or inserted under one of the legs of an iron pot, it allowed a steady stream of coffee to pour into the wide funnel and on into the jug below. From this five-gallon jug, tipped by hand, the smaller coffee pots were filled and the smoking drink carried about to be again emptied into the cups that all the initiate had brought with them.

So says one informant of the use of the great brass jug. Another says that it, and brass funnel, and glass funnel, were used in distilling, to catch and carry the brandy of apple and peach that dropped from the great copper worms of happy memory.

We have no carpet on our stairs nowadays, but in the days between the Civil War and the century's end stair rods of brass held the long strips and runners in place. Later there were brass beds, and to-day all our furniture, antiques or reproductions, has brass about it. There are the drawer pulls on chests of drawers and desks, with their acorns and their grapes, their baskets of fruit or flowers and their eagles. Brass hooks and brass wire hold our pictures on their rails and brass screws hold in place the great sashes that transform our porch into a conservatory.

The brass of hand-rails was bright everywhere in old

days, on locomotives, on steamboats, and on stairways in
public buildings. Bright, too, were footrails of bars. Masefield tells us in *A Mainsail Haul* (1905) that it was his
pride to make such a footrail "to glow like refined gold."
This was in Luke O'Donnell's saloon in New York, in
1896. There has been loud outcry in our land against the
saloon, some of it well taken. It had evils connected with
it, there is no doubt of that, but it was the poor man's club,
a refuge from nagging wife and children, a heart-warming
thought to the lonely traveler dragging his feet along a
muddy road. It has attracted many a good man to it as well
as many a bad man. There are a few of us left who have
pleasant memories of the bar and of its brightly-polished
parts of brass.

I had been to Valley Forge with a friend of mine from
Louisiana. We walked across the Chester Valley after visiting Washington's Headquarters and certain of the entrenchments and the sites of the cabins where the men of Washington's army spent those hazardous months of winter. The
visit had been an emotional experience that stirred him to
the depths. The day was warm, the walk heated us, the ride
in in the train from Berwyn was dusty. We were grimed
and dry when we got out at Fifty-second Street to take the
Park Trolley. We had in mind to get off at Chamounix and
walk up the Wissahickon to Germantown.

As we climbed down the steps from the station—this was
in the good old days—a bock beer sign confronted us in the
window of a saloon. "We have no bock beer in Louisiana,"
said the soft-mannered old gentleman; "I would dearly love
to taste some. I was in Munich when I was young. The
beer was—" I took him by the elbow and we went into the
saloon. As we stood at the bar, one foot on the brass rail
and our arms on the bar, he was overcome with compunc-

tion. "I should have remembered that this was Philadelphia. When I came here we had claret or Rhine wine with our meals, but we soon gave them up. We live in a house with only a thin wall between our dining room and the dining room of the house next door, and as we drank I could feel our neighbors' disapproval coming through the wall. Strange, too, for down home we always had punch for whoever dropped in, and strong enough for a spoon to stand upright in it.

"Dear me! I suppose I have disgraced you by taking you in here. And you don't care for bock beer at that. I can tell by the way you are fiddling at it. I know what will happen. As we go out we shall meet a student of yours coming in, and it will be all over the campus to-morrow that you are a frequenter of saloons."

"Don't anticipate any such thing," I said, "I hardly think we will. We met a student going out as we were coming in, and incidents of that kind do not often happen twice so close together."

He was right about my distaste for bock beer, but it fortified us a little, perhaps, for the walk up the Wissahickon.

Brightly polished as was the brass in saloons, the brass on horse harness, on the guards for oxen's horns, and on the first Ford cars, on their lamps and stay chains and radiators, was polished even more brightly. Brass cannon still make gay certain of our public squares, bringing to most prosaic neighborhoods suggestions of pirates and the Spanish Main. Of brass, too, are certain of the older doorplates, some announcing the name of the family here resident or of the doctor or lawyer or conveyancer here practicing, or of the butcher or baker or candlestick maker here plying his trade.

No uses were too humble for brass. Of it were made brads for pegging shoes and the eyes through which shoes were laced. Three quaint paintings in oil I came on one winter day in northwestern Bucks were painted with such fidelity to detail that the shoe eyes stood out like points of light. The portraits were of one family, of a girl of six in a long white dress, of a girl of eight in a square-necked dress of brownish material, and of a boy of ten in Eton-like jacket and long pants of black broadcloth. There was a background of canyoned river and distant mountains to the girl in white, and about it the suggestion of spring. There was a background of brown tree trunks and green foliage to the girl in brown, and the suggestion of woods in summer. There was a dark and indeterminate background to the prim boy. It was almost grotesque, though, to find your eyes riveted by those shoes, realistic to their last detail under pantalettes and dark trousers, with each brass shoe string eyelet meticulously emphasized.

Bright and flashing as is the display in our own house to-day, it would sink into insignificance could it be placed alongside of that in almost any country house of eighteenth-century Pennsylvania. Years ago I paid a visit with my mother to the homestead built by her Morgan ancestors in eastern Chester County. The truly colonial house of stone above Pickering Creek was pleasantly situated on a gently rising hill. Its mason work had weathered until it was one with the environing landscape; its lines were grateful to the eye, and its dooryard homey and sheltered. There was nothing particularly distinctive about its exterior, and within only the largest kitchen I ever saw in a Pennsylvania farmhouse made its interior notable. This great room, nearly thirty feet long and about eighteen feet wide, had never been ceiled in. Its great oak beams, deep brown with age, were almost oppressive in their heaviness, but they and the deeply recessed windows and built-in cupboards must have been

transformed in the ruddy firelight thrown from the fireplace midway the room's northern side. It was a fireplace
ten feet long, eight feet deep and above six feet high. There
had doubtless been benches set in it in old times, on which
folks could make themselves comfortable about a fire built
in its center. After hard freezing set in I daresay the whole
great fireplace was filled with logs.

How the old brasserie and copper work on hearth of stone
and mantel of oak must have glowed and shone when the
fire was high! On the crane trammels and pothooks held
among iron pots a kettle of copper, perhaps, or a pail of
brass. On the mantel, perhaps, stood a row of basins of brass,
and from pegs on the great beams hung other pots of brass
and copper, from quart to quintal in size, and warming
pans of the same metals. Betty lamps of copper and brass
were slung, no doubt, from hooks above the sink, or rested
on stands on kitchen cabinet and water-bench, giving their
faint light for the offices there to be performed. There, too,
would be hanging the steelyard with its two trays of shined
brass.

On a corner of the great table, beside a coffee pot of copper, must have rested the coffee-grinder, with brass funnel
and brazed turning arm, and with drawer and sides veneered
in mahogany and maple. There, too, would be a spidery
chafing dish of thin and brightly burnished brass. On a secretary bookcase in a corner there stood out, my imagination
tells me, when some one stirred the fire and light shot into
all the corners of the great room, a glass inkwell with brass
top and the brass spectacles great-great-great-grandfather
Morgan used when he had to cipher or to indulge in epis-
tolary labors. By the deskside hung vest and breeches of
buckskin, the brass buttons of the one and the brass knee
buckles of the other catching, too, the firelight, when the

flames flared up. The firelight found particularly bright reflections on the side pieces and wheels of the brass spurs
hanging by their straps from the hook that supported vest
and breeches.

So it may have been in this old room, which I have not
seen since I was young, which may not be in existence now.
It is forty years since we hunted it out, and I have never
revisited it. That great kitchen was certainly a fitting background for brass, filled as it was in daytime with that half
light in which brass most warms the heart, and knowing in
the long evenings of winter that riot of firelight in which
brass and copper flash like jewels. I do not know why the
memory of that room has been so insistently with me this
winter in which I have been preoccupied with brass and
copper and bell metal. One guess is that the bell-metal kettle
which I have, and which I find listed in the inventory of the
estate of my great-grandfather Isaac Thomas, associates all
these utensils of the alloys of copper with the Morgans.
Isaac Thomas was Ann Morgan's husband, and the bell-
metal kettle may have come with her to Milford Mills. I
do know, however, that in the pictures of that great kitchen
above Pickering Creek, firelit pictures that have recurred to
me in all sorts of places and at all times of day, I have
never seen that kettle of bell metal among its brasserie. At
sight of that kettle there rises before me the mill race and
ponds and huddled hills of Milford, with the white houses
at the crossroads; and not this farmhouse, gray and low,
in the sheltered homeyard, on kindly slopes ten miles away.

Brass workers are harder to come on than their work. I
have known well only four all told. One still conducts a
little business, largely of handwork. All three others had
put their journeymen's experience behind them, when I
knew them, having graduated from artisanry into control of

large manufacturing plants. Once, on a train from Chicago
to Denver, I met an undertaker from a town in Illinois
famous for its brass manufactures. He was full of gruesome
stories of brass-makers' disease, and of the total depravity of
brass. So, too, was the brass worker I knew best of recent
years. He had given up the trade he had been bred to from
a boy because of its effects on his lungs. He had become a
back-to-the-lander to recuperate. He was a jack-of-all-
trades. He was a carpenter, the raiser of the best raspberries
I ever ate, the proprietor of a trout pond, the genial host
of a boarding house, a general farmer, and a bee-keeper. As
he carried the sign "Honey" on his station wagon, and
peddled honey about the country he came to be called
"Honey" Lewis. Though I appreciated the carpenter work
he did for me, I liked him best for his stories. He had a
sense of humor and he had the typical American irreverence.
He was no respecter of persons.

He had trouble with "the piscatorial experts" of the state
about his trout pond. He kept it stocked for his own use and
as an attraction for his boarders. He did not sell the fish. The
officials did not want him to put goldfish into the pond as
food for the trout. They were afraid the goldfish would
escape and make the brooks below the pond untenable by
trout.

"Honey" Lewis was very sure the reason trout were scarce
in those streams was that they had little to eat there. The
authorities had cleaned out all the suckers and the trout had
to eat their own young in lieu of the little suckers they had
been used to. He assured the fussy officials, however, that the
goldfish could not escape from his pond. "But," said the fish
warden, "a kingfisher might catch a goldfish and fly with it
to the brook, and drop the fish in it, and fly back to the pond,

and catch another goldfish of the opposite sex, and drop it into the brook, and those two might breed and their progeny crowd the trout out." As "Honey" related this to me he said: "Now is not that a new one, a kingfisher as a propagator instead of a destroyer of fish? I told that warden I was going to breed up a race of educated kingfishers that could distinguish the sex of fish and train them to stock the brooks and oust him from his job. I had the hardest time, to laugh him out of his folly. I had to add a whole lot about educated bitterns and great blue herons, too, before I could persuade him to let me bring in those goldfish from Ohio. Another one of his theories was that the goldfish might revert to carp and eat up all the spawn in the brooks.

"Between those fellows and the bears I have a hard time. The poor creatures up my way are so hungry they climb the bird cherries to eat the caterpillars off them. They have the cherry branches all broken down to get the fruit and the bark of the trunks all scratched off hunting the caterpillars hidden there. There isn't an apple tree left unbroken anywhere, either in the old orchards or those that have grown up in the former pastures and were crowded with cider plums. The mother bears climb them and break down the apples for their cubs. The next thing you know they will be attacking the cattle. There are no huckleberries on the ledges because of the long drought and the bears are nearly frantic for food. They are crazy for honey as you know. I had to take the bells off my three cows and hang them on a line fastened across the hives as they stand in their shed so that the bells will ring when the bears come licking around the hives. That tinkling scares off the brutes."

Among those visualizations of things and of places of past times that come to many of us without will on our part there comes to me one of a winter barnyard full of cattle and feathered stock. As I see the picture I have been driving through wooded country swiftly, in a sleigh, with bells briskly ringing. All of a sudden, at a turn of the road, the woods break away, and there, to the left, is this walled in barnyard of cows and two woolly horses and of fowls of all sorts. The cows are ruddy under the winter sun, the horses bright chestnut, the turkeys silver bronze, the guineas pearl-rose, and the cocks and hens, gaudy bits of many-colored fluff against the yellow-brown litter trampled there.

So, too, there comes to me a picture of a winter noon, Lancaster way, of a shop and store room, close by the pike-side. There is a long sign across the front of the two build-ings, which are clapboarded and painted white, but with that suggestion of a log wall under the clapboards that so many old buildings have. That sign, nicely lettered, but with a certain primitiveness about it, bears the legend: "Kupfer-schmidt und Blechschmidt, und Arbeiter in Eisenblech." Opening the shop door to the left, you are almost dazzled by the products of his copper-smithery and brass work that meet the eye, kettles foremost among them all. There are little fellows of brass and bell metal and great fellows of copper hung from every wall and rafter or nested in every available nook and corner. Here, too, are his forge and bel-lows, his anvil and lathe, his rolling table and molds, his patterns, his hammers, tongs, punches, soldering irons and other tools of strange shapes. In the storeroom are still more kettles, brass kettles of from one gallon to ten gal-lons and copper kettles of from three gallons to forty gal-lons, besides the cast kettles of bell metal. On the shelves are many utensils of tin, coffee-pots of punched tin and of tin molded in relief, and other utensils of perforated tin,

pie-plate shields, lanterns, sides for charcoal-holding foot
warmers, fronts for water-benches and kitchen cabinets.
Here, too, is great store of cooking utensils of sheet iron,
pots and pans, and the like, Dutch ovens, drums and stove
pipe, candlesticks and safes.

There is no painting of tin done here, so there are no gay
colors, no reds and yellows and greens against brown-
burnished or purple-burnished backgrounds, to rival the
silver golds of the bell metal, the yellow golds of the brass
and the red golds of the copper. The shop and store room
are one dazzle of molten gold under the sunlight pouring
in through the south windows, an outburst of warm color
to treasure in the brief December days.

My first visualization, that of the barnyard by the wood's
edge, is, perhaps, a recurrence in memory of a scene recorded
on the inner eye many years ago. And so, too, may the other
be, though I can recall no such shop come on in my jour-
neyings in and about Lebanon, with Uncle Seal, fifty years
ago. I do recall a shop in Newmanstown or Schaefferstown,
a log house white clapboarded, with red roof so low you
could lay your hand on its tiles as you passed by on the
street. The coppersmith's shop with the thousand kettles
goes back, I should say, fifty years beyond the eighteen-
eighties of my wanderings about Lebanon. My knowledge
of that shop must be from ancestral memory, from the
memories of my forbears, if from memory at all. What is
most likely is that it is a visualization from my sight of
that tile-roofed shop in Lebanon County and from the much
brass and bell metal and copper that has come before my
eyes in my many years of collecting.

Of like sort to the joy I had in the barnyard of cattle and
in the storehouse and shop of copper and brass is the joy
I have when I come on an advertisement of a metal shop in

an old newspaper. There is in such a discovery that same sense of suddenness I had in the discovery of barnyard and brazier's shop, a sense of now being without thought of the one or the other, and of now having out of their seeing a full delight of the eyes. I was looking over a file for 1769 of *The Pennsylvania Chronicle* when, on page 231, in the weekly issue of August 7, at the head of a column there stood out:

Benjamin Marshall. Tin Plate Worker.
In Chestnut Street, Philadelphia.

I read on eagerly that he "continues to make and sell all kinds of plain, painted, japan'd and planished TIN WARE, where also may be had a general assortment of best hard metal and common London PEWTER, BRASS and COPPER-WARE, whole sale and retail, at the very lowest rates, viz:"

There are those, I take it, to whom these words, "pewter, brass and copper" will not be lyric, fraught with all kinds of intimations, provocative of romance, as perhaps would be words like "alpine rose" or "edelweiss," landfall or El Dorado, pioneers or high sierras. Those who find dull the catalogues of ships in Homer or in Masefield will find as dull or even duller the long list of utensils of pewter that Benjamin Marshall had for sale. And yet that list, despite the prosaic and lowly uses of many of its items, tells how richly stocked could be the houses of our Pennsylvania countryside even before the Revolutionary War. A thorough survey of this colonial country house to-day, a journey over it from garret to cellar and through its many outdoor offices, or an auction at that country house, stored with the accumulations of two hundred years, will prove to you that certain country families did buy of old copper work or tin work or pewter as largely as even a Benjamin Marshall could wish.

Here is what he had for sale in pewter: "Pewter dishes, plates, basons, slop-bowls; sugar-dishes, tankards, mugs, cullenders, tool and bed-pans, spitting and chamber-pots, tea-pots, cream-jugs, measures from one gallon to half a gill; funnels, water-dishes and plates; sucking bottles, French and ear-syringes, hogshead and bottle cranes, tureens, standishes, ink-pots; soup, table, child, and tea-spoons; candle-moulds, soup and punch ladles; pepper casters, mustard-pots, salt-cellars, pocket-bottles, porrengers, barbers' pots and basons, wash-stand do, worms for stills, etc."

Only he who has hunted for the more out-of-the-way items on this list will realize how comprehensive and all-embracing it is. There are few omissions of familiar objects in pewter, lamps and candlesticks being the only notable ones, but since he lists candlesticks in brass perhaps it went without saying that he carried them in pewter also. Cranes, of course, are the syphons used either in bottles or hogsheads for the removal of liquor. Standishes are inkwells that have rests for quills as well as the glass pots for ink in them. They are apt to have, too, a flattened dish about the bottom of a central inkwell.

Old Benjamin lists few items of copper, only "stills, stew-pans, fish-kettles, Dutch ovens, plate warmers, tea kettles, chocolate and coffee pots, chafing dishes, sauce-pans, jugs, etc." I describe a great jug I have of brass elsewhere in this article. They are, in my experience, very rare, only two or three little jugs in brass, and this one great one I have, ever coming my way. The Dutch oven is a bake-oven in little and on legs that is set just in front of the open fire. It has, of course, a closely fitting lid to cover it, and sometimes, wings of metal angling out at either side of it from a back piece, to catch and convey the heat from the open fire to the back of the oven. If it has these wings and this back, the Dutch oven does not have to be turned in the baking so that both sides of the bread or cake may be evenly done.

Under brass, Mr. Marshall has for sale: "Warming-pans, coffee-pots, scales and weights, mortars and pestles, jaggers; variety of candlesticks; brandy, wine, beer and other cocks; bag-locks, snuffers and stands; flour and pepper boxes; cloak-pins, chaise nails, chafing dishes, curtain-rings, etc." Among these objects few, I think, are unfamiliar to-day. A commoner name for "jagger" is pie-wheel, the wheel used in trimming off the pie dough at the edge of the pie-dish or plate and for ornamenting it with jagged lines of decoration. At the handle's end of the "jagger" is often a crimper to use in putting another design around the edge of the pie. A bag-lock is a padlock.

Benjamin Marshall had much else for sale. He does not classify it, but lumps together, in the longest paragraph of his advertisement tin and copper, brass and bell metal, and steel and iron. It fills eighteen lines of *The Pennsylvania Chronicle*, this omnium gatherum paragraph. It offers: "Tin'd plates, iron, steel and brass wire; bell metal kettles, painted and plain scale beams; money scales and weights in boxes, brass and iron chain, copper and tin'd rivets, bar copper, sheet brass, spelter, bismuth, grain and block tin, emery, putty, lanthorn leaves, rozin, neat 4 and 6 square glass lanthorns, globe and barrel ditto, cases of silver handled knives and forks, variety of scales and weights, shovels and tongs, japan'd plate warmers, waiters and baskets; steel, iron and japan'd candlesticks and snuffers; ivory, buck, bone and other knives and forks, penknives, scissors, cast steel razors, horse fleams, buckles, cork and wood screws, gimlets, augers, files, coat and vest buttons, desk furniture, awl blades, shoe tacks, chest, till, closet and other locks, magnets, coopers and carpenters' adzes, coffee mills, snuff and tobacco boxes, toys, etc., with a great variety of other articles.

"Also the much esteemed hand engines for watering gardens, washing windows, etc.

"All orders executed in the best manner with despatch.

"N.B. The highest price allowed for old copper, brass, pewter and lead."

That is the advertisement, every word of it from A to Z, an advertisement that bespeaks the equipment of our Pennsylvania houses as clearly and fully as any article ever written on colonial times. It is almost self-explanatory, though there are a few terms in it that have passed out of use. Perhaps all the world does not know that "spelter" is zinc, that "lanthorn leaves" are the thin sheets of horn that let through so feeble a light from the old horn lanterns, and that horse fleams are those little sets of folding lancets or cupping tools that one comes across in leather cases wherever one travels through Pennsylvania, bleeding knives that still endangered many lives of horses down into the days of my own youth.

It had been an interesting tour, that of Benjamin Marshall's shop and warehouse. I had been glad, too, to have seen the making of copper kettles at Cropleys or Tryon's in Philadelphia, at John Ihling's in Lancaster, at Jonas Meyers' in Lititz or A. Keene's in Carlisle. I have coveted kettles of all these makers, but I have bought only that marked "Jns. Meyers, Letiz, Pa." Within this kettle I found a postal card with a picture of what is called "Old Miksch Tinsmith Shop, Corner Main and Cedar Streets." On the card is written "House built 1793; Gotlieb Masslich," and "Coppersmith Jonas Meyer." With the card was a slip on which was written "This tea kettle ordered of Jonas Meyers by Miss Rachel Maria Kreiter before she was married, October 26, 1828." It brings back a series of pleasant episodes of long ago, the young girl ordering the tea kettle in the low shop, the making of it especially for her and it taking its place, with the good will of the neighbor who made it, among her *lares et penates*. A full hundred years it served Rachel and her descendants, coming into my hands only in 1930.

It is written that bell metal is an alloy of copper and tin, and brass an alloy of copper and zinc. There are certain brasses, though, that have a proportion of tin in them and there are certain bells that are very close to brass in composition. There are bells, too, that are of iron, and of other metals too. The farm bells that one finds on a post at the kitchen door, or swung above the summer kitchen, or the enclosed back porch, on so many of the old farms in Pennsylvania, are almost always of iron. These bells are sometimes of the diameter of a foot at the bottom and as high as they are wide. If you come on such a one of bell metal, the chances are it came from some ship or some dismantled locomotive of old days. Large bells of bell metal are rare on the farms of Pennsylvania. Bell metal is far commoner, back from tidewater, in kettles than in bells. Every properly stocked home of a hundred years ago had a bell-metal kettle, and until thirty years ago there was always a little stir in the crowd at an auction when one was put up for sale. It generally provoked spirited bidding, being for some reason or other regarded as a particular treasure. Twice I have bought kettles at such auctions and both times I have had compunctions over my purchase, feeling for some obscure reason that I should have left the kettle to some bidder in the family or family connection. The two I so purchased differ considerably in color, the two-gallon one having in it a larger proportion of copper than the two-quart one. Bell metal, from the tin in it, is generally much lighter in color than brass, more silvery, and of a brighter ring.

Bell metal in bells, too, differs in color. A little hand bell with nicely turned handle of cherry is of wide mouth, swelling out from a width of an inch at the top to a width of two and a half inches at the bottom. Its metal part is only an inch and a half high, the handle two and a half inches long. This is of a yellower bell metal than my two famous strings of sleigh bells. Each of these consists of sixteen bells, graduated in size, and mounted on a strap of heavy leather, which, when its ends are buckled together, is four feet long. These bells were not, I hope, used as neck bells, for the sixteen of them on the strap make, altogether, a great weight. Fourteen bells in each string are globe-shaped, with a slit in the lower half and two round holes in the upper half and a marble of metal rolling round inside as a clapper. Two of the bells are what we usually call bell-shaped, each a little more than two inches high and not quite three inches across at the mouth. The globe-shaped bells are beautifully chased, and many of them numbered or lettered too, to what purpose I have only poor guesses. They may have been slung, these strings of bells, between the pole of a two-horse sleigh and the collars of the horses, or they may have been strapped on to the breastpiece of a Dutch collar, or strapped across the saddle of the harness. I have seen bells in all these positions, and strapped, too, across the swingletree, as you more commonly find the bells mounted on a metal strap and non-detachable from it.

There are many other bells found about the old-time homes of Pennsylvania than the great iron dinner bells and the various sorts of sleigh bells. There are all sorts of hand bells, from such a little fellow, suggestive in shape of a tulip, as I have described above, up through big fellows it almost dislocates your wrist to ring. Few can resist them at country auctions. The auctioneers always ring them and inquire dramatically: "What does that remind you of, dinner, or the end of recess at school?" Circus side-shows, or Chautauquas, have brought to most of us Swiss bell ringers, but it is rather our own past lives than the memories of concerts that the auction-offered bells bring back to mind. Great bells recall church, Wednesday evening prayer meeting, old hymns, old folks, old days gone beyond recall. Fire bells of all bells, perhaps, have most excited us, though our fellow Americans, of extra-Pennsylvania residence, often tell us of Philadelphia that our Liberty Bell in Independence Hall is the American bell of bells.

To me, though, cowbells are the bells best loved. I heard tell of them, from Aunt Rachel, in use in Uwchlan, before I ever heard them. There were none in use, in my childhood, in the quiet pastures in and around Germantown. But as soon as I began to visit our Pennsylvania mountain country I heard cowbells. Since I heard them from a distance, just that faint and interrupted tinkle-tinkle, as the slow beasts moved about feeding, so they come to me now. They bring back to me hill pastures in their hundreds in Lebanon County and in Dauphin, in Perry County and in Juniata, in Huntingdon and in Franklin, in Northampton and in Monroe, in Pike and in Wayne. Places on the South Mountain, on the Blue Mountain, and on the Poconos rise before me as I hear the little voices of the cowbells carried so far through the rare mountain air. And of places beyond Pennsylvania, places in the Berkshires, the Green Mountains and the White Mountains.

Only a few of our American cowbells are bell-shaped, like the so much larger and heavier bells used on the Alpine

pastures in Switzerland. Most of our American cowbells are
of wrought sheet metal rather than cast, and they are like a
flattened and truncated cone in shape. The common size is
three inches by two at the mouth and four and a half inches
high. There are those who think the sound of cowbells harsh,
and one good man I know would rather have long hunts for
his breachy cows than bell them. It is not because I hold
cowbells musical, save when they are far off and subdued in
tone, that I so like them, but that they are part and parcel
of that life on mountain farms that I love most of all the
phases of life in America. The tinkle of cowbells is at one
for me with the cattle coming home in the cool of the evening, the scent of woodsy air, the voices of veery and hermit
thrush, and Venus, the evening star, dewy fresh and tender
in the flushed west.

To many people brass means first of all the brass instruments in a band or orchestra, the bell-metal color of the
French horns and tubas and trumpets and cymbals, the rud-
dier brass of the trombones, the clear copper of the kettles
of the kettledrums. As one with a thousand and one concerts behind him, brass means to me the brass of the orchestra, no less surely than that of the household utensils,
of the desk furniture, of the little objects of art, of the turnings of electrical apparatus, of the fireplace paraphernalia,
of the kettles and pots and jugs, of so much hardware, of
the tavern foot rests, of the handrails and sheathings on
boats, of the bravery of old locomotives, and of the harness
trappings and sleigh bells.

There is no brassier brass than that in the famous march
in *Aida*. It is an attempt to express the pomp and splendor
of an Oriental spectacle, and perhaps it does express it. I
am not above such brass. As a boy I liked the Marine band
above any music I heard anywhere, and I envied the boys

that were allowed to march with it the whole length of the Broad Street parades. I like better, though, the brass at the close of Respighi's *The Pines of Rome,* which seems to sum up all the power and might of the greatest empire of old time, all "the grandeur that was Rome." There is nowhere in music that I know such an overwhelming thunder of brass.

It may be Weber that led him to it, but it remains true that it was Wagner who best conjures up old romance by his brass. With unerring instinct Wagner found his way, almost from the start, to subjects as romantic as there are in all legendary lore, the Flying Dutchman, Tannhaeuser, Lohengrin, the Siegfried story, Tristan, Parsifal. He found that the horn was loud in all these old legends, that it was an inseparable part of hunting, of war, of occasions of state. He uses it often to sum up loneliness, unhappiness of lovers long gone, lost hope and foreknowledge of death. The brass is steadily recurrent and loud and beautiful in *The Flying Dutchman.* The French horn sounds the Hollaender motive at the outset, and it reintroduces that motive several times in the course of the opera. Whenever it returns the trumpets and trombones and tuba lift and sustain and add resonance and volume to the motive, and to the noise of the sea that is its undertone. Woodwind and strings and tympani are in the fully-developed theme. It is woven of all the instruments of the orchestra at its height, but it is the horn that initiates it, and suggests its quality. The Hollaender comes to Senta out of the dimness of old time, out of the storm and murk of the sea, a living figure, but stricken and sinister, defiant, tragic and menacing, hardly human enough to love. All this, all that the Hollaender is, is intimated in the opening phrases of the horn. Brass never bore a burden of more memories.

The horn announces, too, the arrival of Siegfried from the perils of his far journey; and a score other comings and goings in Wagner. All his hours recaptured from old romance re-echo with the calls of horns. The great crises in the music dramas would lack weight and volume without the brass. There is no nobler burst of massed brass than that toward the close of Siegfried's funeral march. Horns, trumpets, trombones, tubas, a score of instruments all together crash out the triumph over death that was in Wagner's heart as he saw and heard his hero of heroes borne to the grave.

There is no softer air or more haunting chanted by any brass instrument than that of the French horn in *Der Freischuetz*, the air known to all Americans as "My Jesus, as thou wilt." It is a mistake to associate brass only with great crashes of sound. It can be as gently mellifluous as any oboe or flute or clarinet. The reason that we do associate brass chiefly with overpowering effects is, of course, that without the brass such effects can hardly be achieved.

It is the Russians who pile Pelions on Ossas of brass. Tschaikovsky, Rimsky-Korsakoff and Moussorgsky all love its color and mass and sonorousness. The national hymn of the old regime in Russia brings the *Marche Slav* to its triumphal close, French horns, trumpets and tubas at one in the high lifted crash of sound. It was Ravel, of course, who heaped up the effects of trumpets and horns, trombones and tubas, bells and cymbals at the end of *Pictures at an Exhibition*, but the suggestion for the volleying crescendos was in the piano score Moussorgsky wrote with the Great Gate of Kiev before him. Rimsky-Korsakoff goes completely Asiatic in the splendor of brass in the tumults of *Schehérazade*. The heavy burst of brass at the opening of *Finlandia* is of another sort again. Sibelius has given it the quality of nature in the wildest uproar, the quality of thunder, of waves and wind gone mad, of the breaking of ice jams in rivers or of avalanches loosed from the sides of alps.

That crash of brass in *Finlandia* is too titanic for the last word on what is, after all, a homey and comforting companion of man. Brass, the brass of household gear, needs another farewell than that. It might do to say good-by to brass with the beating of brass kettles to hive bees. More than one memory of that ancient rite is with me. One takes shape as a picture of the homeyard on a May morning. All the family are out in the warming sunshine: mother with a brass kettle and a ladle with which to pound it; cook with the wash boiler of copper and a stove lifter to play a tattoo upon it; the children each with a bell-metal kettle and a spike to waken its clear notes. Father, with ladder, barrel hoop, burlap bag and pruning saw, and half abashed at what is ahead of him, completes the army with designs on the mass of goldey-black bees hanging high up in the Catherine pear. The brazen clamor, or a kindly providence, has brought the whirling hordes to rest, but how now to saw off the drooping branch on which they are lodged and to drop the bunched thousands of the swarm gently into the hooped mouth of the bag?

More intimate to me, though, as symbol of brass, is the saucer candlestick that generations of children have carried to light them to bed. All of such candlesticks as are really old have, I take it, seen this service. They were so used in all Pennsylvania homes, city and country, a hundred years ago, and in many a country home, even to-day, the figure of the child mounting the stairs, driving the darkness before him by the light in his hand, still haunts the memory of his parents now that some far place of the great world has swallowed him up. Many times, too, that experience, that nightly adventure, has, in after years, flashed back into the mind of the man who was that child, when, at touch of a push button, the staircase and the upper rooms of his house have filled with the glare of electric light.

Even in the country houses of old folks the candlestick is passing, though there are enough of us yet left who were born to its uses to keep it the object in brass most closely associated with our experience. As long, however, as short circuits and strikes and lightning may put power houses out of business we must keep candles at hand, and candlesticks. So it may happen that the little figure in the white night-gown, brass candlestick in hand, climbing the stairs to bed, bringing yellow light to upper rooms, white-washed, or to some attic of white pine reddened with age, may recur often enough to keep it a part of the memories of men. The machine age has not yet reached its millennium.

OF SHADBUSHES, SHAD AND
OCTAGONAL SCHOOLHOUSES

for Harry Wharton Shoemaker

IT is said that the shadbush was so named because it broke into bloom while the shad were running up our eastern rivers. In southeastern Pennsylvania it is at its brief height of blow from April 20 to May 1, according to the earliness or lateness of the season. Such shad as still seek the Delaware are most of them at their spawning grounds on the upper reaches of the river by this time of year. It is a waterside shrub, shadbush, or certain varieties of it, often growing along rivers and streams, and it was its presence, no doubt, by the riverside in old days when there were more shad and their runs were longer, that led folks to associate bush and fish.

Shadbush is a name very widely known, and even among people none too learned in shrubs and flowers. My own family were far from being botanists, but both Aunt Rachel and Mother knew the bush. In the days of their youth the run of shad in the Delaware was an event of the year. Fresh fish in winter were far to seek. There was some fishing through the ice, but such pickerel and perch as were thus caught only seldom went further than the families of those who caught them.

In the cities, most folks put up with smoked herring, salt cod and sardines during the winter. So it was that my mother's people, who had left the farm in 1847 for Philadelphia, were glad indeed of the fresh fish that came with the spring. I doubt if they often had shad at Milford Mills, thirty-five miles from the Delaware. Grandfather drove to the city with produce now and then, however, and he may sometimes have brought home a fish or a pair of roes when shad were in season. The consonance of the bush in bloom and the run of fish was just the sort of thing that would interest him, and he, no doubt, told his daughters of the bush. It grows to this day along Marsh Creek and the other streams that feed the Brandywine from the tumbled hill country of the Uwchlans and the Nantmeals.

There was, too, the joy of bargaining in the buying of shad from the city hucksters. Aunt Rachel, particularly, enjoyed a go with such gentry. The hucksters who hawked it about by the wagonload in the day of its plenty were worthy sons of the Delaware front, of Fishtown, or of "the Neck." They thought nothing of demanding a dollar for a shad, and coming down to twenty-five cents as soon as they recognized a doughty opponent in the prospective buyer. At the day's end, if any fish were left in the wagon, they could sometimes be had for ten cents. Mother's folks always went out to the fish peddlers with a great dish of redware, yellow-slipped, made at the Lionville pottery of their Vickers cousins, only a few miles from the old home at Milford Mills. My Cousin Bess still has that dish at her home in Lansdowne, a bit chipped and relegated to a high shelf in the cupboard, but ready for use after a service of nearly a hundred years.

Another similar dish of redware did duty for years in Fishtown itself as a receptacle for shad. It is not a rectangular "chicken-pie platter" like that from Lionville, but a round pie-plate-like affair with sides curved up to prevent the slippery fish from sliding off. The shad must have looked tempting enough, in silver scales, against that background of dark red. There are three bands of wavy slip across the plate parallel to the curled up sides, and three lines of quarter moons on the sharp rise of those sides. The dealer from whom I got it said the woman who sold it him could not for the life of her see how she had never dropped it in one or the other of the many hagglings over shad she had had with the hucksters. She was to the manner born, a foeman worthy of any huckster who ever cried: "Shad! Shad Roe! Oh, Shad! Shad! Shad Roe! Oh, Shad!"

Three photographs I have would have interested all these vigilant bargainers for shad. They are of the Delaware River between New Hope and Center Bridge, and of the days before flood and fire had carried away the two great covered bridges that crossed from these points, respectively to Lambertville and Stockton, in Jersey. The photographs show shad nets reeled on the shore just below Stockton; four men in a boat drawing the seine; and the seine dragged ashore with the shad kicking about in it. There is just the faintest mist of leaves on the trees of the first picture, so there may have been shadbush in bloom hereabouts while the run of fish was on.

We of Philadelphia went more often down river for shad than up river, in the days of my youth. It was to Gloucester in New Jersey we went, in the famous days when Billy Thompson presided over that resort. Whatever else he was responsible for, Billy Thompson was responsible for good planked shad. In the oven in a jiffy after it was out of the water, the shad was served with melted butter and potatoes julienne and—whatever else you wished. It didn't need any washing down, however, that shad, not even that of the unforgettable coffee Billy provided. Even after Billy's day there was good shad to be had at Gloucester, and it may be there are still places that serve it as it should be served. Dex-

trous forkwork and sharp eyes are needed to cope with its
many ribs, and oldsters with dimming vision are forced to
fall back on the tail cut, less herringy with infinitesimal
bones than the rest of the fish. Who will tell me where, in
mid-April, there is the miracle of a perfect shad and a perfect cook found together in one riverhouse or restaurant, will
have done me a service past all payment.

It is the shadbush, however, and not the shad that I remember from a round through the Jersey countryside back
of Lambertville. I was charioteered on that occasion by Mr.
J. A. Anderson, long a pillar of Lambertville and of the
Belvidere Division of the Pennsylvania Railroad. I had
come to Lambertville to be shown covered wooden bridges.
I was shown them, over the Delaware, and over country
streams. The octagonal schoolhouse that so interested my
host was passed on the way to a little bridge over a creek
with a name almost as long as itself, an Indian name, of
course. There was a shadbush by the bridge, on the stream-
side, and another by the schoolhouse. The bush in the latter
situation could hardly have flourished while the schoolhouse
was occupied. The children would, perforce, have stripped
it to give its flowers to teacher. And yet it was one of the
characteristically gnarled specimens of *Amelanchier*, but of
which species I dare not guess. I can fathom the differences
between adult samples of *Canadensis* and *laevis*. The small
bushes of all species, however, are too much for me altogether.

Mr. Anderson was interested in the octagonal schoolhouse
because here his wife had begun her schooling. His theory
of its shape was that in the thirties and forties of last century, when it was built, there was a theory you ought to get
the very most out of your materials for building. A circular
building would encompass most space, but such a shaped

building was very difficult to build. An octagonal building would be almost as economical of material, and its construction would be far simpler. Another theory was that such a building was more easily warmed from a stove in the center than one of any other shape.

I could not help him much. I could tell him of a similar schoolhouse on the North Valley Hill not far from Valley Forge, and, by hearsay, of another on the Harrisburg Pike west of Reading. I could tell him of octagonal apses or ends of churches, of the half octagons carpenters were used to in the framing of hipped roofs, and of eight-sided summerhouses and belvederes that "embellished" the lawns of Italianate houses of a hundred years ago.

Curiously, the day I had first come upon the eight-sided schoolhouse above the Chester Valley was a day of shadbush in bloom. I remembered well that walk from Valley Forge; how hungry we were long before we came to the schoolhouse; the blessed chance meeting with a baker's cart on the crest of the ridge; the delighted purchase, and quick munching, and ambrosial taste, under those conditions, of very ordinary Dutch bread. I remember the little shadbushes by the creeks, the first swallows of the year, the peepers in the swamps as, towards evening, we neared Paoli.

There were shadbushes in bloom, too, that day I first passed the schoolhouse at Sinking Spring, but the rarer bloom of wild plum, come upon in profusion that day, rather minimized the effect of the shadbushes. There were shadbushes in bloom to-day, as I made a country round by Zacharias and Towamencin, by many schoolhouses, but not a one of those schoolhouses octagonal. It is, I suppose, because schoolhouses were in old times so often built on waste land that had been left uncleared, that we find shadbushes by schoolhouses to-day. And yet it may be that the bushes were planted there by some flower-loving teacher of long ago. Sometimes the schoolhouses are on dry ridges, not the chosen haunt of the shadbush. To-day, in that seventy-mile circuit, I saw only three shadbushes transplanted into door-yards, and not one of them so large as the bush I brought home to my own place fifteen years ago. They were not one of the wild shrubs our forbears first tried to bring into cultivation.

The shadbushes were nowhere common about this countryside of lower Montgomery or western Bucks. I saw one thicket of them along the roadside, climbing a hill. Nowhere else did I see more than three or four bushes together. Altogether I doubt whether I saw more than a hundred of them in all the seventy mile round. As I saw none the first ten miles out or the last ten miles in, that means I saw, where they did grow, not more than an average of two bushes to the mile. As a matter of fact there were many miles of the remaining fifty in which I saw no shadbushes. I saw the first shadbush by the Skippack Pike, just beyond where it crosses, with four great arches of red sandstone, the little Zacharias Creek. I saw two or three more, bitten out against the bronze green of cedars, beyond Centre Point, but it was not until I took to a side road I came on any numbers of them. They are one of the fencerow bushes in low places, but in such situations they are ruthlessly done away with in response to that slogan of good farming "Keep your fencerows clean."

If you wish to see more than a shadbush to the mile, take some backroad by woodsedges, and swampy bottoms left as waste land or wood lot. In such countryside, by fences from whose posts sparrow hawks rise as you pass, you will find an irregular row, maybe, of shadbushes, a three or four to some favored hundred yards. In the Towamencin Valley you will find more of them. It was here I found my thicket of them climbing a hill. It was here I saw the one you might really call "lancewood." In a stand of little trees one had pulled up to fifteen feet. It could have been shaped into one of those fishing rods they tell us are fashioned out of its so hard and so tough wood. Almost never, in my experience, does it grow straight in this countryside. The typical bush throws up from two to ten shoots, and twists and straggles up from under some cedar or thornbush. Here in a little flat valley that had long been pasture was the only shadbush I met this day that could be rightly called a tree. Two-stemmed it rose, tufted all over its high and wide top, with the dispersed balls of pure white bloom. The cattle had trimmed this tree in its young years, and now no side branches remained below a height of ten feet above the meadow. The bloom spread out butterfly shape above the yellow-green of springing reeds and the ruddy grass of tussocks not yet quickened into growth. The effect was Jappy, like some tree on a screen out of Yokohama. No birds were about the two-stemmed shadbush, however, to complete its resemblance in composition to the Japanese screen. The place suggested killdeer and fly-up-the-creeks, but neither were in sight, or any other birds. The cold of the morning, only four degrees above freezing at eight o'clock, still prevailed now in late afternoon. It was great good luck the bloom was not browned with frost in this low situation. In not many places in this neighborhood can you come on a shadbush twenty-five feet tall, and in full and perfect blow. In a world washed clean by a day's pelting rain, in this almost frosty air, against the green hillside beyond, this bush in snow-white blow had an inviolate beauty that things within our experience but seldom attain.

The blooms of these shadbushes were most of them of a rather upheaded sort. The bush in my dooryard, which I pulled up with a great sod of earth, not far from the Towamencin, is on its other hand, of a drooping habit. Its flowers hang down in racemes, or short clusters of flowers that are all but racemes. I have great joy in this tree, in the gray bark of its two-twisted stems, in its huckleberry-like fruit, in the yellow and salmon of its leaves in fall. Most of all I have joy, though, in its flowers, the most graceful of all on our flowering trees. My bush is as tremulous as the weeping willow, and, in the white of its pendulous flowers, more arresting to the eye. There is no abatement to the whiteness of shadbush flowers, in the specimens about our countryside. There are no yellow stamens such as those of pear blossoms to lessen the pure snowiness of bloom. The tender beauty of the shadbush is another beauty altogether from that of the stiff primness of our fruit blossoms of white. The bush on my lawn has almost the effect of a white laburnum as it hangs in feathery spray on spray over all the branches, as it sways and trembles and recovers in the little airs that pass.

The name of June berry, by which the shadbush is known in some places, because of the ripening of its fruit in June, is appropriate enough, but the fruit, for all it makes a fair jelly, is not so good as fruit as the bloom as bloom. The scientific name *Amelanchier* is a mouthful. It is said to be a variant of the name of the Savoyan species of the bush. The suggestion of such origin is of Albigensian martyrs and corduroyed leaders of brown bears that dance. It does not take us to aloof woods in late April between the Appalachians and the sea.

A peculiarity of the shadbush is its ability to stand out in its whiteness against the dimming light of late evening. I remember this quality of it from one twenty-third of May on which I went north from Boston. It was gray when we were leaving Tilton, yet a shadbush, close by the waterside, still held enough of its whiteness to be seen for what it was. It is not for this quality that I most care for the shadbush, though it enables the bush to compose exquisitely, in the half-light, against the grayness of the thickets behind it. I like it better under the full sunlight of noon, when its white, dispersed though the bloom is, is of a depth and an intensity and a softness of texture no other bloom can rival.

It is not an assertive bloom. You might easily miss it in a countryside white with thousands on thousands of escapes from cherry orchards. It is only a minor bloom in comparison with the plum and pear and peach bloom that are about in greater plenty or less at the same time. If, however, you care for the detail of landscape you will never miss shadbush once you notice it. Catch a bush of it in full blow of white against distant mountains, purple in the evening light, as I did to-day, and you have an effect in color and decoration to carry with you while you are.

FROM HARZ OR HAVANA, HAHNSTOWN OR HONGKONG?

for George Kern Swank

THERE are some things you take to so quickly when apparently first come upon that they must have had some place in your past. To enjoy them so much you must have enjoyed them before. Or if not in your individual past they must at least have had a place in the past of your people. You have perhaps inherited your delight in them from your forefathers, as you have inherited a way of crossing your hands behind your back, or of shrugging up or hiking up one shoulder, or of smiling with the left corner of your mouth when you are *in extremis*.

There were characteristics of the bird cage to delight me: its shape as of a Conestoga wagon; the neat workmanship of its close-meshed wire covering, and of its drinking cups, the one pewter and the other tin; the wire hinges of its drop bottom; the little drawer hollowed out of a solid block of what seems white pine to hold seeds for its occupants; the wooden sides and ends of its base, brass studded and carved with the conventionalized tulip so common as a symbol on our Pennsylvania barns, and with plants akin to those of our *fractur*. It is nine and a quarter inches by three and five-eights inches at its wooden bottom, it is six and a half inches tall, and it is thirteen inches by six and a half inches on its rounded top of close wire mesh. Three square wire loops at mid top and at the mid-point of either side give its owner a chance to swing it in three ways from hook or nail or staple on wall or ceiling.

None of the features of the bird cage, artistic or mechanical, however, or all of them together, account for all of the extraordinary delight I had in it at first sight. Nor was the thought of two birds billing or quarreling at the slit above the seed drawer and under the thin wooden partition between the two chambers of the cage, a large part of the reason for the joy I had in it. In fact I could not visualize at first glance what sort of birds it first harbored. The work both in wood and in wire seemed native, had the look of Pennsylvania craftsmanship, the earmarks of the loving care of "Dutch" artisans. The wood of the wagon-body-like substructure I could not be sure of.

At one moment I thought the partition was of the so-called cedar, open grained, of Havana cigar boxes. So thinking, I could see in its either compartment a painted bunting, the pair of them netted while wintering in Cuba and brought back home by some sailor out of Philadelphia. There are boys from the Great Valley who go to sea, and Dutch blood has always delighted in such gaiety of color as distinguishes the painted bunting, a gaiety of color that runs nearly the gamut of the spectrum, with bright red and indigo and golden green dominant. Such an old salt might well have spent the long days of the sail home from Havana in carving out the diminutive barn symbols and in hand-weaving the wire and in making and fitting in the two drinking fountains. I have seen similar symbols on a sailor's ditty-box.

Or the two-roomed cage may once have been inhabited by birds picked up in Hongkong, by Java sparrows, common cage birds throughout all the East, and universally loved for their hardiness and friendly ways and for their bright and piebald beauty. Their red of bill and white of ear coverts are set out distinctly against their blue-gray of back and black of poll. Was it, I wonder, some American tea and coffee merchant who had the cage made at home in Pennsylvania and carried out to Hongkong or Batavia for the safe convoy of a pair of pets for his grandchildren?

So many pictures of far-off places and exotic birds rose in my mind as I brooded over the cage I could hardly bargain for it sharply. I was driven to dream rather than to Jewing down. One picture asserted itself with peculiar vividness. It was of an innyard against the outer phalanxes of a great forest of pines in the Harz Mountains of southern Germany. I saw and heard water falling from a wooden conduit into a stone trough. I heard the wind in the pines. I saw jaegers come strutting out of the brown gloom of the pines, jaegers in white uniforms with stiff black hats and with green stripes across their breasts, and I heard "The Hunters' Chorus" from *Der Freischuetz*. I saw the cage in the hands of one tall fellow, clean-shaven and straight as a ramrod, and two canaries in the cage. The next moment I heard them singing full tilt against each other.

That remains the outstanding and recurrent picture conjured up by the bird cage, the innyard at the edge of the pine forest, the resplendent jaegers, and the two Harz canaries. It is from the Harz, I think, that the cage is most likely to have come, with two black and yellow rollers. From the design and workmanship of it, it must have been in old time it came, perhaps more than a hundred years ago. Pennsylvania Dutchland was never wholly cut off from its paternal districts of Germany, folks coming over from generation to generation to join their relatives in America. It must have been some very special occasion, however, for which birds in so pretentious a cage were brought over. The compartments are too small to have housed permanently even so small birds as canaries.

BIRDS AT BUCK HILL

for Witmer Stone

IN the northern part of Monroe County, where the Pocono plateau breaks down into lower lands that roll eastward to the Delaware, is a country that I love. Here at Buck Hill Falls, in a shack in the woods on a low mountain, fifteen hundred feet above tidewater, I spent the three months, June 15–September 15, 1905. The forest about the shack had been burnt through a little more than twenty years before, and was grown up again into a fairly open woods of rock oak, chestnut and hickory. Only here and there were left trees of the previous forest, and there was comparatively little undergrowth on the mountain top, save where the trees had been cut to make way for cottages. There was one cleared space where a farmer lived and worked a few fields before the Friends made a summer settlement there. The building of some seventy cottages had altered somewhat conditions in these woods; it had driven away some birds and brought in others, but, as yet, no English sparrows.

When we arrived on the evening of June 15, you might have supposed you were deep in the woods, so loud was the dusk with whip-poor-wills and ovenbirds and chebecs. As we climbed the steps of our shack a robin fluttered out from her nest under the porch roof, and next morning I found two deserted pewee's nests plastered on the timbers underneath the shack, which was raised high from the ground and left open below, enabling the birds to pass in and out at will. It was slow work going to sleep that first night,

tired as we were, so incessant were the whip-poor-wills. In
the very heart of the night I awakened to the flight song of
an ovenbird; in the gray hours the wood pewees began to
call; and then the chebecs and great-crested flycatchers
joined the chorus, that thus became something very different from our robin chorus in suburban Philadelphia,
although this was partially robin song, for there were many
robins at Buck Hill, too. Red-eyes were about in plenty,
and I had not been long about in the morning when I heard
barn-swallows going over and saw two swifts hurtling by.
Swifts were rare birds hereabouts, however, as they were
everywhere I went within a radius of ten miles. During this
first day I made acquaintance for the first time with the
blue-headed or solitary vireo, which I soon got to know as
one of our most ecstatic and delicious singers—the books
have failed to do him justice. Most of the many wood
thrushes of the neighborhood lived far down the mountain
side, but I heard them singing in the distance, and on the
evening of our second day a hermit thrush came close by
and sang in calm raptures at intervals for half an hour while
the twilight deepened into night. Before many days were
over I had found nests of flickers and indigo buntings and
cedarbirds and tanagers on the mountain top, where, too,
were catbirds and chewinks and chipping sparrows, these
latter chiefly in the brush where the forest had been cut off
to afford a view out over the country.

Looking out from the mountain top I could see that this
Canadensis country—as the natives call the lands of the
upper tributaries of Broadhead's Creek—is a great half-
bowl scooped back into the Pocono plateau, southwest and
west and northwest and north, with little timber of any
size on it, except to northward, but with second growth or
scrub almost everywhere. A higher point, the lookout on the

very top of Buck Hill, a half-mile from our shack, over-
looks most of the country I walked over, and in several
directions, miles further than I walked. From this point you
look upward along the rising sides of the half-bowl over
unbroken woodland as far as the eye can reach. It is somber
and desolate, this unbroken greenness, with something in it
both of the freedom and of the menace of the sea. For
about three miles westward it is growth like that on Buck
Hill, rock oak and chestnut and hickory, grown up since the
great fire of 1882, but with the horizon you come to the
edge of the Pocono plateau, a country of huckleberry barrens, burned over every few years, and having few trees
save scrubby fire-cherries and sassafrases. Eastward the out-
look was over the gorge of the Buck Hill Branch with its
old hemlocks and oaks out into the open valley, and its farmland and over upland farms to the reddish cliffs of Spruce
Mountain and Wismer Mountain and to the green, rounded
outlines of East Mountain, looking lawn-like and smooth at
this distance with its knee-high growth of huckleberries.

At the far end of East Mountain is Goose Pond. Below
the far end of Wismer is Price's Pond, and on this side of
Wismer Gravel's Swamp, but there is no water in sight anywhere. You can see, however, the deep valleys running back
into the Pocono plateau, cut out by the various branches of
Broadhead's Creek—Mill Creek furthest southwestward,
then Rattlesnake, then the Buck Hill, then Middle Branch
and Levis Branch furthest northeastward—all draining
parts of the plateau. The valleys of these creeks I explored,
becoming most familiar with that of the Buck Hill, but
spending a good deal of time on the Middle Branch and the
Levis Branch and hunting up the source of the Goose Pond
Branch in Goose Pond in the pine barrens of Pike County.
This pond is the only piece of water of any size in the

vicinity, Price's Pond being scarcely larger than a country milldam, and the tannery dams on the Rattlesnake being all but empty now. Southwestward and westward are the great ice dams on the Tobyhanna, and eastward the big ponds of Pike County.

Along some of the branches of Broadhead's Creek there is still some primeval forest, but only a bit here and there; the upper courses of all of them run through country burnt over for huckleberries or for grazing for cattle or sheep. Just below the Buck Hill settlement and about Buck Hill Falls are a few acres where the old hemlocks are still standing. There is not here continuous hemlock forest with floor bare save for the hobblebush such as you find in some parts of Pennsylvania, but a tract in which the trees are rather far apart and interspersed here and there with great oaks. Underneath and about them is almost impenetrable rhododendron brush, which not infrequently reaches a height of fifteen feet.

These hemlocks and the burnt-over woods just above them are the hunting grounds of the warblers. The chestnut-sided warbler, in my experience here, is a bird of scrub woods near open spaces in the lowlands; the Maryland yellowthroat I found in his usual swamps, but also high on the huckleberry barrens; the yellow warbler was found in open fields in the lowlands and the black-throated blue warbler I came upon on the high, dry slopes of Spruce Mountain, as well as here in the hemlocks, finding the bird in both places until the time I came home; the black-and-white creeper, too, I found in all sorts of cover, and from the middle of July on they were much in evidence in the dry woods on the mountain tops. I saw two of these birds in far separated parts of the Canadensis Valley, each with a young cowbird. To the hemlocks and rhododendrons along the streams stuck pretty constantly the parulas, the magnolias, the blackburnians, and the black-throated greens, and several others I could not identify. A pair of chats that I came across as I was listening to a veery singing—an overlapping of faunas that was very interesting to me—were as you would expect in a thicket where field and wood met; the only hooded warblers that I saw were in low second growth along the upper waters of the Buck Hill; the Canadian warbler I found, as I had found him in the Berkshires, in high, dry woods, but just over the gorge through which the Buck Hill flows; the Nashvilles, which I did not see until August 12, evidently migrants, were about our shack.

The water thrushes were always along the streams. It was very interesting to find both species along the Buck Hill, and in the breeding season. Later in the summer the northern water thrushes seemed more plentiful than the Louisianas. I got to know the smaller bird's appearance and ways of hunting, as well as I knew the ways and appearance of his southern cousins, for the northern birds were the tamer, often coming within a few feet of me as I sat by the stream and waited for them to come down past me. But I never found their nest as I did that of one pair of the Louisiana water thrushes.

It was in a shallow gully between two tumbling streams that these water thrushes had built their nest. The gully had been scoured out when the snow waters of the spring thaw had turned these little trout streams to torrents no man dare ford. Along the gully's sides the roots of a great hemlock had been washed bare, and in these roots, not fifteen inches above a little pool of water, the birds had built. Overhead a great hemlock towered, against whose rock-binding roots debris had piled up, wreckage of spring floods. Along the Buck Hill all the way to its junction with the smaller stream, Griscom's Creek, a hundred feet below the nest, and on a hundred yards further, great hemlocks pillared a lofty aisle of green gloom over amber water. At intervals the sun broke through, sinking wells of light from the tree tops to the bottom of the clear pools. Upstream a few yards from the nest there was an open space where the sun made its way down to the hemlock roots in early morning and late afternoon, but at other hours no sunlight reached the nest to dry the dampness everywhere about. On the far side of the Buck Hill, rhododendrons lifted pale crowns of bloom high among the hemlocks; the little stream flowed from under a very tunnel of rhododendron. Just above the nest the boulders and pebbles were bare of moss, the sand caught by the little pool telling how the scouring had been accomplished. The brown of the hemlock trunks everywhere about warmed the green gloom their branches made, blending in with the weathered reds and grays of the rocks, and with the grays of the pebbles and sand to make the wood-floor a gray-brown monotone save where the water slid along, wimpled amber, or tossed up in white spray. A little to each side green predominated. Trees and boulders were lichened, the stones in the bed of the little stream were heavily tressed with water-moss, and the trunks of fallen hemlocks were damp and sodden and green with decay. Seemingly everything about was damp but the five young birds sitting closely in the nest in the hemlock roots.

Glad indeed I was to see them, for it was an hour and a half since the anxious cries of the old birds and their full mouths had halted me in my walk upstream with the surety that the nest was near. I found the nest only when there was no other hand-space in an area thirty feet square to look in. Just a foot from my feet in the spot where I first stopped was the nest, but so still were the birds and so like their color and that of the leaves and fibers out of which the nest was molded to that of the debris in the neighborhood that my eye had failed to spot them. There they sat packed in closely, three on the floor of the nest and two back of and half on top of their fellows. All were facing my way, but by not so much as an eyelid's quiver did they indicate their presence, when I stopped within touching distance of them.

I had seen the parents the day before a little downstream from their home and watched them running along the sides of the stream and out into the shallows which extended far into the stream, owing to the very gradual dip of the rock that was here the stream's bottom. Beautiful I had then thought them, their chocolate-brown backs and spotted breasts and clear bluff throats standing out distinctly against the red shale of the shallows. Then I had noticed their habit of flying upstream a certain distance, then hunting downstream, and then flying up to begin the hunt down over the same ground again, just like the European water thrush or dipper that I had first seen in Keimanagh Pass in Kerry. I did not then notice them and I have never noticed them run under water like the dipper, but they chase gnats out into water two inches deep and gather larvae from the stones in midstream, flying out to them and then hunting around them if the water is not too deep or too swift.

Now I had a still better chance to view them, for the longer I searched for the nest the more anxious they became, since all the while the young were going hungry. Both old birds walked about nervously, tilting their tails up like the solitary sandpiper. Worm in mouth as they were, they could utter their complaining "tswit" as sharply as ever. I sat still for a long time and they finally came close to me, tilting themselves about on rocks and logs not ten feet away. The female—as I took it to be because it was the more worried of the two—came the closer, and one time when I had seen the male dart into a cranny of the drift pile and had followed him there in the hope of finding the nest, she got to the nest without my seeing her. I heard the young birds then for the first time, but she was out and walking off some six feet from where I later found the nest before I got my eye on her again. This was the only time the young were fed in an hour and a half. Except for the one time she fed them the female for all the ninety minutes never relinquished the worm she had for them, but the male three times ate his. He would scold around close to his mate, the two often walking the same log or stone, worm in mouth, but after twenty minutes or so the strain or temptation would become too great and he would pound his worm tender on stone or twig and then swallow it.

He sang several times after so yielding, but he was quickly away again and back with a worm in a few minutes. Once he mounted singing in the air like an ovenbird, ending his upward rush by catching a flimsy, big-winged, greenish insect, which he promptly swallowed on his return to the ground. But the restraint of the young seemed to me more wonderful than that of the parents. Time after time in my search I was almost touching them, but they were true to their instinct to keep still. The parents, of course, were in no greater agitation after I had found the nest than while I was hunting for it, for I was as often near it then as now, when I could see it. I did not disturb the young, but when I returned in the afternoon there were but four birds in the nest. The next morning all were gone. I found them less than a hundred yards up the smaller stream hidden in a dense rhododendron thicket. There they remained for three days longer. After that I could not identify any Louisiana water thrushes I saw as this particular family.

I met water thrushes along the stream on and off until August (the young in the nest I found flew on June 25), both Louisiana water thrushes and northern water thrushes. A month later (July 21) after I had been lazing about a half hour on a large rock just below the nest, watching trout in the stream and warblers in the hemlocks, a Louisiana water thrush darted out of the brush just alongside of me, his departure arousing a teetering as of young in the brush. They had evidently been there all that time, taking perhaps their midday rest, for it was now well on towards five o'clock in the afternoon. You could see no more than a few feet into the rhododendrons, and as they were practically impenetrable, I could not find how many young were there. After hunting on the stream for a few minutes the bird that had flown out of the brush flew back into it, and that was the last I saw of him. Even as late as August I usually came upon water thrushes by the Buck Hill if I went there early in the morning, but after the first week in July I never saw one there from ten to four o'clock. They sang on until July 20, late in the evening and early in the morning.

I am not sure I heard the song of the northern water thrush on the Buck Hill, for I never saw one singing, but I got to know well the song of the larger species, and other less fine but unmistakably water thrush songs I put down to the northern bird, and several times I saw this species just after hearing the song I had attributed to it. The place in which the bird sings lends largely to the charm of its song, but the song in itself is the finest warbler song I know. In June I heard it at midday flung out above the pools of dappled amber under the hemlocks, the purring and slucking of the water about the stones muffling its sharpness so that the notes as they reached my ear were clear and pure.

Recall the more musical part of the ovenbird's flight-song and you will have something of its quality.

In late July I heard it at the hour when moonset and sunrise are one. It could not compare with the song of the veery heard at the same time, and doubly precious so late in the season, but I shall always associate it with that song, and with the dawn light over the mountains, and with the moon riding down westward behind the pines. But it was even more memorable to hear it at night. I never heard it at moonlit midnight as I have so often heard the song of the ovenbird, but perhaps I could have heard it then had I been in the Buck Hill gorge at the proper hour. There one evening in early July, I did hear the Louisiana water thrush sing with an ecstasy and abandon I had not heard from it before. Under a high bluff and just far enough below the falls for their roar to be pleasantly dulled, the water thrush sang. Down here in the hemlocks it was darker than twilight, although it was not quite eight o'clock. Perhaps the bluff acted as a sounding-board, perhaps the soft thunder of the falls made a vibration of the air that added intensity to the song. Whatever the cause it rose above the rhododendrons with unwonted volume, still far from a powerful song, but so sweet and appealing that I could not but listen though a glorious-voiced wood thrush was singing not far away.

A bird I saw but once during the summer was near the water thrushes' nest. In one of the hemlocks just above it I watched, on July 16, three crossbills, which after clambering about on the topmost boughs for about a quarter of an hour flew off towards the Tobyhanna barrens. When we arrived at Buck Hill, pewees were nesting along the creek, probably for the second time. I could not help wondering if these were not the same birds that had raised broods earlier

underneath the porch roof of the cottages of the settlement
or under the cottages themselves. There were none on the
mountain top in the middle of June and I saw none there
later. The pewees could hardly have been driven away by
the cottagers, for not half of the people were there at that
time, and few at all had come before June 1. One of these
late stream-side nests was almost reached by the spray of
the falls in its situation under an overhanging cliff; another
in a damp spot the sun never reached on the cliffs above the
swimming hole, very different locations from the dry sites
about the cottages, but probably just as comfortable in this
warmer season. In the former nest the brood was successfully hatched and launched into the world. The fortunes of
the second nest I neglected to follow.

Around this swimming-hole there were veeries two years
ago, but now they have been driven further upstream, where
they sang on past July 20 and one even until the twenty-
third. Now the wood thrushes were *the* thrushes about Glen
Mere and glorious-voiced thrushes they were, too. They
sang on into the thick dusk, until eight o'clock, but higher
up the mountain, although there the light lingers later, they
generally cease their song a half-hour earlier. These higher,
dryer woods were inhabited chiefly by tanagers, of which
there are more at Buck Hill than I have seen elsewhere,
vireos, and the omnipresent ovenbird and whip-poor-will.
Here, too, were a few flickers and hairy woodpeckers. I saw
no downy woodpeckers until September 13 and then only
one, evidently a migrant. Two years before I had seen many
red-breasted nuthatches hereabouts in their September mi-
gration, but this September I saw none.

The kingfishers sometimes came upstream from the open
country, but they were oftener found where meadows run
down to the stream. Everywhere, along the streams, along

the roads, about the houses, in the deep woods, were hum-
ring-birds—they were among the commonest birds of the
locality.

Beyond the Buck Hill, between it and the Middle Branch,
was farming country—bottoms where you found the yellow
warbler and catbirds; orchards busy with cedarbirds and
kingbirds and wrens and bluebirds and Baltimore orioles,
and barns swallow-haunted, with barn swallows within and
eave swallows without. The eave swallows had several large
colonies both here in the valleys and high up the hills, but
you found them on every third barn in the lowlands and
only on every fifth barn in the uplands. One lowland barn
boasted fifty-one nests, forty-four on the southern side and
seven on the northern. There were young in some nests on
June 16 and two months later I still found a few young not
yet flown. On August 17 there were hundreds of them on
the telegraph wires and ridgepoles. After August 20 I saw
none. Every barn and wagon-shed in the country seemed to
have its pair or two of barn swallows and I think there must
have been as many of them all told as of the eave swallows
although, of course, you never saw them in any one place
in such numbers.

In bush-lined fields in the valleys were field sparrows
and indigo buntings and grasshopper sparrows, but these
birds like the robins and redeyes and cowbirds, could not be
said to be more numerous in one kind of country than another. With the grasshopper sparrows I spent a good deal
of time. One place from which I could always flush two
pairs early in the summer was a barren field of sparse grass
below a Moravian graveyard. They were frequently in the
graveyard, and would sing from the tomb-stones and from
the fence posts. But their favorite singing stations were the
tops of dried mullein stalks in the barren field. One windy

June morning I lay here under the lee of a stone wall for an hour watching them. I sought in vain for their nests. All the places they dropped down into were apparently only feeding spots. They scratched up the small stones in the field, presumably to get at some sort of insect life as well as for grass seeds, leaving decided traces of their energetic leg-work. Every few minutes they would mount to the mullein tops with their curious fluttering flight as of young birds and sing, sometimes the grasshopper note and sometimes a fuller song that I can best represent by "tweedle-tee, tweedle-tee, tweedle-tweedle-tweedle-tee." In the graveyard, loved of the grasshopper sparrow, I saw my solitary cuckoo of the summer, a yellowbill.

Climbing the Dutch Hill road that leads from the bottom to the upland between Middle Branch and Levis Branch, you pass a thistle patch where yellowbirds were always to be seen in late summer, but all summer long, wherever I went, I heard them singing in the air as they dropped over. Further up this road I saw on several days between August 8, when I saw it first, and August 16, when I saw it last, a shrike. Which shrike it was I do not pretend to know, probably the migrant shrike, but it was very interesting to watch. For minutes at a time it would sit motionless on the top of the single second-growth chestnut left where the wood lot was cut off; then spying some insect it would swoop down upon it, to return with labored flycatcher-like flight to its chosen station. Sometimes it must have missed its strike or found the prey so small that it could gulp it down without dismembering it, for it would relight on its tower and take up the watch again, without any sign of feeding. At other times I could see it carrying back the insect. These times it would deftly insert the insect under its foot and pressing it down to the limb tear it to pieces hawk-fashion with its bill.

It caught no bird during the several hours I watched it, but I noticed that no small birds were about while it was perched aloft there, though the neighborhood earlier in the season had been thick with indigo-birds, song sparrows and field sparrows, and though later many sorts of sparrows were gathered here in large flocks.

Further up Dutch Hill where the narrow stony road runs between stone walls shoulder-high are buckwheat fields and bare pastures. There were always vesper sparrows, field sparrows and grasshopper sparrows on the ground and walls, and in the air swallows swooping in great circles about the cattle. Toward the middle of August great flocks of bluebirds loitered here on their way to and from the huckleberry barrens northward, filling the air with such gurgling music as I had never heard even in spring. And here on August 18 I came upon my surprise of the summer. I was coming down hill across lots when I heard behind me low calls of "weet, weet, weet," about like those of horned larks in winter, I thought, and turning I saw scudding close to the ground like sandpipers over water a flock of small birds with yellowish breasts marked with black. As they passed me I saw that their backs were grayish and that there was white on their tails. They alighted, some on the ground, some on a stone wall, and walked. I was innocent of the knowledge that prairie horned larks are sometimes seen in northeastern Pennsylvania until I got home to the books, and I was utterly unable to identify the birds. The owner of the lot, lifting boulders out of the ground with a great tripod and lever arrangement, was appealed to. He said, "Only some kind of sparrows," and when I pointed out to him that they walked instead of hopping, he looked at me rather pityingly and said, "Don't sparrows walk?" But I was no nearer an identification than he, although had they not walked I would have thought him not so far from the truth, and guessed dickcissels, for they seemed something like descriptions of these birds I carried in memory, and I had always been hoping that dickcissels might come my way.

At Levis Falls, beyond Dutch Hill, and at Gravel's Swamp under Wismer were solitary sandpipers, for whose nests I looked diligently in June on drift heaps on the margin and on the trees that had rotted off and fallen when the dam-breast was in repair and the dam full of water. It was not until Dr. Witmer Stone came up for a day in August that I learned that the solitary sandpiper nested in old birds' nests in trees and that by my ignorance I had possibly missed a rare find.

What a walk I had with Stone on August 11! It was a day of soaking drizzle, but that did not matter, for Stone's bogging would have gotten me almost as wet on a rainless day. In the swamp to which he took me, way up under the edge of the huckleberry barrens, we made a rare find. The swamp was full of birds, swamp sparrows and others not uncommon in such places in the region, but a number of small flycatchers bothered us. Neither of us had ever seen alder flycatchers in the field, but here were small flycatchers that were not Acadian flycatchers or chebecs and that answered very nearly to descriptions and looked like skins of alder flycatchers. They were not wild at first, and we got several good looks at them. A distinguishing feature was the disclosure of grayish-white as they flew. I had been in this swamp several times before in June and July and I had not seen the flycatchers there, nor did I see others like them afterwards. We had seen them in alder bushes too.

There were interesting birds other than the solitary sandpiper in Gravel's Swamp. Scores of the water-killed trees still stood, and in their rotting trunks scores of woodpeckers had drilled out their nests. I was disappointed at not finding the pileated woodpecker here, for I had seen one at Buck Hill in September, 1903, and I thought this swamp was near enough to the large timber northward to make it possible for the logcocks to come here. The only two woodpeckers I found nesting in the swamp were the flicker and the hairy woodpecker. But in old woodpeckers' holes I found bluebirds and wrens nesting, three pairs of bluebirds and two pairs of wrens. I suppose it was in such places they nested before Europeans came to America to tempt them by boxes and gourds to the homeyard. Here in the swamp were many song sparrows and swamp sparrows, and along its shores some veeries and pewees, and often in the burnt woods above I heard the chickadees, that, by the by, sang their "phoebe" song the whole three months of my stay in Barrett township; and here, too, was seen an occasional crow and bluejay. I was surprised by the comparative rareness of these birds, and I was disappointed in not seeing a raven all summer long. The nearest I got to a record was the statement that there had been caught up in Newfoundland in Pike County seven years before in the winter "a big crow with heavy feathers on his neck that some said was a raven." This bird was kept in captivity a long while in "a big chicken-wire cage." It was not known what had become of him, but "he was not about any more."

In Gravel's Swamp the white-bellied swallows nested, too, in the old woodpeckers' holes. They stayed in the neighborhood later than either of the other swallows, and as late as September 6 I saw six of them hawking about high over the tannery dams at Mountain Home. Here, too, in Gravel's Swamp were redwings, and at Price's Pond a mile away, but there were few in all. Here, too, came great blue herons to fish, but they nested elsewhere, and here, too, I saw one of the only two green herons I came upon all summer. In a grassy swamp a half mile below Gravel's Swamp I sometimes saw the redwings, and in the fields nearby a pair of meadow larks. There were only three places in Barrett township in which I saw meadow larks, and in only one of these places did I ever see more than two. There were no grackles here, but at Stroudsburg, seventeen miles southeastward, at a lower altitude, and at Tobyhanna, eleven miles westward, at a higher altitude, I saw them. The cowbirds were the only orioles at all plenty near Buck Hill.

The huckleberry barrens were very interesting to me. I visited them frequently from the beginning of my stay, flushing ruffed grouse from those parts of them that had a chance to grow up more than knee-high, and always finding on them chewinks and redeyes and bluebirds and flickers and robins— the last three species attracted there no doubt by the berries. On September 13, after I had not seen a wood thrush or a hermit thrush for three weeks, and had concluded they had all worked down to the river valleys, as the theory is, I found one individual of each species on the barrens. A few days earlier I had come upon flocks of chewinks and bluebirds and many flickers and several tanagers—these latter all in green plumage—on the barrens, and in the second week in September on an automobile ride up the Delaware to Milford and back I had seen few birds of any kind, save crows and bluejays. Indeed, during the first two weeks in September the barrens were fairly alive with birds, while in the woods at Buck Hill, five hundred feet lower than the barrens' two thousand feet, there were very few birds. There were occasional brown thrashers to be met with on the barrens, but everywhere about Buck Hill they were scarce.

The bird that drew me most often to the barrens was a small thrush, whose only possible identification would seem to be as Bicknell's thrush. I know the songs of the wood thrush, veery, hermit thrush and olive-backed thrush, and the song of this bird was not the song of any of these. Either I never heard it close at hand or else it is a song of poor carrying quality, for it always seemed as if I but half heard it. I had only one look at the bird at close quarters, but several times I flushed it in the scrub only to have it dive into the thick growth and elude me. I started out several times before daylight and reached the barrens by sunrise, but I was not rewarded by seeing the bird as it sang or even by getting another satisfactory look at it.

The two hard winters of 1903-04 and 1904-05 probably explain why I never came across a quail, but I cannot explain so easily why I never saw the sign of an owl. It was not their noisy season when I was there, but that I heard not a hoot or the startled beating of wings as I came through brush after nightfall or that I discovered no tragedies of the nests to be attributed to owls, struck me as surprising. Hawks were not plenty until late in August, nor as plenty then as I had expected. I identified only three. A red-tail, nailed to a barn door, had noticeably been there long enough to have been a migrant; a pair of broadwings added to their family by at least one during the summer; and these were sharp-shins, of which I saw a good many all summer, but more towards its close. I saw several other kinds I could not identify, one a very long-tailed, large hawk that soared very high, and now and then hung quivering in the air for what seemed minutes.

Towards the end of August came great flights of nighthawks, but in early summer and midsummer I never saw more than two at a time. Their cry was not a typical sound of the night—you would hear it only about once a week. Toward the end of August, too, the doves began to collect in little bunches, but I never saw more than half a dozen together, and it was generally two or three. They were only fairly common.

A refreshing experience was to find familiar birds with songs differing in quality and even in notation from their songs at home. The characteristic robin song of the Buck Hill woods, for instance, was very much more subdued than the characteristic robin song of Germantown. The bird was much less noisy and self-assertive, and since there were no lawns for him to run over, his habits of hunting were different. He ran about on the leaves of the woods floor, upturning one now and again with his bill, and at times even scratching as noisily as a chewink. He came under the shack windows for the boiled barley we threw out, as did, curiously, the white-bellied nuthatches that were about us daily after the middle of July.

The wood thrushes' songs were of more varying quality among themselves than our home wood thrushes' songs. One particular thrush's song had an extra grace note in its second part, and the whole song was of so rich a quality that you would think it some new thrush song, and be sure of it for a while if you heard first its second part. The field sparrows' songs were unusually fresh and full, and the indigo buntings' songs of more body than I had heard before.

After July came in, the evenings and mornings were not nearly so loud with song as were June's. The whip-poor-wills were much quieter, and after the middle of the month they were but infrequently heard. After the middle of August I heard no "whip-poor-will" until there came a springlike night in early September, a night of south wind and soft rain, and then again the whip-poor-wills called and an ovenbird sang its "teacher" song and its flight song as if it were May. The great-crested flycatchers disappeared to a bird with June, and I saw none afterwards on the uplands the whole summer. The chebecs were abundant and noisy after July 1, though less and less noisy as the month wore on, until about the fifteenth they disappeared as the great-crested flycatcher had disappeared two weeks before. However, I saw a chebec and heard him on August 2, and two days later a pair with three young came about our shack. These young were barely able to fly, so they must have come only a little distance from the nest. I suppose some accident had befallen a previous nesting, and the old birds had begun over again late in the season. But if, as I think, they had nested somewhere nearby, they must have been very quiet, which is anything but after their custom. The pewees and wood pewees and kingbirds were still about when we left, fewer kingbirds than pewees and wood pewees, though for that matter there were fewer all season.

Seventy-two species identified is the total of my list, a list that might have been added to considerably by one who knows more birds than I, and who had more time to give to observation. My chief disappointment was in finding so few hermit thrushes and so few veeries. I found that the veeries went higher in this immediate neighborhood than the hermit thrushes. Both species were much scarcer than they are in the southern Berkshires (Mt. Washington Town), a country whose avifauna is much like this of the northern Poconos, but, as you would expect, a little more northern, though scarcely more northern than that of the Tobyhanna district just above Buck Hill. These upper branches of Broadhead's Creek rise in a country that sixty years ago was Canadian in its fauna, and flowing from two to six miles, reach Barrett township, a country then Alleghanian in its fauna, but now that the original forest is almost all gone, largely Carolinian. This forest-cutting began about 1840, and went on steadily until practically all the marketable lumber was exhausted about 1880. So about Buck Hill you find a few stragglers from the Canadian fauna, the survivors of the old Alleghanian fauna and many intruders from the Carolinian. The country was most interesting to me ornithologically in that it gave me the chance to know better three birds I had scarcely known at all, and of a charm that I had not been led to expect—the eave swallow, the Louisiana water thrush and the blue-headed vireo—the last, one of our really notable American singers.

OF AUTUMN CROCUS AND
EASE FOR GOUT

I. M.
James Darrach

THEY have taken away the last solace of those of us who suffer from gout. They have discovered an inflammation in folks who have never known good living so like the ancient and honorable disease in all but its conditions of origin that it is no longer possible for the really gouty to hug to heart the delusion that their affliction, if not aristocratic, is at least allied in some way with a privileged and exclusive life. True, they distinguish the starvelings' ailment as "poor man's gout," but gout it remains in memory for all that, and it dispels the association with old gentlemen of good family and club standing that the mention of gout once evoked.

I know those who find compensation for this loss of prestige in the belief that now that the wholly continent and truly humble have gout of a kind, the victims of the true complaint will be relieved of all suspicion of an incontinent past which the uninitiate sometimes attributed to patrician gout. "You don't have it, do you unless—?" said a concerned but ignorant sympathizer to me when I had just qualified for martyrization by walking thirty yards with an inflamed great toe that throbbed like a toothache. The circumstances were these. Dunsany was lecturing on beauty before a great audience in the hall of the museum of the University of Pennsylvania. No sooner was he under way than two bright electric lights at the back of the hall bothered him. Turning to me, he said: "Can you have those put out?" There was nothing to do but to tramp down off the platform and seek out the janitor. Now the gout was so active in my right foot, that it had been hardly possible for me to stand while introducing his lordship. I did not see how I was going to get down the steps, let alone reach the back of the hall. If walking on hot plowshares were more of a torment to the martyrs than my walking on that gouty great toe, I pity the martyrs. When I found the janitor he tried to tell me that the fire regulations forbade him to put out those lights. The fire in my eyes must have reflected the fire in my foot. He put out the lights. Then I had to hobble back to the stage again, for the lecturer might have other requests to make.

It was just after the lecture was over and I was limping to a taxi that my sympathizer said to me: "But you don't have gout, do you, unless there have been too many hussies and too much port wine in your life?" And that to a college professor who had subscribed to the condition of poverty, chastity, and obedience obligatory on his kind! And that to one with an ancestry of restrained and prudent and godly people who, for the two hundred years we know in detail the family history, walked the straight and narrow way! That inquirer never knew how near he came to feeling the impact of my two hundred pounds and more, back of my fist, on the point of his chin.

We, like our Rhine Valley forbears, have looked on the wine when it was red, but with moderation. Though we knew ourselves to be hard-headed and able for more than most folks, we never put ourselves to the test. We know when to stop drinking. There is a family tradition that none of us have been drunk these two hundred years. Nor has port ever been a favored wine with us. Father brought me up to believe that port and tokay both were too heavy and too rich. Rhine wine or sauterne with dinner; and champagne with fruit cake when neighbors dropped in of an evening or when the family came for Thanksgiving and Christmas feasts; a swig of whiskey when you got your feet wet in cold weather; brandy and soda as a bracer in the morning after you were sixty—that was his code.

It was, I suppose, because father's gout came on him at a time when doctors were giving up the old pharmacopoeia that he was never prescribed the drug made from the bulb of the autumn crocus for his easement. I never take colchisal but I think of him and what pain he might have been spared had he known of it. The dictionaries of yesterday speak of *colchicum autumnale* as a plant from which was formerly made a preparation for use in the treatment of gout and rheumatism. And yet, not so long before that, in the first half of the nineteenth century, it was spoken of everywhere for its medicinal powers. The autumn crocus was then so distinctively the principal crocus that its spring-blooming fellow was referred to as "the vernal crocus."

One wonders how the healing qualities of the autumn crocus were discovered. Did some one see a gouty old dog paw up a bulb and gnaw at it? Was that one an observant wise woman, an herb doctor, a witch wife of old time, Medea herself perhaps, who was learned in so many sorts of hidden lore? It is not mentioned as a medicine in the Bible, but, under the name of saffron, as an herb associated with frankincense and spikenard. The Romans knew it a specific for gout, and it was in common use in Elizabethan England in the treatment of this and allied rheumatic complaints. It is marvelous how efficacious it is in some cases. If I feel the soreness in the joint that is the forerunner of the swelling and sharp pain and immediately begin taking pills of colchisal one by one at intervals of an hour until eight are taken, the attack is weathered with no more serious results than a day's limping. If I walk down Mt. Washington, or up to the pogonia bog on Whiteface and down again, matters of eight and six miles, I may be in for a three days' attack, colchisal or no colchisal. Taken in time, however, and discretion used in walking, it relieves one within a few hours and clears one's blood, for the time being, of the infection that led to the trouble.

The first place in which I ever noted the autumn crocus was at Wonalancet in Birch Interval. It starred the border by the house of an old gentleman whose flushed face and knobbed finger joints pointed to a condition of blood such as quickened the naturally irascible disposition of Major Pendennis. I never heard of this old gentleman being involved in such a bout of wits as that of the Major with his man Morgan, but I would not put past him such an encounter. Whether Mr. Beacon Hill liked the autumn crocuses because in their essense in a drug they afforded him relief from gout I never learned, but I know I think no less of them for that reason. It is their coming into bloom when all else of their immediate kind is gone months earlier that constitutes a large part of their appeal to me. I like them particularly for their untoward blowing in September, as I like Christmas rose and winter aconite for even later blowing.

I have not come on the autumn crocus in many places else than Birch Interval, or nearby in middle and northern New Hampshire. They grace a dooryard in Centre Sandwich, as well as my own here over against Quaker Corners in North Sandwich. They spring up by the doorsteps to my home in Germantown. I cannot recall localities elsewhere made memorable by them, though I have a half memory of seeing them once in a very formal rock garden, at some florist's or nurseryman's perhaps. You will find the bulbs

listed in the catalogues of the larger seedsmen, but, somehow, the autumn crocus has not become widespread in the
States. Like the crown imperial it is a lily loved only of the
few.

The autumn crocus must have been more popular from
old times in the older countries. It is praised as meadow
saffron in the English poets from Chaucer on through the
Elizabethans. I cannot remember mention of it in Herrick,
who has all the earmarks of a gouty person. If he had ease
from gout through *colchicum autumnale,* he did not pay his
debt to it with an epigram. The old herbalists cite it, but
they do not make as much of it as it deserves. Despite its
beauty and the ease the drugs made from its bulb give to
those who suffer from the agonies of gout, it has never come
into its proper fame.

The little blooms of meadow saffron add a poignancy to
these autumn days of amber light. It is northern, very
northern, this evening of late September, with the setting
sun casting long shafts of light over the green rowan of the
hayfields. There are shadows as long, almost, as the shafts
of light. There is frost on the air, but you do not dread it
for these brave flowers. They come, at least by fable, from
that stern country of Medea, from Colchis to the east of the
Black Sea. A light freeze, one that just coats the water in
the sapbuckets on the well-curb, does not hurt them at all.
As yet, only six of the dozen bulbs planted along the foot
of the bouldered bank have shot up flowers. As you look at
them they show no touch of last night's black frost. They
are of varying shades of lavender and light purple and of
different shapes. In some the six petals spread open to form
the very design of the six-petaled tulips on pillared shafts
in Bulgarian graveyards and on the red sides of Pennsylvania barns. In others they still hold the chalice form of the

tulip. These flowers are seven inches high, those only three inches. Their hues of lavender and light purple are at once in perfect accord and in proper contrast to the grays of the great stones of the wall. Their sturdy fragility and known brevity of life endear them all the more to you in the company of those changeless boulders of granite, borne from Labrador perhaps, or from further north and west, in the glacial drift ages ago.

I wish I could bring them before you, these autumn crocuses, in their wax-like and crisp luxuriance, with a flush like that of flesh on their lavenders and purples, in the protection of those so aged and far-borne boulders, come to rest forever on a granite kindred to their own. The amber light is fading, and cold falling on the darkening fields, but the little flowers, with no leaves about them, stand up in full color with a glow as if from within, as if they were self-lighted with the intensity of joy in their so late blowing.

What they are I have striven to say. What they look out upon is scarcely to be told. In the background, a line of mountains cold blue in the oncoming twilight, yet still aureoled with light from the sun we can no longer see. In the foreground, apple trees as red with evenly dispersed fruit as any Christmas tree with glass balls or electrified bulbs, but with the suggestion of late harvest, of winter feasts and nightcaps of cider that no indoor gewgaws can bring. In the middle distance maples reddening to their flaming transfiguration and shorn fields purple in the half light.

And, above all, the sense of wildness, the pathos of a once open and plenteous farmland slipping back to wilderness, the tragedy of man's defeat by nature, the cold that threatens life, the moan of the rising wind, the menace of approaching night. They have been a dread trinity, the night, the wind and the cold, since that far twilight on which man first knew fear of darkness, and trembled in the wind and sought refuge from the cold. It is a moment in which the heart realizes that the world is æons on æons old, man too infinitesmal to matter at all, nothing of any consequence save the escape from thought. And then the sun I believed sunken until to-morrow's dawn again burst through the clouds banked over Bald Knob. The grass and boulders were flooded with amber light, old and mellow and at one with earlier days. The lavender and purple chalices of the autumn crocuses lifted proudly. The gloom of the moment gone was no more than the ancient and inescapable sorrows that have shadowed from the beginning the heart of man. A light shone out from a house across the valley, from another, from a third. I turned to the windows of my home only a rod away. There was security, there was warmth by the fire, there was human companionship. Loneliness of heart, and lonely beauty, were as necessary a part of life as gladness of heart and beauty that is glad. I was reconciled to the night and the cold and the wind.

TUSCARORA NIGHTS

I. M.
Selim S. Thomas

ROUND about us had been from his youth my uncle's land of romance. That was why we were here on the walnut knoll above the Tuscarora. Grandfather Thomas had owned land on Black Log Mountain not far away, a holding that had cost him dear. Thither he had traveled several times when all these valleys and ridges were a true wilderness. He had talked of this part of Pennsylvania so frequently that his son had a keen realization of its wonders and fabled material resources. Money from that mountain was, however, an expectation long dismissed from the mind of Uncle Seal. The Tuscarora country was now to him the place of escape from politics and all the monotony of the daily round in Lebanon.

It was more, though, than that. Here the trout tasted sweeter than other trout; here the sunsets were of warmer gold and brighter crimson than elsewhere; here were more little wonders of out-of-doors than any other place could boast, blacksnakes that could move faster than other blacksnakes, and rattlers that were more courteous in letting you know of their presence than any other rattlers in all their range from east to west. All that happened in the Tuscaroras was transfigured with roseate light and freshened with air out of Eden.

Uncle Seal would have his sisters' sons share the delight of the Tuscarora country with him. That was why Walter

and I were along with him. There was also with us so
thrilling a person as a detective, a man of silences uninter-
rupted save by confidences about the ways of preparing food
and an anecdote now and then about some malefactor of his
acquaintance. There was, too, a negro boy who was supposed
to know how to cook, but who did not, and who could not
even wash dishes. His only accomplishments were cake-
walking and singing comic songs.

There was also with us a keg of beer of which we never
had a taste; two tents; a horse and wagon; much gear for
fishing; and pots and pans galore. There was, just below our
camp, an underground stream of coldest water breaking out
of the limestone cliff, a natural refrigerator as efficient as
any springhouse in the preservation of meat and milk. There
were great old trees of black walnut in the grove in which
we camped, some of them with hearts of rotten wood so
light and dry we could start a fire with a match from chunks
of it cut out and piled up loosely.

The daily routine here was not, as I remember it, particularly interesting, but time never hung heavy on our hands.
My chores were to pull in the outlines set out all night in
the creek; take from the hooks the catch, and place it in the
live box of lath; and to cut the hooks out of the water snakes
that swallowed them and that were always more numerous
than the eels and fish. I had, too, to water and feed and
curry the horse, and to harness him when we had to go in
to Port Royal for supplies. Sometimes, too, I went for the
bread cooked in an out-of-door oven at a neighboring farmhouse. Here, too, we bought eggs and butter and lard, eggs
at twelve cents a dozen and butter and lard alike at twelve
cents a pound. Here we had to run the raillery of a red-
headed young virago, sullen and of a smoldering temper.
Just how we filled in all the long hours of the day I cannot

recall now after nearly fifty years. Chores took a good deal
of our time, and there were fishing and tramping and watching Uncle Seal do a log cabin and coon in charcoal to indicate our allegiance in the campaign for president. The days
have somehow faded out for the most part. What remains is
the memories of the nights.

Those Tuscarora nights were nights of midsummer, many
of them loud with wind and rain, and others hardly less
loud with the roars of the bullfrogs, the chokings and
snapped-out cries of the whip-poor-wills, the quonks of the
night herons, and the barking and screaming of owls. They
were nights of late July and early August, in the last of
which the katydids began to call. All night long there were
creatures lifting up their voices, from the little voices of
crickets to the great voices of the bullfrogs that kept Uncle
Seal from sleeping. None of us slept too well, as a matter of
fact, even the youngsters, for it was either close or cold in
the straw of the tents, and again and again the rain came
through the canvas sufficiently to make us thoroughly un-
comfortable.

Even on those rainy nights, though, there was talk that
was a revelation to boys of seventeen. Uncle Seal had
climbed Pike's Peak in early days after trekking southwestward from Illinois to what is now Oklahoma. He had
painted stage coaches in many places beyond the Mississippi.
He had been caught in Louisiana when the Civil War broke
out, and he had worked his way, after a long hiding, all the
way home to Pennsylvania, but very slowly and without a
moment of real security until he reached the mountains of
Tennessee. He had, too, no end of stories about the farm in
Chester County on which he was born, a subject recurrence
to which always roused lyric feeling in me; stories of the
underground railway; and stories of battles between rival

fire companies in the Philadelphia to which he came as a young man.

There were matchings, too, of stories between the detective and Uncle Seal, but only when the topic was Abe Buzzard, whose Welsh Mountain home was situated between the Milford Mills of Uncle Seal's boyhood and the Lebanon of his later years. I had not then heard of the Doanes of Bucks County, or of Simon Girty, that outlaw of the Susquehanna, but I not only knew of the famous mountaineer but had met him, on a visit to the jail in West Chester, through which I was piloted by a be-sombreroed cousin of mine whose Friendly ancestry would never have been guessed from his port-red cheeks and long black mustachios.

There were the men, too, who jeered as they passed at the Harrisonian banner of log cabin and coon, illuminated by the great fire we kept going all evening long. Sometimes they came in to talk and argue with Uncle Seal. They were afraid he was going to settle in Juniata County and take a hand in local politics. They knew he would make trouble for them by his energy and experience in such matters, and they did not want him as a competitor. They were frank in telling him to keep out, and he, in return, baited them by threatening to establish residence and give them a run for sport's sake, as he had always baited all aggressive folks of every condition.

It is strange that I have no memory of the moon riding up behind the great limbs of the walnuts. We were there two weeks, and you cannot have two weeks without some sort of a moon. The nights that I recall were all of them black nights. It may be that the great fire riveted my attention and gave me little else to see but its red embers. There was a great heart of fire always there among the logs, a heart of fire that cast light surprisingly far about and brought out prominently some fifteen feet of the lower trunks of the freely growing trees. The soil here suited them, and all were in good thrift save the very oldest. From the trees large enough to yield the best of timber down to the younglings only stout enough to be safe from the cattle, they sprang, clean trunked and vigorous, from the kindly limestone. Through the widespread illumination from these red-hearted coals of walnut wood creatures would pass now and then. I remember a belated ground hackie with both cheek pouches stuffed full of some spoil; a night heron, grotesque and griffin-like as he made straight at us in his bewilderment by the fire; and a vixen fetching in provender for her cubs in the cliff below our camp. One time as she passed she appeared to have a rabbit thrown over her shoulder, its white scut and white belly very prominent in the firelight. I noted this passing of the vixen particularly as there is a picture of some English painter of yesterday showing a fox running with a rabbit thrown over its back in just such a position.

Even after the frogs, poor creatures, had the most of them been shot off that Uncle Seal might not be disturbed by them, and even after our fire had begun to scare the owls away, there was plenty of noise at night. The herons flying up and down the creek, the whip-poor-wills all about, and the chorus of the cricket kind made a background of continuous and palpitant sound. There were also sounds less distinguishable: the soft rush of the stream itself, the pull of errant airs in the trees, the stamping of the old horse, the crackling of the fire as it was fed fresh logs of walnut, the darky humming that song that never left his memory, "Oh, see dat watermelyon a-growen on de vine." Such was the background to the voice of Uncle Seal, talking of the thousand and one nights of his life that lay so far out of the experience of the two boys. Sometimes we drowsed from

weariness or the warmth of the fire, but for the most part
we listened eagerly, so different were these adventures from
the citied lives of our own parents, so highly colored, so full
of quick change from one condition to another, so tumul-
tuous and charged with danger.

How we held our breath as he told of those unending
days and nights he was hid in a tumble-down sugar warehouse in Louisiana, supplied with food by a negro who declared the Northerner his friend. Uncle Seal lay, covered
by sacks, in a corner of a room on the second floor, a single
plank stretching across to his place of concealment. This
brought back to me John Balfour in *Old Mortality* and that
crazed Puritan's log to his hiding place in the glen loud
with tumbling water. The army of black squirrels on migra-
tion that Uncle Seal came on once in Kentucky, that, too, I
shall never forget, the lemming-like persistence with which
they drove on their way across country, swimming branches
and refusing to leave the roads before oncoming teams. This
talk was of the sort of things I had not before met in life,
but only in books. And had Uncle Seal the will to write,
what a book his autobiography had been! After his return
from Louisiana he had gone into the Union army, but of
his experiences there he did not talk much. Strain in attempt-
ing to get a provision or ammunition wagon out of the mud
had cost him a rupture that made half his days miserable,
and, in the end, led to his death, in a log cabin in his beloved Juniata County, to which he had retired from the tur-
moil of politics in Lebanon.

He much preferred to talk of his painted dower chests,
bought up about Lebanon, and the porcelain pipes brought
in old years from Germany and preserved as choice heirlooms down the generations between the South Mountain
and the Blue Mountain. These chests and pipes he was par-

ticularly interested in because he had been trained to the
trade of stagecoach painting and found the pictures on pipes
and chests of a kind allied to those of his own craft. Unfortunately for me, I had not then the knowledge that would
have enabled me to cross-examine him about such painting.
He had met and discussed the painting of chests with men
from those districts of northern Lebanon County from
which so many of the finest chests came. Nor had I the
knowledge that would have enabled me to take down what
bits of ballads there were in the talk of the callers at our
camp. It was not until years afterwards, indeed, that I, remembering certain phrases in use by Tuscarora, as I read
ballads collected in Virginia and Kentucky, realized what
treasure trove I had missed in my youth.

It does not look so romantic to me now, this knoll above
the Tuscarora. It was full two days' drive from Lebanon in
1889. It is now no more than five hours by motor all the
way from Germantown. In the years that have passed since
this memorable two weeks in camp all this mountained part
of the world has been leveling itself down to the conditions
of life prevalent everywhere in America. Gas stations and
bungalows mar the roadsides and creek-sides, and all the
little towns have been given common topics of conversation
by the newspapers and the talkies. The stagecoaches I knew
are gone, and the canals, and, I fear, the ballads. There may
be remote coves in the back mountains where conditions are
now as they were three miles from Port Royal in 1889. I
have not, though, come recently upon such a divergence
from the monotony of the centers as I knew by Tuscarora
long ago. I have, blessedly, the memory of it all, and I can
bring back when I will the dankness of that creek valley,
the sense of teeming wild life it imparted to me, the picturesqueness of the speech of its people. And there is clear

before my inward eye the glow of that fire of walnut logs, and distinct in my inward ear the sounds that were so insistent from the darkness beyond its range, the sharp bark of the vixen, the quonks of the night herons, the churning and snapped-out cries of the whip-poor-wills, the barking of the great horned owls, the throbbing of the crickets, and the deep-voiced morum-morum-morum of the bullfrogs.

FORDS AND FERRIES

for Walter G. Sibley

THERE are fewer and fewer fords and ferries as the years go by. Here and there a ford on a by-road that is little used survives because no one has troubled to agitate for its displacement by a bridge. Here and there some great river or estuary of the sea is so wide that its bridging daunts the engineers. And there are ferries that hold on because long-established use and wont have so inured people to their difficulties and delays that they patronize them rather than the bridge or tunnel that rivals them. It is the great ferries and the little fords that survive in Pennsylvania. The little ferries and long fords have all but all of them disappeared.

The rope ferries that were a feature of travel by road in the days of my youth are mostly gone now. Tragic accidents have sometimes been the cause of their discontinuance or of the building of bridges to take their place. I do not recall that such was the cause of the removal of the three I knew on the upper Delaware, even on into automobile days, but I do remember that they came nearer, by situation or background, to making an automobile picturesque than any other agency. Crossing on a flat-bottomed ferryboat, the most modern car took on some of the stateliness and suggestion of yesterday of the stage coach.

There is a little ferry, but for folks and not for teams or cars, at what was the lowest roadhouse on the Wissahickon. It takes those on outings across the stream to the landing where are most of the rowboats, and to the retreats where

320

there are more seclusion and fewer folks than on the team-cluttered drive of the southern bank.

There were other ferries, of course, though not so many of them, that were only for people. These were often, though, not rope ferries. One such was at Shawmont in the old days. Often, when I wished to visit my sister at Bryn Mawr College, during her years there from 1885 to 1889, I would walk over to Shawmont, be rowed across to the landing where Mill Creek fell into the Schuylkill, and walk up the Mill Creek Valley and over the hills to Bryn Mawr. A much-celebrated rowboat ferry was that at Iroquois on the Juniata, not far above its juncture with the Susquehanna, where a small girl grew famous as ferryman. We passed her ferry on our wagon journey from Lebanon to Port Royal in 1889.

There was, very recently, a rope ferry at Laceyville, on the north branch of the Susquehanna. There was just one cable, stretched from shore to shore, to this ferry. Two rings, running on this cable, were attached to ropes fastened on either end of the flat-bottomed ferryboat. To drive the boat across the stream the ferryman took his place at the front of his boat, put his pole with a cleft in the end against the cable, gave a twist to his pole so that it gripped the cable, and walked backwards on the platform along the side of the boat. He thus pulled the boat ahead. Arrived at the back of the boat, he broke the hold of his pole on the cable, walked forward, the boat still under momentum, took another hold on the cable and walked backward again the length of the boat, thus propelling it ahead again. He repeated this process until the river was crossed.

This is a much more complicated procedure than that of the old scow ferry in which the scow with its load is just poled across the stream, sometimes unattached to any cable, but in most instances, for safety's sake, held to its direct court by the short cables attached to sliding rings on a great stationary cable extending from shore to shore.

At Montgomery, on the west branch of the Susquehanna, there have been, successively, ford, ferry and bridge. The bridge is recent, replacing the rope ferry only about 1920. The charge on the ferry was twenty-five cents for man and team, and ten cents for each foot passenger. This ferry, operating in both directions by the force of the current, had not for years been adequate to the demands on it on days of heavy travel. There were times when teams were lined up for two miles, waiting for their turn to cross. In the old, old days, when a ford supplied the only meant of crossing, folks who wished to use it on days of high water were just out of luck. There were periods of a week often, when one could not get across at all, and later, when there were bridges at Milton below and Muncy above, those whose errands were urgent had to make long detours to one or the other place. Even in the ferry days there were floods so great that all crossing was out of the question. It is no wonder fords and ferries on such wide crossings were done away with. It is, indeed, remarkable that the rope ferries should have lasted as long as they did.

There is a neighborhood yarn at Montgomery about an old German, recently come from the fatherland, who was being driven down to the ford in the local doctor's gig. As the horse took the water at the ford the old German jumped out, declaring that he had crossed the sea once, but that he would never trust himself to its crossing again.

In the old ferry at Montgomery the cables at either end of the ferryboat were adjustable, so that each one could be shortened or lengthened as need was to bring the current of the river against the one or other end of the boat's side.

THE WRIGHTSVILLE–COLUMBIA FERRY

When the boat was on the west bank, the short cable from the boat's western end to the cross-river cable was lengthened, and that to the eastern end shortened, and the boat moved east, propelled by the force of the river's current. To move the boat west again from the eastern bank of the river, the cable from the eastern end of the boat to the guide cable was lengthened and that at the west end shortened, and the boat would start west again.

The ferries I have all my life known best are those between Philadelphia and Camden. Some of these boats are great side-wheelers, alike in shape at both ends, but screw-propelled ferryboats are displacing them. Great driveways for teams and trucks pass through the center of the boat on either side of the engine room, and outside of them, on either side of the boat, are the cabins for men and women. In childhood these ferryboats were associated in my mind with our short summer trips to Beach Haven or Barnegat City or Angiesea. There was a certain earnest of romance about the boats. The clanking of the chains that lowered or lifted the floats in the ferry slips, the whistles and bells so different in pitch and quality of tone to those of the locomotives and factories and horse-cars with which I was daily familiar, the river craft and sea-going ships passing on the Delaware, the vendors of strange-shaped glassware from Vineland or Salem, the old colored women from Medford or "de earthly Zion" with their magnolias and marsh pinks and pond lilies—all these were of another world than that of my usual experience, strange, wonderful, new and interesting.

There was a little spice of adventure in the journey, but I was gladder at the sight of the ferryboats on our way home than I had been on our way down to the shore. I could not take my pets with me or my favorite haunts, and they were more to me than the newnesses of the shore, the charms of which wore off so quickly. There was more excitement, as well as more happiness, for me, on my first round of beasts and birds and fish at home, of stable and henhouse and garden, than there had been at the first scent of salt marsh. That scent did excite me in a measure, as did the first sight of a fish hawk's nest, or the first awareness of the old sob of the sea, but I tired of the salt scent quickly, the thought of the wildness and power that great nest and resting bird symbolized could not long content me, and that insistent recurrence of the waves on the beach was never quieting to my nerves. The voices I love are those of the mountains, not those of the sea. Wind in the great gulfs of alps never wearies me, or the monotonous shrilling of snowbirds from the low shrubs and grasses above the timber line. The fall of night under high peaks, sad as it may be, never has for me the poignancy, searching but baffling, of the offshore mirk, and of the lamentable crying of the shore-birds in the half light, and the menace there is in that sea that "seek'st and seek'st, yet never gain'st."

The ferrying from Newburgh to Beacon, or from Kingston to Rhinecliff, on our annual trek north to New Hampshire, before there was a Bear Mountain Bridge, was often a penitential session. You never knew in those self-starterless days for Fords whether the engine would start when it was time to run out of the boat on the other side of the river. Once it would not, despite vigorous cranking, and we had to be ignominiously pushed off by the boat hands, to have the engine spin merrily at the first try of the crank when we were safely out of the road of the line of cars and teams that we were holding back. I liked the ferry from Rhinecliff to Kingston best on our return south in late September when all the driveways of the boat were redolent of the apples going to market in truck-loads of barrels and bushel baskets. Once

we had the great honor, going north in June, to become engulfed in firemen gathering for a parade. We proceeded,
more slowly than I thought possible, behind the Ringgold
Band from our own city of Reading, and we were followed
close by large cohorts of the red-shirted.

Nor can I say I had ever much delight in the long ferry
from Oakland to San Francisco. It, too, like the Camden
ferry of my childhood, was a gate to another world than that
to which I was born. Here, in San Francisco, was an outpost
of El Dorado; here was Chinese pottery that fascinated me;
here were the hoar beauty of the live oaks and the challeng-
ing smell of the red gum trees from Australia; here were
such clashings of civilizations, Spanish-Indian, Oriental, Bret
Hartian and Atlantic American, as I had not known before;
here was the sun setting over the open sea; here was Ultima
Thule. Here, I learned quickly, was much I could take to
heart, and make a part of me, but I was not here long enough
to feel proprietary rights in ferry or bay or bare hills, in
curlews and avocets and strange gulls.

It is a long leap from a wide ferriage like this across San
Francisco Bay to a little ford like that a Milford Mills in
southeastern Pennsylvania, a ford a rod wide, and unused
and neglected by the bridge-side. As long as a covered
wooden bridge carried the road across Marsh Creek the ford
was used and cherished, but on the widening of the road
that accompanied the building of the concrete structure the
ford was pushed aside. This ford at Milford Mills was the
one I heard most about in chilhood, for in the house at the
cross-roads, within a stone's throw of the ford, my mother
was born. I heard of horses brought down to drink of the
pure waters of the creek; of buggy washing here; of the
wading here of the children that set grandfather to quoting
his beloved Burns on paddling in the burn; on the fun of

driving the cows down to it before they were stalled for milking. Cows crossing a ford make a picture that, like that of geese on a green common, has long been close to the affections of men. In *American Scenery* (1872), a book of engravings of representative paintings by American artists, there are more pictures in which creeks and cows are associated than there are pictures on any other subject. They are not all of them of fords, though in most cows are crossing a stream. The conjunction is natural. Water is the life of a landscape and cows the most picturesque of farm beasts. In a country like America, where most of us who are of the old stock are close to the farm, a picture of stream and cows, of mill and streamside road, is sure to be in the experience of us all and to awaken loved memories.

Among our writers Whitman alone has risen to the possibilities of ferries. There is lyric prose of his about night and stars he saw and felt as he crossed and re-crossed from Camden to Philadelphia. "Full Starr'd Night," a record of May 21, 1877, is the best ferry piece I know of. There is more poetry in that than in "Crossing Brooklyn Ferry," cosmic as are the sweep and drive of its freed imagination.

If you had asked me before a certain Saturday night in February of 1932 as to the number of fords in southeastern Pennsylvania I should have said: "They are going, of course, but a good few remain." How few there are was driven in upon me suddenly. Coming up from Gettysburg we swung north from the Lancaster Pike just east of Lancaster, intending to reach home by Blue Ball, Churchtown, Morgantown, Coventryville, Bucktown, Phoenixville, Oaks, Audubon, Jeffersonville, Norristown, Plymouth Meeting and Barren Hill. At Oaks we found the old covered wooden bridge gone, and the new concrete bridge not yet passable. We detoured east. Less than a mile up the Perkiomen the road ran out,

A DAM BREAST FORD ON THE PERKIOMEN

apparently, at our side the stream. Signs told us we were in Indian Rock Park, the Landis Mill of the maps on which I was brought up. A lighted window invited inquiry. The word came back: "Go ahead, and cross on the dam breast, a hundred cars are crossing it every day." We went ahead and crossed it, through water no more than a foot deep. Great loglike stones had been laid across the top of the dam, who shall say how long ago, with their ends up and down stream. Great freshets had failed to budge them, and they carried us over with less bumping than we were to meet on the road on the other side of the Perkiomen.

It was an experience for my friend, a man of thirty-five, the first time he had ever crossed a ford. When he told me it was his first such crossing I began to tot up my own crossings of fords. I remembered one in McCrillis' Interval, in the White Mountains, some ten years before, but none in Pennsylvania since our summers in the Poconos, more than twenty years ago. Before those summers, which began in 1905, I had known fords round about Germantown, and in Montgomery County, Chester County, Berks County and Juniata County, in Pennsylvania, to speak only of my home state.

I remembered that I had been told such dam breasts as this we had just crossed had first carried across Wissahickon to Roxborough the old road from Rittenhousetown and Livezey's Lane from upper Germantown. When I tried to recall other dam-breast fords my memory or my experience failed me. A Frankford friend remembers a two-horse team in a mill wagon being driven across a dam-breast ford on the Pennypack, the sense of power in the great beasts splashing through the water and up the steep ascent on the side from which he watched them being one of the lasting impressions of his childhood.

The fords I knew best in my young years were those by the

side of macadamized roads. And yet I am put to it to remember the location of a single one near home save that which carried Township Line over Cresheim Creek after the old bridge broke down and before the present bridge was built. Curiously, I can remember places in eastern New York, in western Massachusetts and in Rhode Island where we stopped and unchecked the horses and let them drink as we crossed fords. Perhaps I do not remember such places in the country about Germantown because father very seldom watered the horses, when we were out driving, save at watering troughs.

A good many people remember fords anything but pleasantly. When the fords were built up high across deep and slow-moving streams of cloudy water there was a chance you would let the wagon wheels on one side get over the edge and endanger an upset. So a ford on a side road east of Dublin always affected in her childhood a Bucks Countian who is glad fords are a thing of the past. Such fears of fords have been justified again and again. I have heard of no man drowned fording any of the streams I know well, but I have no doubt there were many such accidents in our countryside in old days. I have heard of even a stout horse carried away by a stream in flood and of his rider winning to the bank only with the greatest difficulty.

A glance at any map of the early or mid-years of last century will reveal how many fords there were on all streams of good size. Take the Brandywine for one. There were eleven fords on the main stream and on the east branch, from Chadd's Ford to Downingtown, if we list all the bridges as one-time fords. Their names indicate that two bridges had replaced fords and the chances are that all bridges did. From Chadd's Ford my map of 1847 lists the fords and the bridges as Brinton's Ford, Painter's Bridge, Wistar's Bridge, Buffing-

ton's Ford—thus far the united Brandywine—and on the
east branch Jefferis' Ford Bridge, Taylor's Ford Bridge,
Scott's Ford, Sugar's Ford, Hawley's Ford, and Hoopes'
Ford, or about one a mile. So it was, too, on our larger
streams.

There were many fords across the upper Schuylkill,
Hagy's Ford, Swedes' Ford at Norristown, Pawling's Ford
just below Phoenixville, Long Ford, Royer's Ford, Grater's
Ford, Tower's Ford, Wisemer's Ford, Lawrenceville Ford,
Schantz Ford, Hiester's Ford, Giest's Ford, Parker's Ford,
and so on. So it was with ferries on the lower Susquehanna,
where its mile or so of breadth and its volume of water made
fords impossible. Here were McCall's Ferry, which lasted
down well towards the end of the century, and Wright's
Ferry, Harris' Ferry and Clark's Ferry, which bridges
superseded in earlier years.

A ford I remember but cannot find again these later years
was over some headwater of the Tohickon under Haycock
Mountain. I drove through its glittering shallows of swift
water one bright day of October that followed heavy rain.
It was a Sunday, during the church hours of the morning,
when all the countryside was deserted. There was grass of
Parnassus by one wet roadside, fringed gentian in several
favored spots, and clusters of red leaves on the suckers that
had sprung up from the stumps of white oaks chopped down
the previous winter. Grass of the intensest green was everywhere, and brown leaves carpeted all the woodsides despite
the myriads of them that still clothed the young white oaks.
The expanse of blue sky was broken only by a few white
clouds that went racing by. Your words rang on the air when
you spoke, like a bell's clapper on a bell's rim. The rare
flowers of yellow-green and gentian blue, the green, green
grass, the brown leaves, the red furrows of the fall plowing,

the blue sky, the racing clouds so warm a white, the air like wine, were all good, but my moment of moments that day was when I splashed with my car through the glittering ford. It was a transfigured world I saw through the water sprayed up about the prosaic car, a world of light flashing everywhere in the reflections from a thousand hollows cupping the rain water, a world washed of moil and toil, fresh, clean and heady, a world that lifted the years from your shoulders and freed you of all care.

I resought that ford and failed to find it on a day of February so spring-like that you listened for peepers, but in vain, and on which you did see your first bluebird and did hear your first meadow lark. Haycock was purple blue in the distance that day, aloof for all it was so low, stretching further, it seemed, under its cloak of woods than ever before. We were an hour making the ten-mile circuit of it, via Bucksville, Bursonville, a corners just short of Applebachsville, and Tohickon. A good part of that ten miles had to be taken in low and second, so rough were the roads. Never had Haycock seemed so primitive. Its log houses, its scent of wood smoke, its uncleared reaches, spoke of the eighteen-thirties. Despite the hard times that have driven people back to the country, it had still a number of cellar holes, though there was evidence of rebuilding on them in more than one instance. Some of the old roads were unpassable through the growing up of brush, but men were making others more shipshape by brushing along their edges. A good deal of cleaning up along old walls and of burning of old grass in fields was going on. Considering that the lower slopes of the mountain and the country about it are a wilderness of trap dykes and wet ground and grown up fields and pastures the district is well populated. We met a truck, a couple of cars, and children on the road. It is remote enough, however, this country environing Haycock, for folks not to have to bury a cow that "died on them." We passed one so recently hauled into a wood road that there were yet no turkey buzzards sailing about in the sky above it.

It is a little ford away at the other end of Bucks County, miles south of Haycock, whose description fascinates me almost as much as do the fords I know myself. John Mendenhall loves to recall it, and I have him tell me of it again, because of its lantern. In his boyhood this lantern was nightly hung on a tree at one end of the ford to beckon folks on across it through the darkness. This friendly ford was over one of the branches of the Neshaminy on a road that followed the railroad from Churchville to Newtown.

A ford I know on Plum Creek, in northwestern Berks County is, like so many of its fellows, not cared for of late years. It takes a back road, now unworked by the township, over the creek. The ford's raised bed has been washed out, and you would hardly notice it if it were not for the stepping stones by its side that take foot-travelers across dry shod. There were many such stepping stones across fords years ago, the one that I best remember near Germantown being across Paper Mill Run on the line of Washington Lane. That, however, was so little used by teams you could hardly call it a ford.

Road supervisors and their like are natural enemies of fords. They are afraid of accidents in them and of their own responsibility in the suits that may follow. The ford that existed until a few years ago on the old Callowhill Road between South Perkasie and Perkasie is now banned to the public by a "No Thoroughfare" sign. Here a foot-bridge of wooden planks on cables slung from wooden posts yet carries folks over this branch of the Perkiomen. On my last visit to it, in February of 1932, only one wagon track was cut in the grassy turf of the unworn road that leads down to the crossing. It would be heavy going here now, on both banks of the creek, and perhaps mud so deep in the creek bottom that you would get stuck there. It is a spot that looks better for catfish and eels than for crossing.

Further north, and further west, in old years, I drove across another branch of the Perkiomen, on a ford with stony bottom and swift water sluicing by. This was in a willowed lowland, with a great log dropped across the creek for a foot-bridge and made passable by being adzed flat on top and provided with a handrail.

There is even to-day a water crossing by a stone bridge over the Skippack, on Forty Foot Road, which connects the Sumneytown and Skippack pikes. I saw fresh wheel tracks on both its banks on February 27, 1932, on the day I sought in vain for the ford under Haycock Mountain. I should not dare attempt this Skippack crossing in a car, the roadways down to the water on both sides being decidedly soft.

One sometimes wonders if, after a few years, there will be, in long-settled districts, no fords except for cows. It is the quick spread of road improvements during the past thirty years that has done the fords to death. Fords for the main traffic of roads were pretty well gone, save in the backwoods places, by the end of last century. Those that survived were the fords on byways and on the dirt roads found to either side of the old pikes. The bridge to carry the road often was only the width of its macadamized part, with the dirt roads left to cross, as the old four-track highway had once crossed, by fords at the natural level of the stream. Even in 1932, on so traveled a through route as that from the Lincoln Highway west of York to Hanover, I saw an automobile plowing through such a ford at the west side of the metaled road.

Even the cow fords, though, are threatened. The modern practice of turning cattle out of the stanchions only for exercise has done away, to a large degree, with the necessity of pastures. There are, however, fortunate cows who know what it is to wade to their knees through lush meadow grass, and to eat their fill of it. Even near to Philadelphia cows were, until a recent yesterday, driven to pasture across two fords through a looped bend of the Pennypack. These were shallow fords, in which the cows loved to linger on hot days of summer, their legs in the cooling water and the flies less tormenting above its coolness than in the warm grass.

Further back the years was the joy in cattle fords a friend of mine had in his youth in Erie County, clear across the state diagonally from these Philadelphia County fords. On the Laurie farm, outside of Corry, the cattle were driven to pasture over a ford raised some feet above the bottom of Hare Creek, a rather deep and sluggish stream. At its center the raised roadway of the ford was some eighteen inches under water, but it was constantly wearing off at the sides. Wading here in a pair of hip boots, at the age of ten, our protagonist got off the edge and plunged over his head into the deep pool by the side of the ford. It was a hard job floundering out, half stunned as he was by the suddenness of his fall and weighed down by the water in his gum boots.

Fords, like ferries, have not been praised as they should be. There is, of course, "Ford o' Kabul River" by Kipling, reminiscent of several fights at fords in the old ballads; and there is Whitman's "Cavalry Crossing a Ford." Of the true savor of our Pennsylvania hinterland is an account of a fight of a big bull and a little bull in a ford of Swamp Creek, told me in his old age by him who had witnessed it as a boy. Neither that account, though, nor Kipling, nor Whitman, gives us the quality of little rivers or runs or creeks. The fishy smell is not in these accounts, the dank air is not about them, the noise of the water clucking past the stones is not heard in the cadences of their lines. There are times I would remember fords under such a sunset glow as that in "Light Triumphant" of George Inness, and other times when the glamour of "The Last Gleam" of William Hart is good enough for fords. In the end, however, I come back to that memory of the black creek past the white mill, the piloting lights of the car, the thunder of the water falling sharply at our right, the sense of security that was given us by those guiding stones along the roadway through the fast-moving stream.

THE GREATEST PENNSYLVANIAN

for Bernhard S. Foster

STEPHEN COLLINS FOSTER (1826-1864) has brought more delight to the world than any other man born in Pennsylvania. The verses he wrote are far from poetry, but the sentiments they record, joined to the airs that bear these sentiments so closely home to the hearts of all men, have given his songs an appeal denied to those of far better artists. The best of Foster is, of course, the airs, that since the moment of their publication have never died out of the hearing of mankind. Some one of them, "The Old Folks at Home," "My Old Kentucky Home," or "Old Black Joe" is always sounding somewhere in the world, whistled or sung or played on an instrument. Ask anybody you meet from anywhere if he or she knows one of these songs, and there will be for answer a light of happiness in the eyes before a word of assent is spoken. They are all three as surely universal as "Annie Laurie," "The Marseillaise" or "The Blue Danube."

These three songs I have mentioned of Foster are in "the negro convention." That is, they are occasioned by the sort of song that was popular in negro minstrel shows, they are about negroes, or they are in negro dialect. That is as far as the negro quality of them goes. They are no more negro in kind than those Elizabethan plays in "the Italian convention" are Italian in kind. They are not negro in the sense that "Dance de Juba" is negro, or *Uncle Remus* or Vachel Lindsay's *Congo*, or even in the secondary way that certain of the

335

motives in Dvorák's *New World Symphony* are negro. The
most haunting songs of Foster are haunting as old Scotch
songs are haunting. They all bear a burden of "old unhappy
far off things"; they all hark back to emotions so common
to humanity that they are shared in by all men irrespective
of place and race and time. Their sorrow is the sorrow that
all flesh is heir to.

Foster had Scotch-Irish blood in his veins. There were ballad singers of like blood everywhere throughout the Pennsylvania and Ohio in which his formative years were spent. In
his childhood just outside of Pittsburgh, in his school years
further east and north at Athens, in his brief weeks further
south and west at Canonsburg at which is now Washington
and Jefferson College, he could have heard variants of the
Border stories sung to airs with a burden of old sorrow. They
were as widely disseminated in Pennsylvania as they are still
in the mountain country further south. It may be that such
songs were handed down in his own family. His early life
had, too, it is true, contacts with negroes and negro influences. There was a mulatto servant in the Foster home; there
was a trip that Stephen made down the Ohio and all the way
to New Orleans; there were his visits to the shows of white
men masquerading as negro minstrels; there was his hearing
of the chanties of the negro roustabouts on the Pittsburgh
wharfs.

It was out of himself, of course, that Foster made his
songs, whatever outside stimulus afforded the immediate
occasion of this one or that. It is known, though, that Foster
cared for Scotch things, that as a boy he loved to recite
"Lord Ullin's Daughter," that his "Sadly to My Heart
Appealing," is reminiscent of "Robin Adair," that his girl
"with the light brown hair" is "Jeanie," and that every now
and then a phrase from an air of his falls on your ear with

the very melancholy of Celtic music. There is another sadness than this in his verse, a mid-Victorian lugubriousness
about both words and music. We luxuriated in plangent
melancholy and we wallowed in pathos in the days of
Dickens. There are other influences in all probability than
those of his time and of his racial ancestry to account for the
sadness of Foster's songs. All I would point out is that the
fact of Celtic ancestry must not be forgotten.

There is no doubt of the stout-heartedness of Foster in
early life. He was quick to fight and skillful with his fists.
There was, however, a sense of defeat about him from his
young years, a defeat that his songs confess candidly and
that is writ large in the events of his life. It was an accident
that cut short that life at thirty-eight in New York City,
but it was an accident that his habits provoked. He had fallen
into

> *that pit abysmal*
> *The gulf and grave of Maginn and Burns.*

Burns must not be forgotten as an influence in the life of
Foster. America had taken Burns to heart as England had
not, and Scott, too, was a household familiar in Pennsylvania
all Foster's days. All things Scotch have always been close
to our hearts and daily concerns in the Keystone State.

That Foster left his songs in the comparatively crude state
musically in which we find them has never worried me as it
has so many of his commentators. I am one who likes primi-
tives of this kind "straight"—"Danny Boy" in its early form
rather than in that of the fussed up "Londonderry Air" of
Percy Grainger. The best airs of Foster are perfect in their
undeveloped kind, with the accent of folk song, forthright,
haunting, unforgettable. What if they go only half so far as
tragedy, and purge us with pity only and not with terror.
They succeed in what they set out to do, they bring us a

cleansing of the heart, and a refreshment of the spirit, they capture for us a beauty that no other song-writer of America has in any way approached. Lovingly as their words and music are wedded they are not to be compared to the standards of the men of the old song books to the verse and airs of Campion. It is their airs and their subjects that have carried the songs of Foster around the world. There is neither naïveté nor art in their words.

All this I write I have often talked, and for years, before I have made a note of it on paper. That is the way with all I write: it has been talked first. I speak of the matter because some of my friends say I ought to argue out and justify my assumption that Foster is the greatest Pennsylvanian. Need I so do, or will not affirmation of the belief be all of significance that I have to say on the subject? The roll call of the distinguished Pennsylvanians is a long one, even if there are not more than two or three native sons among them who are undisputed "firsts." We have had scores of learned and talented investigators and men of affairs who have given the state a cultivated public life from colonial times until today, but a paucity of "firsts." John Singer Sargent is a "first," but Pennsylvania did little more for him than give him birth. If Pennsylvania had much to do with his making as an artist, we might have to lower Foster's colors to his, but as things are, we have hardly more claim to him than to the Franklin and Poe and Whitman who spent so many fruitful years among us. Nor was Conrad Weiser wholly Pennsylvanian, Conrad Weiser the frontiersman most picturesque of all the figures in the pageant of our eighteenth century. Our one president, Buchanan, a connection by marriage to Foster, was certainly not a great man, or the state had not allowed the house in which he was born to be removed from Stony Batter to Chambersburg to domicile an antique shop.

There are those who cry up General George G. Meade, who broke the power of the Confederacy at Gettysburg, as our greatest Pennsylvanian, but the man has yet to come forward to declare him one of the great military leaders of all time. Pennsylvania produced, Pennsylvania fostered, Pennsylvania is responsible for Matthew Stanley Quay, the master politician of the United States. Pennsylvania, too, is entirely responsible for Joseph Leidy and Edwin Drinker Cope, great scientists both of them, but researchers in fields that in the nature of things never deeply interest the public. Herman Vezin and Joseph Jefferson were actors born in Philadelphia; Daniel Boone was a frontiersman second only to Conrad Weiser; Robert Fulton was one of the inventors of the steamboat; Benjamin West and David Rittenhouse and Francis Hopkinson bulked big in the eighteenth-century scene, and Robert Morris, the financier of the Revolution and "Mad" Anthony Wayne; Henry C. Lea, Horace Howard Furness and S. Weir Mitchell were all three proficient in the art of life as well as in their specialities: yet it was given to none of these men to leave to the world a gift so great as the songs of Foster.

Stephen C. Foster was of the world's first in the writing of airs with the quality of the folk in them. He had the instinct to keep to himself, and to cultivate jealously, the gift that was given him. He was saved from the fate of many an American with the spark of genius in him, the fate of being smothered by a superimposed European cultivation. A flame of genius nothing can smother, but spark on spark has been extinguished in just this way. It is a very simple, direct, and human appeal, that of Foster. He voiced inimitably the old call of homesickness, a basic call, the call of people and places known and loved in childhood, and the calls of things of yesterday gone from the world.

There are those who think that Foster might have been much greater than he was. So I, too, grant at moments. Let me put the problem this way. Had there been widely prevalent in Pennsylvania, and respected everywhere, a body of folk song comparable to the folk verse Burns found in the memories of his neighbors and in manuscripts and in chapbooks, Foster might have worked up a body of folk music as great as the folk verse of Burns. Burns revamped worn folk verse and gave it an artistry and an individuality it had not had before him. Foster might have done just that for Pennsylvanian folk song could he have collected a great body of old airs in the memories of manuscripts of old folks in log cabins, in the great houses of the river valleys, and in the city homes of Pittsburgh and Youngstown and Cincinnati. Perhaps. Or it might have been that the very excellence and richness of a large treasure of old songs might have discouraged him. I advance the argument to dismiss it. I think Foster could not have been other than he was.

As it is, the airs of Foster, despite the weakness of his verse, give him first place among the song-writers of America. Often, of course, most often it would be hardly too much to say, the folks who sing the airs of Foster do not know who composed them. It is perhaps only the tune they know, not even the words of the lesser ones, "Come Where My Love Lies Dreaming," or "Old Dog Tray," or "O Susanna." That is the way it is, too, largely with the verses of Tom Moore. Those who sing "Believe Me, If All Those Endearing Young Charms" nine times out of ten do not know or care who wrote the words.

A friend of mine who worked as an interpreter on transatlantic liners told me of an episode that proves a worldwide familiarity with one song at least of Foster. It brings him, too, in happy conjunction with Moore and with that earlier American song-writer, John Howard Payne. The ship, with immigrants to the United States from all over Europe returning to the old countries, lay quarantined off Liverpool. The steerage was particularly put to it for something to do. Finally a concert was arranged. Three songs were joined in with by everybody in all the languages aboard ship, whether Mediterranean or Eastern, Slavic or North European. The original verses of all three songs had been written in English, "Home, Sweet Home," "The Last Rose of Summer" and "The Old Folks at Home."

WHY THE TEAPOT DID NOT MATCH

for Spencer Sweet Shannon

IT was in the old days when the hired man was one of the family. He was employed all the year round, at what we to-day would consider a mere pittance a month, but he knew no layoffs, and his wages were always forthcoming, and regularly at that. He sat at table with his employer and his employer's wife and their children. Often the hired man was a relative or "connection by marriage" of either the boss or his missus, and nearly always he was so much younger than either that his employers took a half parental interest in him.

On the farm I am concerned with, a good farm in Tinicum, but outside "The Swamp," the farmhand was a "swamper," and unrelated to his employers. A youth of twenty-two, he was in a way mothered by Mrs. Strawn and he was much boasted of by her. Coming from a district in which the farms were small, and of wet and cold land that was none too good for crops, he was used to scant pickings. The contrast between the lean fare there and the good living on this place of warm loam on the plowlands and rich meadows along the creek made him feel he had a good job. Two barns, great straw piles and stacks of corn fodder around the barnyards, old and long corn-crib roofed with red tile, cider mill and smokehouse and springhouse and rows of straw beehives spoke this corner of back country an oasis flowing with milk and honey. There was the kindly smell of cows about the place, the refreshing scent of hay, the heavy

342

and kindling odor of honeycomb and, on baking days, that so savorsome delight to the nostrils, the widespread aroma of crusty bread done to a turn in an out-of-door oven heated by red coals of hickory.

It was only in the absence of eggs from the table all winter through that Abel Good could find any fault with the farm regime. The fowls were well housed, but the woman of the place did not get the chicks out sufficiently early in the spring to have pullets mature enough for winter laying. It was long before the day of egg farms, and eggs brought good prices from November to March in the country stores. All housewives considered the egg money theirs for the little luxuries of dress and table and tips for children that are so large a part of happiness. He was a rash domestic tyrant who dared meddle with his wife's egg money. He paid for it in more ways than he knew if he sequestered any of it. Michael Strawn let his wife have every cent of the egg money, and, however he felt about it, he never questioned the absence of eggs from the table in the cold months. After all, the old Light Brahmas did not lay very many, and his wife had great satisfaction in all she took to the store.

The young hired man, however, had a taste for eggs. His mother had seen to it, when he was living at home, that there were few days on which he did not get his egg, even in the wildest of Decembers. There was on their few acres a sheltered hillside thickset with cedars, on which the snow melted quickly, and, at its base, a spring that never froze. These so helpful adjuncts for winter eggs were just back of the hen-house, and she let her hens have the benefit of them whenever the weather allowed. Abel missed that tasty bit, even amid all the plenty of the fat farm's table. Yet he faithfully brought to Mrs. Strawn every egg he found, even though such eggs were laid in places she did not know the hens had stolen nests. He had thought, however, that eggs would be provided generously at Easter. That was the custom of the countryside, and he had heard of hearty young men who had made away with as many as a dozen or even fourteen at a sitting.

He was astounded and dismayed to hear Mrs. Strawn say on New Year's Day that one of her resolutions for the coming twelvemonth was that all eggs were to be sold as long as they brought a good price. He had set his heart on eggs galore at Easter. So he made bold to ask Mrs. Strawn if she would boil eggs for him at Easter if he bought them himself. She smiled upon him and said she thought she could do that. He said, maybe he could get enough eggs for all seven of them, herself, the two men of them, and the four children. She beamed upon him and said she surely could boil the eggs.

Abel had failed to shame her into eggs for Easter; perhaps she had not even understood he was trying to shame her into it. And that, indeed, would seem to have been the case. As the weeks went on he heard here and there, when he met some one on the road and stopped for a chat, or at church, or at tavern, or at country store, that Mrs. Strawn was boasting, more and more, of what a wonder of a hired man they had, who was going to provide Easter eggs for the whole family. She talked so much of it that her husband tried to check her, saying that she would spoil the lad, and that, before they knew it, he would be asking for more privileges and more wages.

Since Abel had gotten around Mrs. Strawn in a good many maneuvers he was a bit peeved that he could not edge her into proper position in this encounter. However, he accepted the situation and went about his work as cheerfully as ever. He continued to find eggs in out-of-the-way places and to bring two or three each day to her to add to the store she was saving to sell. One Sunday morning he begged off from going to church with the family, saying that he would like to go down to Erwinna to order the eggs for Easter. He had heard of a farm there where they kept Light Brahmas, and sold their eggs reasonably. Those Easter eggs would, of course, he said, have to be Light Brahma eggs, for none other were so tasty. He was forgiven church, important function though it was. He came home in a chipper mood, all arrangements made for the Easter eggs. He asked off for the Saturday afternoon before Easter to go for the eggs. Mrs. Strawn said he might have it.

That Saturday night Abel was back for supper with his splint basket filled to the brim with eggs. There were four dozen of them, of a deep brown, darker in color, if possible, and obviously larger, than those of the Light Brahmas of the Strawn farm. Mrs. Strawn was delighted. So uniform in color and size were the eggs that she hated to cook them. She alarmed Abel by asking him if he didn't think it would be too bad to boil such lovely eggs, that they ought to be kept for setting. There was one old hen clucking already, and there would soon be the necessary three more to cover the forty-eight eggs. If it hadn't been for the voices of the children shrilly uplifted in protest, the pain in Abel's face would hardly have served to dissuade her from her purpose. The children, fortunately for Abel, had their mouths set for Easter eggs, and Mrs. Strawn had to capitulate to her offspring. After all, Abel had bought the eggs, she reasoned, with his hard-earned money, and, although he was in a manner giving them to her, still he had rightfully some say as to their disposal.

She determined they would all have an even better Easter dinner than she had planned. "Edna and I will stay home from church. You men and the three boys can go, and, mind you, be back at one sharp!" After they left she took her best teapot from the corner cabinet and put it on the table. It was Gaudy Dutch, bordered with blue and gold, blazoned with flowers of salmon red amidst foliage of bright green, and with a yellow butterfly on either side. She had almost a full set of the pattern, her choicest heirloom. She took down, too, the tea caddy of like pattern, took what tea they would need for dinner, and put it in the teapot. She had been inveigled into buying that tea from a peddler at two dollars the pound. After much thought, she put the be-butterflied caddy back into the corner cupboard. It was not worth while to risk two pieces of that precious ware on children and mere men. And yet she loved it so she could hardly help setting the whole table with it just for once.

The men and boys were home at one sharp, Mr. Strawn twinkling. His high spirits led his wife to inquire if Stephen Applebach had passed his flask around after church. Michael assured her Stephen had not done so, and offered to kiss her to prove that he hadn't touched a drop, that the meeting-house sheds were bone dry even on an Easter Sunday. The seven of them ate the meal in high glee. Every egg would have been devoured had not Mrs. Strawn put one aside to keep. It was the very last of the forty-eight, all the others having been tucked away. She rose from the table to put that last egg into the corner cupboard.

She hesitated a moment before opening the arched door of the cupboard, lost in admiration of that set of Gaudy Dutch. As she stood there in a half trance, content with all the world because of the generosity of her perfect hired man, because of the happy children, because of the dinner, and because of the fox grape wine that topped it off, her husband turned to Abel. He said: "I suppose you saw me having a crack at church with that egg man of yours from Erwinna. One of the Pursels, you'll remember Abel said, Mrs. Strawn! It is wonderful how he gets those tender Black Spanish of his to lay so well in winter. He does it by some new-fangled house he keeps them in, and by green food, and by all sorts of coddling. Funny, though, that the long white eggs they lay should have turned brown on the way home. Eh, Abel! You must have come by a house where there were onion peels and the eggs got dyed from the smell of them."

Mrs. Strawn stood there in a quandary, egg in hand. Then the light broke. "And I always gave you the name of being the perfect hired man! You ungrateful boy! And you just kept the eggs back on me week after week until you had the four dozen! And picked out only the biggest, too! They were worth the whole of a dollar, the four dozen, and more, some weeks. And I telling of your generosity all over Tinicum! And the talk of you going out to Nockamixon, and Plumstead, and Haycock, and it's more than likely, to Quakertown and to near Easton! And I calling you the perfect hired man! What will all the folks be saying of Truda Strawn now?"

Her feelings too much for her, she let go that hard-boiled Light Brahma egg at Abel, as, half quizzical, half appalled, he eyed her from the far side of the table. Her aim was low and wide, however, and, instead of hitting Abel, the egg landed plumb and square on the butterfly teapot of Gaudy Dutch and smashed it to smithereens. Luckily none of the bits reached anybody's eyes.

Mr. Strawn said quietly: "I'll buy another one, Truda." But that did not stay her tears. Nor was she at all pacified when Abel said timidly: "Let me buy it." She was thinking of what the neighbors would say about how she was fooled in her perfect hired man.

A week later the two men went together to the Hillpott vendue and did their best. They got a Gaudy Dutch teapot, but it was Indian bonnet pattern, not butterfly.

This is the story Levi Yoder told me at Silverdale when I asked him why the teapot in his cupboard of Gaudy Dutch did not match the rest of the set.

EASTER EGGS AND EGG TREES

for P. A. W. Wallace

THERE were graven images in more than plenty on our Easter eggs of old years. There were some few on the eggs we colored at home in my young years. Aunt Rachel taught us to gather the catkins from the poplars and to make from them a solution that would stain the eggs a yellow-green. It was onion, as I remember it, from which we secured the dye to color them a red-brown, and it was blueing that brought the white of Leghorn eggs and the dark brown of Brahma eggs alike to the cobalt-green of the eggs of the Araucanas or Naked Necks of current celebrity. Mother balked at blueing-blued eggs, however, as she did at the dyes you could buy at the store, for all of these strong colors were apt to go quickly through the shells and to penetrate into the white of the egg's meat, giving that white a poisonous-looking aspect. Such eggs, she felt, should no more be eaten than those of the cockatrice we read of in Scripture.

As I remember it, we always boiled the eggs hard in the dye-laden waters we made to color them. It does not seem as if the decorated eggs of a hundred years ago or there-abouts were so boiled. All that I have come upon are as light as the blown eggs of old collections. They are not blown, though, as far as I can see, but light because their whites and yolks have dried to next to nothing, at their utmost preserved in a ball that rattles around inside so faintly that you can just hear it and no more.

Three Easter eggs, decorated, that I have, come from

Lebanon. Two are of a dispersed brown not unlike the markings on a guinea's egg, but dotted rather than dashed. The other is of a maroon, but whether from onion or not I am not sure. All three are lively with birds and beasts and symbols. I have no key to the whys and wherefores of the ladders and forks and rakes, the trees and dots in squares and bunched loops that adorn them. Some of these shapes or symbols have a meaning, perhaps, handed down from old times, and others, perhaps, are only what a child's fancy dictated to his hand to trace.

The most recently made of these, and the best preserved, is the maroon-colored egg. On one side it bears the name of Calvin Henry Kauffman in white against the warm maroon, the three parts of the name being set the one above the other, and reading down. On the reverse side of the egg from the name is a child's outline of a man on horseback, and just to the left and above it, the date 1873. To the right of the horse, in the order named, are a three-pronged fork, a seven-toothed rake, and a tree with fourteen branches extending out from its central stem. The fork is a half inch long, the rake three-quarters of an inch, and the tree a full inch. A bird is outlined to the right of the name, a bird a half inch long and less than that in height. All this occupies the larger end of the egg, on the very butt of which is outlined a loosely knit gathering of six ovals around a quartered circle that is looped with six lobes. The whole triple arrangement is vaguely like an enlargement of the six-petaled conventionalized tulip of the common barn symbol. Around the pointed half of the egg, and cut off from the upper half by a waved line, is a decoration of four stunted trees.

I do not know whether the decorations were traced on the egg by a quill pen before the egg was dyed, or whether they were etched on the egg by a knife or other sharp point after

DECORATED EGGS AND EGG PITCHERS

the dye was laid on. If they were done after the former method, the quill must have been dipped in something that would so cover the shell that it would not take the dye. That something may have been beeswax, or lard, or tallow. If the decorations were done after the latter method, they were probably traced on the colored egg soon after the dye was set, and before it had penetrated far into the shell. It is very crude work on this egg, with no artistry about it at all, and, with that on its two light-brown companions of 1858 and 1850, is in strong contrast to the artistry of the egg of 1816.

The larger of the brown eggs, the one with the rattly insides, bears the name of John Henry Light written on it lengthways. The "John Henry" makes one line; the "Light," in larger letters, another line below the first. Above the signature, and also lengthways of the egg, is a bird two inches long, but so conventionalized that he would be a hardy soul who would write it down pelican or eagle or peacock. Its bill, bent towards its breast, suggests the familiar attitude of the pelican seeking its blood to feed its young. The spread wings and extended feet are not unlike those of the eagle on certain almanacs of long ago. A figure of a man is outlined to the left of the eagle, a bird and a ladder to the left of the man, a horse and 1850 still further to the left. We have now made the round of the egg and are back again to the signature. On the large end of the egg is a decoration very like, save in its five lobes instead of six, to the familiar barn symbol already referred to. There is a twisting snake between horse and five-lobed decoration.

The other brown egg, the one that doesn't rattle, bears no name. It came, however, from the Light family, a clan large in numbers in and about Lebanon. On the sharper end of the egg, and reaching up its sides, is a decoration of dotted squares and triangles ending in seven little trees, smaller editions of the many-branched tree of the maroon egg. Above this design at the point is such a many-branched tree, with a circular-lobed design to right of it, and, to the right of that again, a rake and 1858, and a bird, a dog, a fork and a twisted snake. The snake has a straight line cross its waviness that makes it look like an abortive dollar mark. On the larger end of the egg is a circular device with eight lines extending out from its center, each of which ends in a little tree. There are crosses and dots here and there to fill in what would else be blank spaces on the egg.

The egg in maroon and whitey buff of Catherine Metz is another matter entirely from these three eggs. It bears the relation to them of the masterwork in *fractur* of the skilled teacher to the school exercises of that master's pupils. This Catherine Metz egg comes from Dauphin County, and is dated 1816. Its design, of tulips and thistles joined in a simple tracery, is a unit, a combined effect that has a very real if modest beauty of the sort one finds in the folk art of many peoples. Enlarged and spread on wall paper, it would make an admirable background for a room with old-fashioned furnishings.

It is no wonder that these old Easter eggs are so rare. They are more perishable than any other forms of the household art of the Pennsylvania Dutch. Even *matzebäume*, the thin cakes with effigies of men and birds and beasts hung on Christmas trees, survive in greater numbers; and the Christmas candies, fragile though they are and tempting to the appetite despite the "niceness" that makes small fry want to keep them as treasures, are come on half a dozen times to the one time you see a decorated egg. There is a superstition, too, in some sections of Dutchland that Easter eggs should be eaten or destroyed shortly after Easter; that it is unlucky to treasure them; and that, specifically, if you keep an Easter egg for more than a year some one in the family will die. It is to Dr. E. M. Fogel that we owe the recording of this last superstition. You will find it in his *Beliefs and Superstitions.*

There were candy eggs, too, made in many places throughout the Dutch counties. Egg hunts for chocolate and sugar eggs were an institution at children's parties round about Philadelphia as late as the eighteen-seventies, and such hunts are to be found preserved as functions in certain families even to this day. Easter, indeed, was such a high day and holiday all the way from Easton to Little Washington that the basketmakers throughout all this countryside made special baskets for egg gathering and for gifts of eggs. These baskets were characteristically little affairs of white-oak splints, melon-shaped and handled, and dyed with a multicolored confusion of hues.

The newly hatched chick, now so usual an association of Easter, was not much in vogue in old days, either in flesh and feathers or in effigies of any sort. The rabbit, on the other hand, bulked large in the celebration of Easter all through the later nineteenth century, as, indeed, it does today. We had not, in my youth, the many pet stores, or the department stores, that made rabbits a feature of the pre-Easter sales. We had, however, rabbits in plaster-of-Paris, in burned clay, in *fractur* and on painted glass, as well as in cakes and candy. We had tin molds with which to make these rabbit-shaped cakes and candies, and for ice cream, and molds, too, of yellow pumpkin ware, rabbit shaped, for cornstarch and gelatin. We had toy rabbits, this one of wood, and that one the stuffed skin of *lepus cuniculus.*

Just what reinforcement of the Old World preoccupation with rabbits came from the Indian rabbit lore the German immigrants found in backwoods places is merely speculation.

"Brer Rabbit" as we know him in *Uncle Remus* has been now for two generations a part of the inheritance of the American child, but it is pretty generally acknowledged that the negroes who gave us this knowing cottontail borrowed him from the Indians. We of Dutchland have certainly borrowed the Indian belief that a rabbit running straight across the road before us is a sign of bad luck, but running across the road bias or down the road ahead of us is a sign of good luck. We have always been quick to combine the culture we brought from the Old World with that we found in the New. We put the American turkey and Indian alongside the peacock and German Uhlan on our powder horns, and the stars and stripes and American eagles on our *matzebäume* alongside the pomegranates and storks we brought from the Rhine Valley.

Though most of our sects were so stoutly Protestant that they would have no effigies in the churches or steeples above them, we still held to a regard for saints' days and for religious or semi-religious observances that some of them seem to reach back even to pre-Christian times. Who knows what old rites are symbolized in the signs and figures that we find on these Easter eggs of yesterday? As there is an earth goddess of orgiac abandon, whose temple is the Hoerselberg, back of Saint Ursula, so there may be hidden wonders involved in the seemingly childish scrawls on these backgrounds of yellow and brown and maroon.

Reaching back into the days of the latest of these Lebanon eggs are those done by Jesse Laros (1823-1902) of Quakertown. Most recently made of these Quakertown eggs is that dated 1901, but some were much earlier than that, the earliest that I can recall of 1865. The old Evangelical minister had practiced this art, as he had that of *fractur*, all his mature years. Save that the dyes for most of these eggs were bought at the store, all were done in the traditional manner, all, that is, of the thirteen it chanced were preserved. There was a bird amid leafage on nearly every egg, and tulips on several of them. After the eggs had been dyed a chocolate-red in color, the designs had been scratched on them with a penknife. Looking at them you realized you were looking on folk art at its best.

A purple goose egg with the figure of a small boy on it is the largest fowl's egg with decorations that I have ever found. Above the boy is the legend "Snooks. Easter 1868." Seventy years ago there was a warm human appeal in those words. To-day they are read without as much as the arching of an eyebrow, save by some sentimentalist or unfortunate burdened with imagination. This egg is amateur work, out of any tradition, ugly, but somehow or other of the appeal there always is in whatever betrays a heart with the great gift of caring.

It is Theodore K. Long in his *Forty Letters* (1931) who has explained to us most fully the legend of the Ostern Hase, or Easter Rabbit, who was supposed to lay the colored eggs so dear to children and on which they were to scratch rude designs. "On Easter night, before going to bed, the last thing we did was to set our caps or hats around the room at convenient places for the Ostern Hase, and some-time during the night, while the children were fast asleep, he would mysteriously appear and deposit the eggs in our caps or hats."

It was in Pfoutz Valley, that land of milk and honey reaching back from the Juniata toward the Susquehanna in Perry County, that Mr. Long spent his childhood. Although an outpost of Dutchland, it was rich in all the lore that makes us so distinctive a people. Mr. Long goes on to tell us that he often used to scratch rude sketches on these eggs stained pink and blue and red and yellow. "Sometimes," he writes, "the sketches would represent things that happened about the farm. As I became older, I learned to make very pleasing sketches on these eggs, using the dull blade of my knife as a sketching tool. We would eat some of the eggs on Easter day and within a few days thereafter. But the engraved ones were put aside and treasured for many months."

Such Easter eggs as survive to-day are generally amateur affairs such as children used often to make just for the fun of the thing. A cheery old body had cooked up a dozen for us one year after she heard us talking of them in their prime. She had put onion peels in the water in which she boiled them, which had turned them a rich and deep red-brown. She had plastered little blobs of beeswax on some of the eggs here and there before she put them in the onion water, so that they came out with splotches of bright yellow from the wax, which had, of course, prevented the onion dye from "taking." Redder than chocolate though the unblotched eggs were, they looked very like the Easter eggs of chocolate retailed in all the stores.

More pretentious, but not works of art, were the pictured eggs done for us by another old lady and her daughters. They are about of the order of excellence of the Lebanon eggs. They did us a round dozen of these. Rabbits are predominant among their decorations, with peacocks a close second and smaller birds only less in number. There are human figures on some of them, too, a man on a statheled hayrick or "barrick," as such a "berg" or mountain-shaped pile is called, both in Dutch and English. Another shows a straw-roofed barn, such as were plenty all about northern Lancaster until the eighteen-seventies. There are potted plants on others, and on one some wheeled vehicle, but whether Amish wagon or hayrack or Ford car I cannot make out.

The limner of one of these eggs confesses that the peacock on the egg she scratched up began as a rabbit, became again, to the derision of her sisters, a cat on the back fence, and was then crested and tailed peacock-wise. Many of these eggs have stars in the sky above their beasts and birds and buildings, their human gazers at the heavens, their trees and plants and flowers.

The round dozen of these fellows grouped on my desk have an appeal to me that must be atavistic. My folks, back along, for generations, must have done such eggs, in Germantown, in Bethlehem, in Nazareth, in Tatamy, in Christian Spring. I like the eggs in their rich red-brown because they are part of the folk art of my people. I like them, too, because of their dark colors, which suggest the eggs of the Light Brahmas of my youth, the Dark Brahmas of my middle years, and the Cornish Indian Games I introduced now and then to keep proper spangling on my Red Dorkings. Despite our knowledge that Leghorns, layers of white eggs, will produce more eggs than any other breed, we of Pennsylvania stick to the brown-egg breeds, believing in our heart of hearts that brown eggs are richer and meatier and more nutritious than white eggs. Whatever the cause, I have a child's delight in this dozen of pictured eggs of "onion brown" or "onion red" that nestle together by the pad on which I write.

Glass eggs, other than plebeian nest eggs of milk white, are not common in rural Pennsylvania. Peddlers and country storekeepers alike must have now and then stocked up with eggs with peep holes in the end through which you could see little putz-like panoramas of the manger at Bethlehem and the rising from the grave. It is years, though, since I have come across such an egg. A Lancaster County auction did bring to light a golden chick just broken from the top of the shell, but still sitting within that "natal chamber" as comfortably as if she were already grown and sitting upon a hatching of eggs herself. This egg of white glass had seen such wear and tear that the gold paint was worn off the top of the chick's head. The "EASTER" in gold on the side of the shell is, too, a good deal worn. It is most fetchingly done, in staggered letters. The egg is of blown glass, of about the size of a turkey's egg and with such an egg's pointed end.

A still larger egg of milk glass has nearly all its gilding worn off. No chick is hatching from this egg, which is so big one wonders whether you should look for gosling or baby ostrich to burst from it. It, too, is of a flat bottom, like the other glass egg of turkey size, to keep it from rolling, and it bears the legend "Easter" on a scroll amid flowers. Another glass egg, gay as a crazy quilt in red, and white, and blue, and mauve, may be a darning ball. It, too, is blown, but hardly, I think, like the others, into a mold.

This last egg is no gayer, however, than a real hen's egg I have, covered with beflowered calico in red and green, blue and gold, pink and green, all overlaid with designs made of the white pith of some marsh plant. There is so outlined an arrowhead, a circle with center of red, and a triangle. This egg is a Berks County product.

It is to Berks County, indeed, that you trace most of the strange ramifications of the egg cult. Perhaps I too much dignify, by the name of cult, the use of eggs at Easter, or in ordinances in one way or another connected with Easter rites and what those rites symbolize. There is, though, so obviously in the egg the germ of life, the triumphant asseveration of life, the promise of a physical immortality in the handing on of life from generation to generation, that there is no wonder the egg becomes the symbol of life and, as such, the key to cult practices. It was in Berks County I first came on the egg tree, a creation to insure motherhood to its maker. It is in Berks, and in those parts of Lebanon and Lancaster just over the border from Berks, that I have found the most cryptically decorated Easter eggs, and it is from Berks, at Mohnton, that have come that trio of "egg-pitchers" so provocative of guessing.

They were discovered for me, as so much else deeply revelatory of Dutch culture, by the Brunners of Reinholds, Hattie the elder running upon them and giving them to me. Each pitcher is made from the shell of one egg, a shell with small end sliced off as you would slice it off a boiled egg set in the small end of an egg cup. This edge of shell is bound over with a piece of calico, for a third of an inch both inside and out. The large end of the egg is bound around with another piece of calico a third of an inch high, so that an even base is provided for the toy to rest upon. Between upper and lower rounds of calico appears a belt of eggshell some three-quarters of an inch wide, a belt, in each case, of warm buff brown. The eggs are not particularly large ones, looking from size and color and shape as if they were pullet eggs of Plymouth Rocks or Rhode Island Reds. From the lower round of calico to the upper round, a handle of calico is bent, in the very shape of those on old pitchers of earthenware. A "lip" of calico, pasted on the top round, carries this verisimilitude even further.

The little pitcher brought into being and decorated by the pink calico is a trifle of true daintiness. It is real old calico of two shades of deep pink that has been recovered from some old chest for this prettifying. The second pitcher is gay in modern calico of gray and green, pink and yellow.

The third is covered with a plain cotton in potter's blue. All three pitchers were made just before the Easter of 1933, for the delight of children, by Mrs. Mary Horning. I have yet to find if they are of her own designing or of traditional origin. Because of my egg all covered by bright old calico I lean to the latter presumption.

It is in the very nature of things that the egg should be a symbol of fertility. It is not only that all the world knows that the egg harbors the life to come, the chick to be, but that all the world recognizes the egg as a concentrated food, a stimulant of vigor, a provocative of creative instinct. That a similar association should exist with respect to the shell of the egg, the blown shell, is not difficult to explain. The belief that there are powers of fertility imminent even in the broken shells of eggs is only one step farther in the orderly progress of the association of ideas. And all the world knows, too, of other powers of eggshells. Boiled in the pot, they clear coffee; returned to the hens, broken into small bits, they inspire Dame Partlet and her sisters to renewed laying; dug into the flower borders they bring more flowers and flowers of brighter hues.

Eggshells are even looked to hopefully to restore trees to a bloom that for a year has passed them by. Dutch country folks who had banished themselves from Pennsylvania to New Jersey had great pride in a magnolia in their yard. For a number of years it bloomed annually, but finally, in 1932, no blooms made their appearance. Perhaps the dry summers of 1930 and 1931 were to blame. The magnolia lovers were in despair. To prevent the persistence of so desolating an absence of bloom the folks collected all the broken eggshells they could, not only from the eggs they themselves used, but also from the neighbors. These broken shells they dug in around the roots of the magnolia. They carefully blew, and preserved intact, save for the holes in either end, all the eggs they used in cooking. These they strung and hung from the tree, where it is said, the blown shells delighted them as much as the flowers, with which, of course, the tree responded after such generous stimulation.

The most curious manifestation of the egg cult that I have come upon in all Dutchland is the Easter egg tree. It is one of the customs that those who resort to it are loath to admit. After I secured a photograph of the tree, however, and spoke of it to all trusty folks I was rewarded with nods and winks and "Ai! Yai! Ais!" and assurances I should hear all about it when there was not so much company present. The Easter egg tree, Exhibit No. 1, is a little tree, leafless, of eight branches, along which are strung eggs, each close to the other, to the number, respectively, of 9, 15, 10, 11, 9, 12, 16 and 11. It is mounted in what looks like a pottery jug set in a tin bucket. It is, judging from the height of the children in the photograph, less than four feet high.

The woman who made the Easter egg tree had been married for more than five years, but she had had no children. She was told to make an egg tree the coming Easter, and before the following Easter she would have a baby. She made the tree I have described. She had the baby. After she felt sure it was going to live she had the tree destroyed. She did not want another baby right away again. The egg tree was so potent in bringing the first child she was afraid it would prove quickly efficacious again, and a second baby soon after the first was not part of her calculations.

From such high offices, it is a descent to the egg tree's use as a thing to delight children at Easter. Easter egg tree, Exhibit No. 2, one with such a function, attracted five hundred visitors in Holy Week of 1936. There were seven hundred eggs hung from the branches of the tree or impaled

on its short twigs or threaded on its thin wythes. The tree
was a water birch cut along Schuylkill's banks for transmogri-
fication into a thing of wonder and delight. One cannot but
question how many who made pilgrimage to the home on
the river front where the egg tree was displayed knew of
its original use.

Courtesy of Mrs. Elmer L. Palsgrove

AN EGG TREE OF READING

THE "DOCTOR'S" INSIGHT

for Ulysses Bickel

THE two of them had come from Easton to consult the "Doctor." He was, of course, not an accredited physician, but just the powwow man of the wide region dominated by the Hexenkopf. They were well on toward their middle years and none too fervent believers in the hidden arts of hexerei. The regular physicians had not had any success, though, in treating the goiter that was enlarging slowly on the neck of the younger woman. She had been pretty in her time, and she was chagrined over the wane of the attention she had once received. She who had kept herself as neat as a wren was now content to go about with unpreened feathers. From one side she was still fair, but that growing disfigurement made her feel fat and more than the forty she had nearly reached.

It had been a tedious drive from Easton in that long, long ago. The old gray had refused to quicken her pace beyond a slow walk. So forbidding was the road up Morgan Hill that they had left the mare hitched to a fence at the mountain's foot, and made their way slowly up the stone-walled lane that led to the doctor's house. The footing on the loose stones of the road had been uncertain and its rise sharp and a half mile long. The pretty woman was more winded than her older and leaner companion when they reached the flat terrace where the powwow man had his shack of logs. As the two approached the bars at the end of the lane they stopped to get breath. The patient to be was exasperated. "No gate to get in by!" she said. "This is a fine entrance to a doctor's office. I wonder if he can be any good at all?" They were city folks and how to slide the long bars so the ends of them could be dropped on the ground and stepped over was too much for them. Her stockings, too, had bothered the younger woman as she had toiled up the steep hill. So disheartened had she been now that the lump on her neck could not be concealed that she had lost pride in her underpinning. She had fallen into that unpardonable sin of a woman with shapely legs—stockings wrinkled on ankles and calves. Her stockings had had to be pulled up several times during the ascent, or they had gotten under her feet.

The two women had an ado to climb the bars, their long skirts getting in the way. Safely over at last, they walked to the door of the house, and knocked. It was more than a minute, though, before the old powwower came to the door. Smiling benevolently and rubbing the sleep out of his eyes, the patriarch admitted them. He stroked his long white beard meditatively as he asked them what he could do for them. The patient, who had kept her pretty profile toward him, turned so as to display the goiter. Now the cure of goiter was one of the "Doctor's" specialties, but he was not going to make any promises before he had found out something about his visitors or had induced the afflicted one to part with the proper fee. So he tousled his old white poll with one hand, and cupped the other so the money could be dropped into it. He then bent forward and gave minute attention to the goiter.

Shifting his gaze to his patient's face, he studied that as carefully. "I am afraid I cannot help you," he said at length. "If I read rightly what is in your heart, you have no faith in me. I can help only those who have faith in me." The woman, impressed by his reading of her thoughts, was reassured and declared she had absolute faith in him. She took her purse from the covered basket she carried and began to finger the silver. "That you may know I have insight and knowledge," he continued gravely, "I now tell you that one of your stockings is held up, more or less, by a rag at the knee, and the other, not much better, by a rubber band." In response to that sally, a silver dollar dropped into his cupped paw.

Perhaps the old man had not been so sound asleep as his appearance at the door indicated while the women had been talking together in the walled lane and had been climbing over the bars.

THE OLDEST LIVING THING?

for Theophilus E. M. Boll

IT certainly does not look its age, this widespread stand of box huckleberry on a hillside of Perry County. The botanists used to say it was established here near New Bloomfield before the big trees of California began to push upward from seed, that it was possibly ten thousand years old, that it might be the most ancient living thing in all the world. The botanists have now drawn in their horns, though, and at present the weight of authority among them is that the plant is some twelve hundred years old. Its extent is hardly a half mile in diameter, but cultivated land to the eastward, in the direction of Little Juniata Creek, may have once known box huckleberry as cover, as the open woodland contiguous still does. Before clearings were made hereabouts the stand may have been a full mile across from advancing edge to advancing edge.

If, as it is said, box huckleberry broadens each year only three inches on each side, or six inches in all, through the extension of its roots and the throwing up of new stems, the patch would grow in diameter only five thousand feet, or less than a mile, in ten thousand years. Whatever its antiquity, this growth of brown stems and box-like leafage of green has been here long centuries, longer centuries than the known or guessed history of any live thing of other than its own kind in this part of our continent. It is awakening to the imagination to stand here on the westward-facing hillside of deciduous trees, and to think of what has happened to the

366

world since the old shrub of burnished leaves began to spread abroad from the seed of it dropped here. This is not a long-settled countryside, its first opening up dating only from 1740. Its pioneers lost many of their numbers in the Indian forays of 1756 and 1763, but they kept coming in, group after group, Scotch-Irish first, and then Germans. There is fertile land, limestone, in certain of the valleys, but there were no such attractions for settlement here as south, beyond Sterrett's Gap, in the broad Cumberland Valley. The box huckleberry grows on a shaley sort of soil, which must be very sour to keep the shrub in such lustihead of bright green. Its altitude above tidewater is between six hundred and seven hundred feet.

The botanists are higher hearted respecting the age of another patch of this same box huckleberry ten miles to the northeastward of the New Bloomfield patch, on the east side of the Juniata, just opposite Losh Run Station. This patch, though not so thick a stand as the one at New Bloomfield, reaches for more than a mile inland from the river. It may be, therefore, of an even greater age than was ever attributed to the first-discovered plant, or some thirteen thousand years old. It is not so picturesque in itself, though, as the longer-known plant, not so obviously one plant, and, now that it has been ravaged by fire, in no way so appealing. I write of it rather to substantiate the claim of *Gaylussacia brachycera* to antiquity than for its own beauty or impressiveness. It doesn't stir me as does the New Bloomfield plant.

The box huckleberry does not seed of itself nowadays. It has been only after its flowers have been fertilized by pollen from other stands of it to the southward, that it has been made to fruit and to mature seed from which little plants of it have grown. It is a scant bloomer here in mid-Pennsylvania. We walked a hundred yards through the New Bloom-field patch before we came on its wax-like flowers of pink and white all but concealed under the topmost ends of its leafage. Nor did we find the Losh Run plant any more prodigal of bloom.

There are no lovelier little heath flowers in America than these of the box huckleberry. They appeal, in their way, as do, in their kindred ways, snowberry, mountain cranberry and pink alpine heather. They have no scent, and they are smaller than arbutus flowers, but they have the arbutus pink and white. The spray of box huckleberry that I pulled up broke off with six inches of main root, to which hung fila-mented tufts of rootlets here and there. It divided into two upright stems. One of these stems separated into two smaller stems. Each of these again separated. There were ten sprays in all at the top of this half of the plant. The other main stem from the root separated into two. One of these two separated into three finials of leafage and the other into five such finials. It is the eight little sprays last referred to, of box-like leaves, that bear the heather-like bells of pink and white. The fullest blown clusters are of fifteen bells, and the smallest of five.

It was a rainy day, a day now of light showers and now of downpours, that we ran west and north from German-town to New Bloomfield, a sixth of May, when appleblow in the orchards and blow of wild plum by the creek-sides and wood-edges were at their height. After such a feast of pink and white, and fluffy white warm-dusted with faint yellow, the stand of box huckleberry seemed lacking in em-phasis, just an undergrowth of light green shining with rain. A month earlier such a hillside growth had been grateful indeed, in the enameled green of its low and box-like leafage.

HEADWATERS OF THE JUNIATA

Perhaps all the box huckleberries were united underground by a root system, but, to the eye, there were spaces
between this drift and that mat that looked to be devoid of
any of the aged shrubbery, below ground as well as above.
It may be that in some old day fire had run through these
woods, burning down into the mold here and there, and
dividing a great stand of box huckleberry into dispersed and
semi-dispersed patches of some ten to twelve acres in all.

I had expected the stand, from the description I had
heard of it, to be one solid mat of circular form, like that
miniature stand of yew a hundred feet in diameter on the
Nockamixon heights above the Delaware. That yew has been
cut for Christmas greens for years, so it rises to-day no
higher than your head, a mass of branches curving up so
close together as to be almost impenetrable. For as much as
a hundred feet here and a hundred feet there, the box
huckleberry did form such a mat, but for the most part there
were path-like places between this stand and that, though
there were in many instances connecting belts of bushes between the stands. The most of the huckleberry bushes rose
about eight inches above the leafy woods-floor. A good few
of them inclined downhill, and when you straightened them
up they would be, the tallest of them, from a foot to fifteen
inches tall. As you looked at the hillside, though, all appeared to be of about the one height of eight inches. There
is little other underbrush in the woods, the most conspicuous
sort being two other heaths, the common blueberry and
laurel.

The little valley off the Little Juniata that you followed
up to find the box huckleberries is narrow and secluded. It
is cleared in its bottom, and it has been cropped until very
recently. The road up the valley, mossed and arbutus
studded on the bank to its left, skirts the foot of the hill-

side on which the huckleberries grow. There are two homes on this road between the New Bloomfield pike and the stand of *Gaylussacia brachycera*. The farm at the juncture with the pike is still a busy place, but the buildings on the upper place are falling into disuse. One cannot but wonder did the folks who lived here years back know crops of blue fruit on the huckleberries. If such fruit there then were, they gathered it, for the detail of their dooryard shows them to have been an up and doing sort. The stone underpinning of their barn is smooth cut and the road by their door well shaled.

There is no tradition, though, in the neighborhood, of harvests here in old times. The patch lies, of course, off a main road, but not a half mile off it, and it is not difficult of access. It is not even known of to-day, for all the sign pointing to it, by people living close by. At Meck's Corners, only two miles away, we were told that this stand of box huckleberry of so hoar an antiquity "must be something new." She whom we questioned said she had lived a long time here but that she had never heard of it. A boy who had gone to school nearby told us he had heard of the patch, that he had seen the sign pointing to it, and that he had directed people to it, but that he had never been there to see the bushes. "They made nothing of it at school," he said. He could not, of course, have gone to the little red schoolhouse where you turn off the New Bloomfield road to visit the patch. Those children have undoubtedly been taught from their first hours in that building of brick that they are privileged to be within hailing distance of the oldest living thing in Pennsylvania.

The patch was discovered by Spencer Fullerton Baird (1823-1887) when he was living in Carlisle, along about 1850. Visited by botanists from time to time, it has gotten no small share of its present celebrity from the writings of

Edgar T. Wherry. The land on which it grows has been presented to the state, forming a shrine to which all faithful lovers of the heaths and of the yesterday of Pennsylvania must ultimately make pilgrimage.

THE UWCHLAN SAGA

for Bess Hokanson

ALL my youth I heard talk of Milford Mills as an Eden from which my mother and her family had been thrust forth. Just what was the agency of that thrusting I never took in. It was not intended, I suppose, that I should understand, for any explanation, no matter how guarded, must have involved some criticism of Grandfather Thomas. He had, as a matter of fact, let the gristmill and farm and country store, a considerable property for its place and time, slip through his fingers. Neither my mother, who was eight when the family moved out of the old home in 1846, nor my Aunt Rachel, who was twenty-one, would have ever admitted there was a flaw in him. Grandfather Thomas was good company; he had a certain presence; he was ready with his quill and his speech; so it seemed to his daughters that it must have been something else than such a paragon that caused the downfall of the family fortunes.

Now that I have read scores of his letters and of letters to him, I know that he had an inveterate passion for speculation in land, that he was always trying to buy or trade land, and that in the end the sharpers picked him clean. I never heard a word of all this, though, even from my uncles. It seems rather remarkable that I did not, for I had two summer outings with Uncle Seal, and talks by campfires at night that might have inspired confidences. The rolling stone's loyalty was too strong, however, and so was that of Uncle Jim who might have told me something revelatory of his father on our trips to Anglesea or Gettysburg. The loyalty of Uncle Pline was equally strong, or the many nights of fall we sat together on the porch and rocked in the darkness and talked of Milford would have given me some inkling of the truth. Uncle Pline always came out from the city to stay with us in Germantown and help Aunt Rachel look after my sister and me and the place while mother and father went on their vacation of three weeks to the White Mountains and Canada. In every reference to him by his children Grandfather Thomas was tacitly assumed to be beyond criticism. Welsh Quaker, Welsh Baptist and Scotch-Irish Presbyterian make a tight-lipped blend.

It was hard luck, I gathered in some dim fashion, that drove the Thomases out of Milford Mills. The younger members of the family, when they were once established in Philadelphia, were really glad they had escaped the country early. Uncle Seal was such a gypsy he would never have stayed at home anywhere. It was only Aunt Rachel and Uncle Pline who keenly regretted the transplantation. What the others lamented was really the fallen fortunes. Uncle Pline, a boy of fifteen, would not go to town with his family in 1847. After that one year of the whole family in the new schoolhouse on the road to the Eagle, the year of 1846-47, he went back to the house across from the mill, to live with his grandmother until she sold the place in 1848. He could not bear to be parted from his Dominique fowls, the very apple of his eye.

It was from Aunt Rachel, who lived with us from as early as I can remember until her death in 1888, that I heard most of Milford Mills, and of its environing countryside in Uwchlan and Nantmeal. The place was a hill farm, but fairly fertile, and both mill and store, properly managed, were paying businesses when Grandfather Thomas came into control of things there. It was not of the family troubles, though, that I heard in childhood from Aunt Rachel. It was of the delights of the place. That was a never-ending chronicle, the delights of Uwchlan. The story went on night after night, for how many years I am not sure, but surely from before I was seven to when I was ten. I know it began before I was seven, for I can recall Aunt Rachel talking to me of Milford in the second-story back room on Church Lane. I was seven when we moved from there. The telling of that saga ended, as a regular feature of the early night's entertainment, when I had to begin to devote a good deal of time to lessons in 1882. It was a never-ending chronicle, because when Aunt Rachel had told me every incident of it that she was willing to tell me of what she could recall, I would ask her to begin it again and tell it all through once more in every detail. As I remember it took about seven nights in the full recital, in sessions, say, of an hour an evening. Incidents, people, pictures of landscape, all figured in the saga.

There was, indeed, much to tell. To many, perhaps, it would not a bit of it have mattered, but I had always the country heart, to which the little affairs of everyday life on farm and in mill and store, against the background of hills and fields and waters, seem far more important than the fates of nations. From the moment of first coming across it I sympathized with Dunsany's contention in *The Golden Doom*, that the play of a child is more important than the throne of a king.

What chances for play there were at Milford Mills, by pond and race and covered bridge, in store and mill lofts and barn, in country rambles, visiting relatives, and going to meeting! There was no end to fun where there were horses and cows and sheep, Dominique hens and guineas and geese, dump carts, spring wagons and gigs, a springhouse, shops and stacks of corn fodder. There was fishing there and fording, plowing and harvesting, gatherings for talk at the store, the drowsy hum of the buhrstones grinding wheat and oats and corn. There was horseback riding, efforts at bareback feats inspired by a circus seen at Downingtown, adventures with running negroes through by the underground railroad, the spectacle of postwoods nearby losing their top branches under the weight of wild pigeons, chestnutting, walnutting, shellbarking, persimmoning, and scores of kindred delights.

Never was a small boy happier than I, sitting up wideeyed I have no doubt, in those winter nights of searching wind, and drinking in that never-ending saga of Uwchlan. The farmer is stronger in me than all else, I think, stronger than teacher, or collector, or writer. I was never wholly content until I owned a farm, not a real farm, perhaps, for I farm it only slightly, but broad acres with a real farmhouse on them, a great barn, hayfields, pastures, timberland —above all elbow room and open spaces for the sun to fill by day and from which you can see the march of the stars by night.

That I never have come into possession of this farm in Uwchlan on which my mother was born has been at times a concern to me. Mother played with the idea of buying it back, but she never pushed the project, for she would not have been happy there save for a few weeks in summer. In her heart of hearts she did not like the country. Then, too, there had been a more modern house built uphill from the farmhouse on the Downingtown-West Nantmeal Seminary Road by those who had turned the gristmill into a cloth mill and had done well with it in Civil War days. After them had come a breeder of Kentucky horses, who had changed the mill into a stable and built long stables onto the barn.

All these changes had given the place another atmosphere entirely from that it had when the Thomases lived there and the Reeds before them.

It was remarkable, though, how long all that was there in the times of my people's occupancy remained as it had been before they left. Until a row of frame houses was built on a site just across Marsh Creek from the farmhouse and store, those buildings, and springhouse and weaver's house, covered wooden bridge and ford by its side, wagon shed and shops persisted pretty much as they were before 1846. The row of houses the McClures built for their mill hands on the west side of the Downingtown Road below the store is unobtrusive and out of the way. Even the great pear tree by the side of the weaver's house is flourishing now more than a hundred years after its planting. The great walnut by the springhouse has, too, defied time.

Situated no more than thirty-five miles away from Philadelphia as it is, it is surprising how few changes there are in Milford Mills from what it was a century ago. Only the gristmill itself and the bridge have changed materially. What else is different from what it was in old times is what is added. If you stand in the shadow of the mill, on the iron bridge that has succeeded the wooden one, and look at what you can see west and south and back of you to the east, only that row of frame tenements looks anything but old timey. The house of the eighteen-sixties, with the tall Norway spruces before it, is hidden behind the mill. So is the barn whose lines have been spoiled by the stables built onto it. The "storehouse" to the left is no longer a store, but a comfortable-looking dwelling house. The old house just in front of you where my grandparents lived most of the time they were here is resplendent in fresh whitewash, but very like what it has been the forty-five years I have known it.

The weaver's house, narrow and four stories high, counting basement and garret, towers up like a white shaft just across the Brandywine road from the farmhouse. The springhouse in the meadow below the "storehouse" is unused, at least in second story and garret, which is all the better, hygienically speaking, if its lowest level is still a place to keep milk.

The stone walls of all these buildings are bound together by that old kiln-burned lime that lasts forever. Their timbers, sawed probably in the sawmill that stood just by the gristmill, were long seasoned under cover before they were put into place. The shingles on all the old buildings were split shingles. They were worthy of replacement in kind, all the roofs of them, some of which have sunk to tin and building paper that remains building paper no matter how glorified. The paint on cornices and all outside trim was originally and for long that old white lead that wears off only by the disintegration of the wood beneath it. All the materials first used here belonged to that old day before labor-saving devices and cheap substitutes and hurry took durability from building.

Aunt Rachel had vivid memories of Milford Mills and of all the country about it in Uwchlan and Nantmeal, and in other townships further away, Brandywine and Pikeland and West Vincent for three. She was born in 1825, so she could remember events clearly from 1830 on. Her parents had married early in 1820, and Grandfather Thomas, who was a miller, had moved into part of the house opposite the mill, a two-family house, shortly after his marriage. Here most of the children were born, and here Virgil Maro died, at one week old, the only one of the nine children not to live to maturity. In 1828 the family had moved from the "mill house," down the Downingtown Road to Happersetts, a stone's throw below the store. They were back again, soon, though, in the "mill house," or farmhouse opposite the mill. There were times, I suppose, when things got difficult, even in a two-family house. At best there would be encounters in the dooryards, and Ann Thomas, Grandfather's mother, was a redoubtable old lady. There were many things to disagree about, even to so slight a matter as in what window the daphne odora would do best.

I take the date of Virgil's death from the family Bible, from which I shall quote, too, the other records necessary to the understanding of this Uwchlan Saga. The Bible was presented to Elizabeth D. Thomas by Morgan J. Thomas, January 20, A.D. 1842. It was printed in Philadelphia three years earlier. All the children were born at this time, and the family still four years short of the debacle in which they lost their home. Grandfather, a good penman, records that:

"Morgan Jones Thomas, eldest son of Isaac Thomas, and Ann his wife, late Ann Morgan, intermarried with Elizabeth Davis Reed, eldest daughter of William Reed and Rachel his wife, late Rachel Davis, March 9, A.D. 1820." Morgan Jones Thomas was then twenty-one, having been born November 30, 1798, and his wife not yet nineteen, having been born June 21, 1801. Their first child, Ann, was born December 11, 1820. Cosmo Eugene was born November 17, 1822; Rachel Davis, October 24, 1825; Selim Saladdin, January 7, 1828; Virgil Maro, August 4, 1830; Pliny Valerian, August 30, 1831; James Belcomb, March 24, 1834; Theora Alethe, June 28, 1836; and Lucy Ellmaker, November 20, 1838.

There were portraits painted of Grandfather and of Grandmother, with Uncle Jim a babe in her arms. The date of the painting, therefore, must have been sometime in 1834, and family tradition has it that it was an itinerant portrait painter did the work. Grandmother has a rather eighteenth-century look and air, but the quick individuality there was in her is not brought out in the painting. She looks gentle and pleasant, but of so little personal savor that you doubt it is a good likeness. Grandfather with stock and open vest, clean-shaven and sandy, is, I take it, a better likeness. He does not look in the portrait, though, the evader of realities that he was. There is no dream in his pale eyes. Full chin and high forehead give him almost the mien of the substantial man he never was.

There is nothing in this portrait of Morgan Jones Thomas that explains certain of the names he gave his children. The first child was named Ann for her paternal grandmother, but the second child, Cosmo Eugene, owes his name to the Medici, of whom his father had been reading just before the first man child arrived. Rachel Davis was named, as the first girl should have been, for her maternal grandmother. Selim Saladdin was so named because his father had been reading *The Talisman*, only three years published in 1828. There has come to me among my grandfather's books the Warton's *Virgil* from the reading of which it is a safe guess, perhaps, came the name of Virgil Maro. Pliny Valerian was the proper name for Uncle Pline, lover of Dominiques and of all other farm fowl and animals, lover of fish and of everything of the countryside, a simon-pure countryman all his forty years of city life.

The middle name of James Belcomb came to Milford Mills all the way across the Atlantic from the cathedral city of York in England. James Thomas, Grandfather's younger brother, took a sea voyage for his health. He was to have looked up, too, the fabulous family fortune in Wales, whence the Thomases had come early in the third quarter of the eighteenth century, in the person of James Thomas, Grand-father's grandfather. James II, stricken while traveling in

England, was taken in and nursed by Dr. Belcomb of York, who arranged for the burial when all his efforts failed to save the traveler. In gratitude to that kindly physician, Grandfather put Belcomb into his son's name, giving him the first name of his brother and of his first American ancestor.

Where Theora Alethe was discovered, I do not know. Perhaps the two names were Grandfather's own adaptations from what Greek he had picked up. The family understood Theora to mean the countenance of God. Alethe is obviously ἀληθής, truthful, honest, frank. Just how the two words together were translated by grandfather we can only guess. Almost everybody thought, of course, that Theora was an incorrect spelling of Theodora. Lucy Ellmaker, my mother, had her middle name from a friend father made in Harrisburg. It may be that the Lucy was the name of that friend's wife.

Such outland names as these, though Cosmo was shortened into Cos, Selim into Seal, and Pliny to Pline, were something of a scandal in that countryside in the Brandywine Hills. It was what you would expect, though, the neighbors thought, from Morgan Jones Thomas. He was never content to be like Tom, Dick or Harry; he was flighty and unsettled, a reputable person but erratic. His own justification for the foreign names was that in a community in which so many names were only juxtapositions of each other, where there was a Thomas Jones Morgan as well as a Morgan Jones Thomas, a Lewis Reese and a Reese Lewis, an Evan Davis and a David Evans, a John Phillips and a Philip John, such a departure as was his from the established order of names was helpful practically to distinguish one person from another as well as refreshing to the spirit.

Grandmother Thomas bore much without protest these

strange names among the great total. Wives then submitted themselves unto their husbands as unto the Lord. No child of hers was named after her, and she was dead before her Theora had a daughter to call Elizabeth. From Grandmother's letters to Grandfather, which he preserved most methodically, and which have come down to us to-day, you learn that her patience was tried at times, especially when Grandfather went gadding to conventions or on land-speculation trips and left her and the children to run farm and mill and store.

There were troubles over potatoes that must be planted or corn that needed harvesting, over shafts loosening in the mill, and dams breaking, over folks that dealt at the store and refused to pay. One of these store incidents leads to a lighter moment than was usual in her correspondence with her absentee husband. She had caught one of her customers at the store stealing tobacco and had jerked the keg away from him. "This afternoon," she writes, "he came back and said: 'I have come to pay for what I stole yesterday. My horse was strained and I was going to try a project [to cure him]. I was to steal three articles, a piece of meat, a plug of tobacco and a bag of string. If I had told you yesterday why I stole the tobacco it would not have had the effect [I desired].' That was a good come off for a thief caught in the very act."

Once her husband fell ill at Harrisburg and she had to go there, piloted by her brother, to nurse him. The neighbors rose to the occasion and helped the older children to look after the younger and the mill and the farm and the stock.

Grandfather would go off when he could find a plausible excuse, to here, there or everywhere, say to Black Log in the Juniata country, for three weeks, and let things go as they would at home. There are troubled letters to him, not only from his wife, but from his daughter Ann and his son Cosmo. The busy mother and her girl of sixteen and boy of fourteen had their hands full with all the three-fold business of the place. For all Grandfather's pleasantness and solicitude for others, he seems to have had no great sense of responsibility. He had an unmitigated faith, too, in human nature, after it had again and again, in this man or that, proved anything but trustworthy. He was forever giving advice, too, whether it was asked for or not.

Grandfather was a good correspondent. He wrote letters to cousins who had emigrated to Iowa, and to neighbors who had joined the Mormons at Nauvoo. In the end the Mormons were anathema to him, for their perfervid oratory persuaded his eldest daughter Ann that she should join them. They took her away from home in his absence, but he was soon on their trail, and he brought her back unharmed the next day. She was a sprightly girl, for whom Kimberton school had done much, and she was her mother's right-hand help in running the place when her father was traipsing about the country. Marrying in 1841, she rode away happily on a pillion behind her husband, since the roads of that day were impossible for wheels in February. A little more than a year later she died, shortly after the birth of her child, a young woman whose letters reveal her bright intelligence and keen sense of humor and stout heart.

Grandfather's quillwork and penmanship brought him some conveyancing to do, the writing of wills and inventories and the like. Even so early a document as the inventory of the estate of his father, Isaac Thomas, who died in 1815, may be partly in his handwriting. The inventory of the personal property of his father-in-law, William Reed, is unmistakably his. I am going to reprint both of these documents, not because they have to do with the possessions of my own people, but because they reveal what were the contents of typical American country homes in the early years of the nineteenth century. Neither of these homes, both in Uwchlan, but the Thomas home unlocatable now, was as fully furnished as homes of folks of equal substance among the Pennsylvania Dutch would have been, but both are fully representative of Welsh and Scotch-Irish stocks. I include first the inventory of the estate of Isaac Thomas:

An Inventory of the Goods and Chattles, Rights and Credits which were of Isaac Thomas, of the Township of Uwchlan, in the County of Chester, late decd. taken and appraised by us the subscribers the 9th day of Feb. A.D. 1815.

1	Mare, Saddle, and Bridle	$70.00
1	White Cow and Calf	20.00
1	Brindle Cow	20.00
1	Black Cow	20.00
1	White Heifer	8.00
12	Sheep	30.00
4	Pigs	16.00
1	Wheel Barrow	3.00
To 1	Shovel & Spade	1.50
To 2	Dung Forks	.80
To 3	Pitch Forks, one made of wood	.75
To 3	Rakes	.40
To 8	Cow Chains	4.00
To 2	Halters, Chains and Straps	2.00
To 1	Half Bushel Measure	1.00
To 1	Old Waggon, Bed, and Lathers	30.00
To 1	Sleigh and Harness	15.00
To a	Quantity of Hay in the Mow	60.00

To 1 Grubbing Hoe and Axe............... $ 3.00
To 2 Weeding Hoes .... .75
To 70 Bushels Oats 28.00
To a quantity of Dry Apples 4.00
To a quantity of Flax 18.00
To 6 Bags 2.00
To 1 old Spinning Wheel................. 2.00
To 1 Square of Iron..................... .25
To 3 Old Flour Barrels.................. .60
To 1 Bushel Buckwheat .... .67½
To 1 Old Side Saddle.................... 10.00
To 1 Oil Cloth Carpet................... 7.20
To 1 Piece Stripe and Linen............. 7.50
To 1 Side Sole Leather.................. 5.55
To 1 Calf Skin 3.37½
To 3 Willow Baskets 1.75
To 2 Cradles 5.50
To 1 Old Bedstead .... .50
To 2 Curry Combs .... .30
To 2 Small Cleavers .... .75
To 1 pair Hobbles .... .50
To a lot of Old Iron.................... .25
To a Saddle Bag .... .75
To 1 Desk and Book Case............... 30.00
To 1 Settey 6.50
To 1 Walnut Breakfast Table............ 6.00
To 1 Small Looking Glass............... 4.50
To his Library 60.00
To 1 Mahogany Bureau 28.00
To 1 Mahogany Stand 3.75
To 1 Chaff Bed, Bedding, Bedsteads....... 30.00
To 1 Feather Bed, Bedding, and Bedsteads,
with Curtains 60.00

To 1 Feather Bed, Bedding and Green Bed-
    stead $40.00
To 1 Feather Bed, Bedding and Red Bedstead   32.00
To 2 New Bed ticks.......................   10.05
To 2 pair Sheets 8.00
To 1 Cradle Cover 1.50
To 1 Large Hair Trunk.....................   4.00
To 1 New Bed Quilt 4.50
To 1 New Counterpane 2.00
To 1 New Blanket 3.50
To 1 Large Looking Glass 9.00
To 15 Yards Linen.........................   12.00
To a Wash Stand...........................   1.50
To 6 New Green Gilt Chairs................   22.00
To 4 Pair Tow Sheets......................   8.00
To a Remnant of Cloth.....................   4.00
To 6 Green Chairs 6.00
To 9 Old Chairs 3.50
To 1 Silver Watch 30.00
To 6 Silver Table Spoons 14.00
To 6 Silver Tea Spoons 5.00
To 1 Silver Cream Jug 16.00
To 47 Delft Plates 6.00
To 7 Bowls 2.00
To 2 Teapots 1.33
To 2 Large Delft Dishes 1.50
To 2 Broken Sets China....................   2.00
To 1 Silver Sugar Tongs...................   2.00
To 1 Pair Salt Bowls......................   1.50
To 3 Tumblers and 3 Wine Glasses.........   .80
To 2 Decanters and 1 Cruit...............   1.50
To 3 Glass Bottles 60
To 1 Japan'd Coffee Pot...................   .87

To 1 Small Bellows .... $ .50
To 5 Table Cloths and 1 Small........... 11.00
To 2 Small Towels 1.00
To 6 Old Towels .... .75
To 9 Pillow Cases 4.50
To 1 Bolster Case and 3 Pillow Cases....... .50
To 1 Barrel Churn 5.00
To 1 Old Walnut Table.................. 1.00
To 1 Ten Plate Stove and Pipe............ 16.00
To 1 Small Pine Table.................. 1.00
To 1 New Spinning Wheel............... 4.00
To 1 Old Reel .... .80
To 1 Large Lanthorn and Grater .... .50
To 1 Small Steelyard 1.00
To 1 Pair Flat Irons................... 1.00
To 1 Old Dresser 3.50
To 1 Large Copper Ladle................ 1.00
To 4 Ladles and 1 Flesh Fork 1.00
To 1 Copper Tea Kettle................. 2.50
To 1 Bell Mettle Kettle................. 1.50
To 1 Iron Tea Kettle................... 1.06
To Cider Buckets 1.00
To 1 Skillet and Small Pot .... .75
To 2 Old Tin Coffee Pots and Funnel...... .45
To 1 Candle Mould .... .60
To 1 Brass and Two Iron Candlesticks...... 1.50
To 10 Pewter Plates 2.00
To 2 Tins and One Quart................ .20
To 1 Iron Pot .... .67
To 1 Kettle 1.75
To 1 Shovel and Tongs................. 1.50
To 1 Bake Plate and Stand.............. 1.00

To 2 Pot Racks	....	$ 2.00
To Frying Pan and Gridiron	....	1.26
To 1 Toaster and One Dripping Pan	....	1.50
To 1 Coffee Mill	....	1.33
To 3 Wash Tubs	....	4.60
To 1 Small Tub	....	.50
To 1 New Barrel	....	1.50
To a Quantity of Lard	....	5.33
To a Small Keg	....	.60
To 4 Large Cream Pots	....	1.00
To a Quantity of Pork	....	28.00
To a Lot of Earthenware and Crockery Ware		1.25
To a Quantity of Beef	....	10.00
To a Quantity of Tallow	....	4.00
To a Quantity of Potatoes	....	10.00
To a Watering Pot	....	.50
To a Saw and Drawing Knife	....	.50
To a Barrel and a Quantity of Whiskey	.....	5.80
To Dough Trough Soap Tub	....	.50
To 1 Stone Jug and Jar	....	1.00
To 6 Bread Baskets & 2 Splint dº.	....	.75
To a Quantity of Indian Corn in the year	....	90.00
To 1 Dozen Knives and Forks	....	2.00
To 5 Pewter Spoons	....	.50
To 4 Strips Ragcarpeting	....	8.00
To 5 yards Cotten Linsey	....	5.62
To Cash in His Desk	....	130.00
To a Small Hatchet & a Small Brush	....	.68
To His Wearing Apparel	....	30.00
To 1 Bond of Lewis Morgan, Fred Davis and Benjamin Thomas, payable at the decease of Sarah Morgan, widow of Isaac Morgan, late deceasᵈ.	....	474.44

To 1 Note of James Ligget, payable
first day of April 1813 for $121.17
Interest up to this 9th day of February 1815 .... 28.03 $149.20

To 1 Note of James Ligget, payable
the first day of April 1814 for $121.17
Interest on the same up to this ninth
day of February 1815 .... 28.03 149.20

To 1 Note of Lewis Morgan, payable the 28
day of August 1814 for................. 73.30
To 1 note of James Thomas............... 25.00
To 70 bushel wheat at 110 cents........... 77.00
To one bond of Jacob Davis payable
31 March 1815 for $1200.00
Interest on the same up to the 9th
day of February 1815 .... 133.77 1333.77

To 1 bond of Jacob Davis payable
31st day of March 1815 .... $1200.00
Interest on the same up to the 9th
day of February 1815 .... 61.77 1261.77

To one bond of Benjamin Davis payable on the 30th day of March
1814 .... $1200.00
Interest on the same up to the 9th
day of February 1815 .... 133.97 1333.97

To two bonds of Benjamin Davis payable each the 30th day of March
1815 each for one thousand dollars $2000.00
Interest on the same up to 9th day
of Feb. 1815 .... 223.28 2223.28

To one bond of Thomas Needs payable the first
    day of April 1815 for.................... $789.35
To one bond Thomas Needs payable the first
    day of April 1819 for.................... 879.08
To one bond of Wm. James payable first day
    of April 1809......................... 225.74
To one bond of Conrad Keim payable the first
    day of April 1811 for.................... 270.75

Much less extensive was the personal property of William Reed, of less acquisitive habits than his daughter's father-in-law. It reads as follows:

An Inventory of the Goods and Chattles, Rights and Credits which were of William Reed, late of Uwchlan Township deceased as taken by us the subscribers this 5th day of November A.D. 1828

Carriage	$25.00
4 old Wheels.............................	5.00
Log Chain	2.50
2 pair Hobbles	.75
1 Stove	5.00
Lot of Old Iron............................	1.00
1 Ladder	.25
Road Waggon	50.00
Fan	11.00
Forked Chain	1.50
2 Halters, Lot Gears, backband & traces	2.00
1 Set Fore Gears...........................	4.00
1 Pair Breast Chains........................	1.00
1 Quiler	1.00
1 Cutting Box	4.00
Shovel and Dung Hook.......................	.50

Wheel Barrow	$ 1.00
6 Cow Chains	1.75
1 Fifth Chain	1.50
1 Iron Bound Meat Tub	.25
1 Lot Logs	10.00
Iron Bar, Clamps, Saw Sets and Files	4.00
Lot of Cherry and Walnut Boards	5.50
3 Ash Plank	3.00
Standing Screen	2.00
1 Cider Barrel	.50
1 Cross Cut Saw	2.00
1 Mill Saw	1.00
Bay Mare	20.00
Brown Horse	20.00
1 Muley Cow	10.00
1 Horned Cow	10.00
1 Muley Heifer	10.00
1 Calf	3.00
2 Hogs	12.00
1 Hog	4.00
4 Shoats	12.00
6 Sucking Pigs	3.75
1 Cart	5.00
1 Corner Cupboard	2.50
Lot of Wool in the Rolls	3.00
Desk	2.00
Bedstead, bed and bedding	5.00
Bedstead, bed and bedding	3.00
Bedstead, bed, and Sacking	7.00
1 Card Table	1.00
1 Bureau	5.00
1 Case of Drawers	2.00
7 Pillow Cases	.70

7 Sheets	$ 3.50
6 Blankets	4.50
1 Pair New Blankets	5.00
2 Bed Quilts and 1 Comfort	3.00
1 Case of Drawers	5.00
1 Arm Chair	.50
1 Round Tea Table	.50
Lot of Old Iron in Garret	8.00
Saddle Bags	.25
44 lb. Flax (swingled)	2.64
1 Large Wheel	1.00
1 Reel	.75
1 Spinning Wheel	1.00
1 Cradle	1.00
1 Tub	.50
1 Bake Plank	.25
2 Meat Tubs	1.00
1 Table	1.00
Pot Hooks	1.00
Bedstead, bed, &c in the Mill	3.00
1 pair Hames Barking Iron and Shell Augur	.75
1 Double and 1 Single Ship Block and Rope	2.00
1 Adze	.50
Scale and Weights	18.00
Desk in the Mill	.75
Lot of Casks	.60
Flour Brands	1.00
Mill Pick, Coal Chisel, Drawing Knife, Hammer	1.50
2 Spindles, 2 Thines, 2 Gudgeons	5.00
1 Sledge	.50
1 Grindstone and Crank	.75
Bushel	.12
6 Sieves	6.00

1 Stove in the Mill	$ 5.00
2 Wheels	.25
Lot of Boards and Scantling in Mill	2.00
Lot of Cogs	5.00
1 Axe	1.00
Crow bar, 2 Picks, 1 Hoe, 1 Sledge, 1 Corn Hoe	3.00
Clock	25.00
Looking Glass	2.00
5 Table Cloths @ 50	2.50
3 Table Cloths @ 50	1.50
6 Napkins	.75
Case of Drawers	2.50
Arm Chair	.25
7 Chairs	1.75
Lot of Pewter	1.50
Churn	1.50
Iron Kettle	3.00
4 Iron Pots	1.25
Coffee Mill and Oil Can	.50
Tea Kettle and Gridiron	.75
Andirons	3.00
Sad Irons	.25

Grandfather had a gift of easy verse, both in the pompously familiar sort of the eighteenth century, and in the Scotch of Burns. He could write a fair prayer. He was best, though, despite inescapable bursts of rhetoric, in the notes he wrote to his daughter Rachel when she had gone for treatment for a broken ankle to Dr. Stephen Sweet's, at Franklin, Connecticut. He even condescends now and then in these to what he calls "small news." The best thing in them, though, is his evident deep solicitude for her condition. He always did the best he could for each of his children when they needed aid at critical moments in their careers.

Grandfather would not have minded if you said he had an "elegant" taste in literature. As will be seen in the letter to his younger brother, which I quote, he pays due tribute to eighteenth century standards in his appreciation of Goldsmith. Milton, too, he greatly admired, with the rest of Puritan America, but it was Burns that really warmed his heart. James Thomas was at Ephrata, home of the Seventh Day Kloster, working in a mill, I gather from a letter of his to Grandfather. Judging from the letter of James, as well as from that from Grandfather I quote, James found himself a stranger in a strange land among the "Dutch" of Lancaster County.

"West Nantmeal, March 12th, 1828
DEAR BROTHER,

I take advantage of the present opportunity by D. Crous of sending you a few books, which if they should fail in giving you useful instruction may at least serve to amuse your leisure hours, and prove a resort when better Society does not offer, which may frequently happen in your present residence.

Chrysal or the adventures of a Guinea contains many tracts and anecdotes of real life and gives 'a birds eye view' of Society in Europe from the King to the beggars; and from the most exalted virtue to the most abandoned villainy. Who the author is or at what particular period he wrote or who were the characters he has represented I have not been able to discover, but I have at times suspected it to be a work of Dean Swift as most of his works were published without his name, and the actors who figure in the works correspond in many respects with those of his time.

The Heart of Midlothian, or Second Series of the Tales of my Landlord has the reputation of being one of the best of Walter Scott's celebrated Waverley Novels. The plot and incidents are founded upon historical facts, but the author has taken the poet's privilege of weaving them into a fictitious narrative of his own.

The Lady of the Lake is written by the same author and receivd the premium of the Edinburgh Litterary Society (I think it was) as being the best work extant descriptive of the manners, customs and scenery of the Highlands of Scotland, a country wild and interesting in the extreme.

Burns's Poems (many of which you have doubtless read and heard sung) stand preeminent in Scottish poetry as a work of native genius and talent unaided by education and unrivalled in sweetness and pathos. Of Goldsmith's works it is scarcely necessary to say anything, his fame is established and time which destroys most things only adds fresh lustre to his name. His Traveller and Deserted Village rank with Gray's Elegy and are equal to any English poetry extant. His plays of the 'Good Natured Man' and 'She Stoops to Conquer' continue amidst all the changes of fancy fashion and sentiment to be favourites at the Theatre even to the present day.

It is needless I trust to mention that Burns, Goldsmith and the Lady of the Lake, being part of my private Library I would wish you to take especial care of them and have them returned as soon as you are satisfied with the perusal of them when I will forward others to you, but should you have a desire to keep any of them let me know and I can replace them when in the City.

We are all well at present. Mother has a prospect of a farmer for the coming year, Stephen Harlan. I am about to remove next week to a house formerly occupied by Malachi

Happersett a short distance below the Mill, where I hope to have more satisfactory accommodations than I have here and may possibly do as good business with the store. Nailor's place will not be sold before next fall I expect, so that we have time sufficient to make any arrangement respecting it if it should be considered an object deserving of attention.

March 29th. This letter will resemble a journal or diary for as I could not get it closed in time for D. Crous to take I shall continue forwarding it. I receivd yours by Mrs. Bowman and am happy to hear of your good health. I have removed my family to my new residence and am now closing my concerns at the store preparatory to removing it by the 1st day of April.

Mother's expected tenant has disappointed her and removed himself in a hurry. Nobody knows where, and few, excepting his creditors care where. She is possibly quite as well without him. John Williams has located himself upon his new purchase. He had a great moving, 12 or 14 waggons. There appears to be much shifting of situations this season. We are all well and thus far pleased with our new situation.

Yours as ever

M. J. T."

I have two two-volume editions of Burns that belonged to Grandfather, both printed in New York and both dated 1825. Every one of the four volumes has its pages worn thin by constant "perusal," despite the eye-killing print. Grandfather did not need to bother over that print in the end, for he had all Burns by heart, the ungodly as well as the godly.

Of the library of Great-grandfather Thomas listed in the inventory of his estate I have only one book with his name in it, a double column little dictionary not quite five inches square. Its title page is lost, but it corresponds so completely in definitions with another little dictionary that has come to me from the Weygandt side of my ancestry that I think it, too, must be *Entick's New Spelling Dictionary*, "for those who read Milton, Pope, Addison, Shakespeare, Tillotson and Locke, or other English Authors of Repute in Prose or Verse."

Dates subsequent to 1815 in most of the little volumes, leather-bound, that have come to me from Uwchlan, indicate that they must have been purchases of Grandfather. The Warton's *Virgil*, which is of 1748, may, of course, have been his father's. It is all the more probable that it is from its bearing on a page top the scription "F. G. Dwight, Reading Academy, Reading, Pennsylvania." Isaac was a merchant in Reading before, towards old age, he moved back to the Chester County of his birth. The Chesterfield *Letters*, in three volumes, were printed in New York in 1824, and *Ossian's Poems*, in that same city, in 1827. Chesterfield and MacPherson! In the two you have the range of the eighteenth century from ultraworldliness to ultraromance. Most of Grandfather's books, though, bear Philadelphia imprints. We know, from his letter to James, that books were one of the delights of his trips to Philadelphia. Some were bought new, but others, no doubt, were picked up at the secondhand shops of that day.

It is "M. J. Thomas" I find on the title page of Tom Moore's *Lalla Rookh*, published in Philadelphia by James Crissy, No. 112 Walnut Street, in 1821. It is the fourth American edition, with engravings. Most of these little old books have illustrations, generally of scenes from their narratives, and generally copperplate work. Pope's *Homer*, in two volumes, bears a New York imprint, W. Borrodaile, No. 114 Fulton Street, 1825. Thomson's *Seasons* was published in Philadelphia, by Edgar T. Scott, at No. 61 North Eighth

Street in 1828. The *Seasons* must have been more widely read in America than any other British poetry than Milton and Burns. I find it everywhere, in libraries of country houses, at country auctions, in the shops of country antique dealers. It is even more often come upon, perhaps, in New Hampshire and Maine than in Pennsylvania.

The largest of the books that I have mentioned are five and a half inches by three and a half inches, and the smallest four inches by two and a half. The gayest bindings are on the two volumes of *Telemachus*, translated from the French of Salignac de la Mothe-Fenelon by Dr. John Hawkesworth. The gilt backs are bright enough in themselves, but the leather covers are truly gaudy, marbled as they are in green and red, brown and blue. Though their date is 1826, they must have been purchased, so immaculate is their condition, after all the little Thomases were grown beyond the destructive age. No small children could have resisted their gewgawish exteriors.

All these books, with enough others to fill the four shelves of the secretary bookcase, were in Aunt Rachel's room in my childhood. That secretary bookcase, mine now, is by me as I write, with a bell-metal kettle, also from Milford, serving as a jardiniere on the window sill. Upstairs is the "standing screen" listed in the Reed inventory. We have held on to our lesser heirlooms pretty well now for a century and more. Such of Grandfather's books as I have occupy the uppermost shelf of the bookcase, perhaps thirty in all. This secretary bookcase housed, no doubt, Great-grandfather Isaac Thomas's library, since it is listed in the inventory of his estate, at $60, just what his three cows and a calf totaled at. "1 White Cow and Calf, $20; 1 Brindle Cow, $20; 1 Black Cow, $20." That bookcase, suggestive of the Empire style, makes it quite possible it was a new piece purchased by

Isaac when he married and went to housekeeping in 1796. If so it escaped the varied experiences of fire and flood that pursued the Thomases from Pottsville to Hamburg and Reading. My daughter Ann has a silver spoon that was given to Isaac's wife, Ann Morgan, on her marriage. That, too, was once in the house at Milford, for, as I have said, the old lady lived there, at times, in one or the other part of the two-family house, while her son and his wife and children lived in the other part. She took over the place after her son and his family moved to Philadelphia and sold it to Joseph M. McClure in 1848, forty-five acres with mills and store and homestead, springhouse, sheds and shops, for $8000. In 1828, with perhaps a larger acreage, it had been valued at $12,000.

It can hardly be said that Grandfather's gifts of spelling and writing are evident in the copybook of his son Selim. I recovered this relic of Uncle Seal's youth in the storeroom of Aunt Ann Buchanan's at Waynesburg on June 22, 1887, as I carefully recorded on its cover. A good deal of stuff had evidently been stored away at the Buchanans' at Milford when the Thomases went to Philadelphia. Leah Ann Reed was my Grandmother Thomas's sister, and the wife of Andrew Buchanan, who, like Grandfather Thomas, liked to function as a public man. It had been as great a change for the Buchanans to leave their farm for a country town as it had been for the Thomases to leave theirs for Philadelphia. I suppose I begged the copybook of the old lady, but I cannot remember. Its covers are blue, almost the cobalt known as potter's blue. On the front cover is a sworded trumpeter on horseback. On the back cover is a long-horned and heavily dewlapped bull. The book was purchased, so it is recorded in the upper left-hand corner of the front cover, for eight cents, perhaps at the Thomas store. It has the usual outlines of dog and soldier scratched in ink on the inside cover. The name of Selim S. Thomas is written on every other page and sometimes twice to a page. The spelling is most uncertain, small boyish to a degree, "buisness" for "business," "whealt" for "wealth," "fowel" for "fowl," and the like. Little "i" is used instead of great I, and the sentences of correct sentiments do not always so marshal themselves that all their words are compressed into one line. Cowper's "I am monarch of all I survey," and Dyer's "Ever charming, ever new" from "Grongar Hill" are the highest flights Uncle Seal attempts to copy. They are found toward the end of the book, which covers October and November of 1841, when its copyist was thirteen years old.

It was a long walk to the schoolhouse on the hill, a full mile and a half. The children, Ann and Cos, Rachel and Seal, used to trudge it twice a day, carrying lunch, and sometimes, in cold weather, a couple of sticks of wood for the school stoves. Sometimes a load of wood was hauled there from Milford, let us hope at the coldest seasons. There must have been many times when it was hard work enough to battle uphill in the face of a northeaster with only yourself to manage. Uncle Seal, though he had always words like the flowing water, and could hold any audience with a story, was not, I am afraid, a prize pupil at the schoolhouse on the hill when he was bringing his copybook into being. Nor did he then, or in after life, always practice all those precepts he copied out laboriously. "Delays are dangerous and sometimes fatal"; "Be active in business and diligent in study"; "Candour should accompany all disputes"; "A fair piece of writing is a speaking picture"; "Either be silent or say something useful"; "Knowledge and wealth flow from industry"; "Poverty and shame follow the intemperate"; "Many men of many minds, many birds of many kinds";

"Good manners in a lad make his parents glad"; "Hard times when money is scarce"; "Beauty and time soon vanish away"—these shall serve as samples of that two-fold training in penmanship and morals on the Chester County hilltop nearly a hundred years ago.

Upstream along Marsh Creek from Milford, beyond the schoolhouse on the Hill, was Wynn's Meadows, the marsh from which the creek took its name. Wynn's Meadows was a haunt of botanists even in these old days, Joshua Hoopes then visiting it and discovering in it some plants not found elsewhere in Chester County. The record of them will be found in the *Flora Cestrica* of Dr. William Darlington, that delightful "attempt to enumerate and describe the flowering and filicoid plants of Chester County in the state of Pennsylvania, with brief notices of their properties and uses, in medicine, domestic and rural economy, and the arts." In Wynn's Meadows Joshua found the wild calla whose red berries make it a delight to the eye; cranberries; the sweet-fruited viburnum; the hedge bindweed, with large white flowers; and a rare reed grass that grows higher than your head.

It was not in the direction of Wynn's Meadows that the Thomases went oftenest afield. They went east for the mail to the Eagle, south to Downingtown to take the railroad, and west to Brandywine Manor Meetinghouse, in whose graveyard many of them lie buried, though Grandfather was not, I am afraid, a strict Presbyterian when he died. His father had been a Baptist, his mother before she married his father, a Friend, but his orthodox Scotch-Irish wife did so far assert herself that their children were brought up as good Presbyterians. It is the Presbyterian Church at Brandywine Manor, the Brandywine Manor Meetinghouse as it figured in the Uwchlan Saga, that I heard most about and

visited oftenest of all the churches in the neighborhood in
my young years. If the folks at Milford did not go there,
seven miles west, they went to the Friends' Meetinghouse
at Lionville, four miles to the southeastward. Ann Thomas's
influence took them there in later years, as did her daughter's
marriage to Thomas Lewis, a Friend. The Friends at Lionville achieved a wisdom unparalleled so far as I know to
reconcile the split in Quakerdom that followed the Unitarian-
Trinitarian discussions of 1826-27. They divided Lionville
Meetinghouse by a board partition down the middle, so that
the Friends could worship on one side and the other Friends
on the other. In course of time "the other Friends" alone
were left and it became wholly a Hicksite Meeting. Here
Whittier worshiped on his visits to the Vickerses at their
pottery on the road from Lionville to the Conestoga Pike.

The Thomases went now and then to the Windsor Baptist
Church at the Eagle, when Baptist relatives were visiting
them. St. Andrew's Episcopal Church at Ludwig's Corners
was not very far away, but I never heard of any of our folks
worshiping there. Hopewell Methodist Church was on the
road to Guthrieville, and Springton Methodist Church in
West Nantmeal to the northwest of Milford. The nearest
Lutheran church shared services, turn and turn about, with
the Presbyterians, off to the other side of Lionville.

There was a good deal of social life connected with the
churches, funerals, of course, bringing about the greatest
gatherings of people. Grandmother writes of one "at the
Lion" which brought out "58 vehicles and 50 on horseback."
This was in 1837. I doubt if the fox hunts brought out as
many. There have always been hunt clubs in all the counties
"contiguous to Philadelphia." In the neighborhood of
Uwchlan the farmers even to-day turn out on old Dobbins
with two hounds apiece and hunt on Black Horse Hill and

Chestnut Ridge. I have had to wait in my car as recently as 1931 for them to cross the Pottstown-West Chester Cement Road.

I have been many times to Milford Mills in the body. I have been there in spirit times beyond number, sometimes without will on my part and sometimes in studying the neighborhood in maps. I have one of 1847, which does not give the names of those who owned the homesteads, but only of those who had mills or forges or potteries or some other sort of manufactory. My map of 1860 has all the names of the farmers, but by 1860 a good many of the other old families of the neighborhood than the Thomases had moved west or to the cities.

Although Uwchlan and Nantmeal are names as Welsh as Taffy, this hill country above the Brandywine was not dominantly Welsh. As a matter of fact, the Thomases and their Jones and Morgan ancestors came from further east in Chester County, in Charlestown and Vincent. Both Uwchlan and Nantmeal are beyond the so-called "Welsh tract." There were, of course, other people of Welsh names than Thomases and Morgans in the neighborhood. There were Merediths and Lewises, Davises and Reeses, Phillipses and Evanses. There were more names of English and Scotch-Irish origin. There were of the former, and largely Quakers in religion, Levises, Smedleys, Fishers, Marises, Vickerses, Phippses, Stricklands, Temples, Kings, Beards and Dolbeys. Of the Scotch-Irish there were Buchanans and Reeds, McClures and McElduffs, Dorlans and Dowlins, Moores and Laffertys, Ralstons and Reas. The Pennsylvania Dutch who settled more thickly north and west of Milford Mills were represented in the neighborhood by such names as Crouse, Beidler, Myers, Stiteler, Slonaker, Sheneman, Rodebaugh, Buckwalter, Acker, and Riter.

There is no value in such cataloguing save to drive home a realization that it was a very mixed people dwelt in this countryside, as in so many countrysides in Pennsylvania. It was a day, that of a hundred years ago, of a fairly equal division of wealth. There were no really well-to-do farmers such as you found in Chester Valley up in the Brandywine Hills. Uncle Israel Davis in his large house and broad acres of limestone out from Howellville was of an affluence nobody in the hills knew, even if Isaac Thomas did have his estate inventoried at more than ten thousand dollars. If by chance a man of the hills was better off, it was generally because he had made his money elsewhere, as an ironmaster, perhaps, and had come back to the hill country of his birth after retirement. A lawyer or two, a doctor here and there, the millers, the country storekeepers, the tavern keepers and proprietors of stage lines, the strong farmers, made up the bulk of the "comfortable people." The artisans lived generally on smaller places, carpenters, cabinetmakers, masons, locksmiths, tinsmiths, ironworkers, weavers and the like. They, too, farmed it a bit, like everybody else. Then there were the farm laborers, not generally, as in the Dutch country, poorer relatives of the farmers, but a distinct class. For one of these farmhands to marry into the family of a farmer was a calamity for the family of the better sort, not only in their own eyes but in the opinion of all the neighborhood. If a farmer's daughter married a farmhand, the wisest course was for the newly-wed pair to go west. They could never be happy in the neighborhood in which they were well known. Such farmhands were very much in the position of "poor white trash" further south, though not so completely ostracized. Odd jobs paid only fifty to sixty cents a day in the twenties and thirties, with the highest unskilled labor rising to as much as eighty-five cents a day.

Do the names of places in the neighborhood of Milford Mills suggest romance to others, or only to me who have since childhood heard them spoken of as if they were outposts of Paradise? Uwchlan for me is haunted by a hundred stories; the Nantmeals I love for their tumbled hills, quick changes of altitude, rushing streams and out-of-the-world atmosphere. That they are threatened with absorption into suburbia troubles me, these Welsh-named places that are watered by "honeybrooks." Indiantown and Indian Run are names burdened with the past, burdened with memories of the vanished red men. Isabella Furnace, named, like Joanna Furnace and Elizabeth Furnace, for an ironmaster's wife, records a fine courtesy that we were the better for, had it survived into our day.

Brandywine Manor Meetinghouse, with its wide view and its graveyard of white soil, where rest so many of my people, is half as much again to me than if it bore any other name. All my days the fall of those words has fascinated me. So, too, have the words, Eagle Tavern, and what they symbolize, been pleasant to my ears and to my imagination, so that I regret I never saw the swinging sign that flaunted with a gallant pride our bird of birds. And that slogan of the boys of Milford, "Dorlan's Mill, Dowlin's Forge and Downingtown!" that shall not be forgotten as long as I am. The Great Valley, too, the phrase, has been to me as a French horn calling, the echoes of which are always reverberating along the low hills that confine the place the name distinguishes. Yellow Springs rises before me again and again with its old bravery of belles and beaux come from country manors and the houses of the city merchants.

The Conestoga Turnpike runs close to the north of Milford, and not so far away were inns with names racy of the soil and of the road. Wildcat Inn, Brick Inn, Buck Inn,

Drove Inn, Fountian Inn, East Nantmeal Inn and Indian
King Inn—how heartening the names; how stunning, no
doubt, the signs; how good the cheer to those coming in to
them, those kindly and unpuritanic times, from the mud and
snow of the roads! Many, too, were the smithies round
about, each with a heart of fire to respond to bellows and
tough muscle, and each a ready rescuer to the traveler with
broken wagon spring or horse that had cast a shoe. Smithy,
forge, furnace, friendly words all! And quiet and fragrant
names there were of places not far away, possum hollows,
woodcock swales and clover mills.

Long slants of light are spilling over the western horizon,
warming the wooded hills a deep purple. A moon that will
be full to-morrow night swims up in front of us, curiously
wan in the pale pink of the sky. So it was I saw the last of
Milford on an evening of late November, the year of which
I have forgotten, but, I should guess, of more than a decade
ago. Another day on which I remember it it was bright noon
of July, years and years ago, when Uncle Jim and mother
and Sara and I drove up by surrey from Downingtown. It
was a day after rain, after a flooding midsummer downpour,
with all the world new-washed and flashing in full sun. That
day was enlivened, too, by memories of the dispute as to
where had stood the mulberry tree in the west pasture. Uncle
Jim was sure he knew just where it stood, straight across
the field from the bars that let the cows into the road.
Wasn't he the one to know, for wasn't it he, and neither
of the girls, Theora or Lucy, who had driven the cows in
night and morning? Aunt Theora and Mother and he and
I had found it, however, on a memorable previous visit, right
by the bars into the road. The womenfolks, alas! were right
and the man wrong. It is only to-day that those of us of the
Uwchlan clan who are left have had the wit to wonder

if there might have been two mulberry trees, or even more of them. Grandfather had set them out by the score in the forties when the *multicaulis* fever attacked him as it did so many Americans of that time. He was going to make a fortune out of raising silkworms, as he was going to make a fortune out of raising merino sheep.

I remember Milford, too, in the rain of a March afternoon, late in the month when spring was in the air. It was homey to me even then, perhaps from thoughts of long ago, though not a soul was stirring out-of-doors and no cars passing on either road. There were no knee-deeps calling; but three bluebirds straggled across the road one after another, each a warm fragment of blue; and a bunch of robins following them shot suddenly down into the top of an unpruned apple tree and burst into song all together as if they had been one bird. Things looked prosperous along the road to Dorlan's, and, though all signs of the forge were gone at Dowlin's, the rain gave a sheen to the myriad leaves of laurel in the steep woods above the Brandywine.

No journeys, though, to Milford, whether the pious pilgrimages with mother and Uncle Jim, or those impelled in me later by the homing instinct that grows with the years, have been to me half so interesting as were Aunt Rachel's stories more than fifty years ago. It is always a winter night that comes to mind as I think of her recitals of the Uwchlan Saga. I can see the Dominiques as they roosted in the Sheldon pear tree by the gable end of the farmhouse, heads tucked under wings and feet covered by the warm fluff of their bodies. It was not of wintry things, though, that she talked most on those winter nights I remember her talking, nights when the wind was up. She gave me pictures of all the seasons and events of all the changing conditions of the year. I can see, from her telling of it, the pile of ashes and the nighthawk's eggs on the pile. I can see the martin box and the friendly birds garrulous about it. I can see Uncle Seal dumping the pickaninny from the blue cart into the mill-dam, and the small kinky-headed one spluttering scaredly to shore. I can see the pink sunbonnet of six-year-old Theora bobbing along the tailrace and the weaver running fast after it and saving the life of the child carried downstream ahead of it. I can see little Cos sobbing his heart out on the desk of the hilltop school from the unmerited scolding of the teacher, poor Cos who all his life long was too gentle to stand up for his rights.

I can see the little drama of the bold and plausible Seal as he was brought to bay in the matter of the sugar-coated almonds. Aunt Rachel had given him a whole ten cents to buy pink-coated almonds at Downingtown. They did not keep them in the store at Milford, but they were her favorite candy, and there were times when she just had to have them. They expected Seal back in three hours. That was time and to spare for the fourteen-mile round trip on horseback. He was gone longer. When he arrived home and gave the al-monds to Aunt Rachel in the spill of blue paper torn from a sugar loaf, she said: "But I asked you to bring me pink almonds!" A little shamefacedly he replied that he thought it was white almonds she wanted. Aunt Rachel knew her brother. "You bad boy," she cried, "I know what you have been up to! You bought pink almonds and sucked every one white on the way home. That's what took you so long. You let old Jerry walk all the way back." Uncle Seal con-fessed. He paid for his trespass by never hearing the end of the story to his dying day.

An adventurous life was his. He was, when he grew up, a stagecoach painter. His mother, put out by his father's feck-lessness, determined that each of her boys should have a trade. Then, no matter what happened, they would always have something more than a mere education to fall back upon. Cosmo was sent off as early as 1838 to Philadelphia to learn architectural drawing at the Franklin Institute so that he could qualify as a boss builder. Pline was apprenticed to a locksmith when he made his delayed joining with his family in 1848. Jim was apprenticed to a daguerreotypist.

It was Seal got the most out of his trade. It took him to the Juniata Valley very early in his journeymanship. Later it took him to the Middle West, and on, with a migrating family, through Missouri and Indian Territory to Texas. On that trek he learned the drover's life, with flocks of sheep and herds of cattle on the roads. The outbreak of the Civil War found him in Louisiana. He had a time getting through to the North so that he might join the Union Army. Sometime or other, too, he had an exciting time on Pike's Peak, in Colorado.

His adventures did not end with the war. About five years after its end, he was summoned by the man he chummed with all through it, to that friend's deathbed at Lebanon. He made Uncle Seal promise to look after his wife. Uncle Seal said he had no money to do that. His friend replied that what he meant was that Uncle Seal should marry his widow. Although Uncle Seal was not the marrying sort, he promised he would, and he did, after a decorous lapse of time. The marriage turned out better than most marriages do.

I had a letter only a few years ago that asked me did I know that there was a painting preserved on a chimney in Lionville that Uncle Seal had done when he was a boy. This must have been the work of an idle hour during a visit of his to his Grandmother Thomas, born Ann Morgan, who had established herself with her daughter-in-law's mother, Rachel Reed, and an old servant, in Lionville after she had

sold the place at Milford to the McClures in 1848. She was
glad to be near the Lionville Meeting, for although she had
gone with her husband to Baptist Church in her early years
of married life, and although she is buried by his side in
the Baptist Church in Vincent, she was never wholly at ease
in her religious moments, save when she was waiting to be
informed by the Inner Light.

I remember that it was owing to her sharp hearing and
vigilance that they discovered who were the chicken thieves
that had been raiding their roosts at Milford. One night the
old lady heard a guinea hen calling over by the springhouse,
where no guinea hen had the right to be at that hour. Investigation proved that it was in a bag with several other
fowls with pulled necks. Its neck, too, had been pulled, but
the muscles were strong enough to snap the vertebra back
into position, and the outraged dignity of the bird had caused
it to lift up its voice in a lamentation of "buckwheat, buckwheat, buckwheat." It was by their own help the Thomases
were being robbed.

I remember Aunt Rachel telling me how Uncle Jim would
stick his bare toes in under one old cow when he went out
on mornings of hoar frost in October to drive in the bunch
for milking. I remember Uncle Jim telling me of his love
of the tomtit. It was some sparrow he so called, or more
likely, several different but related sparrows. It was the song
sparrow or vesper sparrow he so knew at Milford, perhaps
both of them, for he was not one to notice slight differences
between birds. He used to hear the bird, he told me, sing
from the ground or from the walls on the hill pastures of
Milford. He had heard it on the hill pastures at Gettysburg,
singing, in the lulls between the cannonading and the muske-
try fire. He had heard it at all times of day in his long drives
through the Kentucky countryside as he went from place

to place selling notions. He had heard it on the Restigouche, salmon fishing. It had come to the very ridgepole of his tent there, and sung to him just as it used to when he was a boy on that bare hillside in Upper Chester County. Wherever his love of fishing took him, from Pennsylvania to Minnesota, from Kentucky to New Brunswick, that blessed bird had been there. Only in salt water fishing along the Jersey coast had he missed his tomtit. That love of fishing was strong in Uncle Jim from infancy. His older sister Ann writes to his father in letters of 1837 and 1838 what a time she had keeping him out of the water where he would go frogging as a child of three or four.

Aunt Rachel told me that she kept a knife under the counter of the store to stab the pounds of butter brought to trade in. She had to resort to this practice after she had discovered some of the neighbors had sometimes a gill or two of water in the heart of the butter pat. Some such pats lost as much as an eighth of a pound when they were judiciously stabbed.

I was not the only one who loved the Uwchlan Saga. Uncle Jim and my mother, both of them with city hearts, liked to recall their childhood's days at Milford and their later visits to Uwchlan, to Aunt Ann Buchanan's or to Cousin Ann Vickers's at Lionville. Uncle Pline really loved that home in the hollow of the hills as Aunt Rachel did, though he had not so many memories of it. On Uncle Seal's few visits to us there was always lively reminiscing with Mother and Aunt Rachel. There was ceaselessly, in their ears, as they recalled the place, the noise of wind and water. There was, too, the hum of human voices, the voices of the houseful of children, the voices from the folks at the store, the voices from springhouse and shops and stables. For all it was remote, Milford Mills was a little center, something a good deal more than a congeries, of buildings among the close-huddled hills. Through the hollow the wind was always blowing, whistling by the eaves of the farmhouse, filling the two great pines with the round of the distant sea, sending silvery shivers through the willows, laving hot brows with its healing cool. Through the hollow echoed the drone of the mill, the plunge of water over the dam breast and its clucking down the tailrace. That wind and water and drone of mill I, too, have heard, in my heart rather than in my ears, all my days. Those sounds are much to me, but more to me are my memories of those kindly and quick-tempered people, my mother, my aunts and my uncles. These shared with me several gifts of great value from Morgan and Elizabeth Thomas, their parents, my grandparents. Greatest to me of all gifts, though, from these my folks at Milford Mills, and one for which I cry, day after day, "God bless them," is the content that comes from a country heart.

PRIME IN JANUARY

for the trapper of Reinholds

THERE is no denying the insistence of skunks. They obtrude themselves on us, in death and in life, as do no others of the lesser animals. Squirrels and rabbits keep out of our way, and weasels and groundhogs, and raccoons and foxes. Only the hedgehog, with ages of inherited memories of his avoidance by man and dog, shares the skunk's slowness to adapt himself to the automobile age. The porcupine's size, as he looms ahead on the road, and the knowledge the autoist has that the creature's quills may puncture tires, save him from being run over most times that he ventures on a highway where cars are passing. The skunk, in his smaller size and in his black and white, is less discernible in the lights of the car, and we know he will not throw us into the ditch should we chance not to escape him. We generally hardly recognize the skunk for what he is as he calmly stands his ground in the way of the advancing automobile, and so both he and we pay the penalty of his fearlessness, or, it may be, his stupidity.

In runs out the main thoroughfares through the country, on the numbered routes, we probably come upon as many rabbits flattened out as skunks, but that is because there are many more rabbits everywhere than skunks. Rabbits, too, become confused and blinded by the lights, and are often run over because they are powerless to move. The skunk, too, may be nonplused by the car lights, but it is more likely, in most instances when he is hit, that it is because of his standing his ground through his inherited knowledge he is one to be made way for.

On a trip from Germantown to Gettysburg in the late October of 1933 we passed four skunks freshly killed on the road, and on a trip from Philadelphia to Valley Forge in early November we passed two that had evidently lost their lives within the previous twenty-four hours. Even as near home as the entrance to Fairmount Park at Rittenhousetown, there is now and then a crushed skunk on the road.

All of us fated to be closely associated with skunks know how slowly they make way for us, if they make way at all. We who see a mother and four young crossing the road with unhurried grace a hundred yards ahead of our car bring that car to a stop as quickly as we can. We who have a family of five skunks under the barn knock on the door that gives from barn to henyard before we go through it to let the fowls out for the day, or to close them in for the night. We so knock that father and mother and the three youngsters may retire from the pile where we throw the table scraps, and seek the seclusion of those dim areas under the bays and threshing floor and tie-ups. We give the skunks a full minute at least before we open the door. Then, on opening the door, we gently bang it on the barn side in case any one of the family shall have delayed over some delicious tidbit the chickens have neglected. Then we advance cautiously toward the henhouses, giving the place of the skunks' repast a wide berth. With all these precautions we often see some little fellow daintily mincing his way to the hole scooped out under the sill of the barn.

We refrain, too, from setting traps for the skunks when they dig little pits for grubs in the lawn, or uproot our pansies and forget-me-nots in their search for beetles. A neighbor advocates a trap set in the henyard, with thirty feet of chain fastened at the outer end to a peg set more than thirty feet away from the barn. That is, he recommends such procedure if the skunks take to preying on the hens in the daytime. If the skunks prowl only in the early morning and the late afternoon and at night, he advises keeping the hens in until nine A.M., and hooshing them to roost by five in the afternoon, and letting the skunks alone.

Like many another, I had been brought up on tales of how easy to handle skunks were if you only knew how. Uncle Seal had such tales of the farm where he and my mother were born in southeastern Pennsylvania. Such tales were prevalent, too, wherever I went all the days of my youth and middle years. They came crowding in on me in my sexagenarian years in Sandwich. The skunk, all these tales agreed, could not throw his offensive discharge unless his hind feet were firmly braced, on ground, say, or rock, or fence. If you met him on the road all you had to do was to hurry after him as he, with dignity, sidled away from you; lift him from the ground by the tip of his tail; and you had him, disarmed and helpless, pawing the air, yours to do with as you would. I had never tried out any skill I might hope for at the trick, thinking the story, perhaps, one of the many games the innocent farmer man plays on his brother less versed in country things.

Nor was I more convinced when I found it was so fabled the wandering skunk dealer of Montgomery County caught a large part of his skunks. The scent that heralded his approach at the distance of a quarter of a mile proved that, however well behaved his catch were when he picked them up, they were less well behaved after he put them in the wire cage on the back of his little truck.

All along, I have just realized, I have been assuming that the scent of skunk is a disagreeable scent. It is disagreeable to me, though there are many other smells that are more disagreeable. Perhaps some will agree with me that that assumption of mine is not an unwarranted assumption. There are those, though, that think otherwise. There are people, honest folks, who like the smell of skunks. I know two who hold that so distinct and unmistakable and often breath-taking odor is a typical country scent associated with pleasant things, like the ammoniacal smell of covered wooden bridges in the horse age, and of barnyards even in this sanitary day. The man of these two, and not out of affectation, draws the scent of skunk into his lungs, if it is not too strong, with just such a pleasure as he draws in the scent of freshly plowed loam, or the tang of the half stagnant backwaters where reeds and cat-tails grow and where marsh wrens nest.

The girl says: "The smell of skunk is a real country smell. It is real country where you smell skunks. I like that smell as much in one way as I like the smell of clover in another way." I cannot agree with her that you come on the smell of skunks only in real country. I have met it and them not infrequently in suburban places. They cannot adapt themselves to back yards as opossums can, but they can live and prosper wherever there are a few acres of open country with proper cover in it. And although I cannot like the smell of skunks, I like her to like that smell, and to have the courage to own that she likes it. The world is always the better for those who disagree with the world.

There are other folks, too, who, if they do not positively like the smell of skunks, are little troubled by it. I met such a one and irrefragable evidence of the truth of the age-old stories of handling skunks on a trip to northern Lancaster County in the late fall of 1933. It was after a prodigious dinner, featuring chicken potpie and judacaschia pie, and weighing down the table with so many goodies it hurt you to look at them. Exercise was necessary after that meal. By what means else would the parched corn, and the sweet potatoes, and the string beans soused in ham fat, and the coleslaw, and the celery, and the bread and jelly, and the cut raw tomatoes and lettuce, and the coffee accommodate themselves to the dumpling-like potpie and the tasty afterclap of Jerusalem cherries?

Looking out of the front windows of our hosts' house in that state of inaction that is not unknown to postprandial hours, we saw a nice-looking youth in his Sunday best doing a few steps and whistling as he stood on the pavement before his home across the street. "That's the boy that does so well with skunks," said our hostess. "How?" we demanded. "Oh, by catching them and selling their skins," she replied. "Would you like to go over to see them? He would be proud to show them to you."

The procession formed, old and young alike eager to settle the dinner and to see the skunks. Seven strong we descended upon the youth. He was all smiles at the suggestion he display his pets. A golden pheasant delayed us on our way to the shed in the back yard. He was in a cage at the door of the skunks' domicile. Only a faint effluvium of polecat manifested itself as we had joy of the attitudinizing fowl in his coppery mail. We were quickly ushered on, however, to see the important creatures. We stepped with proper caution into the shed. There, within range, was the cage of skunks. A pile of black and white fellows was heaped up in the corner, with two apart from them toward the other end of the cage. These detached beasts hurriedly threw themselves on the pile.

Quivering noses and bright eyes were directed toward us, but nothing more alarming. "Ane unt zwantsig skunk!" the youth declared in gloating tones as he pointed at the pile. That pile heaved and writhed a little, then subsided. "There is no danger at all," said their lord. "They are all tame by now. Look at this big lady!" So saying, he opened the slide in a box not six feet from us. A flat head, white toward the neck, protruded from the open door, waved sideways gently, and was withdrawn. Her ladyship retired to the corner of the box farthest from the door. She was a friendly and gentle soul who did not, we were told, resent having her head scratched.

As we walked up through the yard we asked the master of the skunks how he caught them. "I just go out most times on my bicycle to places where they are. I go when it gets towards dark," he said, "and just pick them up. Sometimes I set live traps for them. Their coats are getting better all the time now. They will be prime in January."

"Do you never have bad luck when you pick them up?" we asked. "Oh, yes!" he answered. "Once I was hit seven times. It stings your eyes so. And oh, boy! it has some taste. It isn't often I have bad luck, though." There was not the faintest scent of skunk about him, or on the air, as we stood talking to him not a hundred feet from where two and twenty skunks were incarcerated.

"They never bother at all," said our host as we returned home. "Not even when he first brings them home. It is a sight to see him riding on his bicycle just before dark, one hand on the handle bars, and the other holding a skunk by the tail. There is no trouble at all. He gets off his wheel still holding the skunk by the tail. The last we see of him he is walking with it to the shed. When it sees the others it is to be put with it is good at once. There is no trouble at all, with that hundred dollars and more of skunks. He kills the most of them in January, and sells the skins. Skunks are prime in January!"

FROM THE FOREST OF THE NIGHT

for E. Wallace Chadwick

THERE is surprise in a belated firefly illumining a narrow space of September dusk with the cold light from his little lantern. There is surprise in the burning eyes of an otter just lifted from the surface of the pool to which he has risen in the blackness of the night. There is surprise when, in the calm of the small hours, moonless and of all-pervading dark, the heavens open and lightning zigzags in broad bands from zenith to horizon. But sunrise, almost daily spectacle though it is, is the greatest surprise of all the many surprises of light out of darkness. Sunrise is all too little noted. Many of those up and about their chores as it works its miracles are too busy to heed it; many are shut out from it by the city walls that hem them in; and many lie abed long after its glory is gone. You look to the east at dawn, and it is a low expanse of whitey gray; you look away, and look back again, and in the interim the east has flushed to high heaven with soft rose. As you watch it that rose deepens to the "morning redness" that so many men all around the world and down the years have worshiped in awe and utter abnegation of self.

There are surprises of equal sharpness when lights shine out of the obscurity of the past. The past that we think of as dead and gone and done may, in certain moods, under the insistence of memory, open like the heavy hours after midnight to lightning, and flash forth revelations bright and dazzling as diamonds of white radiance and rubies of red.

418

Torch-light processions in political campaigns, parades of red-shirted firemen with engines of brilliant brass, and houses and barns in flames on near horizons return to me from those nights of childhood so long ago, nights of wonderment and thrilling strangeness. The glowing coals from the earth-baked piles of the charcoal burners above the Bashbish; the flares from iron furnaces round about Lebanon; and the fiery tails of comets riding high over familiar fields burn their way back from more rapt nights of youth. From later years rise in consciousness and take shape and color before my inward eye the coronation fires for Edward VII on Achill hills off the west coast of Ireland; Nova Scotian forests low belted with flames beyond all control and devastating a wide countryside; and crowds on Philadelphia streets of a New Year's Eve, each individual unrestrained, wild-eyed, riotous, both the ones in costume and those in conventional garb feeling as free and as privileged for license as their ancestors on St. John's Eve or Samhain.

Many fair and flagrant things met in the arts, too, come back out of the nights of the past, things sainted and things of the furies' ruinous sisterhood: Blake's "Tiger," Crashaw's "Flaming Heart," and *Macbeth*; gypsy songs from *Chauve Souris*, the chants that Debussy heard as he envisioned the blessed damozel leaning from the golden bar of heaven, and the fire music of *Die Walkuere*; Bernhardt, luxuriating in the splendor of sin and in the leopardine carnality of *Gismonda*; Calve in *Carmen*, a brand burning; and Regina in *Ghosts* as played in Orleneff's presentation by a Russian actress who made herself the personification of fascination and resistless temptation.

It is not, though, great lights, conflagrations, figurative or literal, illumining darkness, that are now most on my mind, but the little lights that are scarcely more than sparks, and those paled memories of passion and ecstasy that one thinks of when all the world is white and silver under the moon. Sparks, sometimes, by their feebleness, serve only to make more overwhelming the completeness of the obliterating dark. Even so they may be less of the nature of will-o'-the-wisps than the moon with its greater and colder light.

One spark comes to me to-day out of oldtime in the Forks of the Delaware. It is a wooden candlestick from Nazareth, of delicate and cleancut turning. Into a circular base five and a half inches in diameter is screwed an exquisitely rounded upright that rises eleven inches above the base. This base, of walnut, as is all the candlestick, is so heavy there is little likelihood of it being knocked over by a careless elbow or a rush of wind. An inch and a half through where it meets the base, it narrows, after three neat turnings, to a half inch in diameter at a height of three inches. Then it swells out again to a diameter of slightly less than an inch, and narrows again at seven and a half inches above the base to a little less than the half inch to which it was chiseled down below. Its effect, as of an elongated hourglass, is completed by a top two inches across, above other turnings as slenderly perfect as the ankles of a thoroughbred. To this top is fastened by two little wrought nails a flat cup of crimped tin, soldered in the center of which is a tin candle holder an inch high. That the candlestick was used on into later times than those in which candlesticks were the mode is indicated by the spirit-burning peg lamp of glass that was in the candle holder when it was bought from the old Moravian schoolhouse at Nazareth.

Did some teacher of yesterday con by its candle, I can but wonder, that catechism by my ancestor, Johannes Bechtel, who wished to reduce the tenets of Christianity to a common denominator that would be accepted by all Protestants?

Printed by Franklin, it was widely disseminated throughout Dutchland, but without accomplishing its intended purpose of bringing into one body the divergent sects. I can see a Moravian oldster nodding his approval as he reads, and praying that Brother Bechtel's efforts at Christian unity may meet with wide response. Maybe the candlestick was later used to light the long trestle table at which the boys of Nazareth Hall ate in the refectory, and where, after the evening meal, they did their school tasks and stole time to write letters to pals at home.

From the black night that was eighteenth-century Russia came to-day a book that in printing and binding and in high deeds recorded is a little splendor for all time. It is *Geschichte und Thaten der jungstverstorbenen Allerdurchlauchtigsten und Grossmachtigsten Kayserin Anna, Selbsthalterin aller Reussen,* with Petersburg, 1741, at the bottom of its title page. There is regality about the copperplate print of the Empress opposite the title page. There is regality about the binding of the book, its leather in red and gold and its insignia of royalty. There is pomp and circumstance, if not regality, about the very type of the title page, and in the contrast of red and black lettering on the yellowed white of the linen paper, so tough and age resisting.

That book, too, is a spark burning clear in the darkness. So, too, is that drink made of crabapples and too heady to be called wine, that is the choicest creation of Murrell, that little town just this side of Ephrata. Drink it on an empty stomach, and you feel as if you had been hit between the eyes with a hammer. Wiser it is to let it follow down two pretzels or three. Admire its honeyed amber as it rests on the table in a centuried wine glass, lift it against the light and note the rosy glow it then takes on. Play with it as you crunch your pretzels, and then sip it by half spoonfuls. So taken it warms the heart and quickens the memory so that old pleasantnesses by the score bob up in consciousness, delight you one by one, and fade out, leaving you untroubled by thought, genial, sympathetic and at one with the world.

In one mood the joys such as these of candlestick and book and liquor, the joys one may have after sixty, are only sparks in the darkness, little compensation for the many and great joys one knew in early and middle years. That great store of joys itself that was known in the past is less luminous now in retrospect than even the sparks that are what light we have to follow on the road downhill. The heat has gone from the joys that are past. They have grown as pale and cold as moonlight. There is more life and more to lead, perhaps, in the sparks in the darkness that settles down on the man of threescore. And yet, who knows? The sparks in the present may be engulfed and fade out wholly in the moonlight of the remembered past. It is a moot question, this of the sparks and the moon, whether you speak of it plainly or in parables.

The November moon, at its full, buoys up, big as a cart wheel, above the tattered woods. There are enough leaves yet on the sassafras trees and mazzards and oaks for the wind to sound diapason deep as it pulls through them. The wind soon sinks, however, and what leaves are left no more than rustle now as the moon rides into the clear skies above the trees. There is frost on the air and the tannin scent of the loosened leaves that are whirling down on even keels and carpeting the old lane and the lawn. There is a glitter on the hollies and on the rhododendrons and on such fallen leaves of oak and sassafras as have already taken on the film of hoar frost. It is a glitter of moonlight, cold, silver, jewel-like, broken into separate bits by the innumerable angles of reflection assumed by the innumerable leaves. There is a sense of detachment abroad in the night, a chill, a loneliness, an intimation of the dead and cindered world there will be in the end of days. Such is your mood if you pay heed to the moonflooded world, the bare or half-bannered trees, the white disc that seems unloosed from its moorings, so quickly does it climb high into heaven.

Draw the tannined air into your lungs; kick up the leaves laid ankle deep; step briskly eastward facing the moon, giving your blood a chance to quicken its course through your veins, and your low spirits will lighten and lift and blow away. You will recall white nights of boyhood when you went coon hunting, white nights of courting in youth, white nights of later years when your moonlit acres brought you a keener joy of possession and a larger content than if they were literally covered with pieces of silver.

The wind rises for a little and stirs the smoldering bonfire. Sparks are blown into being and travel like fireflies before the wind. They are far from bright in the flooding moonlight, but there is life in them, even if only for the moment. Memories, good as they are, are no substitute for the experiences that life still vouchsafes. Memories, though, have a value and beauty of their own. As life lessens they bulk bigger and bigger in relation to dreams and hopes and expectations. And yet, who knows? The short morrow may be as sweet as the long yesterday.

INDEX